JANE AUSTEN AT 250

Her Art, Life and Times

Christopher Richard Kerr

Amazon

Copyright © 2024 Christopher Richard Kerr

All rights reserved

No part of this book may be used or reproduced in any manner whatsoever without written permission from the publisher.

This book is dedicated to my daughters, Elizabeth Jane and Hannah Rose. May they be inspired by her example.

CONTENTS

Title Page
Copyright
Dedication
Introduction   1
I: Backcloth: Overture   4
II: Antecedents   14
III: Steventon: the early years   22
IV: Childhood   34
V: Education   50
VI: Juvenilia   63
VII: Lady Susan   89
VIII: Backcloth: Entr'Acte   102
IX: Affairs of the Heart   108
X: Bath and Northanger Abbey   131
XI: Steventon: the later years   151
XII: Jane Becalmed   172
XIII: The Watsons   189
XIV: Death and Glory   197
XV: Southampton   209
XVI: Chawton   228
XVII: Sense and Sensibility   237

XVIII: Pride and Prejudice	256
XIX: Mansfield Park	279
XX: Backcloth: Intermission	306
XXI: Emma	313
XXII: Persuasion	338
XXIII: Sea Change	358
XXIV: Curtain	368
Select Bibliography	378
About The Author	409

INTRODUCTION

The road was little more than a dirt track, the earth bleached white by the insistent sun which had been beating down on the back of my neck for the best part of two hours. The road lay straight, cutting through an expanse of fields in which the occasional cow glanced up with contempt as I rode by on my bicycle. Houses, some of them little more than wooden shacks, lined the track, perhaps a dozen or two on each side. Old men sat on benches and watched as the outsider passed by, not with hostility, but with the benign curiosity that the isolated villager will accord to a stranger. There was the occasional wave, and friendly greeting. *"Dzien dobry"*, I replied, my accent doing nothing to abate the curiosity.

And then my thoughts turned to a cold beer. This was by no means an uncommon occurrence as the afternoon approached. However the need for some liquid refreshment, and preferably of the five per cent variety, was becoming more urgent in the midday sun. There was a shack, a grey concrete, communist-era building, not much bigger than a large garden shed. To the side of the shack, away from the view of the road, and in order to escape the attention of the occasional police car, some middle aged men were chatting and drinking beer from cans. They stopped as I approached to look at the stranger, and then carried on as I got off my bike and went into the shop.

It took me a while to adjust my eyes to the dimness of the light. Behind the counter stood a plump woman of about 60.

Her customer service policy owed more to the old, communist way of doing things. In short, she stared sullenly, and said nothing. I took a can of Żywiec from the fridge, relishing the cold against my sweaty and bike-sore hands. I paid, and as the woman collected my change I looked around the shop. Some basic groceries, potatoes, carrots, and turnips – still caked in the dirt from which they had been dug – a row of tinned food, a shelf of packet sauces, some sweets and an ice-cream freezer.

And then I saw a row of books. I went over to have a look. The first one, a paperback, had a picture on the front which attracted my attention; two young ladies in typical English Regency dress; the title – *Rozważna i Romantyczna* – which translates literally as "Balance and Romantic". And then I saw the name of the author – Jane Austen. I opened the book. My Polish is rudimentary but the first line was enough – *rodzina Dashwoodów* – the family of Dashwood. This was *Sense and Sensibility*, Jane Austen's first published novel, issued by Thomas Egerton of Whitehall in November 1811. What was a copy of a translation of a quintessentially English, early nineteenth century novel doing in a remote backwater, deep in the countryside of south-eastern Poland, on the shelf of a little corner shop?

It was the incongruity of this experience, more than all of the novels or the films which they had inspired, that made me appreciate the global reach of this young woman, born in a little village in rural Hampshire, 250 years ago next December; a young woman who never left the south of England, had little formal education, remained unmarried, the daughter of a village parson, and who died at the age of 40. What was it about her, and what was it about her works, which made her stories so universal? I was familiar, of course, with her novels, which I had read, and re-read, since childhood, and most of the television and cinematic adaptations, but I knew next to nothing about Jane Austen herself. As the father of two teenage daughters, I wanted to try and find out.

This book does not pretend to be what it is not. It is not an original work. It is based on primary sources, already explored by others. I am also grateful for many secondary sources of primary information, especially those who have collated the letters, and the familial records. In common with every biographer of Jane Austen, I must acknowledge, for example, huge debts both to Dierdre le Faye and Kathryn Sutherland, and their unrivalled documentation of Jane's life. At the end of this book is a select bibliography in which, I hope, I have set out the principal sources I have used, and to which I am also hugely indebted. What this book does try to do is to combine, unlike other books about Jane Austen and her work, a comprehensive narrative of her life, together with a thorough analysis of her work. In this modest way, I hope that it may serve as a handbook of sorts for both the student of Jane Austen, and the intelligent, and more casual, reader. I also hope it might inspire my daughters!

CK
London
August 2024

I: BACKCLOTH: OVERTURE

We will soon get to her birth, that being generally a good place to start. First we must look, just for a little, into her past, her antecedents, before we survey her life. But to begin we must look into the period into which she was born in order to appreciate the context of her life, and indeed her art, for this was a period in English history which was, at once, an age of stability but also an age pulsing with the potential for revolutionary change.

It is easy to speak, with hindsight, of periods in English history as being revolutionary, and the England into which Jane Austen was born, in 1775, was indeed on the cusp of seismic change in the form of the industrial revolution. However, at the time of her birth this event had not truly begun. Indeed, it might be said that its embryonic state coincided with hers.

The England of 1775 was stable. Society was still essentially an agricultural one. The majority of the people were still employed on the land. There were only two cities in England with a population of over 50,000: London with 750,000, and Bristol with 60,000. The rest of the boroughs consisted of small market towns and ports. The remainder of the population lived in villages.

Industry, in the sense of urban production as opposed to the rural economy, was still nascent, but the capital being accumulated by the expansion of trade had the potential to launch the new processes of production which would ignite the industrial revolution. Larger units of production, particularly in iron and steel, were emerging. In textiles, the centralization of control over cloth production in the hands of capitalists had been growing for a century, and mechanisation, although in its infancy, was becoming evident. The use of the rolling mill, water frames and home jennies were familiar by the end of the 1760s, and the increase in standardization in such industries as pottery, and the manufacture of furniture, were a vital precedent to the advent of mass production.

However, the "industrial revolution", as we now understand it, was still latent at the time of Jane's birth. Textile production, the greatest and oldest of English industries, was still not concentrated in factories. The labour in that industry was largely sub-contracted to small family run workshops. The age of the canals was still nascent. The improvement in road surfacing had not yet matured, and the coach had displaced the pack-horse only on the more important thoroughfares. British industry, by the third quarter of the eighteenth century, was prospering and throbbing with potential, but it was not yet revolutionary. And it was not significantly affecting the rural population.

The population as a whole, at around 6.5 million, was growing slowly at best. At the beginning of the century it was just over 5 million. The birth rate and the death rate were both high but in proportion, and were a function of the population which could be sustained by the agricultural economy. But in the last quarter of the eighteenth century, the death rate began to decline, and the rate of births to increase. In short, an increase in productivity and wealth, both in the agricultural and trading sectors, was providing an increased national subsistence capable of sustaining a larger population. By the census of 1811, the population was nudging 10 million.

There were a number of factors at play. Medical science was slowly and tentatively emerging from medievalism. Although not formally embraced by the medical profession, the concept of inoculation had been conceived, and the practice of exposing oneself to a mild form of a disease to escape the consequences of a full blown visitation was becoming widespread. Indeed the very first trials of smallpox inoculation were spearheaded by the Princess of Wales in 1722. Just over two months before Jane's birth, on 7th October 1775, Queen Charlotte wrote to the royal governess, Lady Charlotte Finch, about the inoculation of her own children.

"I have the pleasure to acquaint you that my dear children underwent their operation with all possible and more than expected heroism, I trust that same providence which has hitherto given me uncommon success in all my undertakings, will not withhold it from me at this time, as I can say with great truth it is not begun without praying for His assistance as the greatest and best of medicines I can put my confidence in."[1]

Another factor was the general improvement in diet. This was driven in part by the economic imperative. Great Britain was a colonial power but more than anything it was a maritime, trading power. Its colonialism was driven, not so much by imperial ambition, but by the need to obtain and create markets for its commerce. The lynchpin of this policy was the navy. One of the principal catalysts of medical research was the need to combat the problem of scurvy amongst sailors. Scurvy was a debilitating disease brought about by a deficiency of vitamin C. James Lind had successfully experimented with oranges and lemons on board a naval ship in 1747. In 1757 the admiralty ordered all pursers to supply "roots and greens to seamen with their fresh meat." Before 1760, fruit was generally regarded as dangerous and the cause of fever. In that year, James Cook, some sixteen years before his landfall in Australia, was experimenting with wort extracted from malt, sauerkraut, carrots, and fruit.

However the main reason for the improvement in the English diet was more prosaic. It was simply an increase in the production of vegetables. White bread, cheese and potatoes were the staples of the great majority of the population, and vegetables were increasingly contributing to a more varied and healthy diet. The agriculturist Jethro Tull had, earlier in the century, perfected the horse-drawn seed drill, a mechanical seeder that sowed efficiently and at the correct depth and spacing. Viscount Townshend, Secretary of State and brother in law of the first Prime Minister Robert Walpole, promoted the system of crop rotation in his retirement. The Norfolk four-course system promoted by him, involving the rotation of turnips, barley, clover and wheat, was a major contributor to the agricultural revolution which took place in the eighteenth century. By the middle of that century, chalk fertilisers were being introduced, and the drainage of the soil was being improved. And, in tandem with the expansion in the production of vegetables, were improvements in stock breeding. Within the century, the average weight of a sheep for sale at Smithfield market in London rose from 28 to 80 pounds. In short, the population as a whole was eating better, and it was growing in consequence.

The costs to be borne by these new agricultural processes gave new impetus to the movement for enclosure. Farmers with short leases and small lots were not likely to make the required investments. The solution was the consolidation of holdings so that each farm was big enough to justify expenditure on such matters as drainage, and new buildings, as well as innovative equipment.

Revolutionary change then was more apparent at the time of

Jane's birth in the countryside, rather than in urban industry. However society remained stable. Incremental changes in the methods of agriculture were not accompanied by resistance, still less by a movement for social change. The social strata remained static. It was a pyramid, with few at the top and many at the bottom. Distinctions in wealth between the top and bottom of this pyramid were vast. A great landowner, at the top and as a member of the territorial aristocracy, could expect an income of £10,000 or more. In the middle of the eighteenth century, this would be approaching a million pounds in today's money. A labourer at the bottom might have to survive on ten. However the gaps between the adjacent strata of this pyramid were small, and so the social order as a whole remained stable and strong. The early nineteenth century commentator David Robinson put it like this, although in a manner we would deprecate today.

"In most other societies, society presents hardly anything but a void between an ignorant labouring population and a needy and profligate nobility...But with us the space between the ploughman and the peer is crammed with circle after circle, fitted in the most admirable manner for sitting upon each other, for connecting the former with the latter, and for rendering the whole perfect in cohesion, strength and beauty."

The élite of English society was, of course, the landed aristocracy, in control of both the state and most of the wealth. It was a small and stable class. Throughout the eighteenth century, until Pitt began to hand out peerages in the 1780s, there were only 160 lords (not counting the bishops). They owned huge estates, encompassing 20-25% of England's landed wealth by 1800, and lived in great houses, such as Stowe, Bowood and Chatsworth. They could enjoy incomes of as much as £60,000 per year, worth over £5 million today, from rents and exploitation of other resources on the land, and perhaps income from estates in

London. They prospered throughout the century, partly from the revolution in agricultural techniques, and the movement towards enclosure, but also from the growing industrial base. The greatest landowners were often sitting on the richest resources: coal, stone, slate, sand, clay and timber.

Only the eldest sons inherited titles, and marriage ties were closely interwoven. It was almost a closed shop but not quite. There was a degree of mobility, albeit arthritic by today's standards, but there was not the structural rigidity in the social order which one would have seen, for example, in Spain or France, and which led in the latter to the tensions culminating in the revolution of 1789, and the Terror which was to follow. It was a society based upon class rather than caste. Through the media of marriage and money, it was possible, though difficult, to move upwards through the social strata. Conversely, because it was only the eldest son of the landed gentry who inherited title, and usually the land, the younger could enter the higher echelons of overseas trade.

Below this echelon of the aristocracy was the much larger class of the landed gentry below the peerage, comprising some 15,000 families, ranging from baronets to squires. In an age of corruption, when high office depended largely on wealth, the wielding of political power was generally beyond them. Whereas the average peer might enjoy an annual income of five to ten thousand, the average squire might have to make do with one thousand pounds or less. With the growing industrial base, though, there were opportunities for them to supplement their landed income with the profits of trade, such as in coal, iron or forestry. Occasionally, towards the end of our period, this was the route to gentrification for some.

Broadly on a par with the minor squirearchy was the lower clergy, the village parson. As well as ministering to their parishioners, they had to make a "living" from a parish. The right to present a living fell to bishops, the Crown, Oxford and Cambridge colleges, or to private patrons, such as Lady Catherine de Bourgh in *Pride and Prejudice.* The value of the living would depend on the tithes to be collected from the inhabitants of the parish, typically ten per cent of income, and the agricultural yield of the glebe, that is the farmland which belonged to the rectory. This could be extended by the renting of additional land. The value of such a living could vary enormously, depending on the size and prosperity of the population of the parish, and the extent and quality of the glebe. Some parsons held several livings at once, employing curates to tend to those parishes they could not administer themselves, or, alternatively, and reprehensibly, leaving them vacant. "Pluralism" in this respect was common, and unofficially sanctioned by the Anglican Church, although deprecated by the growing evangelical movement. Depending on how many livings they enjoyed, a parson could typically have an annual income of a few hundred to a thousand pounds. It was a respectable position in the social order and, as the century progressed, parish priests were increasingly called upon to fulfill the duties of justices of the peace.

Below the landed gentry and clergy were those who worked the land for an income: owner-occupiers, freeholders, smallholders, and tenant farmers. By 1790, about three-quarters of the agricultural land in England was cultivated by tenant farmers. They could do well if sufficiently industrious. Landowners were prepared to let them large holdings, grant long leases, and underwrite capital improvements. They in turn would employ agricultural labourers. Many of the most successful aspired to become gentrified themselves, educating their daughters at expensive boarding schools, sending their sons to the universities, rebuilding their farmsteads and investing in fine furniture, and perhaps even employing the occasional liveried servant. Although the average income of the tenant farmer amounted to no more than about £300 a year at the time of Jane's birth (a little short of £30,000 now), this increased considerably with the inflation in the price of food in the 1790s and early 1800s brought about by the wars with Republican France.

In an age of rapid urban growth and prosperity in trade and manufactures, this "middle class", as it would now be called, was in turn complemented by master-craftsmen and manufacturers, lawyers and physicians, journalists and engineers, financiers and traders, those who provided culture, and shopkeepers. Of course, the term "middle class" covers a very broad spectrum. In 1750, one would have needed a capital sum of around £20,000 to set up as a banker, around £5,000 as a brewer, but only £50 as a butcher. The generality of this class were running a client economy and servicing those above them in the social heirarchy. However the more successful and wealthy of them, such as the City financier, aspired to the gentry themselves, by a good marriage, or by purchasing land.

The younger sons of gentlemen, who would not inherit an estate, may have had to find a profession. A military career would often be at the top of the list. A commission in a good regiment had to be purchased. It could cost as much as £1,500 to join an elite cavalry regiment such as the Life Guards, and £500 even for entry into an infantry regiment. But the army was not an attractive option for those without private means. The salary was low, and there were few opportunities to supplement it. For this reason the navy was a much better option, particularly in a time of war. Although the salary would not make a man rich - £300 or so for a post captain, around £100 for a lieutenant - there was prize money to be won. If an enemy ship were captured, the ship and its cargo would be valued in prize courts, and the money distributed amongst the officers and men in proportions befitting their rank. Ships carrying bullion or other treasure could yield a fortune. Edward Pellew, who became Vice Admiral of the

Fleet, emerged from the Napoleonic Wars with a fortune of £300,000.

Beneath the middle orders, that is those with means but generally without political power, were the lesser craftsmen, the labourers, and the poor. Some of this class were self-employed – thatchers, woodcutters, tinkers and knife-grinders – but by the middle of the eighteenth century, about 40-50% of all English families were wage earners: such as farm labourers, brick-layers, weavers, domestic servants, and factory workers. Some of this population, particularly in the rural sector, would live in cottages provided by their employer. The fortunes of this class did not improve as the century progressed. The increase in the population led to a surplus of labour, and this surplus was increased by technological innovations rendering labour redundant in some sectors. Rising price inflation from the 1760s exacerbated the effects of the resulting downward pressure on wages, although the expansion of manufactures and industry was gradually opening up new opportunities.

Those who were laid off, or could not work due to illness, were dependent on charity from the parish. By 1800 twenty-eight per cent of the population was in receipt of poor relief. By far the largest proportion of those in employment were the domestic servants, of whom there were, on average, between 600,000 and 700,000 throughout the eighteenth century. Although their wages were quite low, they would typically live in, and be provided with their board and clothing, and would receive tips. In 1796, Jane Austen, having stayed at her brother Edward's country house for over a month, was, she told her sister, "in great distress. I cannot decide whether to give [the maidservant] half a guinea, or only five shillings when I go away".

And then at the bottom were the indigent poor, the casual labourers, beggars, thieves, gypsies, vagrants, those hovering between the margins of the black economy and the underworld. A hundred thousand cottagers' families are thought to have lived in scrubby woodland, topping up their irregular income with petty crime.

Now we must look at where Jane Austen, and her wider family, fitted into this pyramidical structure.

II: ANTECEDENTS

The tracing of family trees is a random business. It depends on which branch you choose to follow. A person whose father is called Smith, and whose mother is called Jones, is just as much a Jones as he is a Smith, but there is a natural bias in following the branch called Smith. Likewise, if his maternal grandmother is called Taylor, he is every bit as much a Taylor as he is a Jones or a Smith, but that branch is unlikely to receive anything like the same degree of attention. And so it goes on, back into the mists of time. We are every much the descendants of those distant branches, disappearing over the horizon of recorded history, as we are those branches we choose to follow. Nevertheless, for want of a better solution, we will follow the same bias.

Jane Austen's paternal line came from generations of Kentish farmers who gradually achieved eminence through trade. Her direct ancestry can be traced back to William Astyn of Yalding in the borough of Maidstone, who died in 1522. By the time William's grandson, Robert Austen, died in 1603, the family had moved further to the south-west, to Horsmondem, near Tonbridge. Certainly by the mid seventeenth century, the family was of some consequence. Jane's great-great-great grandfather, Francis Austen, acquired the Tudor baronial manor houses of Broadford and Grovehurst in the parish of Horsmonden in 1647, and in his will described himself as a clothier. The wealth which enabled him to purchase the land appears to have derived from the wool trade, acting as middlemen in the provision of capital and wool for the manufacture of cloth, and its onward sale to merchants for retailing. This was a trade for which Kent had been famous since the time of Edward III.

However, Francis Austen's grandson, John, died of tuberculosis in 1704, predeceasing his father by a year, and leaving seven young children and a pile of debts to his wife, Elizabeth Weller. His father in turn had left little provision for his grandchildren in his will: for his grandsons £40 each at the age of 14 to pay for apprenticeship premiums, and £200 at the age of 21, provided they gave up all claim to Broadford. Jane's grandfather, William, was the fourth of six sons, and, on the face of it therefore, with little prospects. However, Elizabeth Weller devoted herself to giving her children the best opportunities possible, notwithstanding this unpropitious start. She moved to Sevenoaks where she took up the position of housekeeper in the local Grammar School. Her sons received free schooling, and in 1718, three years before her death, William Austen was apprenticed to a surgeon, William Ellis of Woolwich, for the fee of £115, at the age of 17.

In 1727, he married Rebecca Walter, a widow, and the daughter of Sir George Hampson. He had one son in his turn, and three daughters: George (born in Tonbridge in 1731), Hampson, Philadelphia and Leonora. George was Jane's father. The line leading to Jane, however, suffered another blow to its material prosperity. Rebecca died shortly after the birth of Leonora in 1732. Although William made provision for the education and maintenance of his children in a will of 1735, he remarried again the following year and omitted to alter the will. The marriage settlement left all his property to his second wife. Therefore, when he died eighteen months later, there was no provision for his children. His second wife lived on in the matrimonial home in Tonbridge for another thirty-one years, providing no assistance whatsoever to her stepchildren, and declining even to mention them in her will.

And so Jane's father, George, an orphan, rejected by his stepmother, was sent to live with his aunt, William's older sister, Betty Hooper, who had married a Tonbridge lawyer. George is said, however, to have been "blessed with a bright and hopeful disposition which characterised him during the whole course of his life",[2] and to have a "mildness and gentleness of temper" and a "steadiness of principle".[3] This, it seems, served him well, notwithstanding his start in life. He appears to have thrived at Tonbridge School, and, at the age of sixteen, he went up to St John's College, Oxford, with a scholarship.

In 1751, after his graduation, he was awarded an exhibition which enabled him to remain at Oxford to study divinity with a view to ordination. He was ordained in 1754, as deacon in Christ Church Cathedral but shortly thereafter returned to Kent where he served as the curate of Shipbourne, near Tonbridge. The lower clergy of the Church of England, at that time, were effectively appointed (presented with a "living") by the local gentry, quite often a relative. It is likely that George Austen's appointment to the living of Shipbourne was due to the influence of his father's brother, Francis. Francis, an attorney based in Sevenoaks, had, by a combination of hard work and considerable fortune, become very wealthy and influential, having inherited or bought up a great deal of the local estate.

In 1757 George Austen returned to St John's College as assistant chaplain, and in 1760 obtained the degree of Bachelor of Divinity. His position was now secure as an unmarried member of the clergy, and a Fellow of an Oxford College. However, if he wished to marry, he would need to find a "living" of sufficient standing to enable him to support a family. It appears that he turned to a couple of rich relatives for assistance. First, in 1761, he was presented with the curacy of

Steventon in Hampshire by a rather distant, but nonetheless rich, relative, Mr Thomas Knight, who had been elected a Member of Parliament in 1734. Knight was the husband of Jane Monk, who was the grandaughter of George's great aunt. The living had previously been presented by Mr Knight to two of George's cousins. It was only worth about £100 a year (about £10,000 in today's money), and Mr Knight later agreed that George could use the land at Cheesedown Farm, in the north of the parish, to supplement this income. A rather nearer relative, his uncle Francis, the Sevenoaks attorney, had purchased the two livings of Ashe and Deane which were adjacent to Steventon, and George would be able to have whichever of them fell vacant first; and this happened to be Deane.

Clearly George had been rather fortunate in having two livings falling into his lap, but there was nothing unusual in the eighteenth century for the lower clergy to have more than one parish; nor was there anything unusual in absentee parsons. Indeed, George did not fully take up his duties in Steventon until 1764. It was only then, after his marriage to Cassandra Leigh, that he became the first Austen to migrate from Kent into Hampshire with his new bride.

Cassandra Leigh was the youngest daughter of the Reverend Thomas Leigh, the rector of Harpsden, a small village near Henley-on-Thames in Oxfordshire. The Leigh family were descended from wealthy landowners, and were certainly more aristocratic than the Austens. Their ancestry can be traced back as far as Hamon de Leigh, Lord of the Moiety of High Leigh, Cheshire, in the middle of the twelfth century. However, the direct line begins with Sir Thomas Leigh, who was Lord Mayor of London in 1558. He was rich enough to endow both his sons with estates: Thomas with Stoneleigh Abbey in Warwickshire, and Rowland with Aldestrop in Gloucestershire. It was the Stoneleigh branch which was the more distinguished. One day early in the English Civil War,

Charles I was on his way to raise his standard in Nottingham, only to find that the gates of Coventry were closed to him. He rode to Stoneleigh Abbey and received the hospitality of Thomas's grandson, also called Thomas. In gratitude, he was created Lord Leigh of Stoneleigh in 1643.

However, it is the Aldestrop branch which leads to Jane; although this line was distinguished too in its own way. Jane's great grandfather, Theophilus Leigh (1643-1725), married the sister of the future Duke of Chandos in 1689, and had no fewer than twelve children. His second son, also Theophilus, became Master of Balliol College, Oxford and Vice Chancellor of the university in 1736, "a man more famous for his sayings than his doings, overflowing with puns and witticisms and sharp retorts..."[4] His fourth son, Thomas, was elected Fellow of All Souls, Oxford, and in turn became rector of the living which was in the gift of that college, namely Harpsden in Oxfordshire. He married Jane Walker, and although not quite as prolific as his father, had two sons and two daughters, one of whom was Cassandra, Jane Austen's mother.

Cassandra's father must have been brilliant to have been elected Fellow of All Souls, and at a young age. Cassandra appears to have inherited his intellect. "She united strong common sense with a lively imagination, and often expressed herself, both in writing and in conversation, with epigrammatic force and point."[5] According to her uncle, Dr Theophilus Leigh, who visited the family in December 1745, she was already writing verses at the age of six, and a poet of great genius. Her granddaughter, Anne Lefroy (Jane's niece), later wrote this about her.

"The education of my Grandmother had not been, for a person in her station of life, much attended to; but whatever she had the opportunity of learning, there was quickness of apprehension, & a retentive memory to make the most of; whilst her natural talent may well be supposed to have compensated in early life for many school room deficiencies, it certainly qualified her to be the companion of a husband, who had little toleration for want of capacity in man or woman..."[6]

This observation is quite shocking to the modern reader, and rightly so; the suggestion that intellect in a woman was of value only to the extent that it served her prospective husband. It must be appreciated though that, even as late as the latter half of the eighteenth century, it was regarded as remarkable for a lady to advertise her intellect. Very few women achieved any prominence. There were no female parliamentarians, explorers, lawyers, magistrates or entrepreneurs. High public office, the professions and the church were simply closed to women. Women were expected to be the mere shadows of men. Catherine Macauley, who wrote an eight volume history of England between 1763 and 1783, was sneered at for her intellectual pretensions. The poet and classicist Elizabeth Carter, who met Macauley in 1757, described her in a letter to a friend as a "very sensible and agreeable woman, and much more deeply learned than beseems a fine lady..." Lady Mary Wortley Montagu, another poet, advised her daughter to "conceal whatever learning she attains with as much solicitude as she would hide crookedness or lameness." Jane Austen expressed a similar sentiment in *Northanger Abbey*, although from her pen it was dripping in irony, when she wrote that, "Imbecility in females is a great enhancement of their personal charms."

It is not entirely clear how Jane Austen's father met her mother, nor exactly when; although it seems to have taken place in Bath, where Cassandra Leigh's parents moved in later life. It would certainly have been sometime in the early 1760s, probably between 1762 and 1763, because we know that they moved to Hampshire together as man and wife in 1764, but it is reasonable to suppose that any serious courtship would not have occurred before the issue of George's future income had become clearer. Not much is known about their courtship but marriage in the eighteenth century was not generally about love. It involved wider matters of family policy and fortune. Women of the genteel classes had no way of making a living, and would typically be unlikely to inherit much property. In choosing a husband, the choice would usually be the father's rather than the daughter's, and considerations of security, family, title and land would have priority over affection.

However, attitudes to marriage were changing as the century progressed. Increasingly prospective partners were permitted to explore personal affection, although this would not, of course, include physical intimacy, at least not in polite society. Daughters were granted a greater say in the choice, although the parents retained an effective veto with the purse strings. Balls, family parties, and visits to resorts, such as Bath, developed as vehicles to present young women to potential suitors. There is evidence for this cultural shift in the apparent need in 1753 for Hardwicke's Marriage Act, which prohibited marriage for those under twenty-one from marrying without parental consent, and required the publishing of banns. But the best evidence of all that marrying for love was becoming respectable towards the end of the century, and certainly into the beginning of the next, is of course in Jane's novels. Indeed Jane gave this advice to her niece Fanny, shortly after the publication of *Mansfield Park* in 1814: "Anything is to be preferred or endured rather than marrying without affection."[7] However, the precise dynamics of the nuptials between Jane's parents, almost half a century before she tendered this advice, are unknown.

Preparations had to be made for the move to the matrimonial home. The rectory at Steventon itself was apparently in a dilapidated state, and "of the most miserable description."[8] It would not be fit to live in without considerable renovation.

The current incumbent in the neighbouring rectory of Deane, which George was to inherit, lived outside the parish, and so the parsonage at Deane was vacant, and this is where the couple made their first home. George had moved in to the property by the middle of March 1764, in advance of the marriage, to prepare the residence for his bride. Then, on 26th April, a Thursday, the marriage was celebrated in St Swithin's Church in Walcot, Bath. Straight afterwards, they took a coach to Steventon, stopping overnight in Andover, where, one supposes, the marriage was consummated.

III: STEVENTON: THE EARLY YEARS

Steventon was a small village in the north of Hampshire, with about thirty families, in gentle countryside, in a valley between the market towns of Basingstoke and Whitchurch. It was populated by simple folk. The men grew turnips and beans, and the women worked at home, spinning flax, or wool from the sheep that inhabited Hampshire's hills. There was an old maple tree on the village green which formed the focal point of the community. The rectory, its core dating from the late seventeenth century, stood at the end of the village, half a mile along a lane leading uphill to the thirteenth century church of St Nicholas. However, for the first four years of their marriage, the Austens lived in the parsonage at Deane, about two miles to the north, which was let by the absentee incumbent, the Reverend William Hillman who preferred to live at nearby Ashe Park. Absenteeism and plurality in the lower clergy was rife at this time but the example of George Austen was venial enough; the two parishes were very close, and the combined populations of Steventon and Deane numbered only about three hundred; although the plurality would still require the formal approval of the Archbishop of Canterbury when George finally inherited the living of Deane in 1773.

The Austens lost no time in starting their family, and were as prolific as their forebears. We should, of course, be careful not to measure this by the standards of the present day. People of all classes, at that time, had more children than is the norm in the developed world of the twenty-first century. Lady Bristol, who married at the age of nineteen in 1695, had a son in 1696, a daughter in 1697, a son in January 1699, another in December in the same year, and yet another in 1771. She miscarried with triplets in the same year, bore a son and a daughter in 1703, and a stillborn son in 1704. Between 1706 and 1710 she produced three more sons and two daughters, then two sons in 1712 and 1713 respectively, and two daughters in 1715 and 1716. In total she gave birth to twenty children, few of whom lived to maturity.

Although this example is a bit of an outlier even in those days, the reasons for this profundity are prosaic enough. Firstly, infant mortality was far higher in the eighteenth century, notwithstanding the gradual improvements in medicine, sanitation and diet. It was an accepted fact that children were quite likely to die in infancy, and so there was both a primal and an economic imperative to produce more. Secondly, the only birth control were the natural methods of *coitus interruptus* or abstention. Abortifacients, that is drugs inducing abortion, were advertised in newspapers but there is very little evidence of mechanical contraceptives being used by the gentle classes. Condoms were used for protection against venereal disease in houses of ill repute but not as a means of birth control.

The Austens' first child, James, was born on 13th February 1765; their second, George, on 26th August 1766, and their third, Edward, on 7th October 1767. The rural practice in those days, for a genteel family, was to have one's children nursed in a cottage in the village as soon as they were weaned. For this purpose the Austens employed John and Elizabeth Littleworth in Deane. James was sent to be dry nursed by Mrs Littleworth in May 1765, at the age of three months. The Littleworths played a similar role, as we shall see, in the infancy of Jane, and remained loyal servants to the Austen family for many years.

For the second son George this took a different form. The precise nature of his condition is unclear but he suffered from some abnormality and was subject to fits, probably due to epilepsy. In the summer of 1770, George Austen wrote this: "I am much obliged to you for for your kind wish of George's improvement – God knows only how far it will come to pass, but from the best judgment I can form at present, we must not be too sanguine on this head; be it as it may, we have this comfort, he cannot be a bad or a wicked child."[9] George could not be catered for at home, and was boarded out to a respectable family in a village to the north of Basingstoke. But his parents had not abandoned him. Mrs Austen wrote this in the December of 1770: "My poor little George is come to see me today, he seems pretty well, tho' he had a fit lately, it was near a twelvemonth since he had one before, so was in hopes they had left him, but must not flatter myself so now."[10]

What was the social status of the Austens? Clearly they were of genteel stock. They are best described as country gentry but well beneath the aristocracy, and somewhat below the baronets and squires of the wealthy landed gentry. However, George held the respected position of rector, was Oxford educated, and "…in those days a rector who chanced to be a gentleman and a scholar found himself superior to his chief parishioners in information and manners, and became a sort of centre of refinement and politeness."[11] But George was certainly not rich, and had not inherited an estate. In his case, as has been noted, the cascade of family wealth down the generations had been interrupted on more than one occasion. Indeed, his bank accounts reveal that from time to time his finances were in a perilous position. Cassandra was descended from more wealthy, and more distinguished, antecedents but was nevertheless the daughter of a fourth son.

In the marriage settlement, signed in March of 1764, Cassandra brought some leasehold property in Oxfordshire, and the prospective sum of about £1,000 to which she would become entitled upon the death of her mother, an event which happened four years after the marriage. This, together with other family monies, yielded an income of £100 per year. George had the prospect of some land in Tonbridge upon the death of his stepmother. She had done nothing for him in life, and the news of her death in January 1768 cannot have been entirely unwelcome, and when the property was sold later in the year, he received his share of £1,200. In today's money this would be worth about £100,000.

In the summer of 1768, when the Austens finally loaded up their waggon and moved to the rectory in Steventon, George had insured the contents, containing all his worldy possessions, for £300. The lane, we are told, between Deane and Steventon "was a mere cart track, so cut up by deep ruts as to be impassable for a light carriage. Mrs Austen, who was not then in strong health, performed the short journey on a feather bed, placed upon some soft articles of furniture in the waggon which held their household goods."[12] With them, and part of the household, was her mother, Jane Leigh; Cassandra's father having died in 1764. She in turn died in 1768, and so never knew her granddaughter.

The rectory and its surroundings no longer exist, and because of its importance in the formation of the mind and character of the subject of this book, it is important to review what accounts we have of its constitution. Steventon, in those days, was deep in the Hampshire countryside, reachable only by navigating rough and muddy country lanes. There was no transport infrastructure. The living of Steventon included the glebe lands, in other words the three acres of land which surrounded the rectory, the purpose of which was to be farmed specifically for the maintenance of the parish priest.

The rectory itself "stood in a shallow valley, surrounded by sloping meadows, well sprinkled with elm trees, at the end of a small village of cottages, each well provided with a garden, scattered about prettily on either side of the road."[13] It had a carriage drive at the front to bring in vehicles off the road. To the north of the house was the lane from Deane to Popham, and to the south an enclosed garden, "bounded by a straight row of spruce firs, and terrace walk of turf. At one end this terrace communicated by a small gate with what was termed the Wood Walk, which winding through clumps of underwood, and overhung by tall elm trees, skirted the upper side of the Home Meadow. At the other end of the terrace a door in the garden wall opened to a lane that climbed the hill, and led through field or hedgerow to the Church [the 'Church Walk']…near the Wood Walk gate, and garden bench adjoining, was placed a tall white pole surmounted by a weathercock." A silver fir, we are told, grew at the opposite end of the terrace with honeysuckle climbing up its stem.

There was "a well between the house and the Wood Walk… in the square walled-in cucumber garden. The walls of this inner garden were covered with cherry and other fruit trees. On the west side was a garden tool house. On the south a door communicated with the back yard – not far from the granary – another door opened into the larger garden, in the east wall, I think. I remember this sunny cucumber garden well – its frames and also its abundance of pot-herbs, marigolds, etc."[14]

The house itself had a three-storey main block, with two projecting wings at the back. Jane's niece, Caroline, the daughter of her brother Francis, recalled that the house "consisted of three rooms in front on the ground floor – the best parlour, the common parlour and the kitchen; behind these were Mr Austen's study, the back kitchen, and the stairs, above were seven bedrooms, and three attics. The rooms were low pitched, but not otherwise bad, and compared with the usual stile of such buildings, it might be considered a very good house."[15]

Anna, Jane's niece by her brother James, describes "the lower bow window, looking so cheerfully into the sunny garden up the middle grass walk bordered with strawberry beds, to the sundial, belonged to my Grand Father's study; his own exclusive property, & safe from the bustle of all household cares. The dining or common sitting room looked to the front, & was lighted by two casement windows; on the same side the principal door opened into a parlour of smaller size."[16]

An excavation of the site in 2011 revealed that a long passage ran from the front to the back. The best parlour, in effect the dining room, was just over seventeen square feet and was to the left of the door, with two casement windows looking out at the carriage drive. There were two kitchens (back and front) to the right of the door. The back kitchen would have been used for the cooking, and the front for the storage of crockery and other kitchenware, and perhaps for light preparation such as the making of tea.

There were outbuildings too. There was a well, a washhouse, a tool house, granary, brew house, and a barn. There was a yard for poultry, turkeys, ducks, chickens and guinea fowl, and a dairy for making butter and cheese. Cows were kept in the field. The Austens, then, could be called farmers. Mrs Austen, in particular, when she was not giving birth, was the manager of a small business producing meat, dairy and vegetables.

The home, according to Jane's nephew, was "a pleasant and prosperous one...Their situation had some peculiar advantages beyond those of ordinary rectories. Steventon was a family living. Mr Knight, the patron, was also the proprietor of nearly the whole parish. He never resided there, and consequently the rector and his children came to be regarded in the neighbourhood as a kind of representative of the family. They shared with the principal tenant the command of an excellent manor and enjoyed, in this reflected way, some of the consideration usually awarded to landed proprietors. They were not rich, but, aided by Mr Austen's powers of teaching, they had enough to afford a good education to their sons and daughters, to mix in the best society of the neighbourhood, and to exercise a liberal hospitality to their own relations and friends. A carriage and a pair of horses were kept."[17]

The Austens enjoyed then a very respectable status. If one had to fit them into the modern class structure, they would be solidly upper middle class. They would have had maids and manservants, although there is no clear evidence as to how many, or who they were. Most of them would not have lived in but would have come in from the village, as and when required, to take the laundry, do some cooking, and tend to the garden, and so on. Servants did not in those days appear in recorded history, save for the records of their birth and death. However, according to an account of household management, written in 1825, a family with an income of £600 per year, which is roughly the bracket in which the Austens found themselves, could afford to employ three females and one man: a cook, a housemaid, and a nursery maid with "a boy as groom, and to assist in the house and garden."[18]

But what of the Austens's social circle? It appears to have been based primarily on the extended family. The extended family, one must remember, was more important at that time than perhaps it is now. Parents often died before their children reached maturity, in which case it would be the wider family who would take on the responsibility, and in an age which was far less mobile than now, the pool of eligible spouses was much smaller, and would include cousins. The extended family was also of particular importance to the Austens because of their uncertain financial status, and the potential patronage and support which the wider family could provide. Important amongst this extended family was Mrs Austen's elder sister Jane who married the Reverend Dr Edward Cooper (a Fellow of All Souls College, Oxford) in December 1768, and their two children, Edward born in 1770, and Jane in 1771. These were Jane Austen's first cousins, based in Southcote near Reading. In early December 1770, Mr and Mrs Austen visited them for five days, and took little James, then five years old. By December 1771, the Coopers had taken up occupation of a house in the newly built Royal Crescent in Bath.

There were also visits to and from the family of George's mother, Rebecca Austen, by her first marriage to William Walter, although the Walters were still based in Kent. This was a distance of eighty miles, a considerable journey even in the late eighteenth century, requiring an overnight stop and two long days of travelling in a coach. In the spring of 1770, Mr Austen wrote to Mrs Walter, the wife of his half-brother (also William), inviting her to stay at Steventon with her child Philadelphia who would then have been nine years old. They stayed until the end of June. On 26th August, Mrs Austen wrote to Mrs Walter that her sister (Jane) was "tolerably well & the child [Edward] quite so…We talk of going there…in about three weeks time, and shall be absent a full month, shall take both my boys with me…Neddy [Edward] is not so ungrateful to forget so good an Aunt but talks of you very often."[19]

Cassandra was also close to her brother James Leigh Perrot, four years her senior. The adopted name of "Perrot" came from the family of their mother, Jane Walker, who was descended from the Perrots of Oxfordshire. Her childless uncle, Thomas Perrot, left his estate at Northleigh in Oxfordshire to James on the condition that he took the surname and arms of the Perrot family. The Austens visited the Perrots at Christmas 1770, with James and Edward, and in the summer of 1773 the

Perrots came to stay at Steventon for a fortnight.

The closeness and affection in this extended family network is very evident from a letter written by Mrs Austen on 9th December 1770.

"...my little Neddy's cough seems entirely to have left him – he was so well that I ventured to leave him with his maid for a few days, while we went to Southcote, where we found my sister, Dr Cooper and the little boy quite well...We went on Monday & returned last night and found Neddy quite well. The day after Christmas Day we are to go to my brot. Perrot's for about ten days, but there I shall take Neddy as well as Jemmy , there being no little ones there to catch anything bad of us. I wish my dear brother & sister Walter were not more than thirty instead of eighty miles from us, for believe me tis the distance, not the place you live in, which prevents my visiting you so often as I could wish."[20]

The Austens were also in frequent contact with George's sister, Philadelphia. She had been sent to India in 1752 to find a husband, and married Tysoe Saul Hancock, an employee of the East India Company, and appointed surgeon at Fort St David in Calcutta. Their only child, Elizabeth (known as Betsy, and later Eliza) was born in 1761, and was the godchild of Warren Hastings, a business partner of Hancock, and who was to become a leading light of the East India Company. He, together with Robert Clive, were essentially the founding fathers of the British Empire on the Indian sub-continent, with Hastings becoming Governor of Bengal in 1771. The friendship between the Hancocks and Hastings was such that rumours were rife that Eliza was the daughter of Hastings, rather than Hancock.

In June 1765, the Hancocks returned to England, and took up lodgings in London, in Norfolk Street just off the Strand. George went to visit them in July of that year. Philadelphia and Hancock continued to live together in London for three years, but were living well beyond their means, and Hancock had to return to India to replenish his finances in the autumn of 1768. He failed to prosper, and died a few years later in seemingly perpetual ill-health, and financial distress. In the meantime, Philadelphia Hancock and little Eliza remained in London, and had frequent contact with the Austens. In July of 1770 they stayed at Steventon, and Philadelphia came to assist Mrs Austen when she was confined for the births of her son Henry in 1771, and little Cassandra in 1773. We will return to Eliza in due course because her extraordinary life undoubtedly had an influence on Jane, on her personal development, and, in due course, on her works.

In addition to the extended family, the more immediate social circle in Steventon would have included the Reverend Hillman and his wife, of the adjoining parish of Deane, and the very well to do Harwood family, who owned most of the land in that parish. Their property at Deane was worth about £1,200 per year, and had descended through five or six generations of Harwood squires. By the summer of 1771, the Reverend Hillman appears to have returned to the rectory in Deane, and Ashe Park had been let to "two agreable young men."[21] The two young men were James Holder and his brother. Next to the church was the manor house, owned by Thomas Knight who had presented George with the living; although the house had been let to the Digweed family for more than a century. They had four boys, born between 1766 and 1776, who would have been regular playmates of the Austen children.

The first baby to be born in Steventon was Henry on 8th June 1771, and then Cassandra, Jane's beloved sister, on 9th January 1773. Philadelphia Hancock was in Steventon to help with the birth and aftermath, and shortly thereafter Mrs Cooper paid a visit with her two children, no doubt also to lend a hand. A letter from Mrs Austen to her sister-in-law, Mrs Walter, gives us a snapshot of a happy household when Cassandra was just a couple of months old.

"I suckled my little girl thro' the first quarter...I want to show you my Henry and my Cassy [who has been] weaned and settled at a good woman's at Deane just eight weeks; she is very healthy and lively, and puts on her short petticoats today. Jemmy and Neddy are very happy in a new play-fellow, Lord Lymington, whom Mr Austen has lately taken charge of...I have got a nice dairy fitted up, and am now worth a bull and six cows, and you would laugh to see them; for they are not much bigger than Jack-asses – and here I have got duckies and ducks and chickens for Phyllis's amusement."

The reference to Lord Lymington stems from the fact that George Austen's income was insufficient to sustain this growing family. From 1770 he had been selling his holdings of South Sea Annuities. These were exhausted in April 1772. In February of 1773, his brother-in-law made a payment to him of £300 to keep him afloat. In March of 1773, he acquired the second living of Deane upon the death of the Reverend Hillman, worth an additional £110 per annum. However, George still needed to supplement his income. Therefore, from the summer of 1773 he established a school in the rectory to prepare boys for university entrance by teaching them the classics. He was, after all, a scholar of some repute. The intake was broad. Their first boarder was "between five and six years old, very backward of his age, but good temper'd and orderly; he is the eldest son of Lord Portsmouth who lives about ten miles from hence." Then, around November of 1773, Mrs Austen wrote of a "new pupil, Master Vanderstegen [who] has been with us about a month, he is near fourteen years old; is very good tempered and well disposed."[22] Each pupil provided an extra income of around thirty-five pounds each.

The sixth child, Francis, who was to become a most distinguished Admiral of the Fleet, was born, appropriately enough, on St George's Day 1774. "My last boy," Cassandra wrote, "is very stout, and has run alone these two months, and is not yet sixteen months old. My little girl talks all day long, and in my opinion is a very entertaining companion. Henry has been in breeches some months, and thinks himself near as good a man as his brother Neddy.

On 20th August 1775, Mrs Austen wrote to Mrs Walter to say that she was expecting her next baby in November. And then, on 17th December 1775, George Austen wrote this to Mrs Walter.

"You have doubtless been for some time in expectation of hearing from Hampshire, and perhaps wondered a little we were in our old age grown such bad reckoners but so it was, for Cassy certainly expected to have been brought to bed a month ago: however last night the time came, and without a great deal of warning, everything was soon happily over. We have now another girl, a present plaything for her sister Cassy and a future companion. She is to be Jenny…"[23]

And so, Jane Austen is born.

IV: CHILDHOOD

She was baptised privately the very next day. This, of course, was common in a world in which infant mortality was so high. Statistics in rural England are unreliable, and the evidence sparse. Estimates of infant mortality in London from the London Bills of Mortality, and other sources, indicate that the death rate in the first year of life was no less that 35 – 40 % in the early eighteenth century. Although the rate of infant mortality began to fall decisively in the latter part of the century, it was still at the rate of around 15-20% by the 1840s.

The Anglican church required that infants who had been privately baptised should be brought at some later date to be publicly received into the church, and registered. However the winter of 1775-1776 was unusually cold. The Thames was frozen solid that year, and it wasn't until 5th April, on Good Friday, that Jane was publicly christened at Steventon. Her godparents were the Reverend Samuel Cook, the husband of her mother's cousin, Cassandra Leigh; Mrs Musgrove of Chinnor, Oxfordshire, the wife of another maternal cousin, one of the Perrots, and Mrs Jane Austen, the wife of her great uncle, Francis. Some three months or so later, she would have been sent to be dry nursed by the Littleworths, as were her older siblings before her. She would have been visited regularly, probably on a daily basis, by one or other of her parents, and would have had the Littleworths's own children for further diversion, but she would have remained resident with the Littleworths until she could walk. As a toddler she would have had plenty of fresh air and exercise. The ideas of childcare promoted by such enlightenment thinkers as Locke and Rousseau had taken hold by this time, and children were being encouraged to enjoy nature and the outdoors.

The family was completed with the birth of Charles, after a gap of four years, on 23rd June 1779. Jane's place in the family was ideal for her mental and physical development. Both her mother and father were highly intelligent, and loving parents. There is no doubt of that from the surviving letters, some of which have already been quoted. The use of the diminutives "Jenny" and "Cassie", and the reference to Jane's being a plaything for her sister, in George's letter at the time of her birth, are indicative of a hands-on, affectionate father, and not the distant paternal figure often envisaged when one thinks of the past, and in particular the approaching Victorian era.

Jane had older siblings as mentors; Frank, only one year her senior, and her sister as constant companions and playmates; and a younger brother to nurture. Her eldest brother James was a precocious talent, going up to St John's College, Oxford at the age of fourteen in 1779, where he produced a periodical called *"The Loiterer"*. James's son later wrote this about his father. "He was well read in English literature, had a correct taste, and wrote readily and happily, both in prose and verse. He was more than ten years older than Jane, and had, I believe, a large share in directing her reading and forming her taste."[24]

The Austens' second son Edward was eventually adopted by the son of George's benefactor Mr Knight, who was also called Thomas, and who had inherited his father's great estate at Godmersham Park in Kent, and Chawton House in Hampshire. Shortly after Thomas Knight's marriage, in May of 1779, he visited the Austens at Steventon with his new bride, and took along Edward, who would then have been eleven and a half years old, for the rest of their journey. As time went on and their marriage remained childless, the Knights invited Edward to stay with them from time to time, and effectively adopted him as their heir. He went to live at Godmersham, and the adoption was formalised in 1783. George and Cassandra may have been more ready to take this step, given their precarious and uncertain financial position. This strengthening of the bond with the Knights was no mean advantage. The Knight family owned considerable property: Godmersham Park in Kent, a mansion at Chawton, not far from Steventon, and a third estate near Winchester.

Jane's interaction with Edward during her childhood, therefore, would have been limited; although, as we will see, his family was important to her in her later years. At the age of eight, however, the apparent loss of her brother may have made a lasting impression. In Emma Jane has Isabella Knight (admittedly a rather silly character) say this: "I never can comprehend [it]. To give up one's child! I really never could think well of anybody who proposed such a thing." Jane also shows considerable empathy for the displaced child in the trauma of Fanny Price in Mansfield Park, uprooted from her childhood home, and transplanted into the home of the wealthy Sir Thomas Bertram. It was, of course, in the long run, in Fanny's best interests, as indeed was the move to Godmersham in the long term interests of Edward Austen.

Jane's third brother, Henry, only four years her senior, "had great conversational powers, and inherited from his father an eager and sanguine disposition. He was a very entertaining companion...".[25] Her fourth brother, Francis, born in April 1774, and her younger brother, Charles, four years her junior, were sent off to the Royal Navy Academy in Portsmouth, and were both to become distinguished sailors in adulthood. There can be little doubt that they were her companions and playmates in her early years. Jane dedicated one of her earliest works to Francis, "Midshipman on board his Majesty's Ship the *Perseverance* by his obedient humble Servant The Author."[26]

However, it was Cassandra, her sister, to whom Jane was undoubtedly closest. Indeed, she was her companion and soulmate for the whole of her life. One of the first pieces of evidence of this relationship is to be found in the dedication Jane wrote to Cassandra in one of her earliest works: a little short story, with a very silly plot, *The Beautiful Cassandra*. This story contains a reference to Bond Street, and is the earliest known reference to London in all of Jane's writing. For this reason, Dierdre La Faye speculates, perfectly reasonably, that this may have been written around the time of the Austens' visit to Kent to see George's uncle, Francis, in the summer of 1788, when Jane was just twelve.[27] On the way back to Hampshire, they dined with Mrs Hancock and Eliza in London. The dedication to her sister is probably intended to be a little mocking, perhaps of a perceived vanity in her elder sister, but the shared humour and affection shines through.

"Madam,
You are a Phoenix. Your taste is refined, your Sentiments are noble, & your Virtues innumerable. Your Person is lovely, your Figure, elegant, & your Form, majestic. Your Manners are polished, your Conversation is rational & your appearance singular. If therefore the following Tale will afford one moment's amusement to you, every wish will be gratified of Your most obedient humble servant
THE AUTHOR."[28]

Many years later, Jane's nephew wrote this. "Their sisterly affection for each other could scarcely be exceeded. Perhaps it began on Jane's side with the feeling of deference natural to a loving child towards a kind elder sister. Something of this feeling always remained; and even in the maturity of her powers, and in the enjoyment of increasing success, she would still speak of Cassandra as of one wiser and better than herself...They lived in the same house, and shared the same bed-room till separated by death. They were not exactly alike. Cassandra's was the colder and calmer disposition; she was always prudent and well judging, but with less outward demonstration of feeling and less sunniness of temper than Jane possessed. It was remarked in her family that Cassandra had the merit of having her temper always under command, but that Jane had the happiness of a temper that never required to be commanded."[29] One is tempted to draw a comparison with the Dashwood sisters in *Sense and Sensibility* but that would be a superficial reading, as we shall see. Elinor had more sensibility than the title would suggest, and Marianne more sense.

The household, as Jane was growing up, included her father's pupils, whose numbers increased to supplement his income. He charged thirty-five pounds a year for tuition, board and lodging, and by 1779, there were four boarders, in addition to Edward, Henry and Frank who remained to be taught at home after James had gone up to Oxford. With seven bedrooms and three attics it must have been a full house, but there is little doubt that it was a house in which a child with intellectual curiosity could thrive. Mary Leigh, the wife of Mrs Austen's cousin, the Reverend Thomas Leigh, wrote this about a visit they made to Steventon in 1781.

"With his sons (all promising to make figures in life) Mr Austen educates a few youths of chosen friends and acquaintances. When among this liberal society, the simplicity, hospitality, and taste which commonly prevail in affluent families among the delightful valleys of Switzerland ever recurs to my memory."[30]

In 1783, the social circle was considerably extended following the death of the Austens' neighbour, the rector of the parish of Ashe. It will be recalled that this living, together with the parish of Deane, had been bought by George's uncle, Frances.

He now sold it, and the Rectory at Ashe passed to the Reverend George Lefroy. He and his wife Anne Brydges, known as "Madam Lefroy", were to play an important part in the life of the Austens. Mrs Lefroy was, by all accounts, a dramatic, compassionate, expressive and quite remarkable woman. She gave dances, rode donkeys around the locality to visit people in need, set up a daily school for poor children in her home, and was actively involved in the early vaccination movement, personally inoculating around eight hundred of the poor against smallpox.

The Lefroys played a leading role in the life of the community, and formed a strong bond with the Austens, later to be cemented with marriage. The Lefroys' son, Benjamin, eventually married Anna, Jane's niece, the daughter of her brother James. Mrs ("Madam") Lefroy, although twenty-six years her senior, forged, in particular, a strong friendship with Jane. In 1786, Madame Lefroy's younger brother, Egerton Brydges, rented Deane parsonage from Mr Austen, and stayed there for two years. He later wrote this: "I remember Jane Austen, the novelist, a little child; she was very intimate with Mrs Lefroy and much encouraged by her."[31] After Mrs Lefroys death, Jane wrote eleven verses to commemorate her friend. Three of them merit quotation here.[32]

"Angelic woman! Past my power to praise
In language meet thy talents, temper, mind,
Thy solid worth, thy captivating grace,
Thou friend and ornament of human kind."

"I see her here with all her smiles benign,
Her looks of eager love, her accents sweet,
That voice and countenance almost divine,
Expression, harmony, alike complete."

"She speaks! 'Tis eloquence, that grace of tongue,
So rare, so lovely, never misapplied

By her, to palliate vice, or deck a wrong:
She speaks and argues but on virtue's side."

Here, it seems, was humanity and sensibility, under the good governance of sense. It is quite clear that Mrs Lefroy had a profound influence on Jane from the age of seven or eight.

The earliest account of Jane Austen herself comes from a childhood memory of her sister Cassandra which was later recounted to her niece, and Mrs Lefroy's daughter-in-law, Anna Lefroy. It is a touching portrait, from when Jane was still a little girl, of the affection of two sisters for one another, a sister for her little brother, and all three for their father.

"Cassandra in her childhood was a good deal with Dr & Mrs Cooper in Bath – She once described to me her return to Steventon one fine summer evening. The Coopers had sent or conveyed her a good part of the journey, but my Grandfather had to go, I think as far as Andover to meet her – He might have conveyed himself by Coach, but he brought his Daughter home in a Hack chaise; & almost home they were when they met Jane & Charles, the two little ones of the family, who had got as far as New down to meet the chaise, & have the pleasure of riding home in it."[33]

Another feature of Jane's early childhood at Steventon, and also both an indicator and a product of the stimulating familial atmosphere in which her mind was developing, were the amateur dramatics of the kind which were to feature so heavily in the plot of *Mansfield Park*. Amateur theatricals were very fashionable in the upper echelons of English society from the 1770s, and well into the nineteenth century. Many members of the aristocracy would go to the extent of erecting scaled down imitations of London playhouses. However for those without the resources or the inclination to go to such lengths, large rooms would be converted into temporary theatres.

There is no doubt that the family theatricals had a profound effect upon Jane. It fuelled an interest in dramatic art which had an impact on her earliest writings through to her more mature works. Her descriptive art is of a pictorial quality, whilst much of the text is written in the form of dialogue, unmediated by the author. *Pride and Prejudice* is a case in point, and it is no coincidence that it has been adapted many times for the stage and screen. What could make a more dramatic scene than Darcy's first proposal to Elizabeth? Jane also had a keen eye for comic misunderstandings, dramatic irony, and the *coup de theatre*. The scene in *Sense and Sensibility*, in which Edward Ferrars calls for Eleanor, unaware of the presence in the same room as her rival, Lucy Steele, is a perfect example. It is the stage equivalent of the villain behind the arras.

At Steventon, the main parlour on the ground floor was frequently used as a theatre from 1782 to 1784, and a little later so was the barn. Jane's brother, James, would write the prologues and epilogues for these theatricals.[34] According to a manuscript volume of poems written by him, which is now held at the Jane Austen museum in Chawton, the first play performed at Steventon was in December 1782, when Jane was seven. It was *Matilda* by Thomas Franklin, a London preacher and friend of Dr Johnson. It is set in the time of William the Conqueror. Morcar, the Earl of Mercia, and his brother, Edwin, are both in love with Matilda but she only loves Edwin. Morcar imprisons them and decides to have his brother killed. He is foiled, repents, and the lovers are married. This must have made quite an impression on the seven year old girl.

In July 1784, Sheridan's *The Rivals* was staged, which was an ambitious undertaking given that it has twelve principal characters. It is likely that friends and neighbours, and occasionally extended family, would be invited to join in these productions, and perhaps some parts were doubled up, as in the abortive theatrical efforts in *Mansfield Park*. In 1787, one of Jane's cousins wrote that her "uncle's barn is fitting up quite like a theatre, & all the young folks are to take their part." This is probably a reference to a production of Susannah Centlivre's comedy *The Wonder! A Woman Keeps a Secret* which was put on from 26th to 28th December of that year as a Christmas entertainment.

The inspiration for the production of the *The Wonder* was, it appears, Jane's cousin Eliza, the daughter of her father's sister, Philadelphia. Eliza, to whom reference has already briefly been made, undoubtedly played a major role in the development of Jane's imagination, and it is necessary to return to her. It will be recalled that Eliza had been born in India in 1761, the godchild of Warren Hastings. The family came back to settle in London in 1765, but her father, Tysoe Hancock, had to return to India from financial necessity in 1768. His correspondence shows that he regularly sent his wife exotic goods from the subcontinent: curry leaves, pickled mangoes and limes, chillies, balychong and casoondy sauce, attar of roses and fine Indian fabrics, such as silks, chintz and muslin. He also asked her to share the goods with other members of the family, and so it is highly likely that they would have found their way to Steventon. But Hancock never met Jane. Having failed in business, and failed in health, he died in the year of her birth, 1775.

By the time of Hancock's death, however, Warren Hastings, who may very well have been Eliza's biological father, had settled the capital sum of £10,000 on her, and a trust was set up in her name, with her uncle, George Austen, as one of the trustees, and Hasting's brother-in-law, John Woodman, as the other. The capital would yield an income of nearly £400 per year, which would have been a sufficient dowry to allow Eliza to marry well. Hancock, in his correspondence from India, made constant enquiry after the physical and intellectual health of Eliza, and was keen for her to have a knowledge of French culture. Philadelphia, having always lived beyond her means, and knowing that her income would not support her in style in London, decided to fulfill this wish by setting off with her daughter to the continent in late 1777. Firstly they lived in Germany and Belgium, and in the autumn of 1779 settled in Paris. It was indeed an interesting time to do so. The rotting ancien regime was already beginning to stink, and slowly sink under a mounting wave of sovereign debt, sovereign corruption, sovereign excess, and growing discontent among every estate below that of the Crown. The cataclysmic events which would begin at the Bastille in July 1789, and which would engulf the whole of continental Europe for much of Jane's life, were beginning to loom large on the horizon.

It is not evident, however, that Eliza and her mother were too concerned about the march of history. It is clear from correspondence written by Eliza to her cousins in Kent, that they had obtained admission, or at least access, to the highest echelons of the social order, and were as oblivious as those around them to the coming conflagration. How Eliza obtained such access is not clear but she certainly played on her connection to Warren Hastings, whom she referred to as the famous Lord Hastings, "gouverneur de l'Inde".

"We were a few days ago at Versailles & had the honor of seeing their Majesties & all the royal family dine & sup. The Queen is a very fine woman, she has a most beautiful complexion, & is indeed exceedingly handsome, she was most elegantly dressed, she had on a corset & petticoat of pale green lutestring, covered with a transparent silver gauze, the petticoat and sleeves puckered & confined in different places with large bunches of roses, & an amazing large bouquet of white lilac. The same flower, together with gauze, feathers, ribbon and diamonds intermixed with her hair. Her neck was entirely uncovered and ornamented by a most beautiful chain of diamond, of which she had likewise very fine bracelet, she was without gloves, I suppose to shew her hands and arms, which are without exception the whitest and most beautiful I ever beheld. The King was plainly dressed, he had however likewise some fine diamonds."

Eliza met an officer in the Queen's Regiment of Dragoons, Jean-François Capot de Feuillide who styled himself, disingenuously, as "Le Comte de Feuillide", and they became engaged by August 1781. George Austen, as trustee of Eliza's settlement, did not approve. His fellow trustee, John Woodman, wrote to Hastings to report that "she seems inclined to give up to them the sum which was settled on her for life…which we have thought prudent for her sake to decline and Mr Austen is much concerned at the connection which he says is giving up all their friends their country, and he fears their religion."[35]

By December 1781, however, the marriage had taken place. It appears to have been a happy one, and surviving letters from Eliza to her cousins in Kent are full of news concerning her life and times in the higher echelons of French society. She wrote of a kind of fashion show which took place at the monastery of Longchamps in the Bois de Boulogne just before Easter. The stink was beginning to rise.

"It was formerly the custom to go thither to hear vespers the three last days of Passion Week but devotion has given place to vanity. Everybody now goes to Longchamps not to say their prayers but to show their fine clothes & fine equipages… The Queen & Royal Family are generally there, & what much contributed to the beauty of the show this year, several of the Princesses made their appearance in open calashes drawn by six horses."[36]

It was around this time in Paris that human beings first left the surface of the planet. In the spring of 1784, Eliza wrote of

Jean-Pierre Blanchard's attempt to make an ascent by balloon from the Champs-de-Mars, reporting that "he ascended to the height of 1500 fathoms & returned from thence in perfect health & safety to the astonishment of most of the spectators."[37]

Although there are no surviving letters to Steventon, one can assume with some confidence that similar reports were made by Eliza to her cousins in Hampshire, and one can imagine such letters being read aloud in the main parlour of the parsonage after supper; little Jane, with her awakening imagination and keen intelligence, lapping up of every morsel with renewed appetite.

There is another snapshot of Jane at the age of twelve from the rather waspish pen of her cousin Phylly Walter in a letter written to her brother in July 1788. Jane's parents had paid a visit to George's ageing uncle, Francis, in Sevenoaks. They had taken Jane and Cassandra with them. On their way back to Hampshire they stayed for a day or two in London, and dined with Eliza and her mother in Orchard Street, just off Portman Square near Hyde Park. This was almost certainly Jane's first visit to London. However, it was in Sevenoaks that the Walters were also invited to dine. Phylly wrote that she "began an acquaintance with my 2 female cousins, Austens…I may be allowed to give the preference to the eldest who is generally reckoned a most striking resemblance of me in features, complexion and manners…The youngest (Jane) is very like her brother Henry, not at all pretty and very prim, unlike a girl of twelve: but it is a hasty judgement which you will scold me for…the more I see of Cassandra the more I admire – Jane is whimsical & affected."[38]

Either this was, indeed, a "hasty judgment", or Jane was having a very off day. It is certainly out of kilter with the weight of the evidence available. Jane is elsewhere described as pretty and by all accounts had a personality anything but "affected". Her works, included her very earliest writings from around the time of this meeting, show her to be anything but "very prim". From her early teens she had a keen sense of humour, and a biting wit, as we shall see from her earliest works. Perhaps Phylly was just not very fond of children.

Social attitudes towards children were in a state of flux in the eighteenth century. Throughout much of that period, children were not considered to be part of the same circle as adults. They were not allowed to attend social events such as balls. Attitudes, however, were changing, and it is important to note that Jane accords significant roles to children in her novels. Appearances of children are intrinsic to the plot of *Sense and Sensibility*, and right at the beginning of the novel is this sparkling description of the rather lively and mischievous four year old, Henry Dashwood. The whole of old Mr Dashwood's property had been "tied up for the benefit of this child, who, in occasional visits with his father and mother at Norland, had so far gained on the affections of his uncle, by such attractions as are by no means unusual in children of two or three years old; an imperfect articulation, an earnest desire of having his own way, many cunning tricks, and a great deal of noise, as to outweigh all the value of all the attention which, for years, he had received from his niece and her daughters."[39]

It is little Henry Dashwood, then, who drives the plot. A little later when Sir John and Lady Middleton bring their eldest child John, "a fine little boy about six years old", to welcome the Dashwoods to Barton Park, Jane Austen remarks "by which means there was one subject always to be recurred to by the ladies in case of extremity, for they had to enquire his name and his age, admire his beauty, and ask him questions which his mother answered for him…On every formal visit a child ought to be of the party, by way of provision for discourse."[40] When the visit is returned the next day, "Lady Middleton seemed to be roused to enjoyment only by the entrance of her four noisy children after dinner, who pulled her about, tore her clothes, and put an end to every kind of discourse except what related to themselves."[41]

In *Mansfield Park*, Fanny Price is shocked by the condition of her young siblings when she visits her childhood home in Portsmouth after eight years absence. Tom and Charles, nine and eight respectively, "were quite untameable by any means of address...Every afternoon brought a return of their riotous games all over the house; and she very early learnt to sigh at the approach of Saturday's constant half holiday."[42] Her little sister, Betsey, was "a spoilt child, trained up to think the alphabet her greatest enemy, left to be with the servants at her pleasure, and then encouraged to report any evil of them..."[43]

However, it would be quite wrong to interpret this as representing Jane Austen's view of children. The blame is placed very much on the parents. Fanny's mother "was a partial ill-judging parent, a dawdle, a slattern, who neither taught nor restrained her children, whose house was the scene of mismanagement and discomfort from beginning to end..." Her father was no better, having "...no curiosity, and no information beyond his profession; he read only the newspaper and the navy list; he talked only of the dock-yard, the harbour, Spithead, and the Motherbank; he swore and he drank, he was dirty and gross."[44]

Persuasion gives us a wonderfully vivid portrait of the children at Christmas. "On one side was a table, occupied by some chattering girls, cutting up silk and gold paper; and on the other were tressels and trays, bending under the weight of brawn and cold pies, where riotous boys were holding high revel; the whole completed by a roaring Christmas fire, which seemed determined to be heard, in spite of all the noise of others."[45]

But the idea that the devil lies with the parenting and not the child is evident again. Anne Elliott's two nephews, Charles and Walter Musgrove, are almost out of control. It is Captain Wentworth's act of pulling Charles from Anne's back that is the first hint of his enduring love for her. Her brother-in-law explains to Anne that he "could manage them very well, if it were not for [their mother's] interference."[46] Their grandmother tells Anne that she "cannot help wishing [their mother] had a little of your method with those children. They are quite different creatures with you!"[47]

Jane's attitude to the care of children shines out from her references to the little Gardiners in *Pride and Prejudice*. When Mr and Mrs Gardiner leave for Derbyshire with Elizabeth they leave their four children at Longbourne. "The children, two girls of six and eight years old, and two younger boys, were to be left under the particular care of their cousin Jane, who was the general favourite, and whose steady sense and sweetness of temper exactly adapted her for attending to them in every way – teaching them, playing with them, and loving them."[48] Similarly, in *Emma* Miss Woodhouse dotes on her nieces and nephews, and their good behaviour is a product of careful and loving parenting. At the end of *Northanger Abbey*, when Catherine Morland returns to Fullerton, she is welcomed by her parents and her three older siblings and "in the embrace of each…she found herself soothed beyond anything that she had believed possible…In the joyfulness of family love everything for a short time was subdued."[49]

Indeed the characters in Jane Austen's work, and in particular the women, are often judged by the author according to their attitude to children. In Jane's unfinished novel, *The Watsons*, written when she was in her mid to late twenties, the character of Emma Watson is defined by her kindness to Charles Blake, the ten year old boy who is allowed to the ball at Stanton, and is so excited to have been engaged "this week" to Miss Osborne as a partner for the first two dances. His disappointment when Miss Osborne casually abandons him for an officer is palpable. Emma's response is her finest recommendation.

"If the poor little boy's face had in its happiness been interesting to Emma, it was infinitely more so under this sudden reverse; - he stood the picture of disappointment, with crimsoned cheeks, quivering lip, and eyes bent on the floor… Emma did not think, or reflect; - she felt and acted – 'I shall be very happy to dance with you sir, if you like it."[50]

In 1920, Jane's great niece, Mary Augusta Austen-Leigh observed that, "If we try to imagine Jane Austen's novels deprived of their children, we shall see that in some cases they could hardly be carried on at all, while in every instance that sense of simple truthfulness, of warmth, and of life which they now possess would be greatly lessened or altogether wanting."[51]

Jane Austen believed that children should be both seen and heard, should be nurtured, and above all, should be loved. This is perhaps the greatest testament to her childhood.

V: EDUCATION

Jane until the age of seven would have been taught principally by her mother how to read and write. One of the main activities of a female member of a household such as the Austens' would have been to write letters to the extended family. This was, after all, the only practical means of staying in touch in the days before the telegram, telephone and mechanised transportation. She would also have been taught craft and needlework, a principal occupation of well-born ladies of the time. This was not merely a useful pursuit in the making and mending of clothing and other textiles. It was also a recreational pursuit. Ladies would sit together, sew and converse. Perhaps one of them would entertain the others on the pianoforte.

Jane was also brought up to love music and became quite accomplished. Later she was taught by the assistant organist at Winchester Cathedral who would visit pupils in Steventon and other Hampshire villages. She may also have taken in some geography and even natural history. Mr Austen owned an eighteen inch terrestrial globe, and a microscope; although it is likely that these were principally for the use of his private pupils. It is apparent from a letter Jane wrote to her brother Frank in later life, that she was allowed to share history lessons with the boys. She mentions "Ghosts" of historical Swedish figures: "Gustavus Vasa, & Charles 12th, and Christina, & Linnaeus…I have a great respect for former Sweden, so zealous as it was for Protestantism."[52] Goldsmith's four volume *The History of England*, from the earliest times to the death of George II, was used in her father's schoolroom, and was read by her in 1790.[53] Her comments in the margin of the books, which have survived, echo, or pre-figure, her juvenile spoof *"History of England"* with its strong pro-Stuart, Tory sympathies, imbued from her family.

It is quite possible too that she was given drawing lessons by John Claude Nettes, who was to become a famous water colourist. In 1784, George Austen made a payment to Nettes of eleven pounds and nine shillings, not far short of one thousand pounds in today's money. Apparently Jane had "not only an excellent taste for drawing, but, in her earlier days, evinced great power of hand in the management of the pencil."[54]

The Rectory, quite apart from the schoolroom, also had a considerable library, in excess of five hundred volumes; quite a sizeable number for a private collection at that time. Jane's brother Henry Austen, writing shortly after her death in his 1818 Biographical Notice to the first edition of *Persuasion* and *Northanger Abbey*, made this observation about his father, and the literary environment into which Jane was born. "[George Austen] being not only a profound scholar, but possessing a most exquisite taste in every species of literature, it is not wonderful that his daughter Jane should, at a very early age, have become sensible to the charms of style, and enthusiastic in the cultivation of her own language."[55]

Books were expensive before the advent of mass printing techniques, and paperback editions. The volumes had to be printed by a typesetter, and sewn together by hand. Most of the books in the Austens' home would have been of a sacred nature, or of the humanities: history, philosophy, ethics, and household management. Jane was certainly encouraged to learn French. In December 1783 she was given *Fables Choissis*, a little textbook of simple stories in French.[56] In June 1784, she was given a copy of *Mentoria, or The Young Ladies Instructor: in familiar conversations, on moral and entertaining subjects*.[57] Her brother Henry later recalled that "at a very early age she was enamoured of Gilpin on the Picturesque... Her reading was very extensive in history and belles lettres; her memory extremely tenacious. Her favourite moral writers were Johnson in prose and Cowper in verse."[58] Jane acquired a copy of Johnson's *Rasselas* in 1790, and in 1791, the six volume set of *Hayley's Poems and Plays*, containing works by the likes of Pope, Defoe, Fielding and Goethe.[59] She was much influenced, as we shall see, by Fielding, and she also became familiar with that other master of burlesque, Richard Brinsley Sheridan, whose play *The Rivals* had been performed as part of the family's theatricals in 1784.

She was particularly fond of Richardson's epic novel *Sir Charles Grandison* (1754) which tells the story of a young orphaned woman, Harriet Byron, who is confident in her own intelligence and abilities, and unafraid to challenge the prevailing norms of male hegemony. What, asks Harriet, can a woman do "who is addressed by a man of talents inferior to her own? Must she hide her light under a bushel, purely to do credit to a man...The men, in short, are sunk, my dear; and the Women but barely swim." Sir Charles Grandison broke new ground in portraying women as independent agents with independent minds. This proto-feminism had a profound influence on Jane, as it had, in turn, on her six principal heroines.

Jane's first experience of education beyond the home environment was an unfortunate one. It was in the spring of 1783, at the age of seven, that she and Cassandra, together with their older cousin Jane Cooper, the daughter of their mother's sister, were sent to Oxford to be tutored by Dr Cooper's widowed sister, Mrs Cawley, the widow of a Principal of Brasenose College. It may be that the reasoning behind this was simply that the rectory was too small for all the boys George Austen intended to take in. As well as the five Austen children there were by this time five or six pupils. Perhaps it was also felt that it was more fitting for the girls to grow up in a more feminine environment. It must, however, have been a difficult experience for Jane at the tender age of seven, who had only known the countryside, to be thrust into the bustle of a city environment, separated from her parents. "One's heart aches for a dejected mind of eight years old"[60], she later wrote, having heard that two of her nieces were being sent away to school.

Later that same year Mrs Cawley moved the school to Southampton, apparently to avoid an outbreak of measles in Oxford. But it was a short-lived move from the frying pan into the fire. Southampton was a spa town but it was also a military port. In August 1783, troops returning from Gibraltar were billeted there, and brought with them an outbreak of typhus, commonly known in those days as gaol fever. It was common in prisons, and was the product of over-crowding in insanitary conditions, or, as in this case, a sea voyage in confined quarters. Both Jane and Cassandra were infected. Mrs Cawley, for reasons best known to herself, did not think it necessary to inform their parents but Jane Cooper, who was twelve, had the common sense to write to her mother, as a result of which Mrs Austen and Mrs Cooper travelled to Southampton and brought the girls back. Jane was very ill and nearly died. Unfortunately Mrs Cooper also caught the fever, and did not survive. She died on 25th October.

The year following her mother's death, Jane Cooper, aged thirteen, was sent to the Ladies Boarding School in Reading, otherwise known as the Abbey House School. In July 1785, Cassandra, then twelve, followed her. According to Anna Lefroy, Jane insisted on going too, although perhaps, at the age of nine, a little young. Anna wrote that her grandmother had told her that "it was her own doing; she [Jane] would go with Cassandra", and, apparently directly reporting her grandmother's speech,: "if Cassandra's head had been going to be cut off, Jane would have her's cut off too."[61]

The Abbey House School was just about the leading school for the daughters of the gentry and the professional classes in the south of England. It was almost certainly in part the model for Mrs Goddard's school where Harriet Smith had been boarded in *Emma*, a school which did not profess "in long sentences of refined nonsense, to combine liberal acquirement with elegant morality upon new principles and new systems – and where young ladies for enormous pay might be screwed out of health and into vanity – but a real, honest, old-fashioned Boarding-school, where a reasonable quantity of accomplishments were sold at a reasonable price, and where girls might be sent to be out of the way and scramble themselves into a little education, without any danger of coming back prodigies."[62]

The school had something of the Gothic about it, and must have fuelled Jane's imagination in this regard. Part of its premises included the inner gateway of Reading Abbey, which was all that remained intact of the twelfth-century monastery. The rest of the school occupied a large brick house attached to the eastern side of the gateway. There were dormitories for sixty or seventy girls, two to a bed. Downstairs was the schoolroom for prayers, lessons and dinner, and the ballroom for dancing and acting.

There was a "beautiful old-fashioned garden, where the young ladies were allowed to wander, under tall trees, in hot summer evenings"[63], and a view of the romantic ruins of the rest of the abbey. The gateway "had rooms above, and on each side of it a vast staircase, of which the balustrades had been gilt." There were also "many little nooks and round closets, and many larger and smaller rooms and passages."[64] The children's writer, Mary Martha Sherwood, almost an exact contemporary of Jane Austen, was a pupil at the school, and may very well have been there at the same time as Jane. She later recalled her days there with fondness, and in particular the parlour breakfasts, and a "huge plate of toast and butter." She had never been allowed to eat toast and butter before, "nor to come near a fire." She reported herself to be "supremely happy under this new order of things."[65]

The syllabus at the school included writing, spelling, French, history, and geography, needlework, drawing, music and dancing, as well as some elementary arithmetic. The school was well equipped with teaching aids – globes, a magic lantern with historical plates, charts and maps, and scenes for theatrical exhibitions. After morning lessons, the girls were left to their own devices; free to run around in the garden, or explore the old ruins.

They did, of course, come back to Steventon for the holidays, and they also received the odd visit. On 12th October 1785, their mother's cousin, the Reverend Thomas Leigh of Aldestrop, on the way to Mill Hill, dropped in and gave them a guinea. In December, their brother Edward and cousin Edward Cooper came to Reading and took them out to dinner in one of the local inns.[66] However, the Austen girls did not stay at the Abbey House School for long. It seems likely that their father simply could not afford it. The fees were £35 a year for each pupil. In mid-December 1786, the girls were brought back to Steventon for good; their formal education was at an end.

Thereafter, it appears that Jane was essentially self taught, like the Bennett girls in *Pride and Prejudice*: "such of us as wished to learn, never wanted the means. We were always encouraged to read, and had all the masters that were necessary."[67] She made extensive use of her father's library, and her novels are a testament to how well-read she became. She also had her family around her, although reduced by the absence of James and Edward; and Francis too who, by the time she returned from Reading, had been sent to Portsmouth to pursue his naval career. Upon their return, then, Jane and Cassandra would have had Henry, and little Charles, as their daily companions, together with two or three of their father's pupils who were then in residence. Henry, four years older than Jane, must have been something of an influential figure. According to Anna Lefroy he was "brilliant in conversation, and like his Father, blessed with a hopefulness of temper, which in adapting itself to all circumstances, even the most adverse, seemed to create a perpetual sunshine of the mind." John Willing and Charles Fowle, amongst her father's pupils, must also have made an impression upon her young mind, and they became friends well into adulthood.

On 21st December 1786, not long after their return from Reading, their cousin Eliza, twenty-five years old and now Madame de Feuillide, and their aunt, Mrs Hancock, came to stay, along with Eliza's infant son. It seems that her husband had sent her home, whilst pregnant, because he wanted the child to be born in England. She wrote that "he greatly wishes him to be a native of England."[68] Alas, he was born in Calais before they could embark. Eliza had been living abroad since Jane was a baby, and so Jane only knew of her through word of mouth, and the letters she wrote of her glamorous life in Paris. She and her mother had taken a house near Portman Square, and she was leading quite a glamorous life in London too. Their arrival must have made quite the impression on the eleven year old girl.

They brought with them as a present for Jane's eleventh birthday Arnaud Berquin's newly published children's stories of morality, *L'ami des enfans* which, perhaps unusually for the period, were not fairy tales but concerned themselves with events which might happen to children in their every day lives. They encouraged generosity, kindness to servants and animals, charity to the poor, hard work, courage, grace, ease of address, deportment and conversation, and seeking their mother's advice when in doubt. They contemplated childhood reading as a familial exercise; some of the stories are plays with parts for other members of the family. A letter from Mrs Austen, written a few days later, provides a poignant snapshot of the benign and fertile environment in which Jane was to continue her education and reach the milestone of puberty.

"We are now happy in the company of our sister Hancock, Madame de Feuillide & the little boy; they came to us last Thursday Sennet & will stay with us till the end of next month…Madame is grown quite lively, when a child we used to think her too grave. We have borrowed a pianoforte, and she plays to us every day; on Tuesday we are to have a very snug little dance in our parlour, just our own children, nephew & nieces, (for the two little Coopers come tomorrow) quite a family party…Five of my children are now at home, Henry, Frank, Charles & my two girls, who have now quite left school…Every one of our fireside join in love, & duty as due and in wishing a happy 87 to our dear friends at Seal."[69] The "two little Coopers", Edward and Jane, were by then seventeen and sixteen respectively.

Eliza returned to London in the New Year, renting a smart house in Orchard Street. She invited her cousin Henry Austen, still only sixteen and her future husband, to stay with her in April. Later in the year she wrote to her other cousin, Phylly Walter, of her plans for the Christmas season when, it will be recalled, she inspired the theatricals of that year.

"You know we have long projected acting this Christmas in Hampshire & this scheme would go on a vast deal better would you lend your assistance…on finding there were two unengaged parts I immediately thought of you,

& am particularly commissioned by my Aunt Austen & her whole family to make the earliest application possible…Your accommodations at Steventon are the only thing my Aunt Austen & myself are uneasy about, as the house being very full of company, she says she can only promise you 'a place to hide your head in but I think you will not mind this inconvenience…I assure you we shall have a most brilliant party & a great deal of amusement, the house full of company & frequent ball. You cannot possibly resist so many temptations, especially when I tell you that your old friend James is returned from France & is to be of the acting party."[70]

It was during this Christmas season that the rather saucy play, *The Wonder: A Woman Keeps A Secret* was performed twice. Eliza played the part of Violante who falls in love with Don Felix despite her father's wish that she enter a nunnery. It is not difficult to imagine Eliza flirting with both of the Austen brothers who took part, namely Henry and James. It was James who would write the prologue to the plays which were performed, and it was Henry who read the prologue in this case. James gave Henry these words to speak which are almost certainly deliberately suggestive.

"…many a trick and many a gambol neat,
And many a frolic, helped the time to cheat.
Nor yet in lov'd Eliza's golden reign
Did Christmas ever claim its rites in vain."[71]

It was Eliza who spoke James's epilogue, containing another piece of proto-feminism:

"…Woman holds a second place no more…
These Men all wise, these 'Lords of the Creation',
To our superior sway themselves submit,
Slaves to our charms and vassals to our wit;
We can with ease their ev'ry sense beguile'
And melt their Resolutions with a smile…"

In January, John Fletcher's rather saucy Jacobean comedy *The Chances* was put on, followed by Garrick's even more risqué farce, *Bon Ton*, about a couple narrowly saved from vice whilst on the brink of adultery. Eliza played Miss Tittup who declares: "We must marry you know, because other people of fashion marry; but I should think very meanly of myself, if, after I was married, I should feel the least concern at all about my husband." The fact that these plays, with such subject matter, were chosen is, at first glance, perhaps surprising. It must be remembered, however, that standards of public morality were very different in the late Georgian and Regency periods than they were to become in the Victorian era.

Eliza de Feuillide, in any event, was clearly a sparkling, funny and entertaining flirt, and her example surely inspired more than a few of the characters which decorate Jane's fiction. The words of Miss Tittup, and of that feminist epilogue, could easily have been spoken by her early anti-heroine Lady Susan. In the summer of 1788, Eliza wrote to Miss Walter enquiring after her latest beau, asking for a "a full and particular account of all your flirtations...I want of all things a description of his person...is he tall or short, fair or brown, and particularly are his eyes black or blue?...I was last night at a party of about two hundred..." She goes on to describe a Colonel who was as "captivating as ever": "...whom should I see in Hyde Park last Sunday but the charming Baddy in his still more charming curricle – How my heart beat!...Tomorrow I dine with a Tunbridge Lady &CC, by the bye I am more in Love than ever with this &CC."[72] This could be the voice of Lydia Bennett.

Another major influence on Jane at this time was Madame Lefroy with whom, as we have seen, she was "very intimate" and "much encouraged". According to her brother, Egerton Brydges, this must have been a benign influence. "She [Madame Lefroy] had an exquisite taste for poetry, and could almost repeat the chief english poets by heart, especially Milton, Pope, Collins, Gray, and the poetical passages of Shakespeare; and she composed easy verses herself with great facility...The charm of her first address was magical; her eyes were full of lustre; and the copiousness and eloquence of her conversation attracted all ears and won all hearts...She was spotless; and her heart was the seat of every affectionate and moral virtue..."[73]

She was also a poet in her own right. She wrote a number of poems for her siblings, several of which were collected after her death, and published privately by her son in 1812. She also had at least two prose articles published anonymously in the *Gentleman's Magazine*. She took a leading role in promoting the education of children in the parish by setting up a Sunday school, where she taught the basics of reading, writing and scripture, and she played an active part in vaccinating the local population against smallpox. She must have been quite an inspiration to Jane.

And so, perhaps, was Anna Lefroy's brother, Sir Egerton Brydges. He was a published novelist and bibliographer. It seems likely that he saw quite a lot of Jane. He became a tenant for a while at Deane Parsonage, and recorded that her house at Ashe "was always full of company."[74] He specifically recalled Jane in his autobiography as "a little child: she was very intimate with Mrs Lefroy and much encouraged by her."[75]

Jane was exposed to novels. She read Fielding and Richardson. The novel was still a new art form. Although it may have had its origins in the ancient world, its revival in English literature dates from the early stirrings of the romantic movement. It emerged in the form of the Gothic novel, a sensational literature of terror, the essence of which was violent sensibilities and passions, usually arising from themes such as abduction, atrocity, horror and the occult. The term

"Gothic" comes from Gothic architecture which conjures up images of ghouls and ghosts, and things which go bump in the night. Typically the novels were set in remote locations, either in space or time, where the ordinary norms of behaviour were in a state of suspension.

Whatever its origins, the novel as a form was certainly looked down upon by anyone who had intellectual pretensions in the late eighteenth century. The nearest modern comparisons are perhaps with the soap opera, or the slasher movie. Although many a twenty-first century intellectual may enjoy Eastenders, Coronation Street, or Blood of the Vampire, they are unlikely to admit to it. An endearing feature of Jane's father was that he did. He enjoyed reading novels. He presumably had a collection of them, and encouraged Jane to enjoy them too. One of the main themes of *Northanger Abbey* (the first of Jane's mature novels to be written), and the driver of the plot, is the heroine's love of the Gothic novel, and the author's staunch defence of this art form.

And yet, Jane Austen was later to write of her education in December 1815, in a letter to a literary admirer, "I think I may boast myself to be, with all possible vanity, the most unlearned and uninformed female who ever dared to be an authoress."[76] Although she had little formal education, it was no less than most young ladies of her class and time. They would be expected to gain some degree of skill in music, the visual arts, and modern languages. We know that she had a good knowledge of French, and learned a little Italian. She also picked up some Latin, and inscribed the words "Ex Dono mei Patris" ("from the gift of my father") in the second volume of her manuscript juvenile writings, to which we will turn shortly.

For Jane Austen, education in any event was much more than the formal gathering of information. It is clear from her novels that she considered a system of education should be more holistic, should address the whole person, and should be a moral as well as an intellectual training. Maria and Julia Bertram in *Mansfield Park* are "entirely deficient in the less common acquirements of self-knowledge, generosity, and humility". Their father had to learn that he had made a "direful mistake in his plan of education" because "they had never been properly taught to govern their inclinations and tempers." Darcy regrets that "As a child I was taught what was right, but I was not taught to correct my temper." Darcy learns that from Elizabeth, as Fanny Price is perfected by Edmund; Emma by Mr Knightley. The exchange of knowledge about what is right, and how to behave, is often seen as a strong basis for love. Jane, largely taught in the bosom of her family, had this in abundance.

There is, nevertheless, evidence from *Persuasion* that Jane – possessed of such a keen intelligence and brilliant perception – bitterly resented the fact that she was not afforded the same advantages as her brothers. Through the mouth of Anne Elliott she makes the following observation. "Men have had every advantage of us in telling their own story. Education has been theirs in so much higher a degree; the pen has been in their hands."[77] This of course is laced with irony. The pen, notwithstanding the disadvantages of her sex, was very much in hers.

VI: JUVENILIA

The opportunities for women writers had never been greater than in the late eighteenth century. First, it was generally much easier in that era for authors to have novels commercially published than now. Second, the novel, perhaps because of the characteristics of the romantic and the Gothic, rather than in spite of them, was increasingly looked upon as a vehicle in which the female writer could excel. From the 1760s to the 1790s, the number of novels by women which were being published increased by no less than fifty per cent in each decade. However, the seeking of publicity was still regarded as a non-feminine characteristic. It would also conceivably be a risk to a woman's reputation and therefore her marriageability, and so many women writers of the time published their novels anonymously, including Sarah Fielding, Frances Burney and Ann Radcliffe, with the works of all of whom Jane would have been familiar. Their names would appear above their titles only when their reputations had been secured. During her lifetime, Jane's never did.

It is clear that Jane had a burning ambition to be a published novelist from the age of eleven or twelve. Her earliest known compositions, which she began to write in 1787 or 1788, now known as the *Juvenilia*, were later copied and collected in three notebooks, inscribed by Jane herself as Volume the First, Volume the Second, and Volume the Third, and made to appear as published works. We know from the date on the frontispiece, that Jane began to compile the third volume on 6th May 1792. There are twenty-nine separate pieces, amounting to ninety thousand words. The collections were probably assembled for convenience. The Austen family would often read aloud for entertainment, and it is likely that Jane would have read from her own stories. The original manuscript copies, frequently dedicated to family members, would most likely have been given away as presents. It is also reasonable to suppose that Jane enjoyed the thrill of seeing her work in a form akin to publication.

The contents of the volumes are broadly ordered chronologically, although this is not always true. Most of the work in the first volume dates from 1787-1790 but *The Three Sisters* was written in 1792, and the *Fragment* and *Ode to Pity* in 1793. Almost all of the contents of the second volume was written between 1790 and 1792, save for *Scraps* in 1793, and the third volume was all written in 1792. The work falls into three groups: the earliest writings between 1787 and 1790; the two burlesque or parody pieces (*Love and Friendship* and *The History of England*) in 1790 and 1791 respectively, and the later, more mature, writings in 1792 and 1793.

The writings in the first group are all within Volume the First. The notebook itself is dedicated to Jane's friend, Martha Lloyd, "As a small testimony of the gratitude I feel for your late generosity to me in finishing my muslin Cloak, I beg leave to offer you this little production of your sincere Friend." Martha Lloyd (ten years older than Jane), and her younger sister Mary, were the daughters of Mrs Martha Lloyd, a widow who had taking up the letting of the Deane Parsonage from Jane's father after Egerton Brydges had moved out. This was in the spring of 1789, and so the dedication can be dated from when Jane was just 13, at the earliest. However, this is the dedication at the beginning of the collected edition.

The original manuscripts from which the first volume was

compiled would have been written from as early as 1787. Some of the writing is dated, and also the dedications at the beginning of many of the individual works provide a clue as to their date. *The Visit*, a little play, is dedicated to the Reverend James Austen in which Jane hopes that the little drama "will…afford some amusement to so respectable a Curate as yourself." The emphasis on the word "curate" suggests that it was something of a novelty, and therefore may be shortly after her brother's ordination. He was in fact ordained on 10th December 1787. It is most likely, though, that this work was not written until around the end of 1788. It contains a quote from the play *High Life Below Stairs* which was performed that Christmas as part of the family theatricals.[78]

It is believed from stylistic analysis that *Edgar and Emma*, *Frederic & Alfreda* and *Amelia Webster* (dedicated to her mother) are even earlier, and were probably written in 1787. *Jack and Alice* and *The Adventures of Mr Harely* are both dedicated to "Francis William Austen Esq Midshipman on board His Majesty's Ship the Perseverance." Francis left the Royal Naval Academy and joined the Perseverance to train as a Midshipman in December 1788, although he was not officially appointed Midshipman until a year later.

These early writings, in sharp distinction to the bland morality stories of Berquin, consist largely of extravagant, irreverent comedy and knockabout farce, of the kind which a lively and intelligent child of twelve or thirteen tends to revel in now and then, although the principal medium may have changed. It was heavily influenced by her brothers' interest in the burlesque, and in particular by the literary journal they published at Oxford, *The Loiterer*, of which sixty issues were produced between 1789 and 1790, and which was modelled on Dr Johnson's famous periodicals, *The Rambler* and *The Idler*. Another influence was her interest in drama, and in particular the works of Fielding and Sheridan. Fielding's *Tom Thumb* and

Sheridan's *The Critic*, two of the most successful examples of eighteenth century burlesque, are both heavily referenced.

Although much of this delightful work is immature, random, episodic, and clumsily plotted, as one might expect, it contains the earliest flashes of Jane's brilliance: her biting humour and irony, her vivid imagination built upon her personal experience, her distinctive voice, her mastery of paragraph and sentence construction, and the comic distance which is built between the author and her characters; features which enrich the juvenile works, before being refined to perfection in the mature novels. Her main purpose was to create humour and hilarity from the absurd but she was also concerned with the sort of parody championed by Fielding and Sheridan, who were mocking the literary and dramatic conventions of the time.

Most of this first volume consists of short stories. Five of them are styled as novels and arranged into short chapters. The longest extends to no more than twenty pages in the printed text. There are four short stories which consist of a few paragraphs, and a short story *Amelia Webster* which is in the form of the epistolary novel, although but three pages long. The episolary novel, in other words a novel formed of a series of letters, was a very popular form at the time. It had been popularised by Samuel Richardson with his highly successful works *Pamela* in 1740 and *Clarissa* in 1748. Jane was very familiar with both. There are also two little plays, again no more than a few pages long.

The very first work to appear in the Austenian canon is characteristic of these early works. It is styled as a novel in five short chapters: *Frederic & Elfrida*.[79] The central character is Charlotte, whose father is the rector of a village called Crankhumdunberry. She describes, "A Grove of Poplars which led from the Parsonage to a verdant Lawn enamelled with a variety of variegated flowers & watered by a purling Stream...", perhaps not that far removed from the Steventon Rectory but the stream was "...brought from the Valley of Tempé by a passage under ground."

Charlotte and her friends go to visit Mrs Fitzroy and her two daughters, one of whom has an "engaging Exterior & beautifull outside." However, they much prefer the younger sister, "notwithstanding your forbidding Squint, your greazy tresses & your swelling Back, which are more frightful than imagination can paint or pen describe, I cannot refrain from expressing my raptures, at the engaging Qualities of your Mind, which so amply atone for the Horror, with which your first appearance must ever inspire the unwary visitor." Perhaps this is a comment by Jane on the perceived distinction between her, in the early stages of puberty, and her sister Cassandra; so unkindly pointed out by her cousin Phylly in the letter of July 1788. If so, it is a very early and biting example of Jane's wit and her sense of irony.

This little work also contains elements of a parody of the novel, or at least a parody of the features of the novel imagined by their detractors – in other words the excessive sensibilities. Charlotte had become engaged to two men at the same time and "the reflection of her past folly, operated so strongly on her mind, that she resolved to be guilty of a greater, & to that end threw herself into a deep stream which ran thro' her Aunt's pleasure grounds in Portland Place."

Even more dramatically Fredric & Elfrida demand that their friend's mother consents to a marriage. If she agrees, "this smelling Bottle which I enclose in my right hand, shall be yours & yours forever...But if you refuse to join their hands in 3 days time, this dagger which I enclose in my left shall be steeped in your hearts blood." Jane comments, with perfect ironical timing, "Such gentle & sweet persuasion could not fail of having the desired effect." (The eighteenth century equivalent of "an offer you can't refuse".) The story concludes with Elfrida having such "a succession of fainting fits, that she had scarcely patience enough to recover from one before she fell into another."

A recurring feature in these little gems is the deployment of an ironic juxtaposition of formal language with high farcical comedy in order to mock the traditions of sentimental fiction, a technique which goes beyond slapstick humour. George Hervey in *Amelia Webster*, writes to his love, "I saw you lovely Fair one as you passed on Monday last, before our House in your way to Bath. I saw you thro' a telescope, & was so struck by your Charms that from that time to this I have not tasted human food."[80]

In *Edgar & Emma*[81], the eponymous heroine is in love with Edgar, the son of Mr Willmott, a local dignitary. When the family arrive to visit, Emma "continued at her Dressing-room window in anxious Hopes of seeing young Edgar descend from the Carriage". When Mr and Mrs Willmott first appear Emma begins to tremble. When Edgar's siblings descend from the carriage, she turns pale, and when the two youngest girls are lifted from the coach, "Emma sunk breathless on a Sopha." Edgar does not however appear. Here is the dramatic conclusion of this *coup de coeur*.

"Emma had continued in the Parlour some time before she could summon up sufficient courage to ask Mrs Willmot after the rest of her family; & when she did , it was in so low, so faltering a voice that no one knew she spoke. Dejected by the ill success of her first attempt she made no other, till Mrs Willmot's desiring one of the little Girls to ring the bell for their Carriage, she stepped across the room & seizing the string said in a resolute manner. 'Mrs Willmot, you do not stir from this House till you let me know how all the rest of your family do, particularly your eldest son.'" Having been told that Edgar was at college: "It was with difficulty that Emma could refrain from tears on hearing of the absence of Edgar; she remained however tolerably composed till the Willmots were gone when having no check to the overflowings of her greif, she gave free vent to them, & retiring to her own room, continued in tears the remainder of her life."

Some of this is quite saucy stuff to come from the pen of a child, and Jane may very well have been heavily influenced by Eliza, and the theatricals which took place over the Christmas of 1787. In *Sir William Mountague*[82], a farcical little story two pages long, the hero falls in love no fewer than five times. First, he is in love with the Miss Cliftons but "not knowing which to prefer he left the Country and took Lodgings in a small Village near Dover." In Dover he "became enamoured of a young Widow of Quality" Lady Percival. She agrees to be his wife, but he then breaks it off when the day of the wedding is fixed for the beginning of the hunting season. Sir William is sorry to lose her but "as he knew that he should have been much more grieved by the Loss of the 1st of September, his Sorrow was not without a mixture of Happiness, & his Affliction was considerably lessened by his Joy." He then falls in love with his friend's niece. She prefers Mr Stanhope, so Sir William shoots Mr Stanhope and "the lady had then no reason to refuse him…" When Mr Stanhope's sister demands atonement for the murder of her brother, he offers himself instead, and they are married the next day. But after a couple of weeks he sees "a charming young Woman entering a Chariot in Brook Street" and falls "violently in love." On discovering that she is the sister of Lady Percival, he hopes that his acquaintance with her Ladyship will afford him "free access" to her sister. This piece can probably be dated to the autumn of 1788, because the first of September is referred to as "the following Monday", and the first of September was a Monday in that year.

Another literary technique deployed by Jane at this early age is her use of bathos, a form of irony in its own right: an abrupt change of key from the sublime to the ridiculous, often in order to mock pretension or pomposity. And so Mr Willmot "was the representative of a very ancient Family & possessed besides his paternal Estate, a considerable share in a Lead mine & a ticket in the Lottery."[83] In *The Memoirs of Mr Clifford*[84], the eponymous hero was a very rich young man who kept a great many Carriages "of which I do not recollect half." He set off from Bath to London. "However when he was once got to Devizes he was determined to comfort himself with a good hot Supper and therefore ordered a whole Egg to be boiled for him & his servants."[85] Charles Adams, a slightly ridiculous character in *Jack and Alice*[86] is "an amiable, accomplished & bewitching young Man. Of so dazzling a Beauty that none but Eagles could look him in the Face...The Beams that darted from his Eyes" were so strong that "no one dared venture within half a mile of them; he had therefore the best part of the Room to himself."[87]

The title of *Henry and Eliza*[88], again styled as a novel, must have been inspired by the relationship between her brother and her cousin. Although Henry did not marry Eliza until ten years later, after the death of her French husband at the hands of Madame la Guillotine in 1794, they were clearly very close whilst Eliza was staying in England, and she invited him to stay with her in London in the April of 1787. The fact that it is dedicated to Jane Cooper suggests that it was written around the Christmas of 1788. The theatricals that year included *The Sultan* in which Miss Cooper played the part of Roxelana.[89]

The fanciful plot of *Henry and Eliza* has more in common with a nursery tale than any of the others. Sir George and Lady Harcourt find a little three year old girl in the 'thick foliage of a Haycock". They adopt her and call her Eliza, whereupon she lives a life of uninterrupted happiness until she is eighteen when she is thrown out for stealing a fifty pound note. After amusing herself for some hours singing under a tree, she decides to become a lady's companion to a Duchess. Instead she marries Henry, the lover of the Duchess's friend, and leaves a note which is short and to the point, "Madam, We are married and gone. Henry & Eliza." The Duchess sends out an army of three hundred men to bring them back and "have them put to Death in some torturelike manner, after a few years Confinement." Henry and Eliza flee to France. After the death of Henry a few years later, Eliza returns with her two boys, is seized by the Duchess and imprisoned. She escapes, returns to Sir George and Lady Harcourt and is welcomed back with open arms. It turns out that Eliza was their real child all along, Lady Harcourt having left her in the Haycock and forgotten all about her.

Embedded even within this farcical tale, however, are little gems which foreshadow what was to come: examples of comic understatement, and biting, mocking wit. On the imprisonment of Eliza and her children, Jane observes that "no sooner had Eliza entered her Dungeon than the first thought which occurred to her, was how to get out of it again." Having escaped "she began to find herself rather hungry, & had reason to think, by their biting off two of her fingers, that her Children were much in the same situation." On her way back to the Harcourts, Eliza "on turning the Corner at which she was stationed, stopped to give the Postilion an opportunity of admiring the beauty of the prospect." One cannot help but think that this was a friendly dig at her cousin's vanity and reputation as a bit of a flirt.

There are other elements of the grotesque in these earliest works, again reminiscent of the fairy tales of central Europe. In *Jack & Alice*[90], a "lovely young Woman lying apparently in great pain" is found lying by Alice and Lady Williams "beneath a Citron tree". Prevailed upon to relate her life story, she concludes by explaining that upon finally entering the grounds of her beloved's house, she found herself, "suddenly seized by the leg & on examining the cause of it, found that I was caught in one of the steel traps so common in gentlemen's grounds." She screamed "till the woods resounded again & till one of the inhuman Wretch's servants came to my assistance & released me from my dreadfull prison, but not before one of my legs was entirely broken." Lady Williams, observing that the young woman's leg should be set before further delay, "immediately began and performed the operation with great skill which was the more wonderfull on account of her having never performed such a one before." It is not clear whether the character of Alice was inspired by anybody in particular but she was certainly a bit of a soak. "She has many rare & charming qualities, but sobriety is not one of them."

Above all, there is in these earliest of works, a sparkling sense of comedy, naughtiness, and laughter, burnished with a remarkable talent for the succinct aphorism, or turn of phrase. Lady Williams "was a widow with a handsome Jointure & the remains of a very handsome face" who advises Alice to "preserve yourself from a first Love and you need not fear a second."[91] It is a glimpse through the eyes of a brilliant young woman observing the world through a crack in the door, or behind a twitching curtain, and making a good deal of fun out of the foibles and failings of the people around her; not the least of which is a fondness for the bottle. "The Johnsons were a family of Love, & though a lttle addicted to the Bottle and the Dice, had many good qualities…the Bottle being pretty briskly pushed about by the 3 Johnsons, the whole party not excepting Virtue were carried home, Dead Drunk."[92]

Love and Friendship[93], which falls into the second group of the Juvenilia and in the second volume, is dated: "Finis Sunday June 13th 1790". It is dedicated to Eliza, "Madame la Comtesse de Feuillide", who spent some time at Steventon that summer. Jane was still only fourteen years old. It is the second example of an epistolary work by Austen; although this is only form rather than substance. All but one of the letters are from Laura to Marianne, the daughter of Laura's friend, Isabel. Isabel has asked Laura (in the first letter) to give Marianne an account of her life story. Laura then proceeds to relate it in a series of fourteen letters. It is the longest work so far, and extends to over thirty pages in the printed text. It is, without doubt, more sophisticated in its literary humour, although the story is as (intentionally) absurd as most of the earlier works.

A young man called Edward stumbles across Laura's family home. He had refused to oblige his father's wishes as to his future bride, and had left home. Laura and Edward instantly fall in love and are married. They go to Edward's aunt where Laura meets Edward's sister who attempts to turn Edward against her. The arrival of Edward's father is the last straw, and they decamp to Edward's friend, Augustus. His wife, Sophia, instantly becomes the bosom friend of Laura. However this domestic idyll is ruined by the arrest of Augustus who, it turns out, has stolen some money. Edward leaves to go and see Augustus in prison, and promptly disappears. Laura and Sophia then repair to Scotland where Sophia has a cousin called MacDonald. They persuade his daughter to marry against her father's wishes, and, in order to teach MacDonald a lesson, they steal his money. Forced to leave, they take their rest beside a stream when, lo and behold, Edward and Augustus appear in a phaeton. The phaeton overturns and both are killed. Sophia dies of exposure. Laura travels to Edinburgh, and, in the carriage, meets almost everybody still left alive in the story. Edward's father leaves her some money as the widow of his son, and she takes up residence in a "romantic village in the Highlands of Scotland".

This work is a satire on the novel as a form of literature. Its very structure is part of the satire. Although it is arranged as a series of letters, the letters, apart from the first, are all from the same source to the same recipient, who does not respond. This pointless structure is a judgmental comment on how the epistolary novel had become ubiquitous. By the 1780s and 1790s, it had become the most popular form for fiction, merely using the device of the letter as a replacement for chapters.

More than the form, though, *Love and Friendship*, in its substance, is a satire on the late eighteenth century cult of sensibility, and the sentimentalised fiction which was portraying it. As the century drew to a conclusion there was a backlash against this movement. Jane was heavily influenced by Sheridan's trio of burlesques *The Critic*, *The Rivals*, and *The School for Scandal*, and the influence of *The Loiterer* is still palpable, indeed the title itself was most likely inspired by number 27, *Thoughts on Education – A New System recommended*. This issue proffers the following advice to young ladies: "Let every Girl who seeks for happiness conquer both her feelings and her passions. Let her avoid love and friendship." Sentimentalised fiction, a product of the nascent Romantic movement in general, and the Gothic novel in particular, are remorselessly mocked, and with little subtlety. Commenting on the sensibilities of his son, Edward's father, scolding him for his "unmeaning gibberish" opines, "You have been reading novels I suspect."

Love and Friendship is full of overblown sentimental rhetoric which trumps any practical considerations. Laura's only fault, according to Laura, is a "sensibility too tremblingly alive to every affliction of my Friends, my Acquaintance and particularly to every affliction of my own." Laura falls in love with Edward instantly; "no sooner did I first behold him, than I felt that on him the happiness or Misery of my future Life must depend." Edward's marriage to Laura is against the wishes of his father, as a result of which the latter is cast as a monstrous villain. Edward dismisses any practical difficulty caused by the absence of financial support from his father, "What support will Laura want which she can receive from him?" His sister responds archly, "Only those very insignificant ones of Victuals and Drink." He replies, "Does it appear impossible to your vile and corrupted Palate, to exist on Love?"

Such sensibilities are mocked, not just in the context of love, but also in the context of friendship. Sophia, the wife of Edward's friend Augustus, is "all Sensibility and Feeling." The moment Laura and she meet, "We flew into each others arms and after having exchanged vows of mutual Friendship for the rest of our Lives, instantly unfolded to each other the most inward secrets of our Hearts." When Edward and Augustus fly into each others' arms as well, the scene was "too pathetic for the feelings of Sophia and myself. We fainted alternately on a sofa." Nor is this the last time they sigh and faint on a sofa, or "run mad" with emotion.

The emotions though are shallow and artificial, rather than genuine sensibility, even within the context of this parody. The connection between excessive sensibility and hipocrisy is a theme which Sheridan had emphasised in his other great burlesque, *The School for Scandal*. After Augustus is arrested, Sophia protests against being taken to Newgate to see him. "I shall not be able to support the sight of my Augustus in so cruel a confinement – my feelings are sufficiently shocked by the *recital* of his Distress, but to behold it will overpower my Sensibility." The emphasis on the word "recital" is Austen's, not mine. Laura goes on to inform Sophia of a "trifling circumstance" in comparison, namely the death of her parents. The man intended for MacDonald's daughter, Janette, is ridiculed as having no soul because he is "Sensible, well-informed and Agreable...had never read the Sorrows of Werter" and "his Hair bore not the least resemblance of auburn." Later they meet an old widow who has a daughter but "alas she was very plain and her name was Bridget...Nothing therefore could be expected of her."

The dichotomy of sense and sensibility, the clash between Romantic idealism and prudent conservatism, was, of course, a theme which Jane would return to in a rather more subtle way in the future, and the use of the name Marianne perhaps indicates a conscious transition. Although the satire is a little heavy handed in *Love and Friendship*, the wit is beautifully observed and phrased. In the first letter from Isabel to Laura, inviting her to recount her life story to Marianne, Isabel observes that her friend is now fifty-five, and, "If a woman may ever be said to be in safety from the determined Perseverance of disagreable Lovers and the cruel Persecutions of obstinate Fathers, surely it must be at such a time of Life."

Whereas 1787-1790 had seen an early flourishing of Jane's writing career, with the composition of the earlier pieces, up to and including *Love and Friendship*, the year of 1791 does not appear to have been productive in relative terms. Then, in 1792, as we shall see, comes a second flourishing. The reason for this lull, followed by a revival of activity, may be due to two factors: first, the troublesome circumstances of Jane's cousin Eliza and her mother, Mrs Hancock, and, secondly, a shift in the domestic arrangements of the Austen household which followed.

George's sister, Philadelphia Hancock, and her daughter Eliza, had returned from France, and arrived in England on 7th July 1789. Although there is no direct evidence of their motive, it is reasonable to assume that it was to do with the growing crisis in Paris, culminating in the storming of the Bastille just a week later. After staying in Margate for a few months for the health of Eliza's young son, Hastings, they returned to London to live in Orchard Street in the spring of 1791. Soon afterwards, Mrs Hancock developed symptoms of breast cancer, and it soon became clear that the illness was terminal. Eliza's husband was still in France, and, it appears, was unable to leave the continent. In a letter written by Eliza in January 1791, she revealed that her husband had aristocratic sympathies, and had taken refuge in Turin "where the French princes of the Blood are assembled and watching some favourable opportunity to reinstate themselves in the Country they have quitted."[94] It was not until early 1792 that he was able to travel to England, around the time of Mrs Hancock's death on 26th February 1792. However, he was soon obliged to return, or risk being regarded as an emigré, forfeiting his property to the state.

A little later, in August 1792, Eliza went to stay at Steventon, and provides us with a portrait of Jane shortly before her seventeenth birthday. It may be seen from the degree of affection expressed for Jane, that Jane may very well have been pre-occupied by the misfortunes of the de Feuillide family in the previous year.

"Cassandra & Jane are both very much grown. (The latter is now taller than myself) and greatly improved as well in manners as in person both of which are now much more formed than when you saw them. They are I think equally sensible, and both so to a degree seldom met with, but still my heart gives the preference to Jane, whose kind partiality to me, indeed requires a return of the same nature."

There is, however, one very notable, albeit short, exception to the dearth of activity in 1791; namely *The History of England*[95], completed in November of that year. There is a hint in *Love and Friendship* that Jane's mind was already on her History. The overturned phaeton and the Life of Cardinal Wolsey, says Laura, are "an ample subject for reflection on the uncertain Enjoyments of this World." Just as *Love and Friendship* mocks the form and the sentimentalism of the popular novel, the *History* is a parody of the popular historical writing of the time, epitomised by Goldsmith's *History of England* of 1764, in which the style confused the fact with the fiction. The parody begins in the dedication to Cassandra with the self-deprecatory comment: "...by a partial, prejudiced, and ignorant historian." The dedication finishes with: "NB. There will be very few Dates in this History."

It is a short work, being only ten pages or so in the printed text. Each of the chapters is dedicated to the monarchs from Henry IV to Charles I. It is illustrated in Volume the Second with little portraits of each of its subjects by Cassandra. It is quite deliberately littered (or perhaps "bejewelled" is a better word) by partial and prejudicial comments, totally unbecoming of a serious historian, and dipped in the most delicious wit and irony. Much of this is driven by a strong pro-Yorkist and pro-Stuart position. As Brian Southam points out, this is a deliberate counter-point to the anti-Stuart bias in Goldsmith's work. It is also partially a reflection of the traditional Tory sensibilities of the lower gentry of the time, and in particular the Austen family.

According to Jane's nephew, James Edward, when she was a girl Jane "had strong political opinions, especially about the affairs of the sixteenth and seventeenth centuries. She was a vehement defender of Charles I and his grandmother Mary [Queen of Scots]; but I think it was an impulse of feeling than from any enquiry into the evidences by which they must be condemned or acquitted, but she probably shared the feeling of moderate toryism which prevailed in her family."[96] In her copy of Goldsmith's *History of England* Jane had written comments in the margins, most likely at around the same time that she was composing her own *History*. In response to one of the Republican actions, she wrote "Oh! Oh! The Wretches," and then delivers her views about the Stuart family in general: "A family who were always ill-used, betrayed or neglected, whose virtues are seldom allowed, while their errors are never forgotten."[97] These sentiments extended into later life. Her niece Caroline recalled that her aunt "was a most loyal adherent of Charles the 1st, and that she always encouraged my youthful belief in Mary Stuart's perfect innocence of all the crimes with which history has charged her memory."[98]

The tone is set by the first paragraph in which the usurper Henry IV (the scion of the Lancastrian succession) is vilified.

"Henry the 4th ascended the throne of England much to his own satisfaction in the year 1399, after having prevailed on his cousin and predecessor Richard the 2nd, to resign it to him, and to retire for the rest of his life to Pomfret Castle, where he happened to be murdered. It is to be supposed that Henry was married, since he had certainly four sons, but it is not in my power to inform the Reader who was his wife."

As for the feeble minded Henry VI, Jane observes that, "I cannot say much for this Monarch's sense. Nor would I if I could, for he was a Lancastrian." Richard III is acquitted of his traditional role as a monster and an infanticide. She concludes that he "has been in general very severely treated by Historians, but as he was a York, I am rather inclined to suppose him a very respectable Man." Whereas Henry VII, the first of the Tudors, and now generally regarded as a rather good king, if a little parsimonious, is "as great a villain as ever lived", and a "Monster of Iniquity and Avarice."

The greatest bile, however, is reserved for Elizabeth, "that disgrace to humanity, that pest of society… the destroyer of all comfort, the deceitful Betrayer of trust reposed in her, and the Murderess of her Cousin.." Her cousin of course was Mary Queen of Scots, the matriarch of the House of Stuart, being the mother of James I. There is nothing but praise for the Stuarts, and those who supported them. The Duke of Norfolk, although Earl Marshall to Henry VIII, is praised for being "so warm in the Queen of Scotland's cause." The Duke of Somerset was beheaded but even this is regarded as a blessing because "such was the death of Mary Queen of Scotland", and Charles I is vindicated with one argument, "and this Argument is that he was a STUART."

The fact that the work stops well short of the Hanoverian succession of George I in 1714 is probably due to the fact that the expression of such strong pro-Stuart sentiments in that context would be verging on the treasonous. Although, despite the High Tory leanings of the Austens, this was not, of course, supposed to be taken remotely seriously, nor indeed published beyond the family. It was meant to be, and succeeds in being, a thoroughly entertaining and effective parody to be read for pleasure around the tea table, and all this from a girl who had not quite reached her sixteenth birthday. These political leanings, though, would go on to influence her later work. A common thread throughout the mature novels (most obviously in *Mansfield Park*) is the lauding of the Tory values of reason, dignity and moral responsibility, and the satirising of Whiggish materialism.

It was around this time that the Rectory began to be little less crowded. In July 1791, Charles followed Francis to the Royal Naval Academy at Portsmouth, and on 27th December 1791 the first of Jane's brothers was married. Edward, who it will be recalled had been adopted by the wealthy Knight family of Godmersham Park, married Elizabeth Bridges, the daughter of Sir Brook Bridges of Goodnestone Park, Wingham. They settled at Rowling, a small country house provided for them near Goodnestone by Sir Brook. Meanwhile her brother James, recently ordained at Oxford, became the curate at Overton, the nearest town to Steventon. Here he met General Edward Matthew who had served as an equerry to the King, as brigadier-general in New York during the American

Revolutionary War, and as the Governor of Grenada. He was married to the sister of the third Duke of Ancaster. James married their second daughter, Anne, on 27th March 1792. Clearly by marriage, the Austens were moving up in the social heirarchy. With the Austen brothers all departed, there was a little more room at the Rectory. Anna Lefroy, Jane's niece, later painted a vivid picture of the new living arrangements.

"...one of the Bed chambers, that over the Dining room, was plainly fitted up, & converted into a sort of Drawing room; but this transformation did not occur till my Grand Father and Grand Mother had reared a goodly family of children...not probably till my two Aunts, Cassandra and Jane ...were living at home as grown up young ladies. This room, the Dressing room, as they were pleased to call it, communicated with one of smaller size where my two Aunts slept; I remember the common looking carpet with its chocolate ground that covered the floor, and some portions of the furniture. A painted press, with shelves above for books, that stood with its back to the wall next the Bedroom, & opposite the fireplace; my Aunt Jane's Pianoforte – & above all, on a table between the windows, above which hung a looking glass, 2 Tonbridgeware work boxes of oval shape, fitted up with ivory barrels containing reels for silk, yard measures, etc."[99]

George Austen's account at the house furnishing store in Basingstoke shows that he bought a large Wilton carpet and "three remnants" for two pounds twelve shillings on 17th October 1791, and so it is likely that the later *Juvenilia*, perhaps including *The History*, were composed in this newly fitted up dressing room. These new, more spacious living arrangements, more conducive to creative writing, may explain the productivity which followed; for in 1792, Jane wrote four novellas: *The Three Sisters*[100], dedicated to her brother Edward, which was later included in Volume the First;

Lesley Castle[101] in Volume the Second, and *Evelyn*[102] and *Catherine*[103] both in Volume the Third.

The short story *Evelyn* is still in the burlesque tradition. Like *Jack and Alice* it is in the style of a fairy tale, much of which might have come from the pens of the brothers Grimm. It is about a fantasy village called Evelyn in which the fortunate traveller, Mr Gower, has only to ask in order to receive. It also has a touch of the Gothic: "The gloomy appearance of the old Castle frowning on him as he followed it's winding approach, struck him with terror".

In the other three works, however, there is a noticeable movement away from knockabout comedy and burlesque into realism, with a more mature characterisation and plot formation. Thus, character is no longer a function of appearance. "Never was there a sweeter face, a finer form, or a less amiable Heart than Louisa."

However, the pudding is, as yet, half-baked, which makes these works, generally speaking, disappointing in comparision to the earlier writings. Thus, in *Leslie Castle*, an epistolary novella, the letters from Margaret to her friend Charlotte are an attempt to construct a more considered narrative but they are interrupted by the replies from Charlotte, and her friend Lady Lesley, which again venture into the burlesque, and in the latter half, the vacuous. The first letter has Charlotte recounting the story of how her brother has been abandoned by his perfidious wife for another man, leaving their daughter, "our dear little niece the innocent Louisa" in the care of her and her sister. In response, Charlotte recounts the story of how her sister's fiancé has been thrown off a horse and the wedding cancelled. However her chief concern is all the food which has been prepared for the wedding. "Why what in the name of Heaven will become of all the Victuals! We shall never be able to eat it while it is good. However, we'll call in the Surgeon to help us."

It is worth noting, though, that *Lesley Castle* is subtitled, "an unfinished novel in letters", and towards the end, in the very last epistle, there are some glimmers of a plot. The heroine is in London, and her pleasure tempered only by her "sensibility for the sufferings of so many amiable young Men" whom she meets, and her "Dislike of the extreme admiration" she meets with. She also beholds a "Young Man the most lovely of his Sex…From the first moment I beheld him, I was certain that on him depended the future Happiness of my Life." There is also the prospect of a visit to Naples. However, it remains unfinished. It may be that at this young stage in her life Jane did not have the capacity to develop the plot and she simply ran out of ideas.

By far the most substantial and impressive product of 1792, though, is *Catherine*, extending to fifty pages in printed text. This also appears to be the latest of this group of works, included in Volume the Third, and dated August 1792. The dedication to Cassandra suggests that Jane was rather pleased with it, although, as usual, her tongue is quite firmly in her cheek. The novel, she says, "I humbly flatter myself, possesses merit beyond any already published, or any that will ever in future appear, except such as may proceed from the pen of Your Most Grateful Humble Servant."

The central character, Catherine or 'Kitty' Percival has been brought up by her maiden aunt, who seems determined to suppress any pleasure she might get out of life. Indeed, she could be a prototype of the frightful Mrs Norris in *Mansfield Park*. Mrs Percival's relations, the Stanleys, come to stay, and the dubious friendship between Kitty and Camilla, the Stanleys' vacuous daughter, is one of the main drivers of the story. However, the central device of the plot is a ball held by a neighbouring family called the Dudleys. Kitty is initially unable to go because of toothache but recovers sufficiently to go later in the evening. Just before she departs, the Stanleys' son, Edward, arrives from France and accompanies her to the ball. Thereafter, they very nearly fall in love.

Here we have the beginnings of a fully fledged Austenian story. Although clearly still unfinished, it is far superior in terms of plot to anything that had gone before, and shows that a real maturation took place around this period, shortly before Jane's seventeenth birthday. There is also for the first time genuine character development. Kitty is modest, sensible and well-read, although a little flirtatious, perhaps like a rough sketch of Elizabeth Bennett or Emma Woodhouse. Her friend Camilla is ridiculous which is a product in part of her education, and Jane may well have been commenting here, in describing Camilla's education, on the inadequacy of the curriculum typically prescribed for girls at the time.

"...twelve years had been dedicated to the acquirement of Accomplishments which were now to be displayed and in a few Years entirely neglected. She was not inelegant in her appearance, rather handsome, and naturally not deficient in Abilities; but those Years which ought to have been spent in the attainment of useful knowledge and Mental Improvement, had been all bestowed in learning Drawing, Italian and Music, more especially the latter, and she now united to these Accomplishments, an understanding unimproved by reading and a Mind totally devoid either of Taste or Judgement."

The most developed and interesting character is Edward Stanley, a young man just returned from France, "with a vivacity of temper seldom subdued, & a contempt of censure not to be overcome, possessed an opinion of his own Consequence, & a Perseverance in his own schemes which were not to be damped by the conduct of others..." Kitty and Stanley flirt and dance at the ball, and afterwards he toys with her affections. Although having no inclination to marry, or to have any other attachment to Kitty "than as a good natured lively Girl who seemed pleased with him", he nevertheless takes "infinite pleasure" in alarming "the jealous fears" of her aunt by paying attention to her "without considering what effect they might have on the Lady herself." This is very much a foretaste of Henry Crawford.

The lady very nearly falls in love with him, although their characters are very different. He scarcely has a fixed opinion on any subject, and can argue "with temper" on whatever side of a debate he chooses. She, however, is "guided by her feelings which were eager and warm, was easily decided, and though it was not always infallible, she defended it with a Spirit and Enthusiasm which marked her own reliance on it." Stanley leaves to return to France at seven o'clock in the morning without saying goodbye to her, leaving her, if not quite heart-broken, sorely disappointed. Her spirits are revived, however, by the news from his sister that the only reason he did not take his leave was because he could not trust himself to see her, and "wished with all his heart that you might not be married before he came back."

Here, then, is real plot and character development. There is even a sparkling little portrait of the servant, Anne, who opens the door to Edward Stanley. This is a rare instance of a servant being given a substantial speaking part in an Austen novel: "I dared to say that you would wait upon him. Lord, Ma'am, I'd lay anything that he is come to ask you to dance with him tonight, & has got his Chaise ready to take you to Mr Dudley's."

There are themes which are referenced in these works which are developed in the later novels. There is a genuine portrait of young courtship and incipient love in *Catherine* which is almost moving: "Every moment as it added to the conviction of his liking her, made him still more pleasing, and strengthened in her Mind a wish of knowing him better." And later: "…they continued talking to each other…[during the evening]…and such was the power of his Address, & the Brilliance of his Eyes, that when they parted for the Night, tho' Catherine had but a few hours before totally given up the idea, yet she felt almost convinced again that he was really in love with her." In a time before mass media, one can only speculate where Jane would have found the inspiration for such writing at the age of sixteen. Of course, there were the novels of which she was a keen reader but there were still three or four boys boarding at the Rectory. One of them, Richard Buller, would have been roughly Jane's age at this time, and he remained a firm friend until his death in 1806.

There is also, in *Catherine*, the first real sketch of a ball, the event which plays such an important role in the plot, certainly of four, of the mature novels.[104] All the constituent parts are there: the days of anticipation and preparation, the flirting, the jealousies, the politics, the petty slights, and then the aftermaths; the "heightenings of imagination and all the laughs of playfulness which are so essential to the shade of a departed ball"[105].

The Austenian themes of class and wealth emerge too. Kitty is looked down upon by Camilla because, although as an heiress she was "certainly of consequence…her Birth gave her no other claim to it, for her Father had been a Merchant". The sister of Kitty's old friend was forced through financial necessity to take up the offer of a trip to Bengal to "embrace the only possibility that was offered to her, of a Maintenance." This idea must have been inspired by the experience of Jane's aunt, Philadelphia, recently deceased.

In *Lesley Castle* the issue of wealth and marriageability is also explored. Margaret is concerned about her father's second marriage and that if he "should have a second family, our fortunes must be considerably diminished." Lack of fortune of course has implications for the marriageability of daughters but a young woman might yet with "personal beauty, joined to a gentleness of Manners, and an engaging address…stand a good chance of pleasing some young Man who might afford to marry a girl without a Shilling." This theme is developed more fully in *The Three Sisters*[106] with an examination of the subject of whether one should marry for love or money. Notably, this little work is dedicated by Jane to her recently married brother, Edward. Mary, the eldest of the three sisters, receives an offer of marriage from Mr Watts. The difficulty is that she isn't very fond of him.

"He is a quite an old man, about two & thirty, very plain, so plain that I cannot bear to look at him. He is extremely disagreable & I hate him more than anybody else in the world. He has a large fortune & will make great Settlements on me; but then he is very healthy. In short I do not know what to do."

The other factors that Mary has to take into account are her two younger sisters who she could not bear to be married before her, and her mother, a prototype of Mrs Bennett, who is "determined not to let such an opportunity escape of settling one of my Daughters so advantageously." The other, far more sensible, sisters let Mary believe that they will have him if she doesn't, thus deflecting the danger from themselves. In the end, for Mary the deciding factor is Watts's new chaise. "And if he won't let it be as high as the Duttons, & blue spotted with silver, I won't have him." In the end, a compromise is reached, and she does have him.

The point here is the contrast between the absurd, materialistic Mary, who is determined to marry against her feelings for money, and her two sisters who will marry for love. Her sister Sophy expects her husband "to be good tempered & Chearful; to consult my Happiness in all his

Actions, & to love me with Constancy & Sincerity". Mary on the other hand is ridiculed by the author at the conclusion of the story, and consigned to an unhappy marriage. These are themes which were to be developed in the mature novels, and most directly, perhaps, in *Pride and Prejudice*.

After the completion of *Catherine*, there was something of another hiatus in Jane's output, at least in so far as it has come down to us. All that was translated into the manuscripts from 1793 consist of some fragmented pieces of writing known as "*Detached pieces*"[107], and an "*Ode to Joy*"[108], in the first volume, and some "*Scraps*"[109] containing a very short comedy drama, and a few fictional letters which were included in the second.

One should note that the manuscripts in which the *Juvenilia* are contained were revisited by Jane and her family. It is also interesting to note that Caroline Austen, who dabbled as a child with writing stories, recalls her aunt advising her to cease writing until she was sixteen, and saying that, "she herself often wished she had read more and written less in the corresponding years of her own life."[110] It may be that Jane, having rediscovered these manuscripts was less than satisfied with the contents.

It is likely, according to Margaret Doody[111], that Jane rediscovered the manuscripts when she, her mother, and Cassandra moved to Chawton in July 1809. *Evelyn* is supplemented by another hand. Doody opines this was her nephew Edward, and the last paragraph of *Catherine* is also in another hand. Indeed, this supplementation is explicit in *Evelyn*: the last two letters in the series are dated 1809. However, we can be confident, both because of the manuscript form of this body of work, and the immaturity of much of its content, that this was a process of supplementation, rather than revision.

VII: LADY SUSAN

1792 was quite an eventful year in the life of Jane Austen. As we have seen, in August 1792, after the death of her mother, and with her husband holed up in Paris on the verge of the Republican Terror, Eliza came to stay at Steventon. Dr Cooper, the father of their cousin Jane, died soon after, leaving Miss Cooper an orphan – her mother having died of typhus in 1783, following the trip to Southampton. Miss Cooper had just become engaged to a Captain in the Royal Navy. However, she came to stay with the Austens pending her marriage, which took place in Steventon on 11th December 1792. Jane and Cassandra were witnesses.

Another very significant event took place at about the same time. The marriage service between Jane Cooper and Captain Williams was conducted by the Reverend Tom Fowle. He had been a pupil at George Austen's school from 1779 for five years, and therefore a childhood friend of Jane and Cassandra. Tom proposed to Cassandra, around the same time as this marriage service, and she accepted; although the prospect of their wedding was some way off; neither of them had any resources beyond Tom's paltry parish in Wiltshire. Cassandra was almost twenty, and Jane nearly seventeen. It is not difficult to contemplate the mixed feelings which Jane must have experienced on hearing this news; on the one hand the joy at her sister's happiness, and on the other the apprehension of the impending separation from her beloved companion.

It is also in 1792 that Jane came out into society. In the spring of 1792, the Lloyds had had to vacate the parsonage at Deane to make way for James and his bride to be, Anne Matthew. They moved to Ibthorpe, a village fifteen miles or so to the west of Steventon. In the summer of 1792, Jane and Cassandra went to visit them. Whilst there she attended a dance at Enham House, near Andover, the home of Anne Matthew's sister, and also a ball at Hurstbourne Park, the estate of Lord Portsmouth near Whitchurch. Meanwhile, there were assembly balls to be attended at Basingstoke Town Hall every month during the winter season, and there is a record of Jane and Cassandra attending the Hampshire Club Ball at Basingstoke on 4th October, and attending a private ball in the neighbourhood soon afterwards.[112]

The Basingstoke balls were organised by Mrs Martin of the Maidenhead Inn, and they were the centre-piece of the social scene of the Hampshire gentry, and those aspiring to the gentry. They were also, for want of a more refined expression, a marriage market. The balls typically began at nine o'clock, and so there would be the anticipation, and the preparations. The Austen family recipe book includes instructions for "Lavendar Water, Coral Tooth Powder, and Soap for Hands".[113] Then there would come the dressing, followed by dinner, the carriage to the venue, and then the dancing. It was a joyful, energetic business. There was, of course, no intimacy on the dance floor. People would make up sets, and the dances were routines made up of familiar steps: clapping, jumping, forming a ring, or lines, linking hands and arms, moving up and down the sets, and curtseying or bowing. After the dancing would come supper.

It is likely that these balls would have been increasingly attended by the odd officer or two, as well; some of them perhaps the inspiration for George Wickham or Colonel Brandon. Following the declaration of war by Republican France in February 1793, Hampshire included a vulnerable stretch of coastline, including the vital dockyard at Portsmouth. The county was heavily populated with soldiers, sailors and military camps. Humphry Repton, the famous landscape gardener, wrote in his memoir: "Nothing was heard but the dread of Buonaparte, and the French invasion. Beacons, Martello towers, camps, depots, and several species of self-defence alone occupied all minds."[114] There were six-thousand troops stationed in Winchester, with another eight-thousand more in camps in Andover and Basingstoke.

Jane would have been dancing at home from a very early age, long before she ever attended a ball. Dancing at home was one of the principal forms of entertainment amongst her class. After dinner or tea, the furniture would have been pushed back, somebody would have stepped up to the keyboard, and the frivolities would begin. Away from home, the Austen sisters would often have had informal dances at the homes of their neighbours. There were, of course, the Lefroys at Ashe, but also the Bigg-Withers, who in 1789 had moved into the manor house at Manydown Park, near Wootton St Lawrence, around six miles from Steventon. Lovelace Biggs-Withers was a widower with two sons, and five daughters, of whom Catherine and Alethea were of a very similar age to Jane. Then there were the Terrys, who lived in the small manor house at Dummer, within walking distance across the fields, and the Chutes who lived in a grand Tudor manor house, called The Vyne, on the other side of Basingstoke; although visits to the latter would have been infrequent, it being a distance of ten miles or so.

And when Jane came out into society, and began to attend balls, what exactly did "society" see? The only physical likeness we have of her is the watercolour completed by her sister, Cassandra in about 1810. Her niece, Anna Lefroy, was later to describe this as "hideously unlike". She gave her own description of Jane, admittedly at a later stage in life, in the following terms. "The Figure tall & slight but not drooping; well balanced, as was proved by her quick firm step. Her complexion of that rather rare sort which seems the peculiar property of light brunettes – A mottled skin, not fair, but perfectly clear & healthy in hue; the fine naturally curling hair, neither light nor dark; the bright hazel eyes to match, & the rather small but well-shaped nose. One hardly understands how with all these advantages she could yet fail of being a decidedly handsome woman…Her unusually quick sense of the ridiculous inclined her to play with the trifling commonplaces of every day life, whether as regarded people or things; but she never played with its serious duties or responsibilities – when grave she was very grave."[115]

Jane's brother, Henry, wrote this of her in his *"Biographical Notice"* of 1818. "Of personal attractions she possessed a considerable share. Her nature was that of true elegance. It could not have been increased without exceeding the middle height. Her carriage and deportment were quiet yet graceful. Her features were separately good. Their assemblage produced an unrivalled expression of that cheerfulness, sensibility, and benevolence, which were her real characteristics. Her complexion was of the finest texture. It might with truth be said that her eloquent blood spoke through her modest cheek. Her voice was extremely sweet. She delivered herself with fluency and precision. Indeed she was formed for elegant and rational society, excelling in conversation as much as in composition."[116]

And much later, her nephew, James Edward, writing over fifty years after her death, offered his own recollection. "In person she was very attractive; her figure was rather tall and slender, her step light and firm, and her whole appearance expressive of health and animation. In complexion she was a clear brunette with a rich colour; she had full round cheeks, with mouth and nose small and well formed, bright hazel eyes, and brown hair forming natural curls close round her face. If not so regularly handsome as her sister, yet her countenance had a peculiar charm of its own to the eyes of most beholders."[117]

One is left with the image of a woman who, if not a great beauty, had considerable physical attractions, poise, character, charm and elegance, combined with a lively intellect and sense of humour. How did this manifest in Jane as a very young woman, emerging into society? We have a snapshot which gives us an intriguing, albeit probably partial glimpse. It comes from a Mrs Mitford who claimed to have seen her at some time between 1792 and 1795, probably at one of the Basingstoke assembly balls. She described her as "the prettiest, silliest, most affected, husband-hunting butterfly she ever remembered".[118] This description was dismissed as "a fancy piece...substituted for genuine history"[119] by her nephew, James Edward, in a postscript to the first edition of his memoir. Perhaps the truth about Jane's appearance in her mid-teens is more closely captured by her description of Catherine Morland, the heroine of *Northanger Abbey*, at the age of fifteen. "To look *almost* pretty, is an acquisition of higher delight to a girl, who has been looking plain the first fifteen years of her life, than a beauty from her cradle can ever receive."[120]

In 1793, Jane became an aunt for the first time. Edward and Elizabeth had their first child, Fanny Catherine, on 23rd January 1793, and James's wife, Anne, gave birth to Jane Anna Elizabeth (always known as "Anna") on 15th April. James and his family moved from Overton to the parsonage at Deane that same year, and so remained in close proximity. Given the greater importance of the extended family in the late eighteenth century, the births of two nieces would have had a greater significance to Jane than it would to a typical novitiate uncle or aunt in the early twenty-first.

The collection of writings called *"Scraps"* which were later included in Volume the Second of the *Juvenilia* were dedicated to little Fanny. The contents of this collection of four little tales and a short one act drama, are unremarkable, save for the letter from "The Female Philosopher" which advocates the qualities of "Modesty, Sense and Dignity...Grace, Eloquence and Symmetry...Wit and a good humour" in young ladies, and deprecates "Peevishness, Envy and Spite" and vanity, pride and folly. This could have been a template for most, if not all, of Jane's later heroines. The dedication to Fanny itself, although written with tongue firmly in cheek, is a demonstration of the feelings of kinship and responsibility which Jane must have experienced in relation to her brothers' children.

"My Dear Neice, As I am prevented by the great distance between Rowling and Steventon from superintending your Education myself, the care of which will probably on that account devolve on your Father and Mother, I think it is my particular Duty to prevent your feeling as much as possible the want of my personal instructions, by addressing to you on paper my Opinions and Admonitions on the conduct of Young Women, which you will find expressed in the following pages. – I am my dear Niece, Your affectionate Aunt, The author."

Similarly, on 2nd June 1793, Jane dedicated to Anna two little pieces of venal nonsense, later included in the first volume of the *Juvenilia*: "I dedicate to You the following Miscellaneous Morsels, convinced that if you seriously attend to them, You will derive from them very important Instructions, with regard to your Conduct in Life."

In December 1793, Jane and Cassandra went to stay with the daughter of their father's cousin, Elizabeth, who had married John Butler-Harrison, a wealthy and notable resident of the city of Southampton, having served as its Sheriff in 1790, and in due course twice to be elected its Mayor in 1794 and 1811. One evening during their stay Jane and Cassandra danced at the Assembly Ball in the Dolphin Inn, now still standing as a hotel in the centre of the city. It would appear that they stayed for some weeks. On 17th December, Elizabeth's daughter was born, and Jane was one of the godparents at the christening the following month.

It is likely that Jane picked up her quill again, towards the end of 1793, in order to compose her novella *Lady Susan*[121]. This story, told in a series of letters, marks a step change in her literary development, and recounts the misdeeds of the amoral society woman, and outrageous flirt, Lady Susan Vernon. It must be the case that Jane's experience of coming out into society had had a profound effect on her maturation as a writer, both in terms of her style and her content, and had inspired her to produce something which was a far more serious and subtle observation of the behaviour and morals of the class into which she had been introduced.

It is difficult to date the completion of *Lady Susan* with precision. It was not published until 1871 when it was included as part of the Memoir of Jane's nephew, James Edward Austen-Leigh. He had taken the text from a manuscript copy, which included paper watermarked with the year 1805. However, critical opinion, and family tradition, date the original work to 1794 – 1795. In contrast to her previous stories told in the form of letters, and included within the *Juvenilia*, *Lady Susan* is a serious attempt at an epistolary work – much influenced by Richardson's *Clarissa* – which goes far beyond the farce and burlesque of her earlier work.

Almost all of the characters in Jane Austen's mature novels are neither all good or all bad. Fanny Price and Anne Elliot probably come closest to the former category, and perhaps General Tilney to the latter, but all the mature characters are nuanced, shades of grey on spectra between sublime and ridiculous, divine and evil. Lady Susan Vernon, the anti-heroine, "the most accomplished coquette in England", created by Jane when she was about twenty, is, on those spectra of shades of grey, black. Her malice puts Mrs Norris to shame, her vanity outstrips that of Sir Walter Elliott, and her devious self-centredness makes Mrs Elton look like a philanthropist.

At the beginning of the story, Lady Susan has been widowed for four months, and lives with her sixteen year old daughter, Frederica, with some friends, the Manwarings, at Langford. She is, by all accounts, devastatingly attractive: "…delicately fair, with fine grey eyes and dark eyelashes; and from her appearance one would not suppose her more than five and twenty, though she must in fact be ten years older." She is clever, well-read, and witty, "…with a happy command of language, which is too often used…to make black appear white." In short, she has all the charm of a rattle-snake, and uses it expertly for the purposes of seduction, advancement and deceit.

Lady Susan essentially invites herself to stay with her late husband's brother, Charles Vernon, the kindness and naïvety of whom she proceeds to exploit to full advantage. The story is in the form of an epistolary novel, a series of letters, principally between Lady Susan herself, and her offstage friend, Mrs Johnson; between Lady Susan and Charles's wife, Mrs Vernon, and between Mrs Vernon, and other members of her family, who are the wealthy de Courcys. This is the perfect form in which to display the duplicity of the eponymous character; the representations she makes to Mrs Vernon and the de Courcys, are juxtaposed to her true intentions which are revealed in her letters to her amoral and obnoxious friend, Mrs Johnson, to whom she can confidently confide that Mr Johnson is "too old to be agreeable, and too young to die." The absence of a narrative voice also enhances the dramatic quality of the work. Lady Susan is condemned out of her own mouth, or, more accurately, pen.

At Langford, Lady Susan has destroyed the tranquillity of her friends by flirting outrageously with her host, Mr Manwaring, who has fallen desperately in love with her. At the same time, she has been flirting with the intended husband of the Manwarings' daughter, the wealthy Sir James Martin, in order to detach him for her own daughter, Frederica. She declares to Mrs Johnson, without a hint of irony, "The females of the family are united against me." It is for this reason, it seems, that she is forced to leave Langford and find shelter with her husband's brother in the village of Churchill. Although she feels no gratitude for this refuge. "Were there another place in England open to me, I would prefer it."

The situation is further complicated by the fact that there is something of a history between Lady Susan and Mrs Vernon, for it was Lady Susan who did everything she could to prevent Mrs Vernon's marriage to her brother-in-law, for no other motive, it appears, than pure malice and jealousy. But through her subsequent "display of grief, and professions of regret, and all those attractive powers for which she is celebrated", she has been able to soften Mr Vernon's heart but not that of Mrs Vernon. Mrs Vernon, in the form of her letters to her husband, her brother and her mother, is the nearest element to the Austenian narrative voice. She plays the part of a moral anchor in the midst of the moral relativism and corruption of Lady Susan and Mrs Johnson. ("Facts are such horrid things!"). In these respects she is the prototype of Fanny Price and Anne Elliott, observing the conduct of others, and judging it to be improper by objective standards.

Indeed Mrs Vernon is about the only character, apart from Frederica, who is not taken in by Lady Susan's artifice. As well as being an outrageous, scheming flirt, she is also a cold, vindictive and cruel mother and before she goes to stay with the Vernons, she offloads her daughter into the care of a Miss

Summers, who runs a school for young ladies in Wigmore Street, "till she becomes a little more reasonable". Her mother's aim is to make her the wife of the wealthy but ridiculous Sir James Martin, and "to make it her own choice by rendering her life thoroughly uncomfortable till she does accept him." Such are Lady Susan's maternal qualities that Mrs Vernon is of the view that it is "to her [Frederica's] advantage to be separated from her mother".

Having arrived at Churchill, Lady Susan then sets about Mrs Vernon's brother, Reginald de Courcy, who is due to inherit his father's considerable estate. He, having heard of her appalling behaviour at Langford, concludes that this "degree of captivating deceit…must be pleasing to witness and detect." However, far from being free to observe it from a distance, he too becomes a captive of her charm and artifice. She finds "an exquisite pleasure in subduing an insolent spirit, in making a person pre-determined to dislike, acknowledge one's superiority". Her pride triumphs over his prejudice, not by the power of love, as Darcy wins over Elizabeth Bennett, but by the power of pure artifice and deceit. At the same time as she is bewitching Reginald, Lady Susan continues to toy with the affections of Manwaring, writing to him, and passing off the letters as a correspondence with his wife.

Frederica, in contrast to her mother, develops a genuine attraction for Reginald, who is probably closer to her in age, and Mrs Vernon becomes hopeful that her "artless affection" will detach him from her mother. Eventually Frederica falls in love with him. Her mother watches this process and ridicules it, observing that her daughter's feelings "…are tolerably lively, and she is so charmingly artless in their display, as to afford the most reasonable hope of her being ridiculed and despised by every man who sees her…Artlessness will never do in love matters." Like many a villain before and after her, Lady Susan judges all by her own standards.

As in all of the mature novels, there is a happy ending. The story climaxes with an unfortunate meeting between the Manwarings and Reginald de Courcy. The latter then finally appreciates the true extent of Lady Susan's duplicity, and declares that: "The spell is removed. I see you as you are." Frederica is eventually taken into the household of the Vernons, "fixed in the family of her uncle and aunt, till such time as Reginald de Courcy could be talked, flattered and finessed into an affection for her." Her mother is by now happy to see her go, and marries the ridiculous Sir James Martin herself, content with the wealth bestowed by her second choice.

In *Lady Susan*, Jane Austen took a decisive step away from the slapstick of her earliest work, and the burlesque of *Love and Friendship*. This was a serious attempt at the epistolary form which allows the same events to be described and interpreted from a variety of perspectives. Within it, she has created characters with depth, a well-rounded plot with a richness of texture and modulated pace, and scenes of realistic dramatic tension. The plot presents a self-contained society, vibrating with tensions, in which the characters reveal themselves - their jealousies, appetites, insecurities, and moral imperfections – through their own mouths and actions. The text is imbued in irony throughout by the counterpoint between Lady Susan's revelations to her friend, and the manner in which she presents herself to the other characters, and there is the advent of a clear moral voice in the form of Mrs Vernon, a central element in the mature novels.

In *Lady Susan* herself, Jane creates a fascinating, and first class, villain; a character who is the embodiment of artifice, whose external appearance, and overt behaviour, are in extreme contrast to her motives and her inner soul. It is likely that the character was inspired in part by Eliza de Feuillide, whose star shone brightly at Steventon around this period. Eliza was certainly a flirt, and the age gap between Lady Susan and Reginald could certainly have been suggested by the flirtatious relationship between Eliza and Henry Austen, ten years her junior, and eventually to be her husband. But Jane respected Eliza and was much influenced by her. She could certainly not be described as a villain.

Juxtaposed to the character of Lady Susan, is her daughter Frederica; with a reserved and conservative disposition; genuine, kind and loving beyond artifice. It is true to say that Lady Susan and Frederica are to a large extent caricatures of types, rather than the more nuanced *dramatis personae* who were to come, but this early novel is nevertheless a decisive progression; a more mature study in the contrast between the hypocrisy of false sensibility, and the artlessness of restrained and rational love. This contrast was to become more subtle, and to reach full maturity, of course, in *Sense and Sensibility*.

There is a more fundamental sense in which one sees, in this novella, the evolution of Jane Austen's style, in a decisive step towards the art which was to come. It is her last surviving experimentation with the novel as related by a series of correspondents. A three page conclusion at the end of the work appears to be a later addition, probably written around 1805 when the work was reproduced on paper watermarked with that date. It is distinguished from the rest of the novel because it is delivered in the voice of a third party narrator (Jane Austen), rather than in the form of a letter, and it takes the opportunity to mock the epistolary form itself. It concludes: "This Correspondence, by a meeting between some of the Parties & a separation between the others, could not, to the great detriment of the Post office Revenue, be continued longer." This is a deliberate statement in rejection of the epistolary form.

From this point, Jane had moved on from both the purely dramatic and epistolary forms which have no room for the objective, authorial voice. In her mature works, she continued to incorporate theatrical effects into her work, with the creation of scenes which could be reproduced on the stage. However, she principally relied upon, and perfected, the voice of the third party narrator. It is this which is essential to her art – the narrator who is both inside her characters speaking with their voices and also with their thoughts, but, at the same time, the benevolent and omniscient, albeit often mischievous, observer who is able to comment and judge, with exquisite irony, upon their actions, their motives, their hopes and their fears. It is this quality which is the fundamental advantage of the narratorial novel over other literary forms. It was perfected in the work of Jane Austen in a manner which was rarely, if ever, surpassed.

VIII: BACKCLOTH: ENTR'ACTE

The twenty-two years from 1793 to 1815 is a period which occupied over half of the life of Jane Austen. The epochal conflict which took place between those years hardly features at all in her writings, save for occasional references in her letters to the exploits and promotions of her sailor brothers, Frank and Charles, and in her novels to the presence of military camps, such as Mr Wickham's at Meryton, and to fictional naval heroes, such as William Price and Captain Wentworth. However, these are always in the context of social intercourse, character development, or plot devices. There are no direct references to the horrors of war. But this period, which was known as "The Great War" to its contemporaries, and which we now refer to as the Napoleonic Wars, was the defining event of the nation during Jane's adult life.

In that period from 1793 to 1815, Great Britain and Republican France were in an almost continuous state of conflict. There were only thirteen months without active combat, but even these periods of hiatus were really armed truces, rather than genuine peace. The Revolution which had begun with the storming of the Bastille in July 1789, like many a revolution before or since, had begun to consume itself, and descended into a Reign of Terror by 1793. This was enough in itself to cause considerable concern to the monarchies of Europe, but the execution of Louis XVI and his Queen, Marie Antoinette, along with much of the rest of the French royal family, was a threat to the stability of the *ancien regime* which could not be tolerated. Indeed, the National Convention in Paris had expressly declared that any conquered territories would be declared Republics. Even so, London's prime concern was the potential disruption to its Baltic and North Sea trade, and it sought to maintain the peace on terms. But the Convention, frothing at the mouth with revolutionary fervour, rejected Britain's proposals for peace, and declared war on 1st February 1793. Thereafter, Britain built, and sustained, a shifting continental alliance against Republican France, precipitating and maintaining a world war which could only end with the overthrow of its tyrant emperor, Napoleon, at Waterloo, twenty-two years later.

France, motivated initially by the propagation of revolutionary republicanism, under the dictatorship of Napoleon became motivated more by imperialist ambition. Britain was primarily a mercantilist nation, and, although imperialistic, was motivated more by the need to spread its trading base, rather than the extension of its territories. The conflict between the two nations became, therefore, a struggle for naval supremacy. Since the end of the American War of Independence in 1783, the administration of William Pitt the Younger, one of the greatest statesman in the country's history, had maintained the Royal Navy. However, in 1789, there was a dispute with Spain over rights of navigation in the Pacific. As a result, the Admiralty speeded up the repair and re-arming of the fleet. Although the crisis with Spain was resolved by negotiation, the increase in naval expenditure was maintained, and the fleet was in good shape at the outbreak of war with France.

And yet the combined fleet of France, and its principal naval partners, the Netherlands and Spain, was a serious challenge to the hegemony of the Royal Navy, essential to Britain's prosperity and security. In 1797, the Dutch were defeated at the Battle of Camperdown off the coast of Holland, and the Spanish at the Battle of St Vincent, off the coast of Portugal. As a result, Britain gained control of the Atlantic. The French still controlled the Mediterranean but when Napoleon invaded Egypt in 1798, Nelson destroyed the French fleet at the Battle of the Nile, and Britain was the unchallenged master of the seas. It began to seize French and Spanish possessions in order to broaden and deepen its trading base.

The war had a profound effect upon the economy of Great Britain. The national debt after the American war had already risen to a record 243 billion pounds; now it soared further. Although opportunities presented themselves to expand the nation's commercial networks for the longer term, and to build a global, mercantilist empire, in the shorter term its trade was disrupted, and the resources generated by it, severely depleted. The costs to the public purse of prosecuting the war eventually led to the imposition of an income tax in 1799 for the first time in the country's history; a tax which has been levied ever since. At the outbreak of war, government stocks lost a fifth of their value. In March 1793, there was a run on local banks. By mid April over one hundred country banks had failed, and the consequential failure of lines of credit led to many bankruptcies amongst merchants and manufacturers. The works on the palladian crescents of Bath ground to a halt. However, in other areas there was a boom. The number of army agents increased dramatically. Henry Austen resigned his commission in the militia in January of 1801 to take advantage of the commercial opportunities of war, and set up in business in London as an agent. It was also a good time to be a tailor or a cobbler with demand for uniforms and boots at an all time high.

The rural Hampshire of Jane Austen was fiercely pro-Tory, and patriotically in support of the war, but not everyone concurred. There were, of course, republicans in urban centres, and extremist apologists for the French regime, but opposition extended beyond this into the mainstream of British politics. The Whigs, led by Charles James Fox, held the view that the French Republic had been driven to war by the absolutist monarchies on the continent, and that the Tories were exploiting the conflict to bolster the power of the Crown, and the aristocracy, over the House of Commons. Outside of Parliament, dissenters and manufacturers were concerned that the war posed a threat to civil liberties, and the well-being of the lower orders. The temporary fall of Pitt's government, therefore, led to a change of policy, and a peace treaty with France, the Treaty of Amiens, was concluded in March 1802. The news of the preliminary peace agreement, signed in October 1801, had been met with such relief in Basingstoke, that the town was illuminated.[122]

However, hostilities resumed just over a year after the Treaty had been signed. Britain, now with its unrivalled naval supremacy, established a blockade of French ports to protect the convoys to India and the Americas, and to stifle the prospects of invasion. When the Spanish actively re-joined the war in October 1804, the blockade was extended to the Spanish coast. This left the navy over-extended. Britain's erstwhile allies had not yet resumed hostilities with France, and with this Continental peace, Napoleon saw an opportunity to prepare to invade the British coast before another allied coalition could be formed. Over 100,000 troops were concentrated in camps on the French coast around Calais and Boulogne, with a further 100,000 further inland. At Boulogne a huge flotilla of landing craft were being assembled but still needed a fleet of warships to escort it before it could invade. Many of the camps could be seen from the cliffs of Dover, and there was widespread panic in southern England. As Napoleon put it, admittedly with a little Gallic swagger, "...it is necessary for us to be masters of the sea for six hours only, and England will have ceased to exist."[123]

From the very beginning of the war the threat of invasion had loomed. Since the time of the Civil War, the British had always been suspicious of a large standing army under the control of the King. In 1793, there were fewer than forty-five thousand men in the cavalry, foot guards and infantry combined, and two thirds of this army was serving abroad, chiefly in India and Canada.[124] In August, the increasingly totalitarian government of the National Convention announced a *levée en masse*, raising at a stroke an army of eight-hundred thousand men. The government reacted to this alarming development by raising new regiments. An important element of this were the provincial militias of volunteers, around the home counties, a little like the Home Guard nearly a century and a half later.

As early as April 1793, Henry Austen had received his commission as a lieutenant in the Oxfordshire Militia, and was stationed in Brighton. By August there were fourteen regiments, and 10,000 troops, stationed along the coast from Brighton to Hove.[125] In 1794, voluntary subscriptions for the Internal Defence of the Kingdom were encouraged. George Austen gave five guineas.[126] After the resumption of hostilities in 1803, James Austen played an active role in riding around the parishes of Ashe, Deane and Steventon recruiting for the volunteers. He formed a militia of one hundred men. Madam Lefroy busied herself in making the camp colours to mark out the ground for their first meeting. Even Edward Austen dragged himself out of his usual torpor, and became a captain in the East Kent Volunteer Cavalry.[127] His daughter proudly wrote to her governess that he looked "very nice in his red coat, blue breeches, & red sash. He is now sitting opposite to me & I can hardly write my letter for looking at him. The hat is a plain round common one with an oak bough & a Crescent in the middle."[128]

As well as the formations of offensive volunteer corps, the government was concerned to improve and strengthen the defensive fortifications along the east and south-east coasts of England, and new defensive systems were begun in the form of a string of Martello Towers, based on the fortification in Martello, Corsica. These were constructed to house cannons, and small garrisons. So serious was the threat of invasion taken that the government began to construct an alternative seat of government in Northamptonshire, in case London fell to the French. Military infrastructure, and even accommodation for the royal family, were constructed in the village of Weedon Bec, about as far as possible from the sea, where it was contemplated that a last stand against the French could take place.

IX: AFFAIRS OF THE HEART

Jane's immediate family, as we have seen, can best, albeit imperfectly, be described as lower gentry, well below the status of the Darcys of Pemberley, or the Bertrams of Mansfield Park. She did, however, have first hand experience of that social circle through her brother, Edward, who had been adopted by the Knights of Godmersham Park in Kent. Edward had married Elizabeth Bridges, the third daughter of Sir Brook Bridges of Goodnestone Park, Wingham. She had been educated at a boarding school in Queen Square, Bloomsbury, which was run exclusively for the daughters of the nobility and gentry. A country house was provided for them by Sir Brook at Rowling, not far from Goodnestone in Kent. Rowling House, which still stands today, was a sixteenth century manor house of two storeys and an attic, later clad with a Georgian façade.

Jane and Cassandra stayed with their brother often. The first visit, of which there is any clear record, took place shortly after the birth of her brother's second child, a son called Edward, on 10th May 1794. During the summer, Jane and Cassandra travelled to Kent, stopping for breakfast at the Bull in Dartford. In a letter to her sister written in June 1808, describing a trip from Bath to Godmersham, Jane recalled this "...hot journey into Kent fourteen years ago...we went to the Bull, the same inn at which we breakfasted in that said journey, and on the present occasion had about the same bad butter." [129] Then, on 23rd October 1794, Thomas Knight died, leaving his vast estate to his adopted son, Edward Austen Knight. He also left fifty pounds apiece to Jane and Cassandra, a not inconsiderable sum, worth a little short of four thousand pounds each in today's money.

In sharp contrast to the tranquillity of this world of the English gentry in the home counties were the events which were occurring in France, by which the Austens would have become increasingly alarmed, especially with their close personal connection in the form of Eliza de Feuillide and her husband. News, of course, would have travelled slowly but nonetheless surely, not just through journalistic reporting, but also through private correspondence, and from the steady flow of *emigrés* across the Channel.

In September 1792, the revolution which had begun at the Bastille in 1789 moved into a new and more terrifying phase. In September, the National Convention proclaimed the abolition of the monarchy, and the establishment of a secular republic. This event was profoundly shocking to an extent which is difficult to comprehend in the twenty-first century. Even more shocking was the Convention's judgment condemning Louis XVI for treason, and his execution on 21st January 1793. In February came the declaration of war against Great Britain. Counter-revolutionary risings in the Vendée, and in Lyons and Bordeaux brought about a suspension of the Constitution, and the Reign of Terror led by Robespierre and his Committee of Public Safety. Between September 1793 and July 1794, no less than 300,000 suspects were arrested, of whom 17,000 were condemned and executed without proper trial, including Marie Antoinette, and the rest of the royal family. Many more died in captivity.

Eliza's husband became engulfed by this Terror. When a friend of his was arrested for planting grain instead of potatoes on her estate, he tried to bribe a member of the Committee, a man called Morel, to have her released. Morel betrayed him, and he was arrested. Before his inquisitors he swore that he was only a patriotic valet who had murdered the real Comte de Feuillide.

This did not help him. He was guillotined on 22nd February 1794.

1795 was an unfortunate year in the Austen family. The winter of 1794-95 was severe. The Assembly ball in Basingstoke had to be cancelled at the beginning of February[130], and the subsequent thaw brought flooding to Steventon. The Austens' neighbour, Mrs Bramston of Oakley Hall, wrote to a friend that "Mr Austen's family did not descend for two days".[131] In early April, Mr Austen spent more than £11 on some new carpets[132]. Then, on 3rd May 1795, James Austen's wife of four years, Anne Matthew, collapsed and died. Their daughter Anna, still only two years old, was sent by her father to be cared for by her aunts Cassandra and Jane, and she stayed there for much of the following two years, until James's remarriage in 1797. This was probably the nearest Jane came to having a child of her own. Henry had also suffered a disappointment in 1795. He proposed to Eliza whilst she was staying at Steventon, probably that summer. She turned him down.

And it was in that same year of 1795 that Cassandra had to bid farewell to her fiancé Tom Fowle for an indefinite period. The French had begun to foment rebellion in the West Indies. In November 1795, a task force of 19,000 troops sailed from Portsmouth for the colonies. Amongst the convoy was HMS *Glory*, the ship to which Francis Austen, now a commissioned lieutenant, had been transferred that autumn. The task force included the Earl of Craven, Tom Fowle's benefactor, his having bestowed upon him the living of Allington. Lord Craven was the Colonel of the 3rd Regiment of Foot, otherwise known as "The Buffs", and he invited Tom to accompany him as his private chaplain. Naval voyages, especially in times of war, were extremely hazardous, and Cassandra had no certain knowledge that he would return. Indeed, on 10th October 1795, Tom Fowle made his will, and in January 1796 sailed with the *Glory*.

The year 1795 is distinguished, however, by Jane's beginning to write the prototype of *Sense and Sensibility*. It was composed, like *Lady Susan,* as a series of letters. In the previous December, George Austen had bought her a nineteenth birthday present which she was to treasure for the rest of her life: "a Small Mahogany Writing Desk with 1 Long Drawer and Glass Ink Stand Compleat" for twelve shillings. It is likely that it was on this very desk, now in the British Library, that she made this final attempt at an epistolary novel. Jane's sister recalled much later that it was read to the family before 1796[133], and we know that it was called *Elinor and Marianne*. It was re-worked into *Sense and Sensibility* fifteen years later. Beyond this, however, pretty much anything else is speculation; there is no extant manuscript in any form, and we are not able to say the extent to which it represented a significant evolution in her art, or, beyond the names of the two eponymous characters, the extent to which it resembled the mature work. However, we do know that by 1805 Jane had decisively rejected the epistolary form in her appendix to *Lady Susan*, and so it is unlikely that she was satisfied with *Elinor and Marianne*. The plot must also have been very different to *Sense and Sensibility*, if for no other reason than that the epistolary form would have required the principal characters to be separated for much of the time.

It was in the winter of 1795-96, however, at the age of twenty-one, that Jane had her first encounter with affairs of the heart. The nephew of George Lefroy, a little younger than Jane, had come to stay with his relations at Ashe rectory. Tom Lefroy was the eldest son, and one of eleven children, of Colonel Anthony Lefroy, of Huguenot descent, who had served with the Dragoons in Ireland, married the daughter of a local squire, and retired to an estate. Tom had graduated from Trinity College, Dublin, in 1795. The trip to Ashe was for a little rest and recuperation before he started reading for the Bar. The accounts which have come down to us suggest that he was a very fine young man. His great uncle, and benefactor, Benjamin Langlois, wrote of him that he had "everything in his temper and character that can conciliate affections. A good heart, a good mind, good sense and as little to correct in him as ever I saw in one of his age."[134] He was also something of an orator. At Trinity he had joined the College Historical Society and won three gold medals speaking in support of the Tory and Loyalist position in debates.

It is at this point that our insight into Jane's life is illuminated by the first of her extant letters. She was a prolific letter writer but only a relatively small proportion of them have survived. They were not, of course, written for publication and her sister (Jane's most frequent co-respondent) destroyed many of the letters after Jane's death which Cassandra did not want future generations of the family to read. Cassandra also destroyed all of the letters she had written to Jane and sections were cut out of some of the letters which were left. A niece subsequently destroyed another set of letters which had been kept by her brother Frank. But in 1882, Edward Hugessen, the first Lord Brabourne, son of Fanny Knatchbull, Jane's niece and daughter of Edward Austen Knight, found a box containing ninety-six letters written by Jane, together with the manuscript copy of *Lady Susan*.[135] The box and contents had been left to Fanny by Cassandra. There are some more letters which have emerged over the years, from other sources, leaving a total of one hundred and sixty in all.

In the January of 1796, Cassandra was staying with the Fowles at Kintbury in Berkshire so as to be near her fiancé before his departure for the West Indies with Lord Craven. This presented the occasion for Jane to write to her sister about her own encounter with a potential beau, and her flirtations with at least two others. There are two letters, and the first was to Cassandra on her twenty-third birthday, 9th January 1796[136]. Jane writes primarily to tell Cassandra about the ball she attended the previous night, the day of Tom Lefroy's twentieth birthday. It was held by the Biggs-Withers at Manydown. "Mr Tom Lefroy's birthday was yesterday...we had an exceeding good ball last night...I was very much disappointed at not seeing Charles Fowle of the party, as I had previously heard of his being invited." Charles Fowle was the younger brother of Cassandra's fiancé.

Jane was clearly very fond of gossip and of dancing. "Miss Heathcote is pretty, but not near so handsome as I expected. Mr H began with Elizabeth [Bigg-Withers], and afterwards danced with her again; but they do not know how to be particular. I flatter myself, however, that they will profit by the three successive lessons which I have given them."

She then refers to Tom Lefroy, with whom, one suspects, she had conducted the "three successive lessons". "You scold me so much in the nice long letter which I have this moment received from you, that I am afraid to tell you how my Irish friend and I behaved. Imagine to yourself everything most profligate and shocking in the way of dancing and sitting down together. I can expose myself however, only once more, because he leaves the country next Friday, on which day we are to have a dance at Ashe after all. He is a very gentlemanlike, good-looking, pleasant young man, I assure you. But as to our having met, except at the last three balls, I cannot say much; for he is so excessively laughed at about me at Ashe, that he is ashamed of coming to Steventon, and ran away when we called on Mrs Lefroy a few days ago."

Her description of how she and Tom behaved at the ball is meant humourously. However the letter is revealing about Tom's apparent feelings towards her. It appears that he had a bit of a crush. But Tom wasn't the only young man who had attracted her attention. "I danced twice with Warren last night, and once with Mr Charles Watkins, and, to my inexpressible astonishment, I entirely escaped John Lyford. I was forced to fight hard for it, however...We had a visit yesterday morning from Mr Benjamin Portal, whose eyes are as handsome as ever." John Warren was one of her father's old pupils, then a fellow of Oriel College, who was staying at Steventon over the Christmas period. Benjamin Portal was a friend of James and Henry at Oxford, and a contributor to The Loiterer, and Lyford was the son of the Basingstoke doctor[137].

It was Tom, however, who visited the next day, its being a custom for gentlemen to call upon ladies whom they had partnered on the day after a ball. "After I had written the above, we received a visit from Mr Tom Lefroy and his cousin George. The latter is really very well behaved now; and as for the other, he has but one fault, which time will, I trust, entirely remove – it is that his morning coat is a great deal too light. He is a very great admirer of Tom Jones, and therefore wears the same coloured clothes, I imagine, which he did when he was wounded."

Tom Jones, of course, is a reference to Fielding's bawdy novel of 1749 which all but celebrates fornication and sexual promiscuity. The fact that Jane and Tom had discussed this book, and that Jane was eager to advertise the fact to her sister, is indicative that their conversation was suggestive, and that her description of their behaviour at the ball was not entirely flippant. And then on Thursday 16th January, Jane wrote again to Kintbury to tell her sister about the party planned in Ashe the following evening.[138] "I look forward with great impatience to it, as I rather expect to receive an offer from my friend in the course of the evening. I shall refuse him, however, unless he promises to give away his white coat."

The levity with which Jane refers to this "offer" suggests that the observation was meant humourously, and she didn't really expect a proposal of marriage. This conclusion is reinforced a little later in the same epistle. "Tell Mary that I make over Mr Heartley and all his estate to her for her sole use and benefit in future, and not only him, but all my other admirers into the bargain wherever she can find them, even the kiss which C Powlett wanted to give me, as I mean to confine myself in future to Mr Tom Lefroy, for whom I don't care sixpence. Assure her also, as a last and indubitable proof of Warren's indifference to me, that he actually drew that gentleman's picture for me, and delivered it to me without a sigh."

"Mary" is a reference to Mary Lloyd, the younger of the two Lloyd daughters, who was also staying at Kintbury. Charles Powlett was a clergyman serving the nearby parish of Winslade, and appointed one of the Prince of Wales's chaplains in 1790. He was the grandson of the third Duke of Bolton and his mistress, the actress Lavinia Felton, who played the first Polly Peachum in *The Beggar's Opera.*

We can see clearly in these letters that Jane thoroughly enjoyed a ball: the flirting, the gossip, the dancing, and the mischief, and that she drew from them much humour and comical, ironic observation, a technique which was used to such good effect in her novels. One cannot say for sure whether Jane had any real feelings for Tom Lefroy, and Lord Brabourne came to this conclusion.

"I strongly incline to the opinion that, whatever passing inclination she may have felt for anyone during her younger days (and that there was once such an inclination is, I believe, certain) she was too fond of home, and too happy among her own relations, to have sought other ties, unless her heart had been really won, and that this was a thing which never actually happened."[139]

There is a postscript to the letter, written on the following day, in which the subject of Tom is dismissed with levity, and which lends support to Brabourne's opinion. "Friday – At length the day is come on which I am to flirt my last with Tom Lefroy, and when you receive this it will be over. My tears flow as I write at the melancholy idea. Wm. Chute called here yesterday. I wonder what he means by being so civil."

However, there is other evidence which suggests that Jane may have had feelings for Tom which went beyond mere flirtation. Tom's cousins, George and Edward, recalled years later that their "Mother had disliked Tom Lefroy because he had behaved so ill to Jane Austen, with sometimes the additional weight of the Father's condemnation..." If this is a true observation, then perhaps Tom did lead Jane on a little, knowing that, without independent means himself, and ten siblings, he was not in a position to marry a young woman without a substantial dowry. There is a further hint of something beyond mere indifference a couple of years later when Tom was again staying at Ashe. There were no meetings between him and Jane but after he had departed, Madam Lefroy called at Steventon, and Jane wrote this to her sister: "She did not once mention the name of the former [Tom Lefroy] to me, and I was too proud to make any enquiries; but on my father's afterwards asking where he was, I learnt that he was gone back to London in his way to Ireland, where he is called to the Bar and means to practise."[140]

Tom Lefroy married the sister of a college friend in 1799, and fathered seven children. He had an extremely successful career at the Bar, eventually becoming Lord Chief Justice of Ireland, and living to the grand old age of ninety-three. But he never forgot Jane Austen, telling a nephew, many years later, that he had a "boyish love" for her.[141] According to Jane's nephew, James Edward, Lefroy still remembered Jane in extreme old age "as one to be admired, and not easily forgotten by those who had ever known her."[142] His sister, Caroline, was of the view, writing in 1869, that "there was something in it…but nothing out of the common way…and no very serious sorrow endured…I have my story from my mother, who was near at the time – It was a disappointment, but Mrs Lefroy sent the gentleman off at the end of a very few weeks, that no more mischief might be done."[143]

One generation removed, James Edward's daughter, Mary Augusta, later wrote of the end of Jane's "own personal romance, inflicting a wound which was, as we know, not the less but the more likely to have been deeply felt, on account of the silence preserved by Cassandra on this subject many years after her death, and the guarded manner in which she at length alluded to it."[144] Was this a lost opportunity for Jane, and for Tom? It is impossible to say for sure, but it is improbable that Mary Augusta would know better than those who had had direct contact with eye witnesses. In any event, it seems likely that Tom's loss was the literary world's gain, and the experience which she had had in her encounter with him, whether that be a bruise or a whiplash, enriched her insight into the nature of the human condition.

At the age of twenty, however, the thoughts of a young woman in Jane's position would have begun to turn towards marriage. The average age for women to marry in the 1790s was twenty-four[145], but the age was significantly lower in the circles in which the Austens were mixing. Jane Bennett in *Pride and Prejudice* attracts a suitor at the age of fifteen, and Catherine Morland accepts Henry Tilney's proposal in *Northanger Abbey* when she is seventeen. Jane had no independent means, beyond the allowance provided by her father. This was twenty pounds a year, roughly the annual income of a farm labourer, but woefully inadequate as an independent income for a young woman of her class and with her aspirations. If she remained unmarried, the options were uninspiring; seeking poorly paid employment as a governess, or perhaps a teacher, or relying on the charity of relatives. Charlotte Lucas in *Pride and Prejudice*, the daughter of a knight (albeit a knight unable to provide his daughter with an adequate dowry) is forced to prefer the option of marriage to the execrable and ridiculous Mr Collins to the alternative of spinsterhood.

In April 1796, Jane and Cassandra stayed with the Coopers in Harpsden, near Henley on Thames, where their mother had grown up. On 20th April they dined with Tom and Caroline Lybbe-Powys, her childhood friends, and some other neighbours. Charles Fowle was also present.[146] Only six weeks after this dinner, Jane Cooper's husband, Captain Williams, was involved in a naval engagement with French warships off the Scilly Isles. Williams was in command of the frigate HMS *Unicorn*, in which young Charles Austen, still only sixteen, was aboard as a midshipman. The *Unicorn* captured two French frigates, an action for which Captain Williams was subsequently knighted.[147] The battle was the subject of a painting by Nicolas Pocock which now hangs in the National Maritime Museum at Greenwich.

In August 1796, Jane went to stay with her brother Edward in Kent, via London. She set off on Monday the 22nd, accompanied by Edward himself, and also Francis, who was on shore leave. Henry was now engaged to Mary Pearson, the daughter of a naval officer. He was to join the party at Rowling with his new fiancée on the Thursday. They stayed overnight at Staines, and then on the Tuesday morning, Jane wrote to Cassandra from their Mayfair lodgings in Cork Street. It is interesting to note, as Lucy Worsley points out[148], that the great uncle and benefactor of Tom Lefroy, Benjamin Langlois, lived on Cork Street. There were no hotels on Cork Street, which is not a long road (then or now) and it is quite probable that Jane was staying there with a family friend. We do not know if Tom was there at the time. However, as Worsley notes, in August, outside of the term times of the Inns of Court, it is more likely than not that Tom would have been back in Ireland for the vacation.

"Here I am once more in this scene of dissipation and vice, and I begin already to find my morals corrupted. We reached Staines yesterday, I do not know when, without suffering so much from the heat as I had hoped to do. We set off again this morning at seven o'clock, and had a very pleasant drive, as the morning was cloudy and perfectly cool…We are to be at Astley's tonight, which I am glad of."[149]

Astley's Amphitheatre, which Jane was so looking forward to, was a performance venue in the form of a circus ring, opened in 1773. In no longer exists, but it was located on what is now Westminster Bridge Road, on the South Bank next to St Thomas's Hospital. In the early 1830s, Charles Dickens wrote an article about Astley's in *The Evening Chronicle* on 9th May 1835.[150] Admittedly this was nearly forty years after Jane's visit, and after it had burned down and been rebuilt. However, it was before it became the grand circus of the Royal Amphitheatre, and it gives a fascinating insight into the atmosphere of this place.

Dickens describes clowns, "comic performers", "tragedians", "riding-masters" and "highly trained chargers". "As for ma, she was perfectly overcome by the drollery of the principal comedian, and laughed till every one of the immense bows on her ample cap trembled…Then when the man in the splendid armour vowed to rescue the lady or perish in the attempt, the little boys applauded vehemently… [and] the little girls looked very properly shocked when the knight's squire kissed the princess's confidential chambermaid…Between each feat of horsemanship the governess leant across to ma, and retailed the clever remarks of the children on that which had proceeded…For ourself, we know that when the hoop, composed of jets of gas, is let down, the curtain drawn up for the convenience of the half price on their ejectment from the ring, the orange peel cleared away, and the sawdust shaken, with mathematical precision, into a complete circle, we feel as much enlivened as the youngest child present; and actually join in the laugh which follows the clown's shrill shout of 'Here we are!'" There is "the riding-master, who follows the clown with a long whip in his hand" and "humours the clown by indulging in a little badinage", and "introduces Miss Woolford into the arena, and, after assisting her to the saddle, follows her fairy courser round the circle…a burst from the orchestra, a start from the horse, and round goes Miss Woolford again on her graceful performance, to the delight of every member of the audience, young or old…the clown making ludicrous grimaces at the riding master every time his back is turned; and finally quitting the circle by jumping over his head, having previously directed his attention another way."

After what must have been a memorable stay in the capital, Jane stayed at Rowling well into the following month. Her letter of 1st September[151] reveals that the intention was for her to return to Steventon with Henry early that month but that he had been unwell, and had gone to Yarmouth to "consult his physician". His condition, which is not specified, was set to delay their return for over a month. He intended to return to Rowling around the 23rd, and then stay for several weeks more "as he wants very much to have some shooting at Godmersham, whither Edward and Elizabeth are to remove very early in October. If this scheme holds, I shall hardly be at Steventon before the middle of that month." Godmersham was the splendid seat of the Knight family which Edward was to inherit, and in which his widowed adoptive mother still lived.

Quite how Henry was able to travel to Yarmouth and back again, and contemplate a season of shooting at Godmersham, and yet to be too unwell to take his sister back to Steventon, is a mystery. Frank was in no rush to return either. "I could return, I suppose, with Frank if he ever goes back. He enjoys himself here very much, for he has just learnt to turn, and is so delighted with the employment, that he is at it all day long." Turning is craft making with a lathe. Frank had "turned a very nice little butterchurn for Fanny."

One does not get the impression, though, that Jane was too upset by the delay, telling her sister, "I am sorry about it, but what can I do?" She seems to have been thoroughly enjoying herself. She clearly liked being with her little niece and nephew. "I have told Fanny about the bead of ner necklace, and she wants very much to know where you found it." She was also dining with the likes of Lady Hales, the Cages from Hythe, and Elizabeth's parents, the Bridges. "We had a very pleasant day, and some liqueurs in the evening."

On 3rd September, there was a "ball" at Goodnestone, the seat of Elizabeth's family. Goodnestone Park was a splendid, two storey manor house, built in 1704, and extended to three stories around 1790. It had a large, pedimented Greek Doric porch, and was surrounded by extensive landscaped grounds. But the event appears to have been a dinner, followed by an informal dance, rather than a ball. "We dined at Goodnestone, and in the evening danced two country-dances and the Boulangeries. I opened the ball with Edward Bridges [the fifth son of Lady Bridges]; the other couples were Lewis Cage and Harriet, Frank and Louisa, Fanny [Cage] and George. Elizabeth played one country dance, Lady Bridges the other, which she made Henry dance with her, and Miss Finch played the

Boulangeries."[152]

On another evening, they dined at Nuckington, home of the Milles family, near Canterbury, about 8 miles from Godmersham. Mr Scott, Miss Fletcher, Mr Toke and Mr J Toke were there, together with the Archdeacon Lynch. The said "Miss Fletcher" was the subject of Jane's acid tongue, expressed in her letter to her sister from Rowling on the 15th. "Miss Fletcher and I were very thick, but I am the thinnest of the two. She wore her purple muslin which is pretty enough, though it does not become her complexion. There are two traits in her character which are pleasing – namely, she admires Camilla [the new novel by Frances Burney], and drinks no cream in her tea." Later that day they were to dine again at Goodnestone, to meet "my Aunt Fielding from Margate and a Mr Clayton, her professed admirer – at least so I imagine."[153]

By the third week in September, plans were well underway for Jane to return home. Frank had received a new commission, and had to be in town on the 21st. Jane might travel with him into London, and then her father "...will be so good as to fetch home his prodigal daughter from town, I hope, unless he wishes me to walk the hospitals, enter at the Temple, or mount guard at St. James'"[154]. However, whether or not Jane could accompany Frank depended on the movements of Mary Pearson, Henry's fiancée, whom Jane was to accompany to Steventon to meet her parents. Jane appears to have been a little peeved by this inconvenience, and Mary received both barrels in her turn. "If Miss Pearson should return with me, pray be careful not to expect too much beauty. I will not pretend to say that on a first view she quite answered the opinion I had formed of her. My mother, I am sure, will be disappointed if she does not take great care. From what I remember of her picture, it is no great resemblance."[155] It is not clear whether Mary Pearson did accompany Jane to

Steventon but we know that she broke off the engagement to Henry a few weeks later.[156]

During the summer, the recently widowed James Austen was looking for a new wife to run his parsonage and be a mother to his little girl. He proposed to his cousin Eliza but was turned down. The life of a country parson's wife was an unlikely one for her. However, in that same autumn, Mary Lloyd, then twenty-six, was invited to stay at Steventon, perhaps by Mrs Austen with a view to match-making. Sure enough, James proposed to her in the November, and she accepted. Mrs Austen was clearly delighted by the match. "Had the election been mine, you my dear Mary, are the person I should have chosen for James's wife, Anna's mother, and my daughter; being as certain, as I can be of anything in this uncertain world, that you will greatly increase & promote the happiness of each of the three...I look forward to you as a real comfort to me in my old age, when Cassandra is gone into Shropshire, & Jane – the Lord knows where."[157] Jane was also pleased for her brother. According to Eliza, she "...seems much pleased with the match, and it is natural she should, having long known and liked the lady."[158] They were married in January 1797, and settled in James's parish of Deane, not two miles away, with little Anna.

In the summer of 1796, George Austen had divested himself of his remaining pupils, and gave up teaching. That means that the household was reduced to Jane, Cassandra and their parents, along with little Anna before she moved to Deane in the new year. It is likely that Jane had a lot more free time as a consequence. Although the Austens had domestic servants at this time, it is unlikely that more than one or two would have lived in. In a letter to her sister in October 1798, she mentions that "the servants were very glad to see us" after an extended visit to Kent. She only refers to two by name who appear to have lived in: Nanny, who was working in the kitchen, and Molly who had found her mother's spectacles.[159] "Dame Bushell" was taking in the washing, and "John Steevens' wife undertakes our purification". Jane undoubtedly would have had to assist with the domestic duties: the preparation of meals, the laundry, and so on, but with the reduction in the size of the household these duties were now significantly reduced.

It may, therefore, be no coincidence that in 1796 Jane Austen began to write the prototype of *Pride and Prejudice*, a very substantial work of 120,000 words, at least in its finished form. According to a note made many years later by Cassandra, she began the draft of what was then called *First Impressions* in the October, and finished it in the following August[160], which would have amounted to a very impressive rate of work. When she began the draft, she would have been the same age as her principal character, Elizabeth Bennett; "not one and twenty". Again, we can only speculate as to what this draft looked like, and how much it resembled the fully fledged masterpiece. We can reasonably suppose, however, that it was Jane's first attempt at a full length novel in the narrative form; *Elinor and Marianne* having been composed as a series of letters. We can also reasonably suppose that two of the principal characters were called Jane and Elizabeth as a result of a tantalising reference in the *Recollections* of Jane's niece Anna, written when she was an old lady in 1864.

"I have been told that one of the earliest novels (*Pride and Prejudice*) was read aloud in the Parsonage at Dean, whilst I was in the room, & not expected to listen - Listen however I did, with so much interest, & with so much talk afterwards about 'Jane & Elizabeth' that it was resolved, for prudence sake, to read no more of the story in my hearing. This was related to me years afterwards, when the novel had been published; & it was supposed that the names might recall to my recollection that early impression. Such however did not prove to be the case."[161]

Jane may also have been inspired by her visit in the summer to Rowling, Goodnestone and Godmersham Park; the latter a Palladian mansion, every bit as impressive as Pemberley. There is also evidence of a tension between the perceived social status of Jane and her sister, and the circles with which they were mixing in Kent. This may have influenced her description of the class tensions which ripple throughout the mature novel, between, for example, Caroline Bingley and the Bennetts. Many years later, Edward's daughter Fanny wrote disparagingly of her aunts. Admittedly she was only three and a half at the time of the visit in the summer of 1796 but she would subsequently have absorbed collective familial memory.

"I think in later life their intercourse with Mrs Knight [her mother] (who was very fond of & kind to them) improved them both & Aunt Jane was too clever not to put aside all possible signs of 'common-ness' (if such an expression is allowable) & teach herself to be more refined...Both the Aunts were brought up in the most complete ignorance of the world & its ways (I mean as to fashion &c) & if it had not been for Papa's marriage which brought them into Kent...they would have been, tho' not less clever and agreeable in themselves, very much below par as to good society and its ways."[162]

As Park Honan has observed[163], Fanny did have a reason to feel a grievance towards Cassandra in later years. In 1826, her step-daughter eloped to Gretna Green with her younger brother. Although disowned by Fanny, the couple were openly received by Cassandra. However, this does not explain her bile extending to Jane, and even if her words were exaggerated by resentment, they must have contained a kernel of her true opinion.

In the spring of 1797, the Austens were expecting the imminent return of Cassandra's fiancé, Tom Fowle; he who had left for the West Indies with Lord Craven some fifteen months earlier. However, in late April or early May, they received the dreadful news that Tom had died of the yellow fever off the coast of St Domingo in February 1797, and had been buried at sea. In his will made shortly before he sailed, he had left a thousand pounds to Cassandra which, if prudently invested, would have yielded an annual income of about thirty-five pounds, roughly the salary of a governess, but not enough to live independently. Quite apart from the loss of a man she no doubt loved, or at least for whom she had considerable affection, she was now nearly twenty-four, and without independent means. His death must have been a terrible blow, both to her and the wider family. Although, according to Eliza, "Jane says that her sister behaves with a degree of resolution & propriety which no common mind could evince in so trying a situation."[164]

The imminent risk of sudden familial death was, of course, far more prevalent in the England of 1797 than it is now, and there is no sign of the paralysis of despair in the wake of this tragic development in the Austen household. Jane completed her novel in the August, and so impressed was her father with *First Impressions* that he wrote to the London publisher, Thomas Cadell, with a view to getting it published.

"I have in my possession a Manuscript Novel, comprised in three Vols, about the length of Miss Burney's Evelina. As I am well aware of what consequence it is that a work of this sort should make it's first appearance under a respectable name I apply to you. Shall be much obliged therefore if you will inform me whether you choose to be concerned in it; what will be the expense of publishing at the author's risk; and what you will venture for the property of it, if on a perusal, it is approved of? Should your answer give me encouragement I will send you the work."[165]

Mr Austen's coyness in this letter is understandable. Despite the growth in the latter part of the century in the publication of female authors, there was still a great deal of prudishness and snobbery stalking the woman as a novelist. It was not regarded as a feminine pursuit to seek publicity, still less to seek financial reward for it, and male writers sought to discourage competition from the burgeoning market in female fiction. Also, the institutional misogyny of the social order might have encouraged speculation as to the autobiographical origins of the work, and inhibited artistic freedom. Frances Burney, who had published *Evelina* in 1778, along with the likes of Sarah Fielding and Ann Radcliffe, all published anonymously until their reputations had been secured.

However, the process of publication was easier then than now; so long as you had, or could at least risk, a little money. George Austen's suggestion of "author's risk" is a reference to the process of publication then known as "on commission". The author was responsible for the costs of publication, which in the days before mass production could be considerable; the costs of the paper, the physical labour of the typesetting, the printing, and then the advertising and the distribution. The publisher would charge a commission on each copy sold, and if the total sales did not cover the costs of publication, the author would be liable for the difference. For Jane, however, even this route remained closed. Across the top of George Austen's letter, Cadell wrote the words, "declined by Return of Post"[166], apparently without reading a word of the manuscript. Jane, remarkably, was not discouraged. On the contrary, it appears, because in November 1797, she began to rework her epistolary novel, *Elinor and Marianne* into the narrative form of *Sense and Sensibility*, a task which occupied her until the spring of 1798. Her experience of working on *First Impressions* had probably convinced her that the third person narratorial form was a superior vehicle for her art. It had impressed her father, and it must also have impressed Cassandra, who was asking to read it again in January 1799[167].

Having refused the chance to become a parson's wife the previous summer, Eliza de Feuillide, meanwhile, had returned to London, having taken up new lodgings in Durweston Street, near Portman Square. In November 1796, Henry Austen, newly disengaged from Mary Pearson, called upon Eliza, and apparently revived a flirtation which had been going on, in rivalry with the parson's flirtations, for some time. In the following May, Eliza reported to her cousin Phylly Walter that Henry, now captain, paymaster and adjutant in the Oxfordshire militia, had again spent a few days in town. By this stage he had given up any idea of a career in the church. At some point he proposed, and she accepted. The proposal may very well have been during this visit in the spring because towards the end of June, Mr and Mrs Austen dined with Eliza in London.

Eliza told her godfather and benefactor, Warren Hastings, the reasons for her acceptance. Henry had been "for some time in Possession of a comfortable Income, and the excellence of his Heart, Temper, and Understanding, together with steady attachment to me, his affection for my little boy, and disinterested concurrence in the disposal of my property in favor of the latter, have at length induced me to an acquaintance which I have withheld for more than two years."[168] The reference to Henry's agreeing to settle her property on little Hastings is crucial. The boy had been infirm from birth, and had recently not been well. It must be remembered that, until the late nineteenth century, a married woman's property automatically passed to her husband, and the sacrament of marriage amongst the propertied classes was more often the consequence of a transactional relationship, than one of the heart.

Eliza and Henry were married on the last day of 1797, in Marylebone. Then they took a house with a garden in Ipswich. Henry was twenty-six; Eliza ten years his senior. She had lost none of her spirit, and made her views of the balance of power in the marriage known to Phylly Walter: "Henry well knows that I have not been much accustomed to control & should probably behave rather awkwardly under it, and therefore like a wise man he has no will but mine." She was also still an outrageous flirt, adding "...as to my Colonel Lord Charles Spencer, if I was married to my third husband instead of my second I should still be in love with him. He is a most charming creature, so mild, so well bred, so good, but alas! he is married as well as myself and what is worse he is absent." [169] Here indeed was the model for Isabella Thorpe and Mary Crawford, but whatever misgivings the Austen family may have had, George at least, hitherto one of the trustees of Eliza's fortune, was delighted to keep the money in the family. He sent forty pounds to Henry's regiment to celebrate.

It was in late November 1797 that Jane and Cassandra went with their mother to Bath to visit their maternal uncle, James Leigh Perrot, and his wife, who were staying at No 1 The Paragon, a row of thirty-seven terraced houses on the road out of town towards London. Both the Leigh Perrots were in indifferent health; she suffered from bronchitis, and he from gout,[170] and soon they would take up permanent residence in the city for the waters. The *Bath Chronicle* of 23rd November 1797 lists the arrivals for the preceding week which includes "Mr Perrot" and "Mrs and 2 Miss Asten". Jane was genuinely fond of her uncle and aunt. There was also, though, another reason why the extended family had an interest in keeping on the good side of James Leigh Perrot: he had no children, and was enormously wealthy, having himself inherited a fortune from a childless uncle, and having married the heiress to an estate in Barbados. Of more immediate importance, though, is that Jane was able to take in the atmosphere and the culture of Bath, right up until just before Christmas when the Austens returned to Steventon.

Steventon in 1798 was by no means insulated from the war with France. In April, the Defence of the Realm Act was passed which required the collection of information from the provinces, in the face of the ever-present threat of invasion, about the available manpower, weapons, other equipment and provisions. George Austen compiled the return for Steventon. There were thirty-nine able-bodied men between the ages of fifteen and sixty. Thirty would serve on foot; five on horseback; and four with draft animals. There were ten men who were not able. There were no aliens, or Quakers, and seventy-eight non-combatants who would need to be helped with evacuation. No weapons were available but there were ten axes, six pickaxes, 12 spades, four shovels, twelve billhooks and eight saws.[171]

Having returned to this Steventon preparing for invasion, Jane turned her mind to something more pacific. She started work on, what was to become, her first Bath novel, *Northanger Abbey*.

X: BATH AND NORTHANGER ABBEY

The visit in late 1797 was Jane's first recorded visit to Bath, although she would have known of its rather *risqué* reputation from literature. In *The Rivals,* with which Jane was very familiar, Sheridan bases part of the plot on his own experience of eloping from Bath with the woman who was to become his first wife. Jane had already referred to the city, disapprovingly, in her *Juvenilia*. In *Love and Friendship,* she refers to "the unmeaning luxuries of Bath", and in the *Memoirs of Mr Clifford,* it is the home of the eponymous anti-hero. It appears that the visit in November to December 1797 was for health reasons. In the following February, Jane wrote to Eliza to say that her mother had benefited much from the Bath waters but had had a slight return of her complaint.[172]

Bath was founded in the first century by the Romans, principally for the very purpose of exploiting the natural hot springs for their health-giving properties. The waters were rich in iron and radium, and were exploited by the Roman legions to relieve ailments such as backaches. But it was only in the eighteenth century that Bath achieved national, and indeed international, repute as a spa town and a fashionable resort. Up until the early 1720s, Bath was a run down, medieval town. However, it was none other than an ancestor of Mrs Austen, her great uncle, by marriage, the Duke of Chandos, who was responsible for its transformation. He came to Bath in the 1720s, saw it, and decided to conquer it too.

He saw the potential, and had the money to invest. The result was the archetypal Georgian city, the work of John Wood, and his son, John Wood the Younger, Ralph Allen, and Richard Nash, who fashioned its public buildings, and open spaces, in the neo-classical style. By the year 1801, some three million pounds had been spent on the city, a sum that equalled the total investment in Britain's cotton industry.[173]

In the latter part of the eighteenth century, Bath was in its heyday as a health and cultural resort for the gentility, attracting the social and political elite. Men and women of letters, such as Pope, Fielding, Byron and Burney; pioneers of the enlightenment, such as Newton, Locke and Hume, artists such as Gainsborough, and even heroes such as Wilberforce and Nelson, all spent time in the city. In 1765, the records indicate that no fewer than twenty-four peers of the realm came to Bath for the season.[174]

Bath's population, according to the first national census in 1801, was a little over forty thousand, making it the eighth largest city in the kingdom. In a guidebook published in 1819, *Walks Through Bath*, Pearce Egan opined: "In the season, which may be said to be at its height from Christmas to April, it is the opinion of every person who has visited this elegant City, that Bath rises superior to every other place in England."[175] "The houses are all built of the beautiful Oolite, or free-stone, and, from their pale yellow clean appearance, produce an uncommonly interesting effect; but, to the eye not accustomed to such uniformity, it feels impressed with their magnificence and splendour...The situation of Bath is low; but, notwithstanding, the air is considered very salubrious; and the inhabitants, generally, possessing good health and longevity. It stands in a fruitful valley...and is surrounded by an amphitheatre of hills of considerable height...It also abounds with most excellent springs, the water of which is conveyed by leaden pipes into the houses of the city."[176]

According to the painter Julius Ibbetson, "Bath presents to the sight and imagination everything that is united with the idea of perfect beauty; and so strong is the impression it makes upon the mind of almost all people at first sight, that the prepossession is converted into opinion; and when enveloped in those exhalations which arise from its salubrious springs, it is still called to mind in all its loveliness and attractions."[177] The Paragon Buildings on the outskirts of Bath, in which the Austens stayed with the Leigh Perrots, were of more prosaic appearance: "There is more solidity than elegance in the appearance of these houses, although well built"[178] but they did afford a view over the surrounding countryside.

Nevertheless, the beauty and buzz of the city must have made a powerful impression on a young woman from a country parsonage. The entertainment rivalled anything in the capital. First there was the Great Pump Room, in which musical performances were laid on. Newly renovated in 1796, it was eighty-five feet long (including recesses), forty-six feet wide and thirty-four high. There was a gallery for the musicians at the western end. In the centre of the south side was the pump, "from which the waters issue out of a marble vase.[179]" This is where the afflicted came to drink the waters and bathe in them, and their wives and daughters came to be seen. This was open to the public from "an early hour in the morning till four in the afternoon...no etiquette of rank being required to obtain an admission; and the only qualification necessary to join the gay throng, without ceremony, is that of a clean decent appearance...To those persons who are fond of bustle and gaiety, this promenade in the Pump Room will be highly attractive."[180] There were separate rooms for bathing, and for "pouring the hot water on the part affected, instead of immersing the whole body."

Then there were the stunning architectural wonders of the

Squares and the Crescents and the Gardens. The jewel in the crown was The Royal Crescent, where the great and the good came to see, and be seen, in their latest fashions. It consisted of thirty houses in an oval shape, with Ionic pillars, a broad carriage road, a fine lawn enclosed with iron railings, and a "capacious gravel walk for foot passengers."[181] The fields and grounds declined towards the River Avon, and there was a "commanding prospect of the opposite hills." According to Egan, it was an "assemblage of private residences" which was "without an equal in the kingdom." Apparently, one of the grottos, which bejewelled the gardens, was even the place where Sheridan met his lover[182] – although one suspects this little detail was added for the benefit of the tourists. Outside of the city itself, there were also beautiful walks, and views, in the surrounding countryside, for which a young lady might chance upon a young man to accompany her in his chaise.

In the evening, there was The Theatre Royal, established in 1767, and which had proved to be "a nursery for several of the greatest actors, both male and female, that have for the last fifty years adorned the stages of the metropolis with the highest specimens of histrionic talents."[183] There were concerts, both indoors and outdoors, sometimes accompanied by fireworks. In Sydney Gardens there were gala nights with music, singing, fire works and illuminations. The orchestra had a large open space before it, and then there was a gradually ascending walk, leading to a semi-circular stone pavillion, paved and covered in with seating. On a gala night this had "a most brilliant effect, from the numerous variegated lamps with which it is ornamented...The view, when seated in the above pavillion down to the orchestra, across arches covered with lamps, gives it a very captivating appearance."[184] There were even swings "adapted for the ladies…"

Then, of course, there were frequent balls in the Lower and Upper Assembly Rooms. The Lower Rooms, opened in

1730, were designed by John Wood, and commissioned by Richard ("Beau") Nash, who was Master of Ceremonies of the entertainments.The Upper Rooms were designed by John Wood the Younger, an even more elegant suite of rooms, opened in 1771 at a cost of £20,000, the most expensive building of all[185]. They included a card room, a reading room, and a ballroom, one hundred feet long, forty-two feet wide, and forty-two feet high, with five glass chandeliers, the elegance of which "astonishes every spectator"[186]. "At each end of the room are placed, in magnificent gilt-frames, the most splendid looking-glasses that could be procured to give effect to the general brilliant appearance." Egan describes the public amusements held in the Upper Rooms during the season (admittedly some twenty years later).[187] On Monday nights, there was a dress ball, on Wednesday nights a concert, on Thursdays a "fancy ball", and on Friday night a "card assembly". The balls were open to the public (except servants) and cost one pound and ten shillings for three tickets, although three front benches at the upper end of the room were reserved "for ladies of precedence, of the rank of peeresses of Great Britain or Ireland."

And for those with a more sedentary and cerebral disposition, there were no less than six public libraries; although these also served a social purpose.[188]

A typical day which might have been spent by a "fashionable visitor" to Bath is described by Egan. "In the morning from the Pump Room to the Parades – the Crescents – a stroll alongside the Avon; or, a walk in Sydney Gardens – the inviting level path to the village of Weston – visiting the shops – libraries – exhibitions, etc. A peep at Pryor Park, Claverton Down, and Lansdown Hill, etc. After dinner, the Theatre becomes attractive; or to dash off to the Rooms, where dancing and the card table tend to finish and fully occupy...the time of a fashionable visitor at Bath."[189]

Hitherto, I have not turned my full attention to *Sense and Sensibility* or *Pride and Prejudice*, although, as we have seen, the prototypes of these works were written before the book we are about to discuss. The reason is that those drafts may have been no more than shadows, or even mere suggestions, of the completed masterpieces, and were extensively revised by the author as she reached full maturity. In the case of *Susan*, which was later renamed *Catherine* after the eponymous heroine, it is safe to assume that the draft which was written in 1798 to 1799 is essentially the version which has come down to us today as *Northanger Abbey*.

It is true that it was subject to further revision before it was first sold to the publishers in 1803, and there were further minor refinements before its eventual, postumous publication as *Northanger Abbey* in December 1817. At the end of Chapter Five, there is a reference to Maria Edgeworth's novel, *Belinda*, which was published in 1801. At the beginning of Chapter Seven, Catherine Morland accepts Isabella's invitation to go to Edgar's Buildings to see her new hat "through the Pump-yard to the archway, opposite Union passage"[190] but Union passage was not so named by the Bath municipal authorities until 1807.[191] But the fact that the novel was essentially finished at the turn of the century is evident from its style. It is not a cohesive whole; it is essentially in two parts: a comedy of manners in Bath, and a gothic parody at the Abbey, and, although in *Northanger Abbey* Jane found the narrative voice so essential to her art, that voice had still not been perfected. It is uneven, and has not yet been brought fully under control. There is the intrusion of irrelevant comment, and still some elements of the burlesque, and a fixation with literary satire and the Gothic which are hangovers from Austen's juvenile writings. Gothic fiction was going rapidly out of fashion around the turn of the century, and it may be that this is why the publishers, who purchased the rights to the book in 1803, did not go on to publish it.

Its earlier composition is evident too from its cultural references, which are very much of the late Georgian, as opposed to the Regency era. The ladies are dressed in muslin, and wear their hair piled high, which is very much of the 1790s. In her "Advertisement" for the book, written in 1816 for re-submission to the publishers, Jane Austen herself makes its earlier composition clear. "This little work was finished in the year 1803…The public are entreated to bear in mind that thirteen years have passed since it was finished, many more since it was begun, and that during that period, places, manners, books and opinions have undergone considerable changes."

Northanger Abbey is not primarily set in the eponymous building, as is *Mansfield Park*. Most of the action takes place in Bath, and there is no way of knowing if Jane Austen even chose the title herself. By the time the final contract was sealed with the publishers, she was dead. We know that her idea was to name the work after its lead character, at first Susan, and then Catherine; a change probably necessitated by the publication in 1809 of another book called *Susan: A Novel*.

The reason Jane wanted to name the novel after her heroine is because it is principally about the entry into society of a young woman, Catherine Morland, and the tensions between her expectations of the adult world, and the reality. In this respect, although it is not auto-biographical, it must in part be a product of Jane's experiences as she was increasingly coming out into society in the late 1790s. Although it is first and foremost a novel about a young woman's entrée into society, it is much more than that. It is also the manifesto of a young, aspirant writer, and, in particular, a young, female novelist, and it seeks to advance a powerful feminist agenda.

Catherine Morland, the daughter of a village clergyman from

a comfortable background, is invited to Bath for the season by her wealthy friends, Mr and Mrs Allen. Mrs Allen is the recipient of an early turn of phrase at the nib of Jane Austen's pen, a perfect example of her use of irony to make a point. It is at once deceptively gentle, and yet devastatingly effective in the assassination of its subject. She was "one of that numerous class of females, whose society can raise no other emotion than surprise at there being any men in the world who could like them well enough to marry them." The irony which makes this observation so effective emerges from the tension between the seemingly innocuous preface, and the vicious conclusion. It incites the double-take in the attentive reader.

Neglected by the vain and self-centred Mrs Allen, who is only interested in dressing herself well, Catherine is shy, a little gauche, and without a companion. Her initial appearance in the Upper Rooms at Bath is socially awkward. "I wish you could dance my dear. I wish you could get a partner," says Mrs Allen, whilst doing nothing practical to achieve the objective. A few days later in the Lower Rooms, she is introduced by the master of ceremonies to a young clergyman called Henry Tilney, "…about four or five and twenty, was rather tall, had a pleasing countenance, a very intelligent and lively eye, and, if not quite handsome, was very near it."[192] They dance, and at the end of the assembly they part, "on the lady's side at least, with a strong inclination for continuing the acquaintance."[193]

The following day, hoping to encounter Tilney again, she meets the widowed Mrs Thorpe, and her three daughters; the oldest of whom, Isabella, is not only four years her senior, but also has "great personal beauty" and is far more sophisticated and worldly-wise; in short, she is an outrageous flirt worthy of Eliza de Feuillide. Isabella's brother, John Thorpe, is a friend of Catherine's brother, James, who are both up at Oxford. Isabella and Catherine become intimate. "Their conversation turned upon those subjects, of which the free discussion has generally much to do in perfecting an intimacy between two young ladies; such as dress, balls, flirtations and quizzes."[194] It is Isabella who encourages Catherine to read Ann Radcliffe's *Udolpho*, and other Gothic novels: "I have made out a list of ten or twelve more of the kind for you," she gushes.[195]

Isabella is a flawed individual, selfish, vain, and mercenary, "regardless of everything but her own gratification"[196], and Catherine forms a much truer friendship with Tilney's sister, Eleanor, whose "simplicity and truth" and lack of personal conceit, is contrasted with that of Isabella. However, after Isabella becomes engaged to James Morland, Catherine's brother, she tries to encourage a romance between Catherine and her own brother, John, but Catherine is of sufficient judgement to reject him, and her thoughts of romance turn instead to Henry Tilney, the son of General Tilney of Northanger Abbey. General Tilney, under the illusion encouraged by John Thorpe that Catherine has considerable independent means, invites her to stay at the Abbey in the hope that she will make a good match for his son. In the meantime, Catherine's obsession with *Udolpho* has excited "the luxury of a raised, restless and frightened imagination"[197], and she fantasises that Northanger Abbey is the setting of a Gothic horror, and convinces herself, with very little evidence, that the General is in the same mould as Montoni, Radcliffe's arch-villain, and that he must have imprisoned or even murdered his wife.

Henry Tilney, learning of her unfounded suspicions, scolds and disabuses her, and she is left mortified. Worse still, General Tilney, having discovered that her means are neither considerable nor independent, orders her to leave the Abbey that very same night, and make her own way home. Meanwhile, Henry Tilney's dissolute brother, Captain Frederick Tilney, has flirted with Isabella Thorpe, causing her to break off her engagement to James Morland, and then abandoned her. However, things finally work out for Catherine. Realising how badly she has been used, Henry goes after her, and they are engaged. The General, having learned that she will have a substantial income in due course, after all, is reconciled to the match, and Catherine and Henry are married.

As we have seen, not only was Jane a reader of novels, encouraged by her father, but she was also a reader of the Gothic novel. This is a form which was wildly popular in the late eighteenth century, perhaps reaching its apogee in the 1790s, with a plethora of titles which included references to abbeys: *Roach Abbey* (1794), *The Abbey of St Asaph* (1795), *Waldeck Abbey* (1795), *The Abbey of Clugny* (1796), *The Children of the Abbey* (1796), *Munster Abbey* (1797), and *Grasville Abbey* (1798). It was also typically the work of female writers. The plots and the settings followed a standard routine: stories of heroines plunged into worlds of horror, abduction, torture and haunting, couched in absurd, hyberbolic language, with heightened passions and sensibilities, and typically set in environments remote in time or space, such as medieval abbeys, where the usual rules of polite society had long since lapsed into disuse. The form was deprecated by the intelligentsia, and anyone with pretensions to it. In 1796, *The Critical Review*, a High Tory publication of book reviews, remarked snootily, "Since Mrs Radcliffe's justly admired and successful romances, the press has teemed with stories of haunted castles and visionary terrors; the incidents of which are so little diversified, that criticism is at a loss to vary its remarks."[198]

The Gothic novel, then, was ripe for parody and mockery, and in *Northanger Abbey*, Jane Austen revels in it. The parody begins immediately with the description of the leading lady, delivered with deliberate bathos. "No one who had ever seen Catherine Morland in her infancy, would have supposed her born to be an heroine." The Morlands "were in general very plain, and Catherine, for many years of her life, as plain as any".[199] Although her personal appearance improves as she reaches her mid and late teens, there is still nothing heroic about her. She is unaccomplished in drawing, music, and languages. However she has no objection to books, "provided they were all story and no reflection", and "from fifteen to seventeen she was in training for a heroine".

Here the conventions of the novel of overblown sentiment, packed with unrealistic situations and plot development, is turned on its head from the beginning. Catherine Morland is very ordinary, but she is *training* to be a heroine, exposing the formulaic conventions of the Gothic novel as contrived and forced. But when a young lady is determined to be a heroine, "Something must and will happen to throw a hero in her way". That is when the Allens invite her to Bath. Even here, however, her departure is immersed in bathos. Jane, speaking ironically with the authorial voice, supposes that Mrs Morland might warn her daughter about the dangers of being abducted by a baronet, and dragged off to a remote farm house. In fact, her advice extends only so far as to warn her to wrap up warmly at night.[200] And when she sees Mr Tilney with another young lady on his arm, she is able to avoid "turning of a deathlike paleness, and falling in a fit on Mrs Alllen's bosom…"[201] by rationally concluding that she is his sister.

In the second half of the novel, the edifice of Northanger Abbey itself is used to parody the conventions of the Gothic form. When first invited to the Abbey, Catherine is thrilled by the very name, conjuring as it does the names of a list of Gothic novels. "Her passion for ancient edifices was next in degree to her passion for Henry Tilney".[202] Henry Tilney, as they approach the Abbey in his carriage, teases her about her expectations, referring to the horrors that such a building may produce, such as "gloomy passages", "a ponderous chest", an apartment never used since a relative died in it twenty years before, a violent storm, a concealed door leading to vaulted rooms, in one of which "there may be a dagger, in another a few drops of blood, and in a third the remains of some instrument of torture", and an old fashioned cabinet with a secret compartment containing a hoard of diamonds, and a parchment. Catherine pretends to be horrified but in fact is thrilled, "Oh! No, no – do not say so. Well, go on."[203]

In fact the reality is couched in bathos. The Abbey stands so low that she finds herself through the gates before she knows it, "without having discerned even an antique chimney." Nor had the breeze "seemed to waft the sighs of the murdered to her; it had wafted nothing worse than a thick mizzling rain."[204] She had imagined the burning embers of a fire in a darkened room, painted glass, dirt and cobwebs. In fact, the window panes are large, clear and light – "the difference was very distressing".[205] The Abbey is, in fact, well appointed, and fitted up with modern furnishings, much to Catherine's disappointment who "cared for no furniture of a more modern date than the fifteenth century"[206].

The centre-piece of the parody comes when Catherine is alone in her room.[207] Her chamber is light, airy and cheerfully decorated, but determined to find herself in a scene of Gothic terror, Catherine fantasises that an "immense heavy chest" contains a dark secret. In fact, in a wonderful example of the use of bathos, it only contains "a white, cotton counterpane, properly folded" and "might sometimes be of use in holding hats and bonnets." After the dinner party breaks up on her first evening in the Abbey, she returns to her room and wills herself to be frightened, in much the same way that a child derives a thrill from a ride on the ghost train. "The wind roared down the chimney, the rain beat in torrents against the windows, and everything seemed to speak the awfulness of her situation." However a piece of parchment she finds concealed in a mysterious cabinet, just before her candle goes out, and which robs her of half her night's sleep, turns out, in the cheerful light of the morning, to be nothing more terrifying than a washing bill. "She felt humbled to the dust."

Although *Northanger Abbey* undoubtedly parodies the Gothic novel, Jane Austen, in an extensive passage early in the book[208], advances a powerful defence for the novel itself, and also demands nothing less than a sisterhood of novelists. This is no parody, and comes from the heart. Indeed, one can perhaps discern a little of her disappointment and anger at the peremptory rejection of *First Impressions* in November 1797, and her determination not to give up. "Let us not desert one another; we are an injured body. Although our productions have afforded more extensive and unaffected pleasure than those of any other literary corporation in the world, no species of composition has been so much decried." It is an art "in which the greatest powers of the mind are displayed, in which the most thorough knowledge of human nature, the happiest delineation of its varieties, the liveliest effusions of wit and humour are conveyed to the world in the best chosen language."

Her defence of the novel is made all the more powerful by her mockery of other, far less creative and original, forms of literature, regarded as more worthy by those who turn their noses up at the mere novel. "And while the abilities of the nine-hundredth abridger of the History of England, or of the man who collects and publishes in a volume some dozen lines of Milton, Pope, and Prior, with a paper from the Spectator, and a chapter from Sterne, are eulogized by a thousand pens, - there seems almost a general wish of decrying the capacity and undervaluing the labour of the novelist, and of slighting the performances which have only genius, wit, and taste to recommend them."

Jane's manifesto in support of the novelist, and in particular the *female* novelist, is also a condemnation of the misogyny inherent in the critical disapproval of the novel in publications such as the *Review*, and a misogyny which was endemic to the times in which she lived, as reflected in *Northanger Abbey*. Even the most sympathetic male character, Henry Tilney, exhibits what might be called a benign misogyny; the exercise of a soft, more subtle controlling power, over women. Although meant to be humorous, he ridicules what he supposes to be the feminine habit of keeping a journal. "It is this delightful habit of journalising which largely contributes to form the easy style of writing for which ladies are so generally celebrated. Every body allows that the talent of writing agreeable letters is peculiarly female." Having elevated the female talent for writing, he then proceeds to denigrate it. " As far as I have had the opportunity of judging, it appears to me that the usual style of letter writing among women is faultless, except in three particulars…a general deficiency of subject, a total inattention to stops, and a very frequent ignorance of grammar."[209]

He is condescending to both his sister and to Catherine, not just because he considers himself to be intellectually superior, but because of their sex, declaring that he "will prove himself a man, no less by the generosity of my soul than the clearness of my head. I have no patience with such as my sex as disdain to let themselves down to the comprehension of yours."[210] He criticises what he perceives to be Catherine's loose use of language, and is "fearful of wearying her with too much wisdom at once."[211] This prompts Austen's well known ironic observations about the dangers of too much education in women.

"A woman especially, if she have the misfortune of knowing anything, should conceal it as well as she can…though to the larger and more trifling part of the [male] sex, imbecility in females is a great enhancement of their personal charms, there is a portion of them too reasonable and too well informed themselves to desire anything more in woman than ignorance."[212]

Catherine is initially prepared to stand up to Tilney's authority. When she questions his brother's motives in flirting with Isabella, he complains that she is "a very close questioner". But she persists, telling him that she only asks what she wants to be told, "for you must know your brother's heart." But eventually she submits because she believes he must know best, and "remembered his instructions". "She blamed herself for the extent of her fears, and resolved never to think so seriously on the subject again."[213] She is prepared to submit to the authority of a man whom she respects and to whom she is attracted. "His manner might sometimes surprise, but his meaning must always be just: - and what she did not understand, she was almost ready to admire, as what she did."[214]

However, John Thorpe is another matter altogether. He is not only a ridiculous bore, but also an unpleasant, bullying misogynist. Upon greeting his mother and sisters, he mocks his mother's hat, saying that it makes her look like an old witch, and observes that both his sisters look very ugly.[215] Soon after meeting Catherine Morland, he comments upon the looks of every woman they pass "with a short decisive sentence of praise or condemnation." She agrees with him "as long as she could, with all the civility and deference of the youthful female mind, fearful of hazarding an opinion of its own in opposition to that of a self-assured man..."[216] Jane Austen tellingly condemns him out of his own mouth with the words, "I never read novels; I have something else to do," an insensitive response to a polite request which leaves Catherine feeling "humbled and ashamed". In contrast, Austen signals her relative approval of Henry Tilney who declares in response to a similar enquiry: "The person, be it gentleman or lady, who has not pleasure in a good novel, must be intolerably stupid."[217]

It is not only with words that Thorpe seeks to humiliate and control. In the Upper Rooms, acting as Catherine's chaperone, he deserts her, leaving her without a partner, and yet obliged to deny Tilney a dance. The next day he turns up unannounced, protesting an engagement to take a drive. "What a head you have!...Not expect me! That's a good one! And what a dust you would have made if I had not come." He proceeds to invite her into his carriage, but before they set off alarms her by pretending his horse is liable to bolt. Then, when the horse behaves in "the quietest manner imaginable, without a plunge or caper, or anything like one", he puts it down to his own expert horsemanship. A couple of days later, seeing her about to stand up with Tilney, he pretends to have engaged her for the first dance. When she protests that he had never asked her, he says, "That is a good one, by Jove! – I asked you as soon as I came into the room, and I was just going to ask you again, but when I turned round you were gone! – this is a cursed shabby trick."[218] This is behaviour which we would now call gaslighting.

But his behaviour becomes more sinister still. When Catherine refuses a ride with Thorpe on the grounds that she is expecting a call from Henry Tilney and his sister, he deceives her into thinking that he saw Tilney drive off with another piece of "very pretty cattle"[219]. He persuades her upon this false pretence of allowing him to drive her to Blaize Castle, which he represents to be "the finest place in England...the oldest in the kingdom." This is another lie. Blaize Castle was a *faux* medieval folly, consisting of three modern towers surrounding a large chamber, built in 1766 as a party venue by Thomas Farr, a Bristol merchant whose wealth derived from the slave trade.

When Catherine sees Miss Tilney on her brother's arm, she pleads with Thorpe to stop, "Thorpe only lashed his horse into a brisker trot."[220] When she pleads with him again, "Thorpe only laughed, smacked his whip, encouraged his horse, made odd noises, and drove on." It is difficult to avoid the unpleasant conclusion that Thorpe's control of the horse is a product of his psychosexual ambition and desire to control women.

The following Sunday, he and Isabella attempt to brow-beat her into breaking off a prior engagement with the Tilneys. Her sense of propriety prevents her, and Thorpe then feeds Miss Tilney with false information in order to achieve his object. Catherine, mortified by the deception, is physically restrained by Thorpe and Isabella when she attempts to repair the damage.

General Tilney, however, is a real figure of the oppression, not just of male authority, but of the patriarchal state, "poring over the affairs of the nation for hours"[221] after the ladies of the house are asleep. Even Thorpe is a little afraid of General Tilney at first but then comes to have a great regard for him.[222] Indeed, he is a role model for Thorpe. Even upon first making his acquaintance, when he is full of civility and compliments, Catherine feels it "a release to get away from him."[223] On the morning of the departure for the Abbey, he is displeased that Frederick is late for breakfast, and Catherine is "quite pained by the severity of his father's reproof, which seemed disproportionate to the offence"[224]

The journey itself is marred by his obsession with punctuality, and the efficiency of the servants, and Catherine has "difficulty in saving her own new writing desk from being thrown out into the street"[225]. She and Miss Tilney are fearful of being late for dinner. When they enter the dining room they find the General pacing the room, watch in hand, pulling the bell with violence, and ordering, "Dinner to be on table *directly!*" His opinion on the most trivial of matters brooks no contradiction. "The imposing effect of this last argument was equal to his wishes. The silence of the lady proved it to be unanswerable."[226]

Although Catherine's groundless belief that the General killed his wife is proved to be wide of the mark, his son's admission that his mother had "much to bear" and was injured by his father's temper, is telling, and in keeping with what the reader has learned of the General's domineering personality. The personality which he shows to Catherine, on the surface very generous and accommodating, is in fact a façade. It is an artifice to woo her for his son, and what he believes to be her considerable wealth. The façade falls away entirely when he goes to London and is disabused of his illusions surrounding Catherine's circumstances by a resentful John Thorpe. When he returns, he uses a pretext of a forgotten engagement elsewhere to issue instructions, through Eleanor, that she is to leave at seven o'clock the following morning. She is to make her own way by carriage, a distance of seventy miles, without even a servant to escort her part of the way, and were it not for Eleanor's thoughtfulness at the last moment, she would have been turned out of doors without the means to get home. This is bad manners by the standards of today. By the standards of the time, such behaviour towards a seventeen year old, genteel, young lady would have been regarded as nothing short of brutish, shocking and cruel. As Austen concludes, Catherine "in suspecting General Tilney of either murdering or shutting up his wife, she had scarcely sinned against his character, or magnified his cruelty"[227]

Ultimately the Gothic horrors imagined by Catherine are debunked both by the parody of Austen's pen, and the words of Henry Tilney in scolding her for her unfounded fears. "Remember the country and the age in which we live. Remember that we are English, that we are Christians. Consult your own understanding, your own sense of the probable. Does our education prepare us for such atrocities? Do our laws connive at them?" But the residual irony in Austen's novel is that the laws of England, whilst not overtly conniving at torture and murder, most certainly did connive at, install and maintain, a patriarchy in which the rights of women were as nothing compared to the oppressive authority of men in the body of the state, in the body of the social order, and in the institution of the family: represented in turn by the General, John Thorpe, and Henry Tilney.

In the improbably happy and rapid conclusion of *Northanger Abbey*, Austen returns to parody, with no great subtlety, the convention of the Gothic novel in which all the loose ends are tied up, and everyone lives happily ever after: "I fear to the bosom of my readers, who will see in the tell-tale compression of the pages before them, that we are all hastening together to perfect felicity."[228]

However the central truth of *Northanger Abbey* remains, that under the façade of the gentle society into which Catherine Morland and Jane Austen were admitted in the late 1790s, there was an oppressive darkness. Although Catherine does not articulate, or even imagine, her predicament in these terms, she is conscious, during her last night at the Abbey, having been peremptorily dismissed by the General, of the irony of her position. She realises that her chamber "in which her disturbed imagination had tormented her on her first arrival, was again the scene of agitated spirits, and unquiet slumbers".[229] But this time it is different, and in a way even more terrifying, because it is not the mere product of imagination. "Yet how different now the source of her inquietude from what it had been then – how mournfully superior in reality and substance! Her anxiety had foundation in fact; her fears in probability."

Jane Austen's weapon against this oppression was to be the power of the pen, wielded by a proud and confident writer, and more particularly, a proud and confident *female*, writer of *novels*.

XI: STEVENTON: THE LATER YEARS

In the August of 1798, a tragedy occurred. Jane's first cousin, Jane Williams *née* Cooper, and now Lady Williams following her husband's elevation in the wake of his great naval victory, was killed by a runaway dray-horse on the Isle of Wight. She was twenty-seven. She had been friends and playmates with the Austen girls since they were little children, and had been their school fellows in Oxford, Southampton, and Reading. In adolescence and early adulthood, she had often stayed at Steventon, participating in the Christmas theatricals, and sharing in the gossip and the excitement of their first balls. Although there is no record of Jane and Cassandra's reaction, her death must have touched them very closely indeed.

It is possible that it was in response to this tragedy that Mr and Mrs Austen, with their two daughters, were invited to stay for the first time in the great house at Godmersham. Although Edward's adoptive mother, the widowed Mrs Knight, had the estate for life, she had decided the previous autumn to retire to a property in Canterbury, and to let Edward and his family take possession of the property whilst she still lived. Godmersham, about eight miles from Canterbury, which still stands and is open to public view, is a grand, two-storey Palladian mansion with a central block, seven bays wide, and two flanking wings of ten windows. It was sufficiently impressive to attract tourists (much like the Gardiners in *Pride and Prejudice*), and was described in a guide published in 1793 as "a modern building of a centre and two wings; one of which, the Eastern, contains a most excellent library."[230]

Set in a landscaped park in the Stour valley, with walled gardens, an orchard, a Grecian Temple, a Hermitage and a Bathing House in the grounds, it was every bit an equal to the likes of the fictional Mansfield Park or Pemberley. It also had a full complement of servants. *The Complete Servant*, published in 1825, recommends that a gentleman of Edward Austen's standing should employ eight female and eight male servants: a cook, lady's-maid, two housemaids, a nurse, a nursery maid, kitchen maid and laundry maid, with a butler, valet, coachman, two grooms, footman and two gardeners.[231] Edward also needed a governess for his growing family. At Godmersham, then, Jane had an opportunity to observe the detail of life in a grand country estate, experience which was to be put to such good use in her novels.

During this visit to Godmersham, Elizabeth gave birth to her fifth child. When the Austens left towards the end of October, Cassandra stayed at Godmersham to help with the baby. She did not return to Steventon until March 1799. This leaves us with a body of correspondence from Jane to her sister. It was on Wednesday 24th October 1798 that Jane and her parents left Godmersham. On the first evening of their journey, Jane wrote to Cassandra from the Bull and George, a coaching inn on the pilgrim route from Canterbury, at Dartford.[232] Her tenderness towards her brother's children shines through at the end of the letter: "I flatter myself that itty Dordy [her nephew George] will not forget me at least under a week. Kiss him for me."

They had travelled in stages to Sittingbourne, then to Rochester, and on to Dartford, arriving just after four, where they were to stay the night. Much of the letter to Cassandra involves Jane's reassuring her sister about her mother's health, and her fortitude for the journey. "My mother took some of her bitters at Ospringe, and some more at Rochester and she ate some bread several times." But the letter also provides a fascinating insight into the nature of these stage stop-overs. "We have got an apartment up two pair of stairs, as we could not be otherwise accommodated with a sitting-room and bedchambers on the same floor which we wished to be. We have one double-bedded and one single-bedded room; in the former my mother and I are to sleep. I shall leave you to guess who is to occupy the other. We sate down to dinner a little after five, and had some beefsteaks and a boiled fowl, but no oyster sauce."

She also mentions her writing and dressing boxes which had been "by accident put into a chaise which was just packing off as we came in, and were driven away towards Gravesend in their way to the West Indies. No part of my property could have been such a prize before, for in my writing box was all my worldy wealth, 7l [seven pounds], and my dear Harry's deputation [authority from Edward for Harry Digweed to shoot on his land]". Fortunately the landlord sent a man on a horse to fetch the boxes back, and they were restored in half an hour.

The reference to the writing box, which must be the writing desk her father had bought for her nineteenth birthday, begs the question of whether it contained anything else, other than the money and the "deputation". There is every chance that Jane had been working on *Northanger Abbey* during this visit to Godmersham, and there is support for this contention later in the same letter when Jane informs Cassandra that her father is reading the "*Midnight Bell* which he has got from the library." *The Midnight Bell* is a gothic novel written by Francis Lathom. It was newly published that very year, and is one of the novels in the list which Isabella Thorpe had prepared for Catherine Morland. One of Edward's daughters, Marianne, recalled many years later "that when Aunt Jane came to us at Godmersham she used to bring the manuscript of whatever novel she was writing with her, and would shut herself up with my elder sisters in one of the bedrooms to read them aloud...I and the younger ones used to hear peals of laughter through the door, and thought it very hard that we should be shut out from what was so delightful."[233]

On the second night of the journey, Jane and her parents spent the night in Staines where her mother "had not a very good night".[234] They arrived home on the Friday afternoon, and her mother was exhausted by the journey. They had stopped off in Basingstoke where she was revived by "a mess of broth", and also saw a doctor who advised her to take twelve drops of laudanum when she went to bed. With her mother indisposed, and Cassandra away, it seems that Jane took charge of the house. "I carry about the keys of the wine and closet, and twice since I began this letter have had orders to give in the kitchen." She appears to have enjoyed these duties too. "I always take care to provide such things as please my own appetite, which I consider as the chief merit in housekeeping. I have had some ragout veal, and I mean to have some haricot mutton tomorrow. We are to kill a pig soon...I am very fond of experimental housekeeping, such as having an ox cheek now and then, I shall have one next week, and I mean to have some little dumplings put into it, that I may fancy myself at Godmersham."[235] By the Sunday her mother was feeling much better.

Lord Brabourne's opinion of Jane's marriage prospects, that she "was too fond of home, and too happy among her own relations, to have sought other ties, unless her heart had been really won", was tested again and confirmed in the autumn of 1798, in the form of the Reverend Samuel Blackall. Blackall was a fellow of Emmanuel College, Cambridge, and four years Jane's senior. Jane had first met him during the previous Christmas. He had been invited to Ashe by Mrs Lefroy. In November of 1798, Mrs Lefroy had invited him again for the Christmas season but he reluctantly had to decline. She showed his letter to Jane. "It would give me particular pleasure" he says, "to have an opportunity of improving my acquaintance with that family – with a hope of creating to myself a nearer interest. But at present I cannot indulge any expectation of it."[236]

The manner of Blackall's expression instantly recalls the approach of Mr Collins to the Bennett sisters in *Pride and Prejudice*, and it is a safe assumption that he influenced the character of Collins in subsequent drafts of the novel. Blackall's letter suggests that Jane had not been particularly encouraging to him during his previous visit, and Jane's reaction to the letter is confirmation of that. "This is rational enough; there is less love and more sense in it than sometimes appeared before, and I am very well satisfied. It will all go on exceedingly well, and decline away in a very reasonable manner. There seems no likelihood of his coming into Hampshire this Christmas, and it is therefore most probable that our indifference will soon be mutual, unless his regard, which appeared to spring from knowing nothing of me at first, is best supported by never seeing me."[237] Unlike Charlotte Lucas, it is clear that Jane was not prepared to settle for a Mr Collins just for financial security.

Instead, in the run up to the Christmas of 1798, she was probably still working on her first draft of *Northanger Abbey*, quite reconciled with her rather uneventful and unsophisticated domestic life. On 18th December, she described her routine to Cassandra. "We dine now at half-past three, and have done dinner, I suppose, before you begin. We drink tea at half-past six. I am afraid you will despise us. My father reads Cowper to us in the morning, to which I listen when I can. How do you spend your evenings? I guess that Elizabeth works, that you read to her, and that Edward goes to sleep. My mother continues hearty; her appetite and nights are very good, but she sometimes complains of an asthma, a dropsy, water in her chest, and a liver disorder." There is though a hint of frustration with her position: "People get so horridly poor and economical in this part of the world that I have no patience with them. Kent is the only place for happiness; everybody is rich there."[238]

On Christmas Eve, she wrote again[239] to inform Cassandra of some good news received from Admiral Gambier, "in response to my father's application", that Frank's promotion was likely to take place very soon, and Charles had prospects of being moved to a frigate when "it is judged that he has taken his turn in a small ship". The tone of the letter is a demonstration of the great affection both sisters had for their youngest brothers, and their concern for their well-being. "There! I may now finish my letter and go and hang myself, for I am sure I can neither write nor do anything which will not appear insipid to you after this." Four days later came the news that Frank had been promoted Commander, and Charles removed to the frigate HMS *Tamar*.[240] Frank went on to take over command of the sloop HMS *Peterel* in Gibraltar Bay in February of the following year. It was a 24 gun sloop with 120 men.[241]

She went on though to describe a "very thin" ball she had attended, "but by no means unpleasant. There were thirty-one people and only eleven ladies out of the number, and but five single women in the room. There were twenty dances, and she danced all of them, "without any fatigue…in cold weather and with few couples I fancy I could just as well dance for a week together as for half an hour." She lists eight partners, including "a Mr Butcher (belonging to the Temples, a sailor and not of the 11th Light Dragoons), Mr Temple (not the horrid one at all)." There was also a Mr Callard, with whom a little flirting appears to have occurred. Mr Callard "appeared as usual with his hat in his hand, and stood every now and then behind Catherine and me to be talked to and abused for not dancing. We teased him, however, into it at last. I was very glad to see him again after so long a separation, and he was altogether rather the genius and flirt of the evening. He enquired after you."

In late December, Jane was invited by Lady Dorchester to her ball on 8th January at Kempshott Park. This was an estate between Steventon and Basingstoke, and which had been leased by the Prince of Wales. Whilst James was the curate at Overton, he had on several occasions participated in hunts, alongside the Prince and his courtiers. Jane wrote to Cassandra on the day of the ball.[242] She was to wear a marmalone (Egyptian style) cap – "It is all the fashion now" – and a gown "made very much like my blue one, which you always told me sat very well, with only these variations: the sleeves are short, the wrap fuller, the apron comes over it, and a band of the same completes the whole".

She did not supplement the letter the next day with much detail of the ball because she had a weakness in one of her eyes "which makes writing neither very pleasant nor very profitable." However, she did confide that there "was one gentleman, an officer of the Cheshire, a very good looking young man who, I was told, wanted very much to be introduced to me, but as he did not want it quite enough to take much trouble in effecting it, we never could bring it about." One of the Harwood young men took to her "rather more than he used to do", but she sat down for two dances rather than dance with Lord Bolton's eldest son, "who danced too ill to be endured". After the ball she stayed with Martha Lloyd, who "kindly made room for me in her bed" which "did exceedingly well for us, both to lie awake and talk till two o'clock, and to sleep in the rest of the night."

Her reference on 18th December to her brother Edward going to sleep in the evenings, whilst the others were sewing or reading, may relate to a propensity on his part for over-indulgence in wine, food or both. Cassandra had clearly informed Jane of Edward's ill-health, and Jane refers later in the letter to his stomach problems, faintness, sickness, and a "nervous complaint". This wasn't a one-off hangover. There is another reference to it in her letter of 21st January.[243] Charles was about to join the forty-four gun frigate, HMS *Endymion* as second lieutenant[244], and he had had his hair cut short, in the modern fashion. Jane was concerned that Edward, who still had his hair powdered in the late Georgian style, would not approve. She asked Cassandra to conceal it from him for the time being, "lest it might fall on his spirits and retard his recovery". Her father had also sent him a pig, perhaps to keep his spirits up, "already killed and cut up…My mother means to pay herself for the salt and the trouble of ordering it to be cured by the spareribs, the souse, and the lard."

It was, therefore, for his health that Edward and Elizabeth planned to spend a couple of months in Bath for the waters. They came first to Steventon with their two eldest children, and then went on to Bath, arriving on 17th May. A house had been rented at No 13 Queen Square, near to the Pump Room and the Assembly Rooms. Jane and her mother went with them. Jane must have been pleased to return to Bath. She was, after all, still working on her first Bath novel, *Northanger Abbey*. Fortunately for posterity, Cassandra stayed at home, and so there are surviving letters from Jane to her sister. Jane wrote to her that same day.[245] They had spent the night in Andover, where they had had comfortable rooms, and a good dinner of asparagus, lobster, and cheesecakes. They arrived at one o'clock the following afternoon.

"We are exceedingly pleased with the house", she wrote; "the rooms are quite as large as we expected. Mrs Bromley [the landlady] is a fat woman in mourning, and a little black kitten runs about the staircase." Jane and her mother were to have rooms upstairs, the latter being now of sufficient health to cope with a double flight of stairs. Jane's room was as large as her bedroom at home, with "a very nice chest of drawers and a closet full of shelves."

The accommodation was superior to that she had experienced on her first visit. "I like our situation very much; it is far more cheerful than Paragon, and the prospect from the drawing room window, at which I now write, is rather picturesque, as it commands a prospective view of the left side of Brock Street, broken by three Lombardy poplars in the garden of the last house in Queen's Parade." Indeed, Queen Square was described as "magnificent and chaste" by Egan: "...an open and desirable situation, and the north side of which is much admired for the great taste and architectural talent displayed in its erection." In the centre of the square was an obelisk, standing seventy-feet high, dedicated to the Prince of Wales, and erected by Richard Nash in 1787.[246]

The social isolation which afflicted Catherine Morland's first arrival was also to be avoided. "There was a very long list of arrivals yesterday, so that we need not immediately dread absolute solitude; and there is a public breakfast in Sydney Gardens every morning, so that we shall not be wholly starved." The Leigh Perrots were now in permanent residence in Paragon Buildings. The Austens had stopped at Paragon on their way into Bath, with a view to paying their respects, but it was too wet and dirty for them to get out of the carriage.

They spent an evening with a family called the Mapletons, and "...took a very charming walk from six to eight up Beacon Hill, and across some fields, to the village of Charlecombe, which is sweetly situated in a little green valley, as a village with such a name ought to be."[247] There was a Mr Gould of their party who walked her home after tea. "He is a very young man, just entered Oxford, wears spectacles, and has heard that Evelina [a novel by Frances Burney] was written by Dr Johnson." Mr Gould can hardly have been a model for John Thorpe, or Henry Tilney, and the remark gives a hint of intellectual snobbery, sharpened to a point by the razor of her wit, to which Jane had a tendency, and which may have deterred potential suitors throughout her life.

On the evening of Tuesday 4th June, there was to be a grand gala in Sydney Gardens, "a concert, with illuminations and fireworks...even the concert will have more than its usual charms for me, as the gardens are large enough for me to get pretty well beyond the reach of its sound." It appears from the tone of her letters that Jane, perhaps unlike her heroine, was a little under-whelmed by Bath; her head was certainly not turned by it.

On the evening of Saturday 22nd June, the Austen party attended the Theatre Royal to see the pantomime *Blue Beard*, the story of a wealthy man with a habit of murdering his wives, set to music by the Irish composer and theatrical manager, Michael Kelly. They also saw *The Birthday Day*, a translation of August von Kotsebue's *Die Versohnung* ("The Reconciliation").[248]

The main preoccupation for Edward was his health, rather than society. After a couple of weeks, Jane reported that he was about as well as he was back at Steventon. He was drinking the waters from the Hetling Pump Room, was bathing, and also trying electrotherapy. At the time, this was still an experimental treatment, and was not brought into the mainstream until the middle of the next century. A frictional electrical machine was used to charge a patient with static electricity. Jane was sceptical. "He proposed the [electrotherapy] himself to Dr Fellowes who made no objection to it, but I fancy we are all unanimous in expecting no advantage from it. At present I have no great notion of our staying here beyond the month."[249]

By 11th June, Jane was reporting that Edward was pretty well, and that both he and Elizabeth would be glad to get away.[250] She sounds a little bored, complaining that they had "not been to any public place lately, nor performed anything out of the common daily routine of No 13, Queen Square, Bath. But today we were to have dashed away at an extraordinary rate, by dining out, had it not so happened that we did not go." One gets the impression that Edward, who had a touch of the hypochondriac about him like his mother, was perhaps a little bit of a stick in the mud, and old before his years. Indeed, within a week he was complaining of "sick and uncomfortable feelings"[251], and had lost his appetite. It looked like the gout, although Edward's new doctor considered that the "occasional particular glow in the hands and the feet" was only the effect of the waters in "promoting a better circulation of the blood." Edward Austen was to live to the ripe old age of eighty-five.

The Austens arrived back at Steventon on Thursday 27th June, and Edward and Elizabeth left for Godmersham the following Monday. The rest of the summer was spent by the Austens staying with relatives: the Cookes at Great Bookham in Surrey, the Leighs at Aldestrop, and the Coopers at Harpsden in Oxfordshire. They stayed in Harpsden from August to September, which must have been very poignant, being a year since the death of Jane Cooper. Their other cousin, Reverend Edward Cooper, had been offered the family living of Hamstall Ridware in Staffordshire, and the family moved there in October – far too distant for anything other than a very occasional visit.[252]

The century ended with a bizarre episode involving Mrs Leigh Perrot.[253] On 8th August, whilst her husband was in the Pump Room taking the water for his gout, she was in a haberdasher's shop called Smith's, on the corner of Bath and Stall Streets. She had been there the day before to enquire about some black lace. The haberdasher's business was in financial difficulty, and it appears that William Gye, the trustee for Smith's creditors, and Elizabeth Gregory, who ran the business, together with her lover, Charles Filby, who was employed as a shop assistant, conspired to blackmail Mrs Leigh Perrot for money. When she bought the black lace on the 8th August, a piece of white lace was concealed within the parcel. When she and her husband were walking past the shop shortly thereafter, Miss Gregory came out and asked her if she had any white lace. Gregory was shown the parcel, and removed the white lace before returning to the shop. Filby came out and asked the Leigh Perrots for their name and address.

Four days later, having given the matter little further thought, the Leigh Perrots received an anonymous note, addressed to "Mrs Leigh Perrot, lace dealer." It was a blatant attempt at blackmail. "Your many visiting acquaintance" it said, "before they again admit you into their houses, will think it right to know how you came by the piece of lace stolen from Bath St, a few days ago. Your husband is said to be privy to it." Gregory and Filby had, in the meantime, made a formal complaint to the authorities of theft of lace to the value of twenty shillings; a capital offence in 1799, punishable by death, or, more likely, transportation to Botany Bay. On 14th August, Mrs Leigh Perrot was committed to Ilchester Gaol to await trial at the Taunton Assizes the following March. "The Mayor and Magistrates, to whom we were well known, lamented their being obliged to commit me", she wrote, "but to prison I was sent."[254] Jane's uncle subsequently received two anonymous letters from a servant at the Greyhound Inn at Bath, and from one of William Gye's employees, informing him that it was a plot; and that the conspirators had been disappointed that no offer had been made to buy off the witnesses.

It is difficult to exaggerate the shock this event must have caused, not only to Jane's uncle, who was devoted to his wife, but also to the extended family. Attempts to obtain bail were refused; although, because of her social status, Mrs Leigh Perrot was not confined to a cell, but was allowed to stay with her husband in the gaol-keeper's house, but the accommodation was squalid and cramped. The gaol-keeper shared it with his wife, several children, two dogs and three cats. Mrs Leigh Perrot wrote to her cousins in Lincolnshire about the "vulgarity, dirt, noise from morning till night...not bedlam can be half so noisy."[255] Towards the end of the year, Mrs Austen suggested that either Cassandra or Jane could go to stay with her at Ilchester to provide some comfort but Mrs Leigh Perrot refused, feeling that the conditions would be too unpleasant for young ladies.[256]

The trial took place in Taunton on Saturday 29th March 1800. Joseph Jekyll MP acted as her counsel, although was not allowed to speak on her behalf. The evidence, on the face of it, was strong. Richard Austen Leigh, the grandson of James and Mary Lloyd, later wrote that Jekyll (who had presumably seen all of the evidence) believed she was guilty, and considered her to be a kleptomaniac.[257] Miss Gregory gave evidence, describing how Mrs Leigh Perrot "coloured as red as scarlet" on being confronted.

The law at that time did not allow an accused to give evidence in her own defence but she was allowed to read a statement, in which she invited the jury to consider whether at that time of her life, she would risk her reputation, "or endanger the peace of mind of a husband for whom I would willingly lay down my life."[258] More than a dozen witnesses were called to attest to her unimpeachable character, including the Members of Parliament for Reading and Berkshire, and Lord Braybroke, and Jekyll was able, by questioning, and by the calling of other witnesses, to undermine the credit of Gregory and Filby. It turned out that Filby had been bankrupted three times, and had on a previous occasion secreted an extra veil in a customer's parcel, presumably with a view to blackmail. The jury returned after fifteen minutes with a verdict of not guilty. The relief must have been palpable. The Leigh Perrots returned to Bath late on the Sunday, and later in the week Mrs Leigh Perrot told her cousins that "before 10 on Monday morning our anxious friends began coming in…my whole time has been taken up in kissing and crying." Shortly after the trial, Mr Austen invited the Leigh Perrots for a recuperative stay at Steventon but they wanted to settle the expenses of the trial, apparently in the region of two thousand pounds, before going.[259]

There is a scarcity of information about Jane's life in 1800, until in mid-October, her brother Edward, and his oldest son, visited Steventon.[260] They took Cassandra back to Godmersham with them, and so there is a legacy of eight letters which have survived from October, November and January of 1801. Jane talks of the family's visits to neighbours. There were the Bramstons of Oakley Hall in Deane, where they ate "sandwiches all over mustard"[261] and admired Mr Bramston's porter. There were the Harwoods in Deane House, and of course the Lefroys. Fourteen of them sat down to dinner at Ashe. Mrs Bramston talked nonsense, there was a whist and a casino table, Rice and Lucy made love, Mat. Robinson fell asleep, and James and Mrs Augusta alternately read Dr Finnis' pamphlet on the cow pox. "I bestowed my company by turns on all."[262] Some improvements were taking place in Steventon too. Some new tables had been commissioned from Mr Boyle, the cabinet maker, and "the bank along the elm walk is sloped down for the reception of thorns and lilacs, and it is settled that the other side of the path is to continue turfed, and to be planted with beech, ash and lark."[263]

And, of course, there were balls to attend. The Basingstoke ball at the end of October attracted almost sixty people, including Lord and Lady Portsmouth, the Boltons, and the Dorchesters. "There was a scarcity of men in general, and a still greater scarcity of any that were good for much." She still managed to have nine dances out of ten; five with Stephen Terry, T.Chute and James Digweed, and four with Catherine. "There was commonly a couple of ladies standing up together, but not often any so amiable as ourselves."[264]

In November she had over-indulged a little at Lord Portsmouth's ball at Hurstbourne Park, telling Cassandra the next day, "I believe I drank too much wine last night at Hurstbourne; I know not how else to account for the shaking of my hand today. You will kindly make allowance therefore for any indistinctness of writing, by attributing it to this venial error."[265] Charles was on leave, and accompanied her to the ball. They began at ten, supped at one, and were back at Deane by five in the morning. Afterwards, she treated Cassandra to some of her vicious observational humour. Mrs Blount appeared as she had the previous September with a "pink husband and fat neck." In one of the Miss Coxes she "traced the remains of the vulgar, broad-featured girl who danced at Enham eight years ago." Sir Thomas Champneys daughter was "a queer animal with a white neck", and Mr Warren was just ugly, "uglier even than his cousin John."

Frank was going from strength to strength, and rapidly making a name for himself as commander of HMS *Peterel*. He had even attracted the attention of Admiral Nelson.[266] He was on patrol in the Mediterranean between Marseilles and Genoa, and "exposed…to a constant fire from the enemy's batteries, [had] effected the capture and destruction of upwards of forty vessels of various descriptions." On 19th June 1799, he had participated in Lord Keith's capture of a French squadron, and on 21st March 1800, distinguished himself in an encounter off Marseilles. He drove two French ships onto the rocks, and captured a brig of 16 guns and 104 men, after a running fight of an hour and a half, and despite being within point blank shot of two batteries. This feat was achieved without a single loss. When this news reached London, he was promoted to the rank of Post Captain. This was the most important step in an officer's career because, once he was on the Captain's list, he would be sure to advance steadily by seniority. In May he was participating in the blockade of Genoa, and in August he prevented a damaged Turkish ship of the line falling into the hands of the French.[267] The Austens received a letter from him in October which had been written in July, and it appears that by that stage he was still ignorant of his promotion.[268]

Towards the end of 1800, with the advancing age of Mr Austen, now approaching his seventieth birthday, and the continuing indifferent health of Mrs Austen, the momentous decision was made that the Austens were leaving Steventon and moving to Bath. According to Frank Austen, his father felt too "incapacitated by age and increasing infirmities to discharge his parochial duties in a manner satisfactory to himself"[269] Another factor was the increasing financial difficulty in which Mr Austen found himself as a result of wartime taxes, and the agricultural depression. The farm was yielding a paltry annual income of less than three hundred pounds, and the tithes to be collected from the parishioners were diminishing. He had had to let go the family carriage.

Eliza Chute, of the Vyne wrote about the depression in a letter to a friend that: "...the poor are dissatisfied & with reason: I much fear that wheat will not be cheap this year: and every other necessary of life enormously dear: the poor man cannot purchase those comforts he ought to have: beer, bacon, cheese. Can one wonder that discontents lurk in their bosoms: I cannot think their wages sufficient, & the pride of a poor man...is hurt, when he is obliged to apply to the parish for relief, & too often receives harsh answers from the overseers. I own I think our political horizon still lowers."[270]

In addition to the immediate financial constraints, the superior social opportunities afforded in the city of Bath were a bonus for parents who still had hopes of their daughters marrying well. The balls at the Lower and Upper Assembly Rooms served as a marriage market. Beau Nash, although by now long passed into the great Assembly Room in the sky, had decreed that ladies of marriageable age should have a bench reserved for them at the front, and "that the elder ladies and children be content with a second bench at the ball, as being past or not yet come to perfection."[271]

Mrs Leigh Perrot was apparently of the view that there was a more nefarious motive for the move to Bath, and that Jane's parents wished to discourage a growing attachment between her and William Digweed.[272] It is true that Jane had met him on the 23rd January. "On Friday I wound up my four days of dissipation by meeting William Digweed at Deane, and am pretty well, I thank you, after it. While I was there a sudden fall of snow rendered the roads impassable, and made my journey home in the little carriage much more easy and agreeable than my journey down."[273] The language is a little suggestive, and Lucy Worsley draws a comparison with the scene in *Emma* when Mr Elton makes an unwelcome proposal in the carriage on Christmas Eve. But there is no evidence that Digweed accompanied Jane, let alone that there was any intimacy between them; nor is there any reason to suspect that he would have been an unwelcome match. Mrs Leigh Perrot's opinion is probably little more than gossipy speculation, but William Digweed never married.

At the end of November, Jane went to stay with Martha Lloyd at Ibthorpe. She wrote to Martha shortly before the visit. Her mind was as vibrant as ever but there is no sign that Jane was in any way active as a writer at this point. "You distress me cruelly by your request about books," she says. "I cannot think of any to bring with me, nor have I any idea of our wanting them. I come to you to be talked to, not to read or hear reading; I can do that at home; and indeed I am now laying in a stock of intelligence to pour out on you as my share of the conversation, I am reading Henry's History of England."[274] The absence of books, though, was subsequently regretted: "... it is too dirty for such desperate walkers as Martha and I to get out of doors, and we are therefore confined to each other's society from morning till night, with very little variety of books or gowns...Martha has promised to return with me, and our plan is to have a nice black frost for walking to Whitchurch, and throw ourselves into a post chaise, one upon the other, our heads hanging out of one door, and our feet at the opposite one."[275]

She and Martha arrived back in Steventon in early December. This is when the bombshell was dropped. They were met by Mrs Austen who declared that it had been settled that they were to leave Steventon and move to Bath. Mr and Mrs Austen, left to their own devices in the absence of both of their daughters, had taken the dramatic decision without consulting anyone, apart from, probably, the Leigh-Perrots, and James and Mary, who were to move into the Rectory; Mr Austen having effectively sub-contracted the curacy to his son, as he had at Deane. According to Mary, who was at Steventon to see her sister Martha, Jane was greatly distressed by this announcement.[276] There is every reason to think that she was very emotionally attached to her home, and to its environs, as well as to its neighbours. She had been forced to leave her home twice before; once when she was an infant, and once when she was sent away to school, at the age of seven. She may have suffered a similar, or even greater, trauma in hearing the news of the move to Bath. The separation of a heroine from her home is a recurring theme in her novels. Fanny Price is forced to leave her home twice; once from Porstmouth to Mansfield Park, and then, many years later, from Mansfield Park back to Portsmouth. On both occasions it causes her great distress. Marianne Dashwood, on being forced to leave Norland Park in *Sense and Sensibility*, exclaims: "When shall I cease to regret you!...When [shall I] learn to feel a home elsewhere."[277] There are no surviving letters in December, and so we do not know how the news was broken to Cassandra, or how she reacted. It is highly likely that they were amongst the letters subsequently destroyed, which suggests that Jane expresses herself in forceful terms.

Another hint of Jane's reaction is the degree of resentment towards James and Mary which she revealed to Cassandra in her letter of 8th January. Her brother and Mary were to celebrate their wedding anniversary on Friday the 16th. "...a day or two before the 16th", she wrote, "Mary will drive her sister to Ibthorpe to find all the festivity she can in contriving for everybody's comfort, and being thwarted or teased by almost everybody's temper...Fulwar, Eliza and Tom Chute are to be of the party. I know of nobody else. I was asked but declined it."[278] She was also angry at the indecent haste with which James and Mary were usurping her father's place. "My father's old ministers are already deserting him to pay their court to his son."[279] And there was the question of a brown mare which was to go to James when they moved out but "has not had patience to wait for that, and has settled herself even now at Deane...everything else I suppose will be seized by degrees in the same manner." Her resentment is tangible but also understandable. She was being forced to leave her childhood home, and her friends and acquaintances, and move to an urban environment for which she had little affection, and, what is more, had had no say in the matter.

There were three places the Austens had in mind to rent a house; Westgate Buildings, Charles Street, and "some of the short streets leading from Laura Place or Pulteney Street."[280] Money, though, was a factor. The houses near Laura Place Jane thought to be too expensive for their budget. (This is where she was to locate Lady Dalrymple in *Persuasion*); although they were her father's first choice: "...he grows quite ambitious, and actually requires now a comfortable and creditable looking house."[281] Her mother preferred Queen Square again, whilst Jane herself wanted to be near Sydney Gardens; "we might go into the labyrinth every day."[282]

There was also the question of what to do with the property which they would not be able to take with them. The state of the road network meant that it would not be practicable to transport most of their goods. When the Dashwoods move to Devonshire from Sussex, the furniture, including books, and Marianne's pianoforte, is sent round by water.[283] The Austens did not have this option. There were over five hundred books to dispose of which Jane wanted James to take at half a guinea a volume.[284] "The whole world", she wrote, on learning that the books were to go for only seventy pounds, "is in a conspiracy to enrich one part of our family at the expense of another." The pictures, "the battle piece, Mr Nibbs, Sir William East, and all the old heterogeneous miscellany, manuscript, scriptural pieces dispersed over the house" were to be given to James but Cassandra could keep her own drawings, and the "two paintings on tin." The furniture, save for the beds, was to be left. On 10th January, "a party of fine ladies issuing from a well known commodious green vehicle", including Mary Austen, née Lloyd, came to buy Mrs Austen's poultry.[285]

Mrs Austen, along with Jane and Cassandra, were to travel down together, and then Mr Austen was to follow after a couple of weeks, or so. Jane stoically insists that she was getting more and more reconciled to the move. "We have lived long enough in this neighbourhood: the Basingstoke balls are certainly on the decline" but she hints at the trauma by proxy: "Martha has as good as promised to come to us again in March. Her spirits are better than they were." Mrs Leigh Perrot, however, was very pleased; perhaps hoping that to have her sister-in-law in Bath would exorcise some of the demons of her recent experience: "…it is an event which will attach her to the place more than anything else could do, etc, etc."[286]

At the end of January, Jane went to stay at Manydown with the Biggs-Withers for about a month, and while she was there, Edward brought Cassandra to London, where she stayed with Henry and Eliza for about three weeks. Henry had resigned his commission in the Oxfordshire Militia, and set himself up as an army agent and banker, with an office in Cleveland Court in St James's. He and Eliza were now living in Upper Berkeley Street.[287]

Cassandra returned home in February. March and April were spent in making the final preparations for the move to Bath. Edward and Elizabeth came for a valedictory visit in April, and Frank also paid a farewell visit. Poignant occasions, no doubt, but at least the Rectory was to stay in the family, and these visits need not have been the last. At the beginning of May, there was an auction for the sale of "valuable effects" at Steventon Parsonage which took place on site over the course of three days, including household contents, chariot and harness, nag-horse, three cows and hay.[288] Even Jane's piano, and her beloved books, were sold off.[289] In the meantime, Mrs Austen and her daughters had left Steventon and went to Ibthorpe to stay with the Lloyds. Mr Austen and Frank went to London, and then on to Godmersham. On 4th May, Jane and her mother, leaving Cassandra with Martha Lloyd for now, departed Ibthorpe for Bath.[290]

XII: JANE BECALMED

Steventon had been the setting for a prodigious output from Jane Austen: the *Juvenilia* in the late 1780s and early '90s, *Lady Susan* in the mid 90s, followed by *Elinor and Marianne,* and *First Impressions,* and then *Northanger Abbey* at the turn of the century. This impressive and very promising beginning, however, stalled, almost completely, for another decade. Apart from an uncompleted novel, *The Watsons*, to which we will turn in due course, and some minor tinkering to *Northanger Abbey*, and the draft of *Lady Susan,* there was no authorial activity from Jane until she revised *Elinor and Marianne* into *Sense and Sensibility* in 1809. There was no genuinely new output until she started work on *Mansfield Park* in 1811. What happened?

There had, of course, been some trauma in the family: the death of Jane Cooper, the ill-health of Mrs Austen, which probably occupied much of Jane's time, and the bizarre episode with her aunt, Mrs Leigh Perrot. Jane was also increasingly involved in society and travelling, most notably to Godmersham and Bath. But this cannot really be held up as a sufficient explanation for her inactivity as a writer. She had, of course, had the disappointment of the peremptory rejection of *First Impressions* but this cannot be said to have deterred her, because she set to work almost immediately on *Northanger Abbey.* Claire Tomalin argues persuasively[291] that it was the move to Bath which silenced Jane: the disruption, the loss of familiar places and faces, friends and family, favourite possessions and books, and the move from a pastoral idyll, to a bustling and pretentious urban jungle for which Jane had little affection. With this analysis, it would be difficult sensibly to disagree.

Lady Russell in *Persuasion*, a character who is not unambiguously sympathetic, prefers the bustle of Bath to the country: "the dash of other carriages, the heavy rumble of carts and drays, the bawling of the newsmen, muffin-men and milk-men, and the ceaseless clink of pattens." Jane's views, however, are personified in Anne Elliott who "caught the first dim view of the extensive buildings, smoking in rain, without any wish of seeing them better."[292] Anne, just like Jane, "looked back, with fond regret" on the loss of her pastoral home. Although Bath boasted a number of circulating libraries, to which she subscribed, Jane was also deprived of her private collection of books, and her music, which were probably important creative stimulants. Her niece, Anna, recalled almost seventy years later, that she had no piano throughout the entirety of her time in Bath, and that "she felt the loss of the amusement."[293]

She also perhaps suspected that her parents' intentions were to do with the diminishing prospects of marriage in Steventon. She was now twenty-five, and the prospects of spinsterhood loomed large, together with the relative penury to which she would be exposed upon the death of her father. Mrs Austen's parents had behaved in the same way towards her. They had moved to Bath, together with their two daughters, both unmarried and in their twenties. It was in Bath that Cassandra Leigh met George Austen, and it was in that very city that they were married. Jane perhaps resented being manipulated in the same way.

Jane and her mother arrived in Bath on 5th May 1801. The journey was a comfortable one but there are still signs of tension between her and her mother. "We had charming weather, hardly any dust, and were exceedingly agreeable, as we did not speak above once in three miles."[294] They were to stay with her aunt and uncle in Paragon Buildings whilst they were house hunting. Mr and Mrs Leigh Perrot had apparently recovered from their ordeal, and looked very well, although Mrs Leigh Perrot had a violent cough. Jane had her own comfortable room, up two flights of stairs, but her spirits had not lifted, and she was in no mood to like Bath any better. "The first view of Bath in fine weather does not answer my expectations; I think I see more distinctly through rain. The sun was got behind everything, and the appearance of the place from the top of Kingsdown was all vapour, shadow, smoke and confusion."

That same evening, Jane went for a walk with her uncle to the Pump Room. They looked at a house in Green Park Buildings, which, according to Egan, was "an elevated situation, railed in, and also a delightful residence...the look-out from the above buildings across the river, added to the distant hills intersected with trees...is very fine."[295] It pleased Jane very well, with a large dining room, and drawing room, and an apartment, divided into two, one of which could serve as a bed-dressing room. She must have been thinking of the sleeping arrangements for her and Cassandra. Her only concern was symptoms of dampness. Afterwards, they all had a walk by the canal.[296]

Even a ball did not raise Jane's spirits. It was a dull affair. She dressed herself up in all her finery, "much admired at home", but before tea, there was only one dance with four couples. "Think of four couple, surrounded by about an hundred people, dancing in the Upper Rooms at Bath."[297] The next day, there was another "stupid party" with only enough people to make up one card table, "with six people to look on and talk nonsense to each other." She was in no mood to make the best of things. "I cannot anyhow continue to find people agreeable," she said. A Miss Langley was "like any other short girl, with a broad nose and wide mouth, fashionable dress and exposed bosom". Admiral Stanhope was gentlemanly enough, but his legs were too short.

After tea, however, things got more interesting at the ball, and Jane indulged in a little gossip about a Mr Evelyn, a married man with a wandering eye. "I then got Mr Evelyn to talk to, and Miss T to look at; and I am proud to say that though repeatedly assured that another in the same party was the *She*, I fixed upon the right one from the first."[298] A couple of weeks later it was Jane who was receiving his attentions. The fact that she did not repel them shows what a strong minded woman she was, and not much bothered about what others might say. However, she seems to have been distinctly underwhelmed by him, and was dismissive of his slightly rakish reputation. "I assure you in spite of what I might choose to insinuate in a former letter, that I have seen very little of Mr Evelyn since my coming here; I met him this morning for only the fourth time, and as to my anecdote about Sydney Gardens, I made the most of the story because it came into advantage, but in fact he only asked me whether I were to be in Sydney Gardens in the evening or not. There is now something like an engagement between us and the Phaeton, which to confess my frailty I have a great desire to go out in; but whether it will come to anything must remain with him. I really believe he is very harmless; people do not seem afraid of him here, and he gets groundsel for his birds and that." The next day she had an "airing in the very bewitching Phaeton and four. We went to the top of Kingsdown and had a very pleasant drive."[299]

Almost three weeks after their arrival, they were still house hunting. They had looked at a place in Seymour Street but Jane did not think much of the small rooms, and the western aspect.[300] Green Park Buildings were rejected because of the damp. There were reports of "discontented families and putrid fevers".[301] Some houses in New King Street were smaller than Jane expected. One of them was "quite monstrously little; the best of the sitting rooms not so large as the little parlour at Steventon, and the second room in every floor about capacious enough to admit a very small single bed."[302] Cassandra and her father were expected at the beginning of June, but even this did not improve her mood much. "When you arrive, we will at least have the pleasure of examining some of these putrifying houses again, they are so very desirable in size and situation, that there is some satisfaction in spending ten minutes within them."[303]

As expected, Mr Austen travelled back from Godmersham in order to collect Cassandra, and then, in early June, they were reunited with Jane and Mrs Austen in Bath. Shortly thereafter, they finally settled on No 4 Sydney Place, in a row of terraced houses completed in 1792, four storeys tall, across the river at Bathwick estate, facing east. It was three hundred yards from the town centre, across the Pulteney Bridge, and yet on the edge of the open countryside.[304] Another great advantage of the location was that it benefited from springs on the hills behind, and so the Austens would be able to experience running water at home for the first time. The supply was turned on for one day in seven, filling up the cistern for the rest of the week.[305]

The Austens took a short lease of the property with an unexpired term of three and a quarter years which had been advertised in the *Bath Chronicle* on 21st May. "The situation is desirable, the rent very low, and the landlord is bound by covenant to paint the two first floors this summer." The house faced the newly laid out Sydney Gardens, Jane's preferred location.[306] It had two rooms on each floor, and three bedrooms: one for Jane and Cassandra, another for their parents, and a third as a guest room. There were three rooms for the servants in the roof.[307]

After taking the lease, the Austens took a holiday in Devon for the summer. The opportunity for spending the summer months by the sea in the West Country, or in Wales, was just about the only thing Jane was looking forward to as a result of the move to Bath.[308] For time immemorial, the generality of people had been afraid of the sea. It was seen as a dangerous and menacing element, fit only for sailors and fishermen. However, in the latter part of the eighteenth century, it became fashionable to holiday by the sea, and the concept of the seaside resort was born. Sea bathing became popular, and the sea was believed to have health giving properties, as a kind of cold water counter-point to the hot springs of Bath. As early as 1707, Joseph Browne published an *Account of the Wonderful Cures Perform'd by the Cold Baths.* This prescribed a plunge into cold water as a cure for rickets, scrofula, "weakness of erection", and "a general disorder of the whole Codpiece Economy." Later the benefits of bathing in the sea, in particular, was lauded, and by 1803 it had become "the rage to make annual excursions to the coast."[309] Few people could swim in those days, but ladies would be taken out from the beach, far enough into the sea to immerse themselves, in a sort of mobile shed, the ancestor of the modern beach hut.

In January, Jane had reported to Cassandra that the family was planning a trip to Sidmouth[310], a seaside town in East Devon, on the Jurassic coast, about midway between Exeter and Lyme Regis. It was a mere village, until the fashion for coastal excursions, and sea bathing, had developed, and it became a bustling and popular resort. There is no recorded detail of their stay, but it is likely that they would have visited Mr Austen's former pupil, Richard Buller, who in 1801 was the incumbent of the large Tudor vicarage in Colyton, a small town about nine miles along the coast from Sidmouth. He had invited them in the November of the previous year.[311] At the end of September, they had returned to Hampshire and were staying with James and Mary in their old home at Steventon. They spent a day with the Lefroys. Then, at the beginning of October, they returned to Bath; according to Eliza they returned in time to supervise the fitting up of the house in Sydney Place.[312]

By the spring of 1802, they had settled into their new surroundings. George Austen bought a copy of Richard Warner's new travel guide, *Excursions from Bath*.[313] In February and March, Mr and Mrs Lybbe-Powys came to Bath for an extended stay, and regularly saw the Austens. Almost immediately upon their departure, Edward and Elizabeth arrived, and were followed on 19th April by James and Mary, with their daughter, Anna, now nine years old, who stayed for a month.[314] The Treaty of Amiens, between Britain and France, had also brought about a short hiatus in the wars (Napoleon broke the treaty eighteen months later), and almost half of the navy and army were immediately demobilised. Charles was released from active service on the *Endymion*, and joined the rest of the family in Bath too.[315]

During the summer, the Austens, together with Charles and the girls, again took a holiday in Devon, probably staying in Teignmouth, and certainly paying a visit to the nearby town of Dawlish. Afterwards they went to Wales.[316] Mr and Mrs Austen returned in mid-August, via Steventon, where they stayed until well into September. They took an excursion to Portsmouth to see Frank, now flag-captain in the squadron of Admiral Gambier, aboard HMS *Neptune*. For reasons unknown, Jane and Cassandra returned separately. They arrived in Steventon on 1st September for two days, a visit of unusual brevity, perhaps reflecting a residue of simmering resentment. Then they left for Godmersham with Charles, and were joined by Frank who was now on leave. Charles brought them back to

Steventon on 28th October.[317] On the 25th they went for a visit to the Biggs. Their good friends, Alethea and Catherine were still single. Elizabeth Heathcote, their sister, had returned home with her baby son, William, following the untimely death of her husband, and their brother, Harris, now twenty-one, had returned to the family estate, having finished his education at Worcester College, Oxford. Then, out of the blue, on a subsequent visit in the December of 1802, Jane received her one and only proposal of marriage from none other than Harris Bigg-Wither.

It was in 1789 that Mr Lovelace Bigg, a widower since 1784, inherited Manydown Park from his cousin, the last of the Withers, who had held the estate for generations. As a token of his thanks, and as was not uncommon at the time, he added the name Wither to his and his sons' names. Manydown was set in the picturesque village of Wootton St Lawrence, about six miles from Steventon. It was a very considerable estate, with over five hundred acres of parkland, and four thousand acres of plantations.[318]

Jane had known the family since she was thirteen, and the Austens had socialised with them regularly. Indeed, it was at Manydown, in 1796, that Jane had flirted with Tom Lefroy, and she and Cassandra were close friends with the three younger daughters, Elizabeth, Catherine and Alethea. There were three surviving older daughters, and also two sons, the younger of whom was Harris, whom Jane had known since he was eight. His elder brother had died when he was thirteen, and he became the heir to the estate.

Jane would have danced with Harris in the past. In January 1799 she referred to a dinner party at Deane. "…the Biggs and Mr Holder dine there tomorrow, and I am to meet them. I shall sleep there. Catherine [Bigg] has the honour of giving her name to a set, which will be composed of two Withers [Harris and his father], two Heathcotes [Elizabeth Bigg and her husband], a Blackford, and no Bigg except herself."[319] A couple of weeks after this, Mr Bigg-Wither Senior fell ill in Winchester, and Catherine, Elizabeth and Harris had to miss a ball to go to him. Jane regretted that the incident had "deprived" them of the Biggs. Although her regret may just as well have been attributable to the absence of Catherine and Elizabeth, as to the absence of Harris, it is notable that she makes no distinction between the three of them, and there is no evidence at all of any aversion from her towards him. She had stayed at Manydown in the early part of 1801, before the move to Bath, and there is no surviving correspondence to tell us what, if anything, happened during this visit.

Details of Harris's proposal are not known but it came on the evening of 2nd December, one week into their visit. It seems probable that he had discussed the matter with his sisters beforehand, and that the news would have been shared with Cassandra. They may very well have been the ones who came up with the idea, and encouraged him to make the proposal, and they would have made arrangements for him to be alone with her. They must have approved, and why not? On the face of it, it was a very desirable match. Jane was now twenty seven, approaching the "years of danger", as she described it in *Persuasion*. She was on the threshold of becoming a candidate for the status of an "old maid" which had become a bit of a joke, as well as a stigma, at around this time. In 1786, William Hayley, the biographer of Cowper, Jane's favourite poet, had even written an essay on old maids, "reduced to the shelter of some contracted lodging in a country town, attended by a single servant."[320] In 1809, a governess was to write in her journal, probably from personal experience, that "an old maid is a stock of everyone to laugh at. Boys play tricks on them, and are applauded. Girls sneer at them, and are unreproved. Upon my word, I think I will write an essay upon the pitiable state of old maids."[321] Bigg Wither's proposal would, at a stroke, if accepted, remove Jane from this prospect, and ensure the security, not just of herself, but probably Cassandra too, for the rest of their lives, and would unite in marriage two families who already enjoyed close bonds of friendship. And, as expected, on the evening of the 2nd, Jane accepted.

Then, for reasons which are not entirely clear, Jane withdrew her consent the next morning. In the clear light of day, she had obviously thought better of it. According to Caroline Austen, the daughter of James and Mary, writing years later, Harris Bigg-Wither "was very plain in person – awkward, & even uncouth in manner – nothing but his size to recommend him – he was a fine big man – but one need not look about for secret reason to account for a young lady's not loving him – a great many would have taken him without love. I conjecture that the advantages he could offer, & her gratitude for his love, & her long friendship with his family, induced my Aunt to decide that she would marry him when he should ask her – but that having accepted him she found she was miserable & that the place and fortune which would certainly be his, could not alter the man – She was staying in his father's house – old Mr Wither was then alive – To be sure she should not have said yes – over night – but I have always respected her for the courage in cancelling that yes – the next morning – All worldly advantages would have been to her - & she was of an age to know this quite well – My aunts had very small fortunes & on their father's death they & their mother would be, they were aware, but poorly off – I believe most young women so circumstanced would have taken Mr W & trusted to love after marriage."[322]

Caroline, who no doubt had been told all about it by her mother, seems to have put it rather well. The head said that she should have accepted him, and the heart not; another example that Jane Austen was not prepared to settle for anything less than love. The idea that marriage should be primarily for love, rather than for social advantage, was an unconventional one, and was the product of the emerging Romantic movement in all art forms. There can be little doubt that it was an idea adopted and held by Jane, and shared by her heroines, even the socially conservative Fanny Price. Edmund praises Fanny's decision to reject Henry Crawford on the simple ground that she did not love him, and that therefore, "nothing could have justified your accepting him." Only Emma, of the principal heroines, resists the idea, but this is more in her advice to others, rather than advice to herself. Some years after this proposal, Jane wrote about marriage to her niece Fanny. "Nothing can be compared to the misery of being bound without love, bound to one, & preferring another. That is a punishment which you do not deserve."

After the withdrawal of Jane's consent to the marriage, she and Cassandra returned straight away to Steventon. They could hardly have stayed at Manydown any longer, and insisted on returning to Bath the next day. James was obliged to accompany them in the absence of anyone else. It appears that the incident passed off without lasting damage. Jane remained close friends with the Bigg sisters for the rest of her life. Harris married two years later, and moved into a house of his own, not returning to live there until 1813 when he inherited the estate, and so Jane could still visit Manydown without worrying about any awkward encounters. Harris didn't seem to mind either; he had ten children.

Catherine Hubback, James's daughter by his first wife, wrote to James Austen-Leigh about the episode in 1870, when he was preparing his second edition of the biography of his aunt. She had read some letters, now destroyed, which alluded to the subject. "I gathered from the letters that it was in a momentary fit of self-delusion that she…accepted Mr Wither's proposal, and that when she settled eventually, and the negative decisively given she was much relieved – I think the affair vexed her a good deal – but I am sure she had no attachment to him." The reliability of this observation, however, is undermined by what follows it: "If ever she was in love it was with Dr Blackall."[323] If this is a reference to Dr Samuel Blackall, then her contention seems most improbable from the available evidence.

There is a snapshot of Harris Bigg Wither a little later in life which casts further light on his nature, traits of which may already have been observable in 1802. His grandson, Reginald Bigg Wither, published a history of the Wither family in 1907. It paints an ambivalent portrait of his grandfather's character. He was "diligent in magisterial work, kind to the poor, and beloved by his family...[but] owing to his stammering, he was a man of few words, and rather avoided society." He was also quick-tempered. Reginald tells a story of a time when he invited some friends to dinner after some dispute over his right to cut down timber in the park. He gave directions to his butler to make up a bowl of punch by mixing the bottles of wine which had been served at dinner. The mixture was indifferent. After everyone had tasted it, he apparently said, "Gentlemen, my punch is like you. In your individual capacity you are all very good fellows, but in your corporate capacity you are very disagreeable."[324]

The next couple of years were passed unremarkably enough. The Austens alternated between Bath, holidays by the sea, and visits to Godmersham, and to the Lefroys at Ashe. It is in the autumn of 1803 that Jane made her first visit to Lyme Regis, the seaside resort that plays such an important role in *Persuasion.* Jane later recalled that they had seen a fire in the town.[325] According to local records this broke out on 5th November 1803, the very same month that her heroine, Anne Elliott visited the town. Lyme enjoyed a mild winter climate, and was even known as "The Naples of England". It was quite fashionable, and there was a direct stagecoach from Bath. The Regency courtesan and *memoiriste*, Harriette Wilson, described it as "a sort of Brighton in miniature, all bustle and confusion, assembly rooms, donkey-riding, raffling, etc."[326]

There is a suggestion, from an account of Caroline Austen, the daughter of James and Mary Lloyd, that Jane had a romance during one of these holidays. This was also in a written account prepared in 1870 for her cousin James Edward. In 1828, eleven years after Jane's death, Cassandra was staying with Caroline and her mother. They met "a Mr Henry Edridge of the Engineers [who was] very pleasing and good looking." Afterwards, her aunt told her that he reminded her of a gentleman they had met one summer by the sea. "I think she said in Devonshire; I don't think she named the place, and I am sure she did not say Lyme, for that I should have remembered – that he seemed greatly attracted by my Aunt Jane – I suppose it was an intercourse of some weeks – and that when they had to part…he was urgent to know where they would be the next summer, implying or perhaps saying that he should be there also, wherever it might be. I can only say that the impression left on Aunt Cassandra was that he had fallen in love with her sister, and was quite in earnest. Soon afterwards they heard of his death…I am sure she thought that he was worthy of her sister, from the way in which she recalled his memory, and also that she did not doubt, either, that he would have been a successful suitor."

If this is a reliable account from Caroline, and her aunt's recollection was correct, then this must have been a significant event in Jane's life. The "intercourse" apparently went on for some weeks, and marriage was in prospect. There is no record of any other such relationship in Jane's life. We know nothing from Jane's pen what her reaction was to Mr Edridge's death, and one imagines that any letters from her touching upon the subject would have been amongst those destroyed by her sister. It is perhaps telling that there is no mention of Jane's reciprocating his love, but perhaps he was too much of a catch (unlike Harris Bigg-Wither) to let such sentiments stand in the way of a practical marriage. But even James Edward, himself, who typically portrays Jane as a bit of a prig when it came to romantic relationships with men, concedes that "if Jane ever loved it was this unnamed gentleman; but the acquaintance was short, and I am unable to say whether her feelings were of such a nature as to affect her happiness."[327]

There is another account of this episode from Jane's great niece, Louisa, the daughter of Anna and Benjamin Lefroy. She claims that the romance took place during the stay in Sidmouth in the summer of 1801, and that Jane and the gentleman "fell in love". The reliability of this account is questionable. The information would have originated with Cassandra, and she may have exaggerated Jane's feelings in re-telling the story. According to Park Honan, the young man's untimely death gave Cassandra some gratification. She had never forgotten the death of her fiancé, Tom Fowle, and may have embroidered the reality of the affair in order to create a counterpoint to her own loss. Some substance to this theory comes from the account of Fanny Lefroy, who opines that the death of Jane's friend strengthened her bond with Cassandra. "The similarity of their fates endeared the two sisters to each other and made other sympathy unnecessary to each. No one was equal to Jane in Cassandra's eyes. And Jane looked up to Cassandra as one far wiser and better than herself. They were as their mother said 'wedded to each other.'" This theme of a sisterly bond forged by mutual loss must have originated from Cassandra years after Jane's death, and it may well be that she had exaggerated Jane's affections for this suitor in order to propagate it.[328]

There is no hint of this episode in contemporary records, although we do not know precisely when the young man died.

If the romance did take place in the summer of 1801, there is no trace of it in the letters Madame Lefroy wrote to her son that autumn whilst the Austen sisters were visiting. On 30th September, she merely reported that "the Miss Austens spent the day here – next week they mean to return to Bath & after that I suppose it will be long before they again visit Steventon." Three days later, she said that they had dined at the Rectory to take their "leave of Mr and Miss Austen who are to return to Bath on Monday next."[329] It seems improbable that Madame Lefroy, a great confidante of Jane, would make no mention at all of Jane's romance, if it had occurred that summer, and still more improbable if it had been swiftly followed by tragedy. It is quite possible, of course, that she was simply being discreet. In any event, whether this episode was a tragedy for Jane, or a mere disappointment, and precisely when it occurred in the period from 1801 to 1804, we shall never know for sure. Whether or not she was ever truly in love is perhaps best judged from the content of her works.

We do know from the diary of Jane's niece, Fanny Austen, the daughter of Edward, that Mrs Austen was unwell again around the turn of 1803, but had recovered by the spring.[330] Then, in the mid-summer of 1804, the Austens gave up the lease of the property in Sydney Place, which only had a few months to run, and decided once again to tour the Devon and Dorset seaside for the season. They were accompanied by Henry and Eliza. They had returned from France, where they had been attempting to recover some of the property of Eliza's late husband. Henry had returned just before the resumption of hostilities in May 1803 but Eliza had stayed on. She was saved from a lengthy period of internment by her flawless French which enabled her to pass off as a native.[331]

During this tour the Austens returned to Lyme Regis in the late summer. Early in September, Henry and Eliza went on to Weymouth, and Jane and her parents stayed on in Lyme for several weeks longer. It is obvious from her last novel, *Persuasion*, how much affection Jane had for this place and its environs. She devotes an extended, stand-alone passage to lauding the delights of the town, its walks and surroundings: its beach "animated with bathing machines and company"; its "green charms" and "romantic rocks", "the flow of the tide for sitting in unwearied contemplation." There is nothing else like it in any of her work.

There is a surviving letter from Jane to Cassandra, as the latter was about to leave Weymouth to return to stay with the Lloyds in Hampshire. She complains about the "general dirtiness of the house & furniture & all its inhabitants" where they were staying. She had been a little unwell but had indulged in some sea bathing, then regarded as a panacea for many ailments, and felt better. She had walked on the Cobb, the massive stone semi-circular pier which juts out into the sea on the far side of the harbour, and where Louisa Musgrove had her near death experience in *Persuasion*, and she had attended a pleasant ball at the Assembly Rooms, which were situated right on the shore, with a "charming marine view as far as the Isle of Portland eight miles off." They were furnished with s card room, billiard room, and a ballroom "of large dimensions containing three chandeliers and neat orchestra".[332] "Nobody asked me the two first dances" she said. "The next two I danced with Mr Crawford - & had I chosen to stay longer might have danced with Mr Granville...or with a new odd looking man who had been eyeing me for some time, & at last without any introduction asked me if I meant to dance again."[333] The whole family returned to Bath around 25th October. They had rented another house in Green Park Buildings, the street which had been rejected in 1801 because of the damp.[334]

Jane's pen remained relatively silent during this period. Her narrative voice apparently stunted by the disruption in her domestic circumstances. Egerton Brydges, Madame Lefroy's younger brother, who recalled her at this time, knew nothing of her being an aspirant writer. "When I knew Jane Austen I never suspected that she was an authoress; but my eyes told me that she was fair and handsome, slight and elegant, but with cheeks a little too full. The last time I saw her was at Ramsgate in 1803; perhaps then she was about twenty seven years old. Even then I did not know that she was addicted to literary compositions."[335] At that time, it would appear, she was not. To use a naval expression, which would have been familiar to Frank and Charles, she was becalmed: if a ship is becalmed, it cannot move because there is no wind in its sails.

XIII: THE WATSONS

In 1803, Jane finally made an important step towards becoming a published writer. As has been seen, Jane had made some minor revisions to her novel *Susan*, which was eventually to be published as *Northanger Abbey*. It is likely that she had been encouraged to do this by her brother Henry, because in the spring of 1803 his lawyer arranged for the sale of this manuscript to the London publisher, Benjamin Crosby & Son, for the sum of ten pounds. The connection may have been due to the fact that it was Crosby who had published a pamphlet about the trial of Mrs Leigh Perrot, and, in addition, Crosby's agent, a Mr Cruttwell, happened to be a printer in Bath.

Having bought the rights to Susan, Crosby then advertised it as a forthcoming publication, in his *Flowers of Literature for 1801 and 1802*, a miscellany or magazine of extracts from other publications; a little like *Readers Digest*. Crosby, however, having purchased the rights, sat on it, and it was not published. It is likely that, after further consideration, he thought better of it. His principal output was Gothic novels, and, crucially, Ann Radcliffe's *Mysteries of Udolpho*. He may have concluded that Jane's satirising of that *genre*, and in particular that novel, would not endear him to his usual *clientele*. It is also evident that Crosby was in financial difficulties. In the whole of 1804, he only published one book.[336] Nevertheless, this partial and anticipated success seems to have encouraged her to try again. In 1804, she began work on a novel which has subsequently become known as *The*

Watsons.

Emma Watson, with one or two exceptions, the only sympathetic character in the story, has been brought up by her aunt and uncle in Shropshire, in prosperous circumstances. She is sensible, and has a strong sense of propriety. After an absence of fourteen years, she returns to the Surrey home of her father, now a widower, and her rather silly, husband-hunting sisters, Elizabeth and Margaret. Her two brothers, Sam and Robert, and her oldest sister, Penelope, are no longer at home. The circumstances of her aunt and uncle had been much more comfortable than her father's, and they were able to raise her in refinement, until the death of her uncle, and the imprudent re-marriage of her aunt. We see, therefore, the familiar theme in Austen of the importance of the place where one feels at home, and the trauma of separation from it. In the case of Emma Watson's character, there is a prototype of Fanny Price, and in Emma's dislocation, one sees a premonition of Fanny's move from the comfort of Mansfield Park to the less refined circumstances of her childhood home in Portsmouth. It is also a sad reflection of Jane's own dislocation from her childhood home in the move to Bath.

The centrepiece of the story is a ball at the Assembly Rooms in an unnamed Surrey town, probably Croydon. Emma is taken by her sister to the home of the Edwards family, where she is to stay the night and dress. She attends the ball with Mrs and Miss Edwards, and there is the subject of the attentions of the rakish Tom Musgrave. The ball is also attended by the much grander Osbornes from Osborne Castle: Lady Osborne; her son, the lascivious Lord Osborne; his sister, and their friends from the Osborne parish parsonage, Mrs Blake and her brother, the parson, Mr Howard. The rest of the story consists of the ramifications of the ball, the half-hearted attempts of Tom Musgrave and Lord Osborne to woo her, and the visit of her thoroughly unpleasant brother, Robert, and his equally unpleasant wife.

It is a short work, just seventeen thousand words long, no more than the equivalent of half a dozen chapters. It is unfinished, not formally divided into chapters, and containing some unnecessary dialogue which appears to amount to little more than padding. It is clear that the manuscript which has come down to us, although much corrected, needed further revision. Although short and incomplete, it is a work of considerable significance because it is the only original work coming from Jane Austen's pen between *Susan (Northanger Abbey)* at the end of the previous century, and *Mansfield Park*, begun in 1811. Its interest, perhaps, lies principally in its biographical, rather than its literary, value, because it is a powerful indicator of the state of Jane's mind at this stage in her life.

The principal town in the story is described as "D" at the beginning, and then referred to as "R" later on. The story ends very abruptly, and the reasons for this can be explored in more detail a little later. It was unnamed in her lifetime, and only published at the instigation of her nephew, James Austen-Leigh, as an appendix to the second edition of his biography of Jane in 1871. According to Austen-Leigh, she did, at least at some stage, have a plan to complete the novel. Apparently Cassandra showed the manuscript of *The Watsons* to some of her nieces, and told them how her sister intended to finish the story. Mr Watson was going to die and Emma would become dependent upon her brother Robert for a home. She was to turn down Lord Osborne, and eventually marry Mr Howard instead.[337]

The first thing which strikes one about *The Watsons* is its lack of humour, and its prevailing tone of pessimism. If it were a piece of music, it would have been composed very much in the minor key, unlike every one of Austen's other works, with the possible exception of *Lady Susan*. Even *Lady Susan* is laced with dark humour; *The Watsons* has almost none. Much of it appears to reflect a conversation that Jane was having with herself, and perhaps with Cassandra, about the close encounters she had had with marriage, the choices which she had made, and the situation in which she now found herself. There is a hint of a rueful tone of regret, at the same time as an attempt to justify those choices to herself.

Elizabeth, Emma's sister, and her senior by ten years, had been very much attached to a man called Purvis, but he had married someone else. "Everybody thought it would have been a match...It has been the ruin of my happiness," Elizabeth says.[338] Was Jane thinking of Harris, or more likely, Tom Lefroy? And then there is this poignant observation from Elizabeth which must have really hit home both for Jane and for Cassandra: "...you know, we must marry. I could do very well single for my own part – A little company, and a pleasant ball now and then, would be enough for me, if one could be young forever, but my father cannot provide for us, and it is very bad to grow old and be poor and laughed at."[339] The last few words could well have come from the pen of William Hayley in his essay on old maids.

But then Jane fights back, through the mouth of Emma, as if to justify to herself the choices she had made. "To be so bent on marriage – to pursue a man merely for the sake of situation – is a sort of thing that shocks me; I cannot understand it. Poverty is a great evil, but to a woman of education and feeling it ought not, it cannot be the greatest. I would rather be a teacher at a school (and I can think of nothing worse) than marry a man I did not like."[340] Emma Woodhouse tenders similar advice to Harriet Smith in *Emma*, albeit much later in Jane's career. "I shall not be a poor old maid; and it is poverty only which makes celibacy contemptible to a generous public! A single woman, with a very narrow income, must be a ridiculous, disagreeable, old maid! The proper sport of boys and girls; but a single woman, of good fortune, is always respectable, and may be as sensible and pleasant as anybody else."[341]

Another theme is status, a product of Jane's pre-occupation with the challenging position in which she was likely to find herself upon the death of her father. At the top of the pyramid are the Osbornes. On the tier below the Osbornes, are the Edwards, who live in the best house in town. "The door will be opened by a man in livery with a powdered head, I can tell you."[342] Below the Edwards are the Watsons. They are "poor and had no close carriage".[343] Their only servant is "Nanny" who both serves the meals and answers the door. Elizabeth has to attend to the washing herself. Their status, it seems, is only just sufficient to permit their attending the ball. Even since there had been balls, the Edwards had been accustomed to invite them to dress, dine and sleep at their house. Having been used to so many of the elegancies of life with her aunt, Emma was "fully sensible of all that must be open to the ridicule of richer people in her present home."[344]

It is striking that all of the men, and in particular the potentially eligible men, with the exception of Mr Howard, are, at best, of highly dubious character. Perhaps this was a subconscious, or even an intentional, justification by Jane of the choices which she had made, and the fate to which she found herself subject: a depiction of the male sex as unworthy, and fit, with rare exceptions, only to be rejected. Tom Musgrave is introduced as a rather dissolute character who has taken a bedroom within the inn where the ball is to be held. As Emma and Miss Edwards pass along the gallery to the Assembly Room, they are "accosted" by him; "a young man in a morning dress and boots, who was standing in the doorway of a bedchamber, apparently on purpose to see them go by."[345] He tries to bully her into accepting a lift in his carriage, and then enjoys teasing her sisters by leaving them in the dark as to whether he is going to make another appearance the next day.

Lord Osborne's attentions are surreptitious, and even creepy. Under the pretence of talking to someone else, he stands close for the purpose of looking at her. He then goes to stand at the end of a table in order to "gape without restraint"[346], and later returns to the ballroom, under the pretence of searching for his gloves, in order to look behind her. A day or two afterwards, when he makes an unexpected visit to her home, he sits in silence for several minutes, contemplating her. Even Mr Edwards speaks inappropriately of his past associations with Emma's aunt, before she made "her second choice." In contrast, Mr Howard receives the approval of Jane Austen. Mr Watson attends his sermon, and praises his fine delivery, "without any theatrical grimace", and he is kind to Mr Watson in helping him to climb a flight of steps. Fanny Price, herself, would have approved.

The only source of light and humour, and the only melody in the major key, is in the form of Charles Blake, the ten year old son of Mrs Blake, who has accompanied his mother and uncle to the ball. In fact his little cameo is one of the most delightful in the whole of Austen's output. He is described as a fine boy who is uncommonly fond of dancing. Emma finds herself seated amongst the Osborne party, and is "immediately struck with the fine countenance and animated gestures of the little boy, as he was standing before his mother, wondering when they should begin." Miss Osborne had promised the first two dances to him but then thoughtlessly abandons him when she gets a better offer from Colonel Beresford. The passage which follows is one of the most insightful, affectionate, almost moving, portraits of a child in English literature.

"If the poor little boy's face had in its happiness been interesting to Emma, it was infinitely more so under this sudden reverse; - he stood the picture of disappointment, with crimsoned cheeks, quivering lips, and eyes bent on the floor. His mother, stifling her own mortification, tried to soothe his...but though he contrived to utter with an effort of boyish bravery, 'Oh, I do not mind it,' – it was very evident by the unceasing agitation of his features that he minded it as much as ever. – Emma did not think, or reflect; - she felt and acted – 'I shall be very happy to dance with you sir, if you like it,' said she, holding out her hand with the most unaffected good humour."[347] Later he exclaims to Mr Howard, "Oh" Uncle, do look at my partner. She is so pretty!"

In Charles Blake one sees, perhaps, the author reflecting ruefully on the rapidly diminishing prospects of her having children of her own, and on the source of her vicarious maternal joy, namely her nieces and nephews, of whom she was, undoubtedly, very fond. Save for this, the work is unremittingly pessimistic and depressive. It reflects the period of her life in which she was writing *The Watsons*. She had rejected the offer of Harris Bigg Wither, which would have secured the security and comfort of herself, her mother and sister. She was still grieving for her childhood home, and she was contemplating the prospect of spinsterhood, relative poverty, and loss of status. She had also been becalmed as an aspirant writer. With *The Watsons*, she was trying again, but she was unable to summon the wit, the wisdom, the humour, the lightness of touch, the irony, which sparkles through all of her earlier work.

And then she stopped writing again. With the departure of Robert, and his unpleasant wife, from the Watson abode, she laid down her authorial pen for another seven years. Her final observation of Emma is fixated on the death of her uncle, her diminished social status and lifestyle, and her uprooting from her family home. "From being the first object of hope and solicitude of an uncle who had formed her mind with the care of a parent...from being the life and spirit of a house, where all had been comfort and elegance, and the expected heiress of an easy independence, she was become of importance to no one, a burden on those, whose affection she could not expect... surrounded by inferior minds with little chance of domestic comfort, and as little hope of future support. It was well for her that she was naturally cheerful; for the change was such as might have plunged weak spirits in despondence."

There is also another side to the cameo of Charles Blake, which is less cheering but no less relevant. Emma's dance with the pre-pubescent boy is symbolic of her marginal status in the marriage market. Miss Osborne, of far higher social status, feels no compunction in rejecting the boy in favour of Colonel Beresford. Emma, however, not only accepts Charles, but she assumes the male role in inviting him to dance with her. In doing so, she suggests the potential for an alternative social categorisation for herself as a woman, namely as a proxy mother or aunt, and spinster. The more one analyses *The Watsons*, the more one is driven to the conclusion that it is essentially a conversation which Jane was having with herself about her condition. It is a piece of psychological self-reflection which amounts to something approaching, what we would now call, a nervous breakdown.

And so why did Jane lay down her pen again? There are, perhaps, a number of reasons which, in combination, silenced her. First, her depressive state of mind meant that she was unable to find her style. Writing in 1939, the critic Mary Lascelles put it rather well when she said that Jane "seems to be struggling with a peculiar oppression, a stiffness and heaviness that threatens her style."[348] This, if anything, is an understatement. Austen's style was crippled in *The Watsons*. In short, it just wasn't working. Second, Jane, already wounded by her dislocation, and by her future prospects, sustained a series of cruel blows upon the bruise, and they occurred in quick succession.

XIV: DEATH AND GLORY

On 16th December 1804, Jane reached the age of twenty-nine. On that same day, her dear friend and *confidante*, Madame Lefroy, rode from Ashe to do some shopping in Overton. She met James Austen in the town and complained to him about her horse, and that she could hardly make it canter. Later, after reaching the top of Overton Hill, the horse bolted, and Mrs Lefroy fell. She died of her injuries a few hours later.[349] This must have been grave news for Jane when it finally reached Bath. The only record we have of her reaction are the verses, some of which are quoted above, which she wrote in memory of her friend on the fourth anniversary of her death. "The day returns again, my natal day; What mix'd emotions in my mind arise! Beloved Friend; four years have passed away; Since thou wert snatched for ever from our eyes."[350] Mrs Lefroy was indeed a remarkable woman. An obituary was published in the *Reading Chronicle* on Christmas Eve. "The splendour of her talent, her powerful and energetic language, the beaming and eager benevolence of her countenance" and her ministrations to the poor had made her "a good angel."[351]

This was closely followed by another blow. On 19th January 1805, Mr Austen fell ill with "an oppression in the head with fever, violent tremulousness, & the greatest degree of feebleness." It may well be the case that the move in the previous autumn to Green Park Buildings, near the river, and afflicted with damp and "putrid fevers", was the cause. Malaria is a distinct possibility. In Georgian times, mosquitoes carrying malaria were not uncommon in damp, low-lying areas. Dr Gibbs and Mr Bowen of Gay Street were summoned, and towards the evening Mr Austen appeared to recover. He had "a tolerable night, & yesterday morning was so greatly amended as to get up and join us at breakfast as usual." He was able to "walk about with only the help of a stick, & every symptom was so favourable that when Bowen saw him at one, he felt sure of his doing perfectly well." [352] But the fever returned.

Mr Austen died on 21st January, and Jane broke the news to her brother Frank in a letter written the next day. "Your affectionate heart will be greatly wounded and I wish the shock could have been lessened by a better preparation; but the event has been sudden and so must be the information of it. We have lost an excellent father. An illness of only eight and forty hours carried him off yesterday morning between ten and eleven. He was seized on Saturday with a return of the feverish complaint which he had been subject to for the last three years. A physician was called in yesterday morning, but he was at that time past all possibility of cure; and Dr Gibbs and Mr Bowen had scarcely left his room before he sunk into a sleep from which he never woke…Except the restlessness and confusion of high fever, he did not suffer, and he was mercifully spared from knowing that he was about to quit objects so beloved, and so fondly cherished as his wife and children ever were. His tenderness as a father, who can do justice to?...The serenity of the corpse is most delightful. It preserves the sweet benevolent smile which always distinguished him…My mother bears the shock as well as possible; she was quite prepared for it and feels all the blessing of his being spared a long illness. My uncle and aunt have been with us and show us every imaginable kindness"[353]

James and Henry arrived to comfort their mother, and Mr Austen was buried the following Saturday in the crypt at Walcot Church, the scene of his marriage over half a century before. There was talk of the Austens returning to Steventon but they had the house in Bath for another three months, and Jane expected that they would remain there until the end of that period. Their situation was now potentially difficult. Mr Austen had left everything to his wife but his means had been very limited, and his livings at Steventon and Deane transferred to his son James, the new incumbent. The church made no provision for the dependents of its departed clergymen.

Jane's brothers stepped in to help. Frank, newly appointed to the captaincy of HMS *Canopus*, an eighty gun ship of the line, pledged one hundred pounds a year. Mrs Austen would only accept half. James, and Henry, still operating as an army agent in London, pledged the same amount. The much wealthier Edward would have been expected to contribute more. With the income from Cassandra's legacy from Tom Fowle, and her mother's modest income from her family inheritance, they would have a reasonably comfortable income of around four hundred and fifty pounds per year; although Jane had no independent means at all. It was anticipated for the future that Mrs Austen would remain in Bath, whilst paying frequent summer visits to her children and other relations.[354] The stark fact for Jane remained that she was penniless, dependent on the charity of her family, and, at the age of thirty, without a realistic prospect of marriage.

At the end of March 1805, the Austens gave up the lease on Green Park Buildings in Bath, and moved into Gay Street, the road which leads from Queen Square to the Circus in the centre of the city. Jane's mood had hardly lifted. "It is March and April together," she wrote on 8th April, "the glare of one and the warmth of the other. We do nothing but walk about."[355] She even made a wry joke about their reduced circumstances, referring to the invitations they were receiving to tea parties. "Our tea and sugar will last a great while. I think we are just the kind of people and party to be treated about among our relations; we cannot supposed to be very rich."[356] Another good friend from Jane's childhood, Mrs Lloyd, was sick. "May her end be peaceful and easy as the exit we have witnessed." [357] Her death followed a few days later, but from this, at least, there was a positive development. With her mother's death, and her sister married to James, Martha Lloyd was now alone. She was invited to live with the Austens in Bath, and would become their companion for the rest of Jane's life.

In the summer of 1805, Mrs Austen and her daughters went to stay at Godmersham, together with Jane's niece, Anna. Her eldest niece, Fanny, Edward's daughter, now twelve years old, kept her diary during this visit. On 25th June she recorded that they had had a whole holiday, and her aunts and grandma had played school with them. "Aunt C was Miss Teachum, the Governess, Aunt Jane was Miss Popham, the teacher…G mama, Betty Jones the Pie Woman & Mama the Bathing Woman. They dressed in character & we had a most delightful day – After dessert we acted a play called Virtue Rewarded. Anna was Duchess of St Albans, I was the Fairy Serena & Fanny Cage a shepherdess Mona. We had a bowl of syllabub in the evening."[358] *Virtue Rewarded* was the sub-title of Richardson's *Pamela*. It may be that this is a reference to an *impromptu* dramatisation of the novel, or perhaps a performance of some of the various stage adaptations of the book which had been put on in France and Italy.

This holiday must have been a welcome relief indeed from recent events. There were plenty of theatricals. On the 30th

June they put on *The Spoilt Child* and *Innocence Rewarded*, "afterwards we danced & had a most delightful evening."[359] The reference to *Innocence Rewarded* is unexplained, but a play called *The Spoiled Child*, a farce in two acts, had been licensed in 1790, and first performed at the Theatre Royal, Dublin. It was one of the biggest hits of the London stage.[360] It was also during this visit that Jane became friends with the children's governess, Anne Sharp, a friendship which was to last the rest of her life.

Fanny Knight's diary shows that Mrs Austen and Anna left Godmersham on 31st July, but that Jane and Cassandra stayed, enjoying the society of East Kent, and attending balls in Canterbury during the mid-August Race Week. A flavour of it comes from the entries for 15th and 16th August, a Thursday and Friday. The schedule sounds exhausting. On the Thursday, "Papa, Mama, Aunts C & Jane, went to Canterbury to the Cathedral & then dined at Mrs Milles's & afterwards went to the ball. They met Aunt Deedes, & Aunt Harriot...after Mama was gone to Canterbury in the morning, about one o'clock Uncle H Austen came here dined with us, drank tea, & went off to Canterbury at six to meet them at the Ball, & then went to Sandwich." Her mother and Jane went to another ball in Canterbury that same evening.[361]

In late August, Cassandra stayed for a while at Goodnestone with Edward's mother-in-law. This yielded a number of letters from Jane, which have survived. They had paid a visit to George Hatton and his wife Elizabeth at the very grand Eastwell Manor, near Ashford, now owned by Champneys, the luxury spa hotel chain. As so often, she enjoyed the company of the children. George was a fine boy but "Daniel chiefly delighted me. The good humour of his countenance is quite bewitching. After tea we had a cribbage-table, and he and I won two rubbers of his brother and Mrs Mary."[362] Back at Godmersham she played with her nephew William at battledore and shuttlecock, an early form of badminton. George and Henry were animating them "by their races and merriment", but Little Edward was unwell, and unlikely to return to school with his brothers. A trip to Worthing was planned, and if the doctor recommended sea-bathing he would stay there with them.

At the end of August, Jane swapped places with her sister, and went to Goodnestone. There was talk of a grand ball at Deal to which 'no gentlemen but of the garrison are invited." The death of the King's brother led to this being cancelled. This did not bother Jane. "The Duke of Gloucester's death sets my heart at ease, though it will cause some dozens to ache." There is a suggestion that she was of interest to Lady Bridges's son, Edward, four years her junior. He had been due to play in a cricket match but, according to him, was too late to play. He came home, instead of dining with the other players, perhaps to take more advantage of her presence. "It is impossible to do justice to the hospitality of his attentions towards me;" wrote Jane, "he made a point of ordering toasted cheese for supper entirely on my account." [363] There is a hint, albeit a little cryptic, that Jane returned this interest. Three days later, a Friday, she wrote this, with the suggestion that she was postponing her return to Godmersham in order to see him again. "Edward Bridges dined at home yesterday; the day before he was at St Albans; to day he goes to Broome, and tomorrow to Mr Hallett's, which latter engagement has had some weight in my resolution of not leaving Harriot [his sister] till Monday."

Then there was the trip to the fashionable seaside resort of Worthing, at the foot of the South Downs in Sussex. Worthing had been an agricultural and fishing hamlet until the new fad for sea bathing had begun to attract wealthy visitors in the 1750s. The King's youngest child (his fifteenth no less) Princess Amelia had stayed there in 1798. She was suffering from a pain in her knee joint, and it was hoped that the waters, and the sea air, would help. The whole of Edward's family went to Worthing in the September of 1805, with Mrs Austen and her daughters. Martha Lloyd went too. They enjoyed walks along the sands, and a visit to Brighton. They even went to a raffle one evening, and, according to Fanny, "Aunt Jane won & it amounted to 17s [shillings]."[364] Edward and his family returned to Godmersham on 23rd September, but the Austen party remained in Worthing until at least early November.[365]

Frank had written to Jane whilst she was in Kent and Sussex that late summer. From the July of 1803 until the spring of 1804, he had been helping to organise coastal defences along the south-eastern coast. Whilst living in Ramsgate he had met Mary, the daughter of a John Gibson, who had a comfortable house in the High Street. In 1804 they became engaged, and then he returned to his command, HMS *Leopard*, which was part of the blockading fleet off the coast of Boulogne. As the *Leopard* was the flagship, there were more opportunities to call in at Dungeness or Spithead to collect and deposit bundles of post. It is striking that his letter to Jane, which arrived in the middle of August 1805, by which time he had taken command of the *Canopus*, led her to conclude that her brother was "in a great hurry to be married." The reason is that the war with France had reached a crisis point, in which the Royal Navy was to play a decisive and heroic part. In the meantime, Jane had found Cassandra's mittens; "they were folded up within my clean nightcap, and send their duty to you."[366]

The period of crisis did not start auspiciously. In the summer, Pierre de Villeneuve, the admiral of the French fleet, managed to break out of the British blockade of the port of Toulon with eighteen ships, and sailed for Martinique, thus posing a considerable threat to Britain's possessions and trade routes in the Caribbean. Nelson pursued in the *Victory* with a squadron of warships, including Frank Austen's *Canopus* with Nelson's second in command, Rear Admiral Louis, on board. It was to be the longest nautical pursuit of the war; over six thousand miles across the Atlantic and back again, but Villeneuve managed to evade Nelson, and took fourteen merchant ships with cargoes of sugar.

This was followed by another failure, which was to lead to the court-martial of Vice Admiral Sir Robert Calder. As a result, Nelson's reputation took a hit. It is difficult to believe with hindsight that the following assessment appeared in the *Naval Chronicle* in the August of 1805. "Should the mad project of invasion ever be attempted, the public would feel additional security from having the Hero of the Nile off our own coast. But we greatly lament that ill-judged and over-weening popularity which tends to make another demigod of Lord Nelson at the expense of all the other officers in the Service, many of whom possess equal merit and equal abilities and equal gallantry with the noble Admiral."[367]

Meanwhile, Frank returned to blockade duties outside the Spanish port of Cadiz. The *Canopus* was one of a squadron of five ships ordered to keep close in shore to monitor the enemy's movements. By the autumn of 1805, Napoleon had assembled a formidable armada to invade the coast of Great Britain, his plans depended upon the breaking of the British blockade of the French and Spanish ports, because no invasion could succeed without a fleet of friendly warships in control of the English Channel. On 16th September, Frank reported in his log that they had been able to count thirty-three ships of the line and five frigates, a very considerable force. On 28th September, Nelson arrived on the *Victory*. He gave orders for the *Canopus* to sail for Gibraltar in order to re-stock on water.[368] Rear Admiral Louis, and undoubtedly Frank Austen, were concerned that the enemy would come out and they would miss the battle.

Nelson replied that he had no other means of keeping the fleet in provisions other than by sending detachments to re-supply. "The enemy will come out, and we shall fight them, but there will be time for you to get back first."[369]

On 15th October, Frank wrote to Mary, his *fiancée*, on board HMS *Canopus* off Gibraltar. The wind being against them, they had not been able to reach Gibraltar until the 9th. They had provisioned, and were now waiting for a favourable wind to take them back into the Atlantic. "We are of course, very anxious to get back to the fleet for fear the enemy should be moving, for the idea of their doing so while we are absent is by no means pleasant. Having borne our share in a tedious chase and anxious blockade, it would be mortifying indeed to find ourselves at last thrown out of any share of credit or emolument which would result from an action."[370]

A westerly wind, on the evening of the 15th, unfortunately kept them in the Meditarranean. Then, on the evening of the 17th, a frigate arrived with new orders for the *Canopus* to protect a convoy bound for Malta until it had passed the Spanish port of Cartagena. Frank's frustration was palpable. "It puts us completely out of the way in case the enemy should make an attempt to get to sea, which is by no means improbable..."[371] The *Canopus* did not leave the convoy until the 21st. They did so a little prematurely because they had received intelligence two days earlier that the enemy fleet was preparing to come out of Cadiz. Frank was furious.

"Our situation is peculiarly unpleasant and distressing, for if they escape Lord Nelson's vigilance and get into the Mediterranean, which is not very likely, we shall be obliged, with our small force, to keep out of their way; and on the other hand, should an action take place, it must be decided long before we could possibly get down even were the wind fair, which at present it is not. As I have no doubt but the event would be highly honourable to our arms, and be at the same time productive of some good prizes, I shall have to lament our absence on such an occasion on a double account, the loss of pecuniary advantage as well as of professional credit. And after having been so many months in a state of constant and unremitting fag, to be at last cut out by a parcel of folk just come from their homes, where some of them were sitting at their ease the greater part of last war, and the whole of this, till just now, is particularly hard and annoying." Frank did at least have the insight to acknowledge that his *fiancée* must have been delighted: "You, perhaps, may not feel this so forcibly as I do, and in your satisfaction at my having avoided the danger of battle may not much regret my losing the credit of having contributed to gain a victory; not so myself…I shall ever consider the day on which I sailed from the squadron as the most inauspicious one of my life."[372]

As a very brave and fiercely patriotic naval man, Frank was right to be frustrated. Just after noon, on Monday 21st October 1805, off the coast of Southern Spain, not far from Cadiz, the French warship, the *Fougueux*, fired a broadside at the nearest British ship, HMS *Royal Sovereign*. The *Fougueux* was overcome by the British fleet and was taken, but the Battle of Trafalgar had begun. The thirty three ships of the line moved out from Cadiz, and engaged the British blockading fleet of twenty-seven. The slaughter on both sides, from cannon and musket fire, was immense. The entire crew of the *Berwick* was drowned, and almost everyone on Collingwood's ship was hit. Nelson, who had insisted on coming on deck dressed in his full regalia, was a standing target, and was mortally wounded. Mercifully, he knew that his triumph was sure before he succumbed. In total over four thousand were dead, but so was the enemy fleet. Seventeen of the enemy ships were taken, and even the ships that survived were crippled and didn't see action again. Britannia ruled the waves, undisputed, for the best part of the rest of the century.

Frank's reflections were bitter sweet. "I am truly sorry to add that this splendid affair has cost us many lives, and amongst them the most invaluable one to the nation, that of our gallant, and ever-to-be-regretted, Commander-in-Chief, Lord Nelson, who was mortally wounded by a musket shot, and only lived long enough to know his fleet successful. In a public point of view, I consider his loss as the greatest which could have occurred; nor do I hesitate to say there is not an Admiral on the list so eminently calculated for the command of a fleet as he was. I never heard of his equal, nor do I expect again to see such a man. To the soundest judgment he united prompt decision and speedy execution of his plans; and he possessed in a superior degree the happy talent of making every class of persons pleased with their situation and eager to exert themselves in forwarding the public service. As a national benefit I cannot but rejoice that our arms have been once again successful, but at the same time I cannot help feeling how very unfortunate we have been to be away at such a moment, and, by a fatal combination of unfortunate though unavoidable events, to lose all share in the glory of a day which surpasses all which ever went before..."[373] He did receive some consolation in the following February when he was part of Sir John Duckworth's triumph over the French in the West Indies, at the Battle of St Domingo; the battle in which Captain Wentworth had also distinguished himself in *Persuasion*.

In the days before the telegraph, news, even from close to home, took a long time to come. It was not until 4th November, a full two weeks after the Battle of Trafalgar, that the schooner HMS *Pickle* docked at Falmouth with the despatches from Admiral Collingwood. The London papers circulated throughout the country in the following days. The headlines proclaimed the Glorious Victory; the sub-headlines the Death of Nelson. The emotions of the country must have been mixed. The victory was indeed glorious. The ever-looming threat of invasion had been lifted indefinitely, but Nelson had been a national hero, drawing crowds greater than that of the royal family whenever he made a public appearance.

A hundred thousand people flocked to see him lying in state in the Painted Hall of what is now the old Royal Naval College. According to Robert Southey, Nelson's biographer, writing nine years after the event, the death of Nelson was felt "as something more than a public calamity; men started at the intelligence and turned pale, as if they had heard of a loss of a dear friend."[374] His state funeral was unprecedented for a commoner, and unmatched until that of Sir Winston Churchill in 1965. On the eve of the funeral, the royal barge, followed by a flotilla of sixty vessels, transported the body from Greenwich to Whitehall. The banks of the river were packed with spectators; nobility, commoners, and Parliamentarians alike.

The next day, 9th January 1806, the funeral cortege processed from the Admiralty to St Paul's. The bier, designed to resemble Nelson's flagship, was followed by admirals, Greenwich pensioners, and the veterans of the *Victory*. In the cathedral, a congregation of seven thousand watched as the great man was laid to rest. There he lies still.[375]

XV: SOUTHAMPTON

The reaction of the Austens to news of the Battle of Trafalgar must have been even more mixed than that of the general population, and this time with anxiety. They had no means of knowing if Frank and Charles were safe, and they would not know for weeks. When they eventually found out that they were safe, their joy may have been a little tempered by the knowledge that neither had participated in the battle. Parliament had voted no less than three hundred and twenty thousand pounds to be distributed around the fleet. Each captain, involved in the battle, would receive three thousand three hundred pounds (about one hundred and fifty thousand in today's money) and that was in addition to any prize money. If the winds off Gibraltar had been a little kinder to Frank, all his concerns about money would have been over.

In the January of 1806, after a sojourn with James and Mary at Steventon, Mrs Austen, now joined by Martha Lloyd, returned to Bath. Jane and Cassandra spent a few weeks with their friends at Manydown – no longer occupied, of course, by Harris Bigg Wither and his new bride – before joining their mother in Bath. They had taken rooms in Trim Street, in the commercial district of the city, which contained the Unitarian Chapel but was "conspicuous in no other respect."[376] It was entirely different to the accommodation they had enjoyed before. Even Green Park Buildings was near green spaces. Trim Street was devoid of greenery. It was narrow, dark and lined with commercial buildings which were about a hundred years old.[377] Although intended to be temporary lodgings whilst looking for more suitable accommodation, this was an indication, and the product, of their reduced circumstances. Five years before, when the Austens had been looking for a property in Bath, Jane had written to Cassandra about their mother's view, and by implication Cassandra's view too, of Trim Street. "In the meantime she assures you that she will do everything in her power to avoid Trim Street, although you have not expressed the fearful presentiment of it which was rather expected."[378]

In July, however, came a complete change of plan. Frank, buoyed by the victory at St Domingo, finally married his fiancée, Mary Gibson. Anticipating another imminent posting, and not wanting his bride to be on her own, he suggested that she move in with his mother and sisters, and Martha Lloyd, and that they all move to Southampton, just twenty-three miles from Steventon, where they would be within easier distance of the dockyards. Jane was not displeased. She had never been enamoured of Bath. They left that place, for the last time, on 2nd July. In 1808, Jane was to write of her relief: "It will be two years tomorrow since we left Bath...with what happy feelings of escape."[379]

Initially they stayed in Clifton, not fifteen miles from Bath, and then on to Mrs Austen's cousin, the Reverend Thomas Leigh, at the rectory in Aldestrop, in Gloucestershire. On the same day that they left Bath, a more distant cousin, the Honourable Mary Leigh died. The fact that the Austens quitted Clifton for Aldestrop, soon afterwards, may be no coincidence. Mary Leigh was the last of the Stoneleigh branch of the family. She had inherited from her brother, the unmarried fifth Lord Leigh, the great estate of Stoneleigh Abbey in Warwickshire. Stoneleigh Abbey (originally "Stoneley") had been in the Leigh family for seven generations. The first Thomas Leigh, as we have seen, was elevated to the peerage after giving shelter to Charles I. The third Thomas Leigh, in contrast, was despatched to Coventry by the Parliamentarians after they had captured the site – thus giving rise to the phrase "sent to Coventry".

The fifth Lord Leigh made his will in 1767, after embarking on the Grand Tour. Unmarried, and without issue, he left the entire estate to his sister. What happened during the Tour is not known but when he returned he had gone mad, and was being treated by a Dr Munro, the physician to Bedlam hospital for the insane. He died in 1786 at the age of forty-four, a "lunatic of unsound mind," and his unmarried sister duly inherited.[380] More problematic was what was to happen after her death. His will provided, somewhat cryptically, that the estate should then devolve "unto the first and nearest of his kindred, being male and of his blood and name, that should be alive at the time."[381] The eldest Leigh at the time of her death was Mrs Austen's first cousin, Thomas Leigh, who appeared to have the superior claim. On 5th August, Mr Leigh, with his sister Elizabeth, and his lawyer, set out for Stoneleigh to take possession. The Austens went with him. Clearly they had a very keen interest in whether such a near relation was to inherit such a vast estate.

More importantly, it was more than possible that Mrs Austen's brother, James Leigh Perrot, could assert an arguable claim. As a result, the suggestion was made that he might give up his claim in return for a lump sum of twenty-thousand pounds, and an annuity of two-thousand pounds per year. Thomas Leigh wrote to his lawyer, Joseph Hill, on 20th July, to say that he would like his nephew, James Henry Leigh, to inherit but on terms that he was to pay Mr Leigh Perrot the lump sum and annuity, and that he in turn could then provide financial assistance to the Austen and Cooper families. Hill then proposed to Leigh Perrot that, if he had the twenty-thousand, eight-thousand could be settled on the Austens and Coopers, but he resisted and nothing was agreed.[382] This proposal would have solved all of Jane's financial concerns, and the fact that it came to nothing must have been a bitter disappointment.

In a letter of 13th August to Mary Lloyd, Mrs Austen described the grandness of the house in tones which suggested they were a little overwhelmed. "And here we all found ourselves on Tuesday...eating fish, venison & all manner of good things, at a late hour, in a noble large parlour hung round with family pictures – everything is very grand & very fine & very large. The house is larger than I could have supposed...I had no idea of its being so beautiful, I had figured to myself long avenues, dark rookeries & dismal yew trees, but here are no such melancholy things. The Avon runs near the house amidst green meadows, bounded by large and beautiful woods, full of delightful walks...Behind the smaller drawing room is the state bed chamber with a high dark crimson velvet bed, and alarming apartment just fit for an heroine...There are 26 bed chambers in the new part of the house, & a great many (some very good ones) in the old."[383] The reference to an apartment fit for a heroine, one supposes, must have been inspired by the draft of *Susan*, eventually to be published as *Northanger Abbey*. There was also a private chapel.

It is a safe contention that Jane's vision of Pemberley, its grandeur, and its good taste, which begins to turn the feelings of Elizabeth Bennett from prejudice to love, was to some extent, at least, inspired by Stoneleigh. Jane also enjoyed herself there. According to her mother, "Poor Lady Saye & Sele, to be sure, is rather tormenting, tho' some times amusing, and affords Jane many a good laugh – but she fatigues me sadly on the whole." Saye and Sele is a peerage held by the Twistleton-Wykeham-Fiennes family, and the Dowager Baroness in 1806, a cousin of the Leigh family, was a rather ridiculous figure; perhaps a blend of the absurdities of Mrs Allen, Mrs Bennett, and Lady Catherine de Bourgh. Jane also attracted the attention of another Leigh, Robert Holt-Leigh, who was a Member of Parliament: "a single man the wrong side of forty; chatty and well bred, and has a large estate." He apparently became "a great admirer" of her "pretty face", and gave her some "tributes of admiration."[384] Jane was probably no longer interested. She was settled into spinsterhood, with her fellow spinsters, her sister and her friend. After she left Stoneleigh she never met him again.

From Stoneleigh, the Austens, after a visit to Warwick Castle, went to Hamstall Ridware in Staffordshire, on the fringes of the Peak District, where Jane's cousin, the Reverend Edward Cooper, held the living. He had invited them to stay for the summer back in April.[385] They were in Hamstall for about five weeks, and then, after a stay for a few days in Steventon to visit James and Mary, they finally moved on to start their new life in Southampton on 10th October[386], taking lodgings whilst looking for more permanent accommodation. Southampton in those days was still only a small harbour town of eight thousand. It was attractive enough, still surrounded then by its medieval walls. It was also something of a seaside resort. Although there was no beach as such, there was a tree planted "beach walk", running for half a mile, along which the bathing machines took people into the sea, and with views of Southampton Water. There was a High Street running from north to south, lined with brick built shops, an assembly room for dancing, and a number of circulating libraries.

In December, Cassandra went for an extended stay at Godmersham. Edward and Elizabeth had just had their tenth child, Cassandra Jane, and Elizabeth was increasingly calling on her name-sake to assist with child care. The assistance was all one way. It had still not occurred to Edward that perhaps, with his multiple estates, he could assist his mother and sisters with accommodation. Nevertheless, Cassandra's absence leaves us with three surviving letters from January and February 1807. James and Mary had been staying at Southampton, and by 7th January Jane was glad to see them go. She had never much liked Mary, and Jane had recently recovered from a bout of whooping cough which she had apparently caught from the Cooper children in Hamstall Ridware. She sounds irritable. "I shall be left to the comfortable disposal of my time, to ease of mind from the torments of rice puddings and apple dumplings, and probably to regret that I did not take more pains to please them all."[387] Her dislike of Mary also infected her feelings for James, still aggravated by her resentment at being kicked out of Steventon. "I am sorry and angry that his visits should not give one more pleasure; the company of so good and so clever a man ought to be gratifying in itself; but his chat seems all forced, his opinions on many points too much copied from his wife's, & his time is spent here I think in walking about the house & banging the doors, or ringing the bell for a glass of water." One has the impression that he was a little under the thumb of his wife. She referred to him as "Austen" in her diary, as the awful Mrs Elton refers to "Knightley", and drawing the disapproval of Emma in doing so.[388]

By the beginning of 1807, the Austens had taken a "a commodious old-fashioned house in a corner of Castle Square"[389], very close to the Dolphin Inn where Jane had danced in 1793. They began their residence in Southampton quietly enough, but their acquaintance was increasing, not necessarily to Jane's liking; and the unsociable side to her character, more prominent as she grew older, is evident. There was Admiral Bertie, who had recognised Frank, and his daughter Caroline. There were the Browns, and then there were the Lances whose house was in a beautiful location about a mile and three-quarters from the town. Mrs Lance offered to introduce them to others but they "gratefully declined". They lived "in a handsome style and are rich, and she seemed to like to be rich, and we gave her to understand that we were far from being so; she will soon feel therefore that we are not worth her acquaintance." But she liked Captain Foote who had been to dine over a boiled leg of mutton which was underdone even for James. It seems that he liked his mutton rare but Captain Foote not, "but he was so good-humoured and pleasant that I did not much mind his being starved."[390]

During the day, Frank, patiently waiting for a new posting, indulged in some skating on the frosty meadow by the beach, and the ladies treated themselves to a passage on a ferry, presumably to the Isle of Wight. Their evening entertainment was reading aloud. They had tried a translation of a novel by the French moralist the Comtesse de Genlis, *Alphonsine*, but "were disgusted in twenty pages, as, independent of a bad translation, it has indelicacies which disgrace a pen so pure." They turned instead to the *Female Quixotte, The Adventures of Arabella*, by Charlotte Lennox; a burlesque of a Gothic novel published in 1752, in which the heroine, at one point, throws herself into the Thames in an attempt to flee from horsemen whom she mistakes to be "ravishers". Jane cannot resist another dig at James's wife: "the other Mary, I believe, has little pleasure from that or any other book."[391]

The Austens had not benefited at all from the Stoneleigh inheritance, save for three rings worth a total of twenty guineas.[392] Jane's uncle, James Leigh Perrot, had taken the twenty-four thousand pounds, and the two thousand a year for surrendering his claim. After his death, the annuity would be paid to his wife for life. It was only upon her death that the money would go to James Austen, and a legacy of a thousand pounds each would be paid to each of James's siblings, including Jane.[393] Unfortunately for them, Mrs Leigh Perrot was in very good health, and the legacy seemed a distant prospect. In the meantime, the Leigh Perrots, despite the support they had received from the Austens after the unpleasantness in Bath, made no provision whatsoever for their relatives. They could very well have been an inspiration for John and Fanny Dashwood.

Jane reports, however, that her mother was not disappointed by the settlement, and was satisfied with the comfortable state of their finances. They had begun 1806 with sixty-eight pounds, and 1807 with ninety-nine (about five thousand now), and that was after an unspecified purchase of stock for thirty two pounds. They were able to keep three maidservants: but Jenny had been absent for a while, and the catering had taken a turn for the worse. "Our dinners have certainly suffered not a little by having only Molly's head and Molly's hands to conduct them; she fries better than she did, but not like Jenny."[394] Frank was satisfied with his finances too, but it was, nevertheless, still a bit tight, and "much increase of house rent would not do for either."

In the letter of 8th February 1807, there is an intriguing snapshot of Jane's writing desk. They had a "little visitor", Catherine, whom Lord Brabourne identifies as the daughter of Captain Foote. Frank had called for her after church, "and she is now talking away at my side and examining the treasures of my writing desk drawers – very happy, I believe." This suggests two things. First that the writing desk contained Jane's drafts – *Susan, Marianne and Elinor,* and *First Impressions* – it is unlikely that she would have referred to her letters as treasures; and, secondly, that the writing desk, and its contents, were very much in her thoughts, and her presence. Her ambitions were not entirely dormant during this period in Southampton, and it is likely that she was continuing to tinker with her drafts.

By this time, the Austens were in the final stages of fitting up the house, into which they finally moved in mid March. Frank and Mary were choosing furnishings. There was a man to tender the garden, and they had heard that the house was admired by many, and that the garden was the best in town. They were going to procure some roses to border the gravel walk, some syringas, and a laburnum. "The border under the terrace wall is clearing away to receive currants and gooseberry bushes, and a spot is found very proper for raspberries." According to Jane's nephew, who would have been nine or ten at the time, the garden was bounded on one side by the old city wall, and the top of the wall "was sufficiently wide to afford a pleasant walk, with an extensive view, easily accessible to ladies.This must have been a part of the identical walls which witnesses the embarkation of Henry V before the battle of Agincourt..."[395]

The view was afforded even greater interest by the imposing castle built by the eccentric Marquis of Lansdowne, just opposite, where he lived with the Marchioness, formerly his mistress. Originally of Norman origin, the ruined keep had been remodelled by him into a Gothic fortification in 1804. Jane's nephew later recalled looking down from the window and seeing the "fairy equipage" of the Marchioness's phaeton "drawn by six, and sometimes by eight little ponies, each pair decreasing in size, and becoming lighter in colour...as it was placed farther away from the carriage." He described the castle as "a fantastic edifice, too large for the space in which it stood, though too small to accord well with its castellated style...Like other fairy works, however, it all proved evanescent."[396] On the death of the Marquis in 1809, it was pulled down.

Alterations and improvements were taking place inside too: a dresser was being constructed out of a large kitchen table. Jane was able to tell Cassandra that the garret beds had been made, presumably for the three maids, and that "ours will be finished today...This week we shall do more, and I should like to have all the five beds completed by the end of it. There will then be the window curtains, sofa-cover, and a carpet to be altered."[397] Jane also spent two pounds and thirteen shillings on the hire of a piano. She was not going to be without music again, as in Bath.

Frank, unlike James, and always of a practical disposition, had lent a hand by making a fringe for the drawing room curtains. However, in late March he was appointed to HMS *St Albans* to conduct convoy duties in the East Indies and China[398]. He left his wife in the good care of his mother, Jane and Martha Lloyd, whilst he supervised preparations. Around the beginning of April, he was replaced by Cassandra, who returned from her long stay at Godmersham. Frank missed the birth of their first child, a girl called Mary Jane. It was a difficult birth. Fanny recorded in her diary that Mary was "so ill as to alarm them extremely."[399] However, Frank returned for the christening in May, and stayed until June when he sailed for the Cape of Good Hope.[400]

Although Jane certainly preferred Southampton to Bath, she did not really regard either as her home, in the sense that Steventon had been. It was in the late summer of 1807 that Jane was to become first acquainted with the place which was to become her second proper home, and where she composed her greatest works, namely Chawton. Her brother Edward, as well as inheriting Godmersham from the Knights, had also inherited a second estate in Hampshire, including a manor house, and an associated cottage. In April, the tenant of Chawton had vacated the property, and Edward went to stay in Chawton Great House at the end of August. Mrs Austen and her daughters also went, and James and his family joined them. The Great House was a manor built in the first half of the sixteenth century, and, in the middle of the next century, two red brick wings had been added. There was a large hall, and a gallery, and, according to Fanny Knight, "such a number of old irregular passages that it is very entertaining to explore them, & often when I think myself miles away from one part of the house I find a passage or entrance close to it, & I don't know when I shall be quite mistress of all the intricate, & different ways."[401] During this stay she made several shopping trips with her aunt Jane to the nearest town of Alton, a walk of a couple of miles from Chawton.[402]

In 11th September, when the Austens returned to Southampton, Edward and Elizabeth, together with Fanny and her brother William, went with them. The visit was recorded by Fanny in her diary. On Monday the 14th, Cassandra and Jane accompanied them to the theatre to see "The Way to Keep Them." By this, Fanny must have meant *The Way to Keep Him*, a comedy by the Irish writer, Arthur Murphy which had premiered at the Theatre Royal, Drury Lane in 1760. The next day they hired a boat to call on Mrs Palmer, the mother-in-law of Charles, who had been recently married to the daughter of a former attorney-general in Bermuda. "Mama, to everybody's astonishment, was of the party, and not at all sick. In the evening Uncle Henry A came. Aunts C & J walked in the High Street till late." On the Wednesday, save for Elizabeth, clearly not well, they took another boat and went to Netley Abbey, "the ruins of which are quite beautiful." Netley, near Southampton Water, is the most complete surviving abbey built by the Cistercian monks in southern England. Almost all of the thirteenth century walls still stand, and the perfect medieval ruin was an inspiration for Romantic writers and poets, and, perhaps, also for those who sought to parody them. "We eat there of some biscuits we had taken and returned quite delighted. Aunt Jane and I walked in the High Street till late."[403] The next day, Henry, who had also come down to Southampton, took them all for a drive in the New Forest, and they took some cold partridges with them. Jane stayed at home.[404]

Little is known of Jane's life towards the latter end of 1807, and the first half of 1808. She and her sister were rarely apart. Over the Christmas and New Year periods, they both went to stay with their friends at Manydown, paying the occasional visit to Steventon. By the end of February, they were staying with the Fowles in Kintbury, Berkshire. Fulwar Fowle, the pupil of Mr Austen, who had been friends with Jane and Cassandra as a child, had married the sister of Martha and Mary Lloyd, and was the vicar of the parish, and also the Lieutenant-Colonel of a large company of riflemen that formed part of the Berkshire Volunteers. He had six children, the eldest of whom, Fulwar Junior, gave this sparkling description of Jane thirty years later. "She was pretty – certainly pretty – bright & a good deal of colour in her face – like a doll – no that would not give at all the idea for she had so much expression – she was like a child – quite a child very lively & full of humour – most amiable – most beloved."[405]

In the spring of 1808, Jane spent some time with Eliza and Henry. Henry had expanded his banking business, and he and Eliza now had a house in Michael's Place in Brompton, at that time just outside of London. Jane stayed with them from mid May until 14th June, when she joined James and Mary for a trip to Godmersham. They had been staying at the Bath Hotel in Picadilly, which, apparently, her brother had found most uncomfortable – "very dirty, very noisy, and very ill-provided." Henry escorted Jane there in the morning, and she and Mary set off at half past seven, travelling via Deptford Hill, Blackheath, and Dartford. They breakfasted at the Bull, where they had the same "bad butter" she had experienced in 1794, and then set off again at half past ten, reaching Sittingbourne by three. After a short pause, they "drove, drove, drove, and by six o'clock were at Godmersham."[406]

James and Edward were waiting for them outside the house as they arrived, and Jane's nieces, Fanny and Lizzy, met them in the hall "with a great deal of pleasant joy." Jane was given the "Yellow room." "It seems odd to me to have such a great place all to myself", she wrote to her sister. Fanny stayed with her whilst she dressed. Elizabeth was now expecting her eleventh child, and still did not look well. Jane offered to be of assistance in looking after the children. She clearly missed Cassandra. "I feel rather languid and solitary – perhaps because I have a cold; but three years ago we were more animated with you and Harriet and Miss Sharpe. We shall improve, I dare say, as we go on."[407]

Her sharp wit, however, was as sharp as ever: "Mr Waller is dead, I see. I cannot grieve about it, nor perhaps, can his widow very much."[408] She spent two or three hours alone in the Yellow room every day after breakfast, no doubt with her writing desk, composing her letters, and perhaps working on the treasures within its drawers. Towards the end of June, the weather was so cold that she was moved down into the library for the sake of the fire. Mr Leigh was again in town, and Henry met with him. Jane thought it was to do with the legacy, of which she had not entirely abandoned hope. "Mrs Knight is kindly anxious for our good, and thinks Mr L.P. [Leigh Perrot] *must* be desirous for *his family's* sake to have everything settled. Indeed I do not know where we are to get our legacy, but we will keep a sharp look-out."[409]

Jane had been pressed to stay a little longer at Godmersham, and Henry had offered to take her back in September, but she wanted to return in July. "I have felt myself obliged to give Edward and Elizabeth one private reason for my wishing to be at home in July. They feel the strength of it and say no more, and one can rely on their secrecy. After this I hope we shall not be disappointed of our friend's visit; my honour as well as my affection will be concerned in it."[410] Lord Brabourne, in his commentary on the letter, was puzzled by this reference but, according to Lucy Worsley, it was to do with the fact that they were expecting Catherine and Alethea Bigg at Southampton for a visit. Jane had to confide in her brother because she did not want to be late in case this was interpreted by her friends as a continuing resentment or embarrassment arising from Harris Bigg Wither's proposal.[411] This is as good an explanation as any.

However, Jane's feelings about the prospect of her return to Southampton were mixed. She appreciated the luxury of living at Godmersham, but she missed the familiarity of those closest to her. On 1st July she wrote: "In another week I shall be at home, and there, my having been at Godmersham will seem like a dream, as my visit at Brompton seems already…The orange wine will want our care soon. But in the meantime, for elegance and ease and luxury, the Hattons and the Milles' dine here today, and I shall eat ice and drink French wine, and be above vulgar economy. Luckily the pleasures of friendship, of unreserved conversation, of similarity of taste and opinions, will make good amends for orange wine."[412] On 8th July, Edward and Jane left early in the morning for Southampton, with a stop overnight in Guildford.

In September, it was Cassandra's turn again to go to Godmersham to help her sister-in-law with her ever burgeoning family; the eleventh having just arrived. Meanwhile the Southampton social circle was continuing to grow. There was a party at Mrs Maitland's with a quadrille and commerce table [card games], and music in another room. "There were two pools at commerce, but I would not play more than one, for the stake was three shillings, and I cannot afford to lose that twice in an evening."[413] Jane was even match-making: "I have got a husband for each of the Miss Maitlands; Colonel Powlett and his brother have taken Argyle's inner house, and the consequence is so natural that I have no ingenuity in planning it. If the brother should luckily be a little sillier than the Colonel, what a treasure for Eliza!"[414]
In the evenings Jane was reading aloud the recently published

"Letters from England" by Robert Southey. Southey was writing under the pseudonym of a fictional Spaniard called Don Manuel Alvarez Espriella who is journeying through England, and writes home about every aspect of British society. Jane didn't like him. She thought Exprella to be "horribly anti-English. He deserves to be the foreigner he assumes."[415]

Frank and Mary had now taken lodgings in Yarmouth. The Peninsular War, Napoleon's attempt to subjugate Spain and Portugal and bring them within the Continental System, had begun in the summer of 1808. Rebellions had broken out across the Iberian peninsular, and the British saw an opportunity to strike on land, and in particular to drive General Junot out of Lisbon. HMS *St Albans* had been involved in the escort of troopships to the Portuguese coast, and on 5th August twenty-three transport ships had landed supplies and soldiers at Mondego Bay. On 21st August, Frank observed the Battle of Vimeiro from his deck, recording in his log: "Observed an action between the English and French armies on the heights over Merceira." He was then involved in taking off the wounded, and French prisoners: "Anchoring there at noon of the 21st, remaining until the 24th, my boats being all that time employed in landing provisions and stores for the army, and embarking a number of French prisoners and wounded British soldiers on board such of the transports as had been appropriated for their reception."[416] After the battle, the *St Albans* required servicing in the port of Great Yarmouth, and Mary joined her husband there. "Our Yarmouth division seem to have got nice lodgings, and, with fish almost for nothing and plenty of engagements and plenty of each other, must be very happy."[417]

The Austens still did not feel settled in Southampton. Rents were increasing, and Frank now had his own family to support. Mrs Austen was expecting to move to Alton, near to Chawton. Henry had entered into a banking partnership with a local firm, and through this contact Mrs Austen was hoping to hear of "something perfectly unexceptionable." The weather had been cold and windy in Southampton, and Jane had had some kind of ear infection, although Mr Lyford's prescription of cotton, moistened with oil of sweet almonds, had cured it. But she was still out of sorts. She was not even cheered by the prospect of Martha's return, for which some spruce beer had been brewed especially. "I do not know how to think that something will not happen to prevent her returning by the 10th; and if it does, I shall not much regard it on my own account, for I am now got into such a way of being alone that I do not wish even for her."[418]

But on 4th October there was some drama to break the monotony. "On Tuesday evening Southampton was in a good deal of alarm for about an hour: a fire broke out soon after nine at Webb's, the pastry cook, and burnt for some time with great fury. I cannot learn exactly how it originated; at the time it was said to be their bakehouse but now I hear it was in the back of their dwelling-house, and that one room was consumed. The flames were considerable: they seemed about as near to us as those at Lyme[419], and to reach higher. One could not but feel uncomfortable, and I began to think of what I should do if it came to the worst; happily, however, the night was perfectly still, the engines were immediately in use, and before ten the fire was nearly extinguished, though it was twelve before everything was considered safe, and a guard was kept the whole night. I am afraid the Webbes have lost a great deal, more perhaps from ignorance or plunder than the fire; they had a large stock of valuable china, and, in order to save it, it was taken from the house and thrown down anywhere. The adjoining house, a toyshop, was almost equally injured, and Hibbs, whose house comes next, was so scared from his senses that he was giving away all his goods, valuable laces, &c., to anybody who would take them. The crowd in the High Street, I understand, was immense."[420]

At the end of June, shortly before leaving Godmersham, Jane had reported that Elizabeth (Edwards' wife) had improved in looks since they had arrived, and apart from a cold did not seem at all unwell. However, she was not thriving in her eleventh pregnancy. On 27th September, Fanny recorded, "Mama as usual very low." Then, on the 28th, "About three this afternoon to our great joy, our beloved mother was delivered of a fine boy and is going on charmingly."[421] On 4th October, she got up for dinner, and by the 7th, Edward's forty-first birthday, Cassandra had reported that Elizabeth had made a recovery; although apparently far from complete because Jane hoped "to hear of its advancing in the same style" with Cassandra's next letter.[422]

But, by the time of that letter on the 13th October, Jane had already learned of Elizabeth's death from a letter Martha had received from her sister. "Oh! The miserable events of this day!", Fanny wrote on the 10th, "My mother, my beloved mother torn from us! After eating a hearty dinner, she was taken violently ill and expired (may God have mercy upon us) in ½ hour!!!!"[423]

Jane expressed her condolences to her sister, who was still at Godmersham. "We need not enter into a panegyric on the departed, but it is sweet to think of her great worth, of her solid principles, of her true devotion, her excellence in every relation of life." Her first thought was of Edward and she was consoled by the thought of his having a "religious mind to bear him up, and a disposition that will gradually lead him to comfort." Her second thought was of her favourite niece.

"My dear, dear Fanny, I am so thankful that she has you with her! You will be everything to her; you will give her all the consolation that human aid can give."[424]

Ten days later, her brother's two eldest sons, Edward (14) and George (13), came to stay for a few days from Winchester College, on compassionate leave, to relieve some of the burden. A letter from their father was read to them. "George sobbed aloud. Edward's tears do not flow so easily; but as far as I can judge they are both very properly impressed by what has happened."[425] Jane tried to keep them amused with some games – paper ships, riddles, cards – watching the river, and taking the occasional stroll. They took the ferry up the Itchen river to Northam to look at a warship in the middle of construction, and then walked home again, and planned another trip to Netley.

By this time, it is clear that Edward had offered Chawton Cottage to his mother and sisters. Whether this was as a result of Elizabeth's death, or whether the plan had been formed at an earlier stage, is not entirely clear, but by the end of October, they had all become "quite familiarised to the idea", and Mrs Austen wanted Mrs Seward, the occupant of the Cottage, to move out by Midsummer. Cassandra had described the property, apparently in glowing terms: "…everything you say about it in the letter now before me will, I am sure, as soon as I am able to read it to her, make my mother consider the plan with more and more pleasure."[426] There were six bedchambers, and garrets for storage, one of which was going to be fitted up for a manservant, and Jane was also determined to have her music. "Yes, yes, we *will* have a pianoforte, as good a one as can be got for thirty guineas, and I will practice country dances that we may have some amusement for our nephews and nieces, when we have the pleasure of their company."[427]

Jane wanted to make the most of the last few months in

Southampton. "A larger circle of acquaintance, and an increase of amusement, is quite in character with our approaching removal. Yes, I mean to go to as many balls as possible, that I may have a good bargain. Everybody is much concerned at our going away, and everybody is acquainted with Chawton, and speaks of it as a remarkably pretty village, and everybody knows the house we describe, but nobody fixes on the right." One of the balls was in the Dolphin, in the very same room where they had danced in 1793 when Jane was eighteen. She reflected wistfully on the passage of those years. "I thought it all over, and in spite of the shame of being so much older, felt with thankfulness that I was quite as happy now as then." [428]

XVI: CHAWTON

By the New Year, the plan was to leave Southampton on Easter Monday, 3rd April 1809, and then to stay at Godmersham before Chawton became available.[429] Preparations were well under way. Mrs Austen was hopeful that Mrs Seward, the outgoing tenant, would get the garden cropped for them, and William, Edward's ten-year old, was making a footstool for the cottage, "but we shall never have the heart to put our feet upon it. I believe I must work a muslin cover in satin stitch to keep it from the dirt."[430] Cassandra returned in February for the final six weeks or so of their time in Southampton. Then there is a hiatus of two years before we hear Jane's epistolary voice again.

The journey into Kent was delayed by Mrs Austen's ill-health. On 12th March, Fanny received "a very bad account of Grandmama Austen." Although she was rather better a couple of days later, the journey was postponed. Nevertheless, the prospect of the move into a proper home appears to have stimulated Jane, and on 5th April, two days after the date of their planned departure, she wrote to Crosby & Co, the publisher who had bought the manuscript of her novel *Susan* in the spring of 1803. She sounds angry, as if a re-awakened ambition had made her realise she had been ill-used. In this letter she reminded them of the purchase, and offered to supply another copy of the manuscript if it had been lost "by some carelessness", and then would "engage for no farther delay", otherwise she would seek to have the book published elsewhere. She signed herself as "Mrs Ashton

Dennis" at the Post Office in Southampton which, whilst preserving her anonymity, also gave her the excuse to finish the letter with the memorable line, "I am Gentlemen &c &c MAD". The response she received was, perhaps unsurprisingly, less than courteous; "there was not any time stipulated for its publication, neither are we bound to publish it. Should you or anyone else, we shall take proceedings to stop the sale. The MS shall be yours for the same as we paid for it."[431]

The Austen party finally left Southampton around 20th April, and travelled to Kent via Alton, perhaps to take a look at the state of the cottage, but there was another delay. Fanny recorded in her diary that her grandmother had again fallen ill at Alton. She was recovering, and had moved from the inn to the cottage in the town where Frank's wife, Mary, was now lodging, her husband having returned to sea. "It is very uncertain whether she will be well enough to continue her journey, before their future residence at Chawton will be ready for them, & then I conclude they will not come at all, which will be a great disappointment for all parties."[432] These fears proved to be unfounded, and Mrs Austen and her two daughters arrived at Godmersham on 15th May, and stayed until the end of June. On 22nd June, Eliza de Feuillide joined the party, the first time she had visited Godmersham since 1801, followed by her husband Henry a week later. She and Henry were in the process of moving from their house in Brompton into a larger property in Sloane Street. Eliza's French connections had quite the impression on Fanny, now sixteen, recording in her diary her departure, and the birth of Frank's first son. "Uncle & Aunt HA went away *ce matin. Quel Horreur*!! *Un lettre de ma tante C* – announcing the birth of Mrs FA's *petit garcon.*"[433]

It was on 7th July that the Austens entered their new home,

Chawton Cottage. This, according to her nephew, was only Jane's "second home" because in Bath and Southampton, "she was a sojourner in a strange land, but here she found a real home amongst her own people."[434] She was back in her home country of Hampshire, only fifteen miles from Steventon, and closer to the rest of her family. Edward was now spending much of his time at the Chawton Great House. Frank had settled his family in the nearby market town of Alton, and Henry's bank, Austen Gray & Vincent, had a branch in Alton High Street. Charles also frequently stayed in the Great House when he was on leave, and Jane was relieved of much of the financial pressures that she, her mother and sister had been subject to – the cottage was provided to them rent-free.

Chawton was near open downs, in beautiful, undulating countryside, in the north-east of Hampshire; although all of the land had been enclosed. The Cottage itself had been built in the late seventeenth or early eighteenth century and originally belonged to the farmer of a small piece of freehold land. It had then been sold to Thomas Knight in 1769 for £126 when it became an inn. It was, after all, at a busy cross-roads, namely the junction of the routes which led to London, Portsmouth and Winchester. By 1791, the house was occupied by Mr Knight's bailiff, Bridger Seward, and upon his death the remaining occupant was his widow.[435] The building still stands today, restored by the Jane Austen Society, and a museum dedicated to her memory. It is L-shaped, the long arm parallel to the road, with two stories, and two attic dormers.

The location was not as peaceful as Steventon. It was so close to the busy road that the front door opened upon it; "while a very narrow enclosure, paled in on each side, protected the building from danger of collision with any runaway vehicle."[436] People in carriages could even see through the windows. Mrs Knight wrote to Fanny, shortly after the Austen party had moved in, that she had "heard of the Chawton Party looking very comfortable at breakfast, from a gentleman who was travelling by their door in a post-chaise."[437] There was a pond on a green immediately outside the property.

The accommodation itself had been much improved by Edward. He had spent eighty pounds in refurbishing the house; a "labour of love" according to Jane's nephew. "A good-sized entrance and two sitting rooms either side made the length of the house, all intended originally to look upon the road, but the large drawing room window was blocked up and turned into a bookcase, and another opened at the side which gave to view only turf and trees, as a high wooden fence and hornbeam hedge shut out the Winchester road, which skirted the whole length of the little domain."[438] The dining room, however, did look upon the road, and Mrs Austen and the grandchildren enjoyed the lively scene. Caroline Austen, Jane's niece by his second wife Mary Lloyd, and a frequent visitor to Chawton as a child, recalled Collyer's Flying Machine, the stage-coach from Southampton to Ludgate Hill which went by every day, except Sundays. "Collyer's daily coach with six horses was a sight to see! And most delightful was it to a child to have the awful stillness of night broken by the noise of passing carriages which seemed sometimes even to shake the bed."[439] Edward's sons, who were at Winchester College, would frequently break their journey on Collyer's coach with a stay at Chawton, and Fanny often refers to travelling "by Collyer" in her diary.

Upstairs, Mrs Austen and Martha each had a bedroom to themselves. There was a spare room for guests. Jane and Cassandra continued to share a room with two beds. It had a fireplace, and room for an armchair too. Jane would read to her sister at night while they undressed.[440] There was a good kitchen garden and a large court, afforded by the L-shape, and out-buildings too. "Trees were planted each side to form a shrubbery walk, carried round the enclosure, which gave a sufficient space for ladies' exercise. There was a pleasant irregular mixture of hedgerow and gravel walk, and orchard, and long grass for mowing, arising from two or three little enclosures having been thrown together. The house itself was quite as good as the generality of parsonage houses then were, and much in the same style; and was capable of receiving other members of the family as frequent visitors. It was sufficiently well furnished; everything inside and out was kept in good repair, and it was altogether a comfortable and ladylike establishment, though the means which supported it were not large."[441]

There were about four hundred inhabitants in Chawton, about sixty families, most of whom were agricultural labourers employed by the local gentry. It was with the latter, of course, that the Austens would socialise. The Prowtings lived in a larger house to the rear of the Cottage, and set back from the road. They had two unmarried daughters, a little younger than Jane and Cassandra, who became good friends. At Chawton Lodge, a little further along the Winchester Road were the Hintons, brother and sister. The rector was Mr Papillon who also lived with his sister, and then there was yet another spinster, Miss Benn, who, in a reduced state, had rented a rather dilapidated old cottage. Such was the immediate circle.[442] The tenant of the Great House was a widower, John Middleton, who lived with his six young children, and his spinster sister-in-law. Charlotte-Maria, one of those six children, writing over half a century later, gives us a snapshot of Jane Austen at this time, now approaching her fortieth year.

"I remember her as a tall thin spare person, with very high cheek bones, great colour – sparkling eyes, not large but joyous and intelligent, the face by no means so broad and plump as represented…her keen sense of humour I quite remember, it oozed out very much in Mr Bennett's style – Altogether I remember we liked her greatly as children from her entering into all games &c...We saw her often. She was a most kind and enjoyable person to children but somewhat stiff and cold to strangers. She used to sit at table at dinner parties without uttering much, probably collecting matter for her charming novels which in those days we knew nothing about – her sister Cassandra was very lady like but very prim, but my remembrance of Jane is that of her entering into all children's games & liking her extremely."[443]

James Edward Austen-Leigh, who would have first got to know Jane at around this time, recalls her as "very attractive; her figure was rather tall and slender, her step light and firm, and her whole appearance expressive of health and animation. In complexion she was a clear brunette with a rich colour; she had full round cheeks, with mouth and nose small and well formed, bright hazel eyes, and brown hair forming natural curls close round her face. If not so regularly handsome as her sister, yet her countenance had a peculiar charm of its own to the eyes of most beholders. At the time of which I am now writing [the early Chawton years] she never was seen, either morning or evening, without a cap; I believe that she and her sister were generally thought to have taken to the garb of middle age earlier than their years or their looks required; and that, though remarkably neat in their dress as in all their ways, they were scarcely sufficiently regardful of the fashionable, or the becoming...I have collected some of the bright qualities which shone, as it were, on the surface of Jane Austen's character, and attracted most notice; but underneath them there lay the strong foundation of sound sense and judgment, rectitude of principle, and delicacy of feeling, qualifying her equally to advise, assist, or amuse."[444]

His sister Caroline also remembered her frequent visits to Chawton. It sounds like a very happy environment, and, crucially, one in which Jane Austen was beginning to recover her *joie de vivre*. "Aunt Jane was the great charm – As a very little girl, I was always creeping up to her, and following her whenever I could, in the house and out of it...Her charm to children was great sweetness of manner – she seemed to love you, and you loved her naturally in return – This as well as I can now recollect and analyse, was what I felt in my earliest days, before I was old enough to be amused by her cleverness – But soon came the delight of her playful talk – Everything she could make amusing to a child – Then, as I got older, and when cousins came to share the entertainment, she would tell us the most delightful stories chiefly of fairyland, and her fairies had all characters of her own – The tale was invented at the moment, and was sometimes continued for 2 or 3 days, if occasion served."[445]

Jane would typically begin her day at Chawton with music before breakfast. Caroline liked to stand by her and listen to the pretty tunes she played every morning. At nine o'clock, she made breakfast, "that was her part of the household work – The tea and sugar stores were under her charge – and the wine – Aunt Cassandra did all the rest..." Then Jane would generally sit in the drawing room until lunch, chiefly at work – "she was a great adept at overcast and stitch...she could throw the spilikens for us, better than anyone else, and she was wonderfully successful at cup and ball." After lunch they would go for a walk, sometimes to Alton for shopping, or to make a visit to the great house when one of their brothers was staying, or to Chawton Park, or just to visit a neighbour. "They had no carriage, and their visitings did not extend far – they were upon friendly but rather distant terms, with all." The observations she made of her neighbours unsurprisingly informed her writing. "The laugh she occasionally raised was by imagining for her neighbours impossible contingencies – by relating in prose or verse some trifling incident coloured to her own fancy, or in writing a history of what they had said or done, that could deceive nobody." Caroline recalled that her aunt's writing desk was kept in the drawing room, and often saw her writing letters on it. "I believe she wrote much of her novels in the same way – sitting with her family, when they were quite alone but I never saw any manuscript of that sort, in progress."[446]

The Cottage was far from perfect. One suspects that the scene in *Sense and Sensibility*, in which Robert Ferrars goes on and on about how lovely it must be to live in a cottage, to the irritation of Eleanor Dashwood, was inspired in some part by Chawton. However, it was in Hampshire. It was near her family. It was free. It had the feel of permanence as opposed to transience, and she was happier than she had been in a long time. On 26th July 1809, she wrote a poem for her brother Frank on the occasion of the birth of his first son. The last verse, which is about herself, is unmistakably optimistic for the future, and for Chawton.

"As for ourselves, we're very well;
As unaffected prose will tell.
Cassandra's pen will paint our state,
The many comforts that await
Our Chawton home, how much we find
Already in it, to our mind;
And how convinced, that when complete
It will all other Houses beat
That ever have been made or mended,
With rooms concise, or rooms distended."[447]

In short, it was enough to rouse her from her long period of stagnation, and she determined, once again, to be a published writer; Crosby & Co be damned. She had sorted out some of the stories she had written as a girl, which may very well have been unearthed as a result of the preparations for the move. She added the date "August 18th 1809" to *Evelyn*, and updated some of the references in *Catherine*, both of which she had written when she was sixteen.[448] More important still, she set to work in earnest in those "rooms concise, or rooms distended", on the drafts of *Sense and Sensibility* and *Pride and Prejudice*. Her nephew, writing from memory half a century later, gives us a glimpse of the author at work; although his description has more of the museum tableau about it, than it does of reality.

"She was careful that her occupation should not be suspected by servants, or visitors, or any persons beyond her own family party. She wrote upon small sheets of paper which could easily be put away, or covered with a piece of blotting paper. There was, between the front door and the offices, a swing door which creaked when it opened; but she objected to having this little inconvenience remedied, because it gave her notice when anyone was coming."[449]

The truth is more prosaic. She had been allocated the light duties, of making the breakfast, and looking after the key to the wine cupboard. Cassandra, Martha and the servants did the rest. In the meantime, Jane was hard at work in revising those texts, begun at the end of the previous century, into manuscripts ready for submission to a publisher at the dawn of the Regency Age.

XVII: SENSE AND SENSIBILITY

There was no separation between Jane and Cassandra during the crucial period of July 1809 to April 1811, and therefore no word directly from Jane's pen to enlighten the picture. We do not know precisely how she came to return with a will to her aspirations as a novelist, how or when those first drafts came to be in their final form, or the details of how they came to be published. However, according to Caroline Austen, the first year at Chawton was "devoted to revising and preparing for the press"[450] *Sense and Sensibility* and *Pride and Prejudice.* It is certainly the case that, at some time over the winter of 1810-1811, the manuscript of *Sense and Sensibility* was accepted by Thomas Egerton of Whitehall for publication at the author's expense. Why did she choose to publish this first, rather than *Pride and Prejudice*? The original draft of *First Impressions* had, of course, been peremptorily rejected in 1797, despite Mr Austen's best efforts. On top of this, Jane may have considered that *Sense and Sensibility* was the more conventional novel. The character of Elizabeth Bennett was, perhaps, just a little too self-assured and independent for the Regency palate. Even *Sense and Sensibility* had to be toned down for the second edition in 1813. In the first edition, Mrs Jennings is quite express in her belief that Colonel Brandon has an illegitimate daughter. It may very well be that this was a little too racy for some – by the second edition the suggestion is, at most, implied.

There were, in the early years of the nineteenth century, four ways to get a book published. The first was by subscription, in other words by soliciting family, friends, and members of the public, to contribute to the costs, and a list of their names would be printed in the book. If you were a well known writer this could be lucrative. Frances Burney made a thousand pounds from subscriptions to *Camilla* in 1796; and one of the subscribers listed in the first volume is one "Miss J Austen, Steventon". But Jane, of course, was not yet in Miss Burney's class, and would not be anywhere near it during her lifetime. The second method of publication was profit-sharing. The publisher would pay for the printing and advertising, and would recoup these costs from the sale of the first copies. Any profit over and above these costs would be shared with the author. This method depended on the publisher's having a certain level of confidence in at least a minimum of sales. The third method was by selling the copyright to the publisher – this is how *Susan* had been sold to Crosby & Co. The fourth was on commission. This meant that the author was responsible for all the expenses of publication – paper, printing, and advertising – while the publisher was responsible for distribution, and would take a commission, typically ten per cent, on all copies sold.[451] The modern equivalent of this is self-publication. This is how *Sense and Sensibility* was sold to Thomas Egerton. It was a bit of a risk, and the cost would have been somewhere in the region of one to two hundred pounds to print and publish the book.

Happily for the literary biographer, at the end of March 1811, Jane went to stay with her brother Henry and Eliza at their new house, No 64 Sloane Street, in order to ready her proofs for publication. This is indicative that it was Henry, the banker and the man of business, based in London, who had arranged the deal with Egerton, and this is confirmed by the subsequent correspondence which Jane maintained with her sister, Cassandra, who had gone on to Godmersham. It was Thomas Egerton who had distributed *The Loiterer* for James Austen, and he and Henry were certainly known to each other. Egerton was primarily a publisher of military books, and Henry's role as an army agent may very well have drawn them together. According to Henry's biographical note on his sister, written in 1818, Jane was so lacking in confidence that "its sale would not repay the expense of publication, that she actually made a reserve from her very moderate income to meet the expected loss."[452] It is probable, however, that Henry agreed to underwrite any loss. The cost of printing and publishing the book would have been somewhere in the region of one to two hundred pounds, and Jane could simply not have afforded it. Whether the deal would ever have been done without this personal connection, and whether Jane would ever have been published without it – who can say, but it is surely doubtful.

In her letters, Jane sounds in very high spirits, buoyed by the fact that she was to become published at last, and buzzing with the London social scene. Eliza and Henry held a party for over eighty people with five professional musicians. It went extremely well, with the rooms dressed up with flowers. Jane spent the greater part of the evening with George and Mary Cooke. The drawing room grew very hot, so they placed themselves in the connecting passage which was cool, allowed them to enjoy the music, and also to have the "first view of every new comer." Then, she "was quite surrounded by acquaintances." The music was very good, and between the songs there were lessons on the harp, or harp and pianoforte together. "The house was not clear till after twelve."[453] She was noticed by Mr Wyndham Knatchbull, Mrs Knight's brother, who described Jane as "a pleasing looking young woman." She was pleased enough with that compliment: "... that must do; one cannot pretend to anything better now; thankful to have it continued a few years longer!"[454]

She went shopping for muslin and silk stockings, going to house-parties, ("I find all these little parties very pleasant"), for walks in Kensington Gardens, to museums, and to art galleries, "though my preference for men and women always inclines me to attend more to the company than the sight." Some of the company consisted of some French emigrés friends of Eliza; the D'Entraigues, and the Comte Julien. "It will be amusing to see the ways of a French circle." [455] And there was also the theatre. Jane was looking forward to seeing *King John* but they went to see *Hamlet* instead, and then *Macbeth* the day after. They also went to see *The Hypocrite* at the Lyceum. Jane was hoping to see the most famous actress of the time, Sarah Siddons, but she was not on stage that night. "I should particularly have liked seeing her in 'Constance', and could swear at her with little effort for disappointing me."[456]

But it is clear that *Sense and Sensibility*, and its impending perfection and publication, were very much on her mind. "I am never too busy to think of S and S, and I can no more forget it than a mother can forget her sucking child; and I am much obliged to you for your inquiries. I have had two sheets to correct, but the last only brings us to Willoughby's first appearance. Mrs K [Mrs Knight] regrets in the most flattering manner that she must wait till May, but I have scarcely a hope of its being out in June. Henry does not neglect it; he has hurried the printer, and says he will see him again to-day. It will not stand still during his absence, it will be sent to Eliza." She was gratified by Mrs K's interest and thought that "she will like my Elinor, but cannot build on anything else."[457]

Jane left London in early May. She went to Streatham, then a village about eight kilometers to the south of London, to visit her friend, Catherine Bigg, now married to the Reverend Herbert Hill, rector of the parish, before returning to Chawton. She was pleased to be back in the country. "You cannot imagine

– it is not in human nature to imagine – what a nice walk we have round the orchard. The row of beech look very well indeed, and so does the young quickset hedge in the garden. I hear today that an apricot has been detected on one of the trees."[458] She was alone with her mother upon her return but the house soon filled up. On 20th June, Cassandra left Godmersham to stay for a while with Henry in town, before returning to join her mother and sister in Chawton. Martha, who had also been staying in London, was to return with her. At the beginning of August, they were graced again by the presence of Eliza de Feuillide, and a few days later, Charles arrived with his wife and two children.[459] It was seven years since Jane had seen her brother, and the first time that she had met his wife and children – she had been living with her husband on board his ship. Cassandra wrote to their cousin Phylly Walter: "…you may guess the pleasure which having him amongst us again occasion'd. He is grown a little older in all that time, but we had the pleasure of seeing him return in good health & unchanged in mind. His Bermudan wife is a very pleasing little woman. She is gentle & amiable in her manners & appears to make him very happy. They have two pretty little girls."[460]

Towards the end of September, it appears that a firm date for the publication of *Sense and Sensibility* had been fixed. There is an entry in Fanny Knight's diary for 28th September indicating that she had received a letter from her aunt Cassandra begging them not to mention that her aunt Jane was the author of the work. Then, on 30th October, the first advertisement for the novel appeared in the London newspaper, *The Star*, and the next day there was another in the *Morning Chronicle*. Jane finally became a published writer in that November of 1811. The novel appeared, as was normal for the time, in three volumes, and it is likely that around seven hundred and fifty to a thousand copies were printed.

Jane chose to remain anonymous. There was nothing unusual about that, especially amongst female writers before they had made a name for themselves. As Jane's contemporary put it, Mary Brunton, the author of *Self Control*, published in 1810: "To be pointed at – to be noticed & commented upon – to be suspected of literary airs – to be shunned, as literary women are, by the more unpretending of my own sex, & abhorred, as literary women are, by the more pretending of the other! – My dear, I would sooner exhibit as a rope dancer."[461] The title page of *Sense and Sensibility* simply said, therefore: "By A Lady. Printed for the author by C Roworth, Bell-yard, Temple-bar, and published by T Egerton, Whitehall 1811." It cost fifteen shillings (about thirty-five pounds), and most of the copies sold would have been purchased by circulating libraries, very popular at the time amongst the literate classes, rather than by individuals.

After the publication of *Mansfield Park* three years later, Jane made some notes about the reaction of the people in her immediate circle, which afford some insight into the reception of *Sense and Sensibility*. It was just about the favourite of Jane's niece, Anna. She liked *Mansfield Park* better than *Pride and Prejudice*, but not so well as *Sense and Sensibility*. Mr Creed preferred it to *Mansfield Park* too. On the other hand, Mrs Augusta Bramstone "owned that she thought S & S and P & P downright nonsense."[462] Beyond the opinions of her immediate circle, Jane would have been ignorant of the critical reaction, but the novel clearly achieved a good circulation quite quickly. The Countess of Bessborough, the mother of Lord Byron's lover, Lady Caroline Lamb, and friend of Sheridan and the Prince of Wales, wrote to Lord Gower on 24th November: "Have you read 'Sense and Sensibility'? It is a clever novel. They were full of it at Althorp, and tho' it ends stupidly I was much amus'd by it."[463] It was even read by Princess Charlotte, the Regent's daughter: "…it certainly is interesting,

& you feel quite one of the company. I think Maryanne & me are very like in disposition, that certainly I am not so good, the same imprudence, &c, however remain very like. I must say it interested me much."[464]

The first published reviews, of which Jane would have been aware, came out early the following year. They must have given her considerable satisfaction. *The Critical Review* considered it to be "well written; the characters are in genteel life, naturally drawn, and judiciously supported. The incidents are probable, and highly pleasing, and interesting; the conclusion such as the reader must wish it should be, and the whole is just long enough to interest without fatiguing. It reflects honour on the writer, who displays much knowledge of character, and very happily blends a great deal of good sense with the lighter matter of the piece."[465]

The British Critic described it as "a very pleasing and entertaining narrative…The characters are happily delineated and admirably sustained…An intimate knowledge of life and of the female character is exemplified in the various personages and incidents which are introduced…We will, however, detain our female friends no longer than to assure them, if they please, many sober and salutary maxims for the conduct of life, exemplified in a very pleasing and entertaining narrative…"[466] This sounds insufferably condescending to the modern reader, but, by the beginning of July, she was able to write to Frank, "You will be glad to hear that every copy of S and S is sold, and that it has brought me £140 besides the copyright, if that should ever be of any value."[467] Jane must have been delighted, and mightily encouraged.

In the period during which this novel was drafted, revised, and perfected, from the year 1797, when *Elinor and Marianne* was first conceived, until 1811, when the finished work was eventually published, the world had changed, and was in the process of changing, dramatically. In the field of geo-politics, the *ancien regime* of the eighteenth century had been shattered by the aftermath of the French Revolution. Although it was to be patched up at the Congress of Vienna, and held together with sticking plaster for another few decades, it was mortally wounded. The Age of Absolutism was giving way to the Age of Nationalism. In the realm of the arts, the revolutionary symphonies of Beethoven, the introspective poems of Wordsworth and Byron, and the naturalism of painters such as Turner and Blake, were splitting the classical world from top to bottom. The Age of the Enlightenment was giving way to the Age of Romance. Another way to express it would be to say that the Age of Sense was giving way to the Age of Sensibility.

The plot of the novel centres around Elinor and Marianne Dashwood. Their father has died, and his rich estate in Sussex, Norland, is left to a son by his first marriage, John Dashwood. The two sisters, together with their mother, and younger sister Margaret, are left in reduced circumstances. Although John made a promise to his father that he would provide for his half-sisters, he is convinced by his execrable wife, Fanny, that his father was not referring to any financial assistance after all.

John and Fanny move to take up possession of Norland, and for a few months Mrs Dashwood and her daughters remain there too. Fanny's brother, Edward Ferrars, comes to stay. When Fanny perceives a growing attachment between Edward and Elinor, she makes it quite clear that if Edward were not to marry well, their mother would cut him off without a penny. Mrs Dashwood, revolted by Fanny's behaviour, is determined to move. Fortunately, she receives an invitation from her cousin, Sir John Middleton, to come and stay at his estate of Barton Park in Devonshire. They are offered the comfortable cottage on the estate at very reasonable terms.

Sir John lives with his wife and children, and also his mother-in-law, Mrs Jennings. He gives the Dashwoods a warm welcome and has more in common with Mrs Jennings than with his wife. Mrs Jennings and he are both, although a little vulgar and convivial to a fault, warm and kind-hearted, whilst Lady Middleton, although well-bred, is cold, and has nothing to say for herself "beyond the most common-place inquiry or remark."[468] Sir John's friend, Colonel Brandon, is a perfect gentleman, wise, kind and "on every occasion mindful of the feelings of others."[469] At the age of thirty-five, he is considered by Marianne to be ancient, and well past marriageable age, especially when he complains of rheumatism, and talks of flannel waistcoats, but she is "perfectly disposed to make every allowance for the colonel's advanced state of life which humanity required."[470]

Within a few days, Marianne meets somebody she finds far more glamorous, John Willoughby, a dashing twenty-five year old who is to inherit the nearby estate of Allenham from an elderly relative, Miss Smith. She slips and twists her ankle whilst walking in the rain, and he picks her up and carries her home. She soon becomes besotted with him, and he appears to feel the same way about her. Colonel Brandon, who has fallen in love with Marianne, is left out in the cold. He arranges a picnic at Whitwell, the estate of a friend, but this has to be cancelled when he is called to town on urgent business.

Elinor and Mrs Dashwood are both convinced that Marianne is engaged to Willoughby, but Elinor cannnot understand why it has not been declared. One morning, Willoughby asks for a private audience with Marianne. When Elinor and her mother return, they find Marianne in a state of great distress. Willoughby explains that he has been sent to town by Miss Smith and that he must leave immediately with no plans to return. After he has left, Elinor is puzzled but is still convinced of the engagement.

Edward Ferrers comes to stay at Barton but is evidently out of spirits. His reserve towards Elinor is contradicted by the occasional animated look. The answer to this riddle is in the form of the cunning Lucy Steele, a relative of Mrs Jennings. Lucy, feigning friendship with Elinor, but in fact jealous of her relationship with Edward, tells her that she and Edward have been secretly engaged for four years since he was a young man under the tutelage of her uncle in Plymouth. Although devastated by the news, Elinor rightly supposes that all of Edward's affections are in fact for her, and that he has long considered his engagement to Lucy as an unwelcome burden. "With his integrity, his delicacy, and well-informed mind [how could he] be satisfied with a wife like her – illiterate, artful and selfish."[471]

After Christmas, Elinor and Marianne accompany Mrs Jennings to London, where she has a house near Portman Square. Marianne is hopeful of seeing Willoughby but her notes to him are left unanswered. At a party she eventually sees him. Clearly ill at ease, he snubs her. Marianne writes, demanding an explanation, and he responds with a curt note, denying that there was ever an understanding between them, and stating that his affections had long been engaged elsewhere. Marianne is devastated. Mrs Jennings finds out that Willoughby has been in financial difficulty and has become engaged to a Miss Grey who has a large fortune. Colonel Brandon is now free to reveal the truth about Willoughby to Elinor, in the hope that it will eventually ease her sister's suffering.

Brandon was in love with a girl called Eliza as a young man but Eliza was married off to his brother. The brother treated her unkindly, and when they were divorced, Eliza was discarded. She fell into bad company and, before succumbing to consumption, she had an illegitimate daughter, also called Eliza. Brandon took on the care of the little girl and became her guardian but young Eliza disappeared at the age of seventeen. The first news of her whereabouts had reached him on the morning of the Whitwell picnic, and that is why he had had to leave so suddenly. He traced young Eliza, and found her abandoned, in great distress, and pregnant. The scoundrel who had seduced her was none other than John Willoughby.

In the meantime, Mrs Ferrars has discovered Edward's secret engagement to Lucy Steele, and threatens to cut him off without a penny. Although no longer feeling any affection for Lucy, he is determined to honour the engagement, thus gaining further admiration from both Elinor and Marianne for his principled stance. Elinor asks Colonel Brandon to make the living of Delaford available to Edward when he is ordained. Brandon is happy to do so.

Marianne, in even greater distress when she learns of Willoughby's marriage to Miss Grey, insists on returning to Barton. On the way they break their journey at Cleveland, the estate of Mr Palmer, Mrs Jenning's son-in-law. Careless of her health, Marianne walks around the grounds in wet weather and develops a violent cold. Willing herself to be miserable, her condition worsens and becomes dangerous. Brandon becomes more in love with Marianne than ever. She reminds him of Eliza. He performs the valuable service of bringing her mother to Cleveland, and Marianne recovers. She begins to respect and admire him.

Events then quickly resolve themselves into a happy ending. One of the Dashwoods' servants brings news that he has seen Mr Ferrars in town with Lucy Steele, and that they were married. Elinor, who still harboured faint hopes, is deeply saddened. However, Edward arrives at Barton, and they discover that it his brother Robert who has married Lucy; her, out of self-interest, having transferred her affections to the brother who would inherit. Marianne, tempered by her illness, gives way to good sense and marries Colonel Brandon.

Sense and Sensibility deals for the first time in the mature novels with the theme which recurs throughout Austen's work; the injustice of the dependency of women. There is a clear comparison between the plight of the Dashwoods, and the situation of Jane and her sister, dependent upon their brothers. John Dashwood intends to leave his three sisters one thousand pounds each. This is the same amount as had been left to Cassandra by her fiancé. John's awful wife, Fanny, calculates that they will have five hundred pounds a year, almost exactly the income of the Austens after their father's death. Austen reflects ironically on the inadequacy of such an income through the cruelty of Fanny's mouth. "What on earth can four women want for more than that. They will live so cheap! Their housekeeping will be nothing at all. They will have no carriage, no horses and hardly any servants; they will keep no company, and can have no expenses of any kind! Only conceive how comfortable they will be!...They will be much more able to give you something."[472]

John Dashwood is the personification of this unjust dependency. He is at pains to absolve himself of any responsibility for his half-sisters. Perceiving an attraction between Brandon and Elinor, he develops a prurient interest in advancing any prospects of their marrying. When he first meets the Colonel, he only wants "to know him to be rich to be equally civil to him."[473] This is motivated by no fraternal compassion, only by cold self-interest. He impresses on Elinor the expenses he has had to incur since moving into Norland, such as replacing the china, prompting Austen to observe, with rich irony, "having now said enough to make his poverty clear, and to do away with the necessity of buying a pair of earrings for each of his sisters...his thoughts took a cheerfuller turn."[474]

As well as being the physical cause of his sisters' dispossession, everything is valued by him, including people, according to its economic worth. "He never wishes to offend anybody, especially anybody of fortune."[475] Perceiving Marianne's looks to have declined after Willoughby has deserted her, he questions whether she will now be able to marry a man worth more than five or six hundred a year. Women, in particular, are viewed as vehicles for economic advantage. When the plan to marry Edward Ferrars off to the wealthy Miss Morton founders, John assumes that the deal will simply be transferred to his brother, Robert, provoking Elinor to remark that "…it must be the same to Miss Morton whether she marry Edward or Robert"[476], Miss Morton being a mere commodity.

John Dashwood's cold, practical self-interest is rational in economic terms. It is an example of reason, or "sense", in an extreme and corrupted form. But what Jane Austen is exploring in this novel, is that neither sense, nor sensibility, taken in a pure form, is what it is to be fully human. The novel explores the nature of reason and feelings through its characters, and, in particular, Elinor and Marianne. For that reason, it must have been a particularly appropriate treatment for the epistolary form in which it was originally drafted. However, even in the narrative form in which it has come down to us, it remains a deeply subjective novel, and Austen, even in using the narratorial voice, is almost always speaking through her characters. The conclusion is unmistakeably that any well-rounded human being needs to have both sense and sensibility.

Marianne is presented, for most of the novel, as a young woman governed by her feelings, rather than by reason. She is the embodiment of the Romantic movement. Her tendency to commune, or to fancy herself at one, with nature is a central element of this facet of her character. On the day that she meets Willoughby, she declares as fact that the day will be lastingly fair, and that every threatening cloud would be drawn off from the hills, as if it is a truth for her to command. When it rains, she is "chagrined and surprised,"[477] and, tellingly, this failure of Romantic idealism is the very occasion of her ill-fated meeting with Willoughby.

Conversely, Elinor is portrayed as a woman who is *governed* by reason and not her feelings. Marianne reminisces about the fallen leaves at Norland, in a romanticising of nature worthy of Keats, Byron or Shelley. "What feelings are they, the season, the air altogether inspired!" she declares. Elinor, in a deliciously bathetic moment, responds, "It is not every one… who has your passion for dead leaves." Edward Ferrars, whose temperament mirrors Elinor's, observes, just as prosaically: "It is a beautiful country…but these bottoms must be dirty in winter." When Marianne asks him how he can think of dirt with such objects before him, he responds, "Because…among the rest of the objects before me I see a very dirty lane."[478]

Marianne's attraction for Willoughby is fuelled by his perceived romanticism; his apparent oneness with nature, his spontaneity, his tendency to act on impulse, motivated by his appetites and not his reason. It is the rapidity of thought in his action of carrying her into the cottage on the day of their first meeting that first recommends him to her, and he then makes himself even more interesting by leaving in the "midst of a heavy rain".[479] She prescribes for him those qualities which she sees within him, and which receive her approval: "Whatever be his pursuits, his eagernesss in them should know no moderation, and leave him no sense of fatigue."[480]

Elinor initially sees a resemblance between Marianne and Willoughby, "of saying too much what he thought on every occasion, without attention to persons or circumstances."

However, the resemblance between them is only superficial, and this becomes more apparent towards the end of the novel when the true nature of Willoughby's character becomes known. His nature is wholly untempered by restraint. "Too early an independence and its consequent habits of idleness, dissipation and luxury"[481] had corrupted his mind and character. This is sensibility taken to a corrupted extreme.

In the end, Marianne's character is in fact revealed to be more in tune with Willoughby's nemesis, Colonel Brandon. Brandon is the opposite of Willoughby in almost every respect. When Elinor upbraids Willoughby for slighting Brandon, she describes the latter as "a sensible man, and sense will always have attractions for me." Willoughby's reaction is to complain that she is trying to disarm him with *reason*.[482]

Marianne's marriage to Colonel Brandon is less of a paradox than it at first appears because her sensibility is often more virtual than real, and by the end of the book, tempered by her illness, her true character has been formed. "She was born to discover the falsehood of her own opinions, and to counteract, by her conduct, her most favourite maxims. She was born to overcome an affection formed so late in life as at seventeen, and with no sentiment superior to strong esteem and lively friendship, voluntarily to give her hand to another."[483] The verb "born" has been chosen advisedly. At the end, even Mrs Dashwood appreciates that Marianne has far more in common with Brandon than she ever had with Willoughby. His manners "…their gentleness, their genuine attention to other people, and their manly unstudied simplicity is much more accordant with her real disposition, than the liveliness – often artificial and often ill-timed of the other."[484]

In truth, it is the ideal, or the appearance, of sensibility which holds such attraction for Marianne, and not the reality. She confuses the *appearance* of virtue with the inner quality of virtue. Thus she censures Edward for the way in which he reads Cowper. "His eyes want all that spirit, that fire, which at one *announce* virtue and intelligence...his person and manners must *ornament* his goodness with every possible charm [emphasis added]".[485] In contrast, Elinor sees his "innate propriety and simplicity of taste, which in general direct him perfectly right."[486] Similarly, Marianne condemns Elinor, not for what she feels for Edward, but for the way in which she expresses it. "Esteem him! Like him! Cold-hearted Elinor! Oh! Worse than cold-hearted. Ashamed of being otherwise. Use those words again and I will leave the room this moment."[487] Indeed, the exaggerated language Marianne uses in her condemnation is itself a parody of sensibility as an artifice. When they are forced to leave Norland Park, Marianne demands that Elinor *demonstrate* distress. "When does she try to avoid society, or appear restless and dissatisfied in it?"[488]

Although Marianne is genuinely distressed when deserted by Willoughby, the distress she feels does not quite measure up to her ideal of the suffering Romantic. She has to aggravate it by artifice. She was "feeling and encouraging as a duty" a violent sorrow.[489] She makes sure that she does not sleep the night after his departure, not because she cannot sleep, but because she thinks it would be inexcusable to sleep, and she would be ashamed to look her family in the face the next morning. She tries to gain sadness like a commodity, and as a "nourishment of grief."[490] This is a tendency she shares with her mother who resembles Marianne much more closely than Elinor. After the death of their father, "The agony of grief which overpowered [Mrs Dashwood and Marianne] at first, was voluntarily renewed, was sought for, was created again and again. They gave themselves up wholly to their sorrow, seeking increase of wretchedness in every reflection that could afford it, and resolved against ever admitting consolation in failure."[491] The reality of grief has to be augmented in order to live up to the ideals of the person of sensibility. "Misery such as mine has no pride...I must feel – I must be wretched."[492]

In sharp contrast, Elinor tries to manage and contain her distress when Edward leaves after his stay at Barton Cottage, having once again left his affections for her undeclared. Unlike Marianne, she does not "augment and fix her sorrow, by seeking silence, solitude and idleness."[493] It would be a mistake to see Elinor as the opposite to Marianne. She is not. She feels every bit as much as her sister, perhaps more. This is particularly evident when Marianne's health recovers from danger towards the end of the book. "The past, the present, the future, Willoughby's visit, Marianne's safety, and her mother's expected arrival, threw her altogether into an agitation of spirits which kept off every indication of fatigue and made her only fearful of betraying herself to her sister."[494]

However, unlike her sister, Elinor tempers her feelings with reason. "Marianne restored to life, health, friends, and to her doating mother, was an idea to fill her heart with sensations of exquisite comfort...but it led to no outward demonstrations of joy, no words, no smiles. All within Elinor's breast was satisfaction, silent and strong."[495] This facet of her character is made clear in the opening passages of the novel. Elinor "possessed a strength of understanding, and coolness of judgment, which qualified her, though only nineteen, to be the counsellor of her mother, and enabled her frequently to counteract, to the advantage of them all, that eagerness of mind in Mrs Dashwood which must generally have led to imprudence. She had an excellent heart; her disposition was affectionate, and her feelings were strong; but she knew how to govern them."[496]

When Elinor discovers that Edward is engaged to another, and that she is ostensibly in the same situation as Marianne, she suffers every bit as much, but she consciously controls her emotions with sense. She feels "in no danger of an hysterical fit, or a swoon...[her] security sunk; but her self-command did not sink with it...She struggled so resolutely against the oppression of her feelings, that her success was speedy, and for the time complete."[497] When she is finally able to tell Marianne of Edward and Lucy's secret, she lectures her sister on the importance of self-control. "The composure of mind with which I have brought myself at present to consider the matter, the consolation that I have been willing to admit, have been the effect of constant and painful exertion; they did not spring up of themselves."[498] When she finds out at the end that Edward is free "it required several hours to give sedateness to her spirits, or any degree of tranquillity to her heart."[499]

John Dashwood, as has been seen, personifies sense taken to its extreme and corrupted form. Lucy Steele resembles him in her ruthless pursuit of a cold, economic self-interest. Austen's judgment of her is brutal. She is an individual who "may be held forth as a most encouraging instance of what an earnest, an unceasing attention to self-interest, however its progress may be apparently obstructed, will do in securing every advantage of fortune, with no other sacrifice than that of time and conscience."[500] Whereas Willoughby represents the corruption of sensibility, John Dashwood and Lucy Steele represent the corruption of sense. All three characters are condemned unequivocally by the author.

In *Northanger Abbey*, Jane Austen had parodied excessive sensibility in the form of the Gothic novel. In *Sense and Sensibility*, this parody is broadened into a critique of the Age of Romance, not only its excesses but its insincerities and its dangers. The moral triumph of order over chaos, moderation over excess, propriety over indiscretion, and reason over distraction, are themes which recur throughout her work, and it is reasonable to suppose that the advent of the new age is not something of which she instinctively approved. Nowhere is this more explicit than in Jane's gentle condemnation of Mrs Dashwood's shortcomings. "...common sense, common care, common prudence, were all sunk in Mrs Dashwood's romantic delicacy."[501]

Ultimately, however, *Sense and Sensibility* is more subtle than this. Its irony runs from the title to the last page. It appears to set up a dichotomy between sense and sensibility, personified by Elinor and Marianne, but by the end this proposition is turned on its head. Elinor has successfully managed her feelings without corrupting them, and Marianne has tempered her Romantic sensibilities with reason. The conclusion which is reached is that humanity requires a *synthesis* of sense and sensibility; the one without the other is doomed to failure.

XVIII: PRIDE AND PREJUDICE

After the publication of *Sense and Sensibility*, there is little news of Jane until the spring of 1812. In April, Edward, and his daughter Fanny, now acting effectively as her father's escort, went to stay at the Cottage for a couple of weeks. They spent their time visiting the neighbours, the Middletons in particular at the Great House, walking to Alton, and in Chawton Park Wood. On 21st, Fanny wrote in her diary that "Ats. Cass. & Jane, F [her cousin] and I walked with Miss Middleton to Farringdon & back."[502] Farringdon was a village just a couple of miles south of Chawton. On the 25th, they had planned to go to the Alton Fair, but it rained all day. In June, Jane went with her mother to Steventon for a week or so. When they left, they took Anna with them, and she stayed at Chawton until the beginning of October. She and Jane were closer than ever. It was of this visit that Anna wrote, as an elderly lady, some fifty-two years later.

"This has brought me to the period of my own greatest share of intimacy [with Jane]; the two years before my marriage, & the two or three years after, when we lived, as you know almost close to Chawton when the original 17 years between us seemed to shrink to 7 – or to nothing. It comes back to me now how strangely I missed her; it had become so much a habit with me to put by things in my mind with a reference to her and to say to myself, 'I shall keep this for Aunt Jane.' It was my great amusement during one summer visit at Chawton to procure novels from a circulating library at Alton, & after running them over to relate the stories to Aunt Jane. I may say it was her amusement also, as she sat busily stitching away at a work of charity, in which I fear I took myself no more useful part. Greatly we both enjoyed it, one piece of absurdity leading to another, till Aunt Cassandra fatigued with her own share of laughter would exclaim 'How can you both be so foolish?' & beg us to leave off."[503]

She recalled her mother, Mary Lloyd, describing an incident which must have been a joke she had played on her aunts, apparently during the same visit. "It was in searching this library that my mother came across a copy of *Sense and Sensibility* which she threw aside with careless contempt, little imagining who had written it, exclaiming to the great amusement of her aunts who stood by 'Oh that must be rubbish I am sure from the title.'"[504]

The success of *Sense and Sensibility* gave Thomas Egerton confidence in the commercial value of Jane Austen's work. As a result, he was now prepared to take the risk upon himself and purchase the copyright to her next book, *Pride and Prejudice*. Jane had had to change the title because a novel with the title *First Impressions* had been published in 1800. Egerton bought the copyright for one hundred and ten pounds in November 1812. Jane had hoped for one hundred and fifty. On 29th November, she wrote to Martha. "P.&P. is sold. – Egerton gives £110 for it. – I would rather have had £150, but we could not both be pleased, & I am not at all surprised that he should not chuse to hazard so much. – It's being sold will I hope be a great saving of trouble to Henry, & therefore must be welcome to me. – The money is to be paid at the end of the twelvemonth."

Again, the deal would have been struck by Henry Austen, and, given that *Sense and Sensibility* went on to net a profit of one hundred and forty pounds from the first print, Jane might have had reason to feel a little short changed. And yet, it was a pretty good deal for a relatively unknown writer. Copyright in those days only lasted for fourteen years, extended for another fourteen if the author was still alive. After all, Oliver Goldsmith had sold *The Vicar of Wakefield* for sixty pounds in 1766, and Fanny Burney had only received thirty pounds for *Evelina* in 1778.[505]

Pride and Prejudice was published in the January of 1813, in three volumes at the price of eighteen shillings, and described on the title page as being by the author of *Sense and Sensibility*. Jane must have been thrilled by the sense of momentum, and this shines out from her letter to Cassandra, now at Steventon, on 29th January. She was even making plans for her "two next".

"I want to tell you that I have let go my own darling child from London; - on Wednesday I received one copy, sent down by Falknor, with three lines from Henry to say that he had given another to Charles & sent a 3d by the Coach to Godmersham... The advertisement is in our paper to-day for the first time: 18s. He shall ask 1l.1s for my two next, and 1l.8s for my stupidest of all. Miss Benn [the spinster sister of the Rector of Farringdon, fallen on hard times] dined with us on the very day of the books coming, & in the eveng. we set fairly at it & read half the 1st vol. to her - & I believe it passed with her unsuspected. – She was amused, poor soul!...but she really does seem to admire Elizabeth. I must confess that I think her as delightful a creature as ever appeared in print, & how I shall be able to tolerate those who do not like her at least, I do not know. There are a few typical errors; and a "said he," or a said she," would sometimes make the dialogue more immediately clear; but "I do not write for such dull elves" as have not a great deal of ingenuity themselves. The 2d vol. is shorter than I cd.

wish – but the difference is not so much in reality as in look, there being a larger proportion of narrative in that part. I have lopt & cropt so successfully however that I imagine it must be rather shorter than S. & S. altogether."[506] One sees here that the unmediated dialogue in much of the dramatic scenes of *Pride and Prejudice* did not, as Mr Bennett might have said, "proceed from the impulse of the moment" but was "the result of previous study".

A few days later she was still full of her new "darling child", although not beyond a little self-criticism, and an ambition to improve, but with her tongue firmly in her cheek. "Our second evening's reading to Miss B. had not pleased me so well, but I believe something must be attributed to my mother's too rapid way of getting on.: though she perfectly understands the characters herself, she cannot speak as they ought. Upon the whole, however, I am quite vain enough and well satisfied enough. The work is rather too light and bright and sparkling: it wants shade; it wants to be stretched out here and there with a long chapter of sense, if it could be had; if not, of solemn specious nonsense, about something unconnected with the story, - an essay on writing, a critique on Walter Scott, or the history of Buonaparte, or something that would form a contrast, and bring the reader with increased delight to the playfulness and epigrammatism of the general style…The greatest blunder in the printing that I have met with is in page 220, v.3, where two speeches are made into one. There might as well be no suppers at Longbourn; but I suppose it was the remains of Mrs Bennett's old Meryton habits."[507]

She was particularly pleased with her sister's and Fanny's reaction, although Cassandra must have heard the draft being read more than once. "I am exceedingly pleased that you can say what you do, after having gone through the whole work, and Fanny's praise is very gratifying. My hopes were tolerably strong of her, but nothing like a certainty. Her liking Darcy and Elizabeth is enough. She might hate all the others, if she would."[508] In Fanny's diary, her friend, Mary Oxenden, scribbled across the page: "This morning we finished 'Pride and Prejudice' – I will resolve on [illegible] perfection!!!"[509]

She must have been even more delighted with the first review which appeared in *The British Critic* that February of 1813. "It is very far superior to all the publications of the kind which have lately come before us. It has a very unexceptionable tendency, the story is well told, the characters remarkably well drawn and supported,, and written with great spirit as well as vigour…we have perused these volumes with much satisfaction and amusement, and entertain very little doubt that their successful circulation will induce the author to similar exertions."

The Critical Review was equally fulsome, praising Elizabeth's "archness and sweetness of manner." The work, in its opinion, "rises very superior to any novel we have lately met with in the delineation of domestic scenes. Nor is there one character which appears flat, or obtrudes itself upon the notice of the reader with troublesome impertinence. There is not one person in the drama with whom we could readily dispense – they have all their proper places; and fill their several stations, with great credit to themselves, and much satisfaction to the reader." Although the *Review* rather overlooked the paean to feminism embodied in Elizabeth Bennett when it concluded bathetically that the novel "shows the folly of letting young girls have their own way…"

It was the talk of literary society. Susan Ferrier, working on her first novel, *Marriage*, said, "I should like amazingly to see that same 'Pride and Prejudice' which everybody dins my ears with." Sheridan, much admired by Jane, considered it to be one of the cleverest things he had ever read, and the educational reformer and philanthropist, Anne Milbanke, who was to marry Lord Byron the following year, thought it "a very superior work. It depends not on any of the common resources of novel writers, no drownings, no conflagrations, nor runaway horses, nor lap dogs and parrots, nor chambermaids and milliners, nor *rencontres* and disguises. I really think it is the most probable fiction I have ever read…I wish much to know who is the author or -ess as I am told."[510] The novelist Maria Edgeworth was told about it by her friend Pierre Dumont, the Swiss scholar then in London. In May she wrote to her brother, "I am desired not to give any opinion of *Pride and Prejudice* but to beg you all to get it directly and read it and tell us what [your opinion] is."[511]

In that same month, Jane was staying at her brother Henry's house in Sloane Street, probably to liaise with Egerton. They went to an exhibition in Spring Gardens of the Society of Painters in Oil and Water Colours. Jane's mind was clearly full of her novel. She entertained herself by fancying that she could see likenesses of some of the characters in the portraits. "It is not thought a good exhibition," she told Cassandra, "but I was very well pleased, particularly (pray tell Fanny) with a small portrait of Mrs Bingley [in other words Jane Bennett], excessively like her. I went in hopes of seeing one of her sisters, but there was no Mrs Darcy…Mrs Bingley's is exactly herself – size, shaped face, features, and sweetness; there never was a greater likeness. She is dressed in a white gown, with green ornaments, which convinces me of what I had always supposed, that green was a favourite colour with her. I dare say Mrs D will be in yellow." The painting which inspired this reflection has not been identified. Some days later they went to an exhibition of the work of Sir Joshua Reynolds. Jane joked that she was disappointed to find nothing resembling Mrs Darcy there either. "I can only imagine that Mr D prizes any picture of her too much to like it should be exposed to the public eye. I can imagine he would have that sort of feeling – that mixture of love, pride, and delicacy."

The first edition of *Pride and Prejudice* sold about fifteen hundred copies by the July of 1813, and Egerton put out a second edition in the autumn of the same year. Its success had a knock-on effect on the sales of *Sense and Sensibility* too, and a second edition of that was also issued a few weeks later. I wonder, if perhaps, it was just a little galling to Jane that she had, beyond her immediate circle, no public recognition for this stunning achievement. If so, she gave no indication of it. Indeed, she appears to have been rather anxious at the thought of being outed as the author, and of the resulting publicity. That May in London, she was invited to meet a Miss Burdett. She wrote to Cassandra that, "I should like to see Miss Burdett very well, but that I am rather frightened by hearing that she wishes to be introduced to me."[512] She also refused an opportunity to meet Madame Germaine de Staël, woman of letters and veteran of the French Revolution, who was in London in the winter of 1813-14.[513] According to her brother, "To her truly delicate mind such a display would have given pain instead of pleasure."[514] The reluctance was probably more to do with a natural reserve than delicacy, but Jane Austen was certainly ambivalent about fame.

As we speculate about the identity of Banksy, or the Secret Barrister, the literary classes of Regency England speculated about the identity of the author of *Pride and Prejudice*. Henry Austen, in his memoir of 1833, recalled that "a gentleman, celebrated for his literary attainments, advised a friend of the authoress to read it, adding, with more point than gallantry, 'I should like to know who is the author, for it is much too clever to have been written by a woman.'"[515] If true, Jane's feelings on hearing this would have been bitter sweet but one can be confident that she had a good laugh about it.

Mr and Mrs Bennett live in the village of Longbourn, of which they are the principal inhabitants. Mr Bennett's estate is tied to the male line, and his cousin, a clergyman called Collins, is to inherit. Mrs Bennett, "a woman of mean understanding, little information, and uncertain temper"[516] is obsessed with finding husbands for their five daughters. Lydia, her favourite, is an out of control flirt who thinks of nothing but the officers in the nearby garrison town of Meryton. Kitty is under Lydia's malign influence, and Mary is plain and serious, and attempts to compensate by pretending to be an intellectual. It is only the two eldest daughters who have emerged from their childhoods unscathed by their mother's flaws. Jane, the eldest, is good natured and kind, with a gentle disposition, and beautiful too. Her only fault is to find no fault in anybody. Elizabeth, the heroine of the piece, is intelligent, compassionate, and pretty, with a razor sharp wit, and a "lively, playful disposition which delighted in anything ridiculous"[517] but with "more quickness of observation, and less pliancy of temper than her sister."[518]

Charles Bingley, a young man of considerable means, rents the nearby estate at Netherfield Park, bringing with him his two snobbish sisters, and his friend, Mr Darcy. Straight away, Mrs Bennett entertains hopes of Bingley marrying one of her daughters. He is introduced to the Bennetts at the Meryton Assembly ball, and is instantly attracted to Jane, and the feelings are mutual. Mr Darcy, although just as wealthy and handsome as Bingley, does not share his friendly and easy manner, and gives every appearance of being proud and condescending. When Bingley suggests that he dance with Elizabeth, who has no partner, Darcy says, "She is tolerable but not handsome enough to tempt me, and I am in no humour at present to give consequence to young ladies who are slighted by other men."[519] Elizabeth overhears this, is deeply offended, and forms an instant dislike.

However, over the following days and weeks, as their paths cross at social events, Darcy begins to find himself attracted to Elizabeth. He discovers that her face, far from being merely tolerable, is "rendered uncommonly intelligent by the beautiful expression of her dark eyes." What is more, he is attracted to her mind, he admires her manners, and their "easy playfulness".[520] At a party given at the Lucas's, Darcy even asks for the honour of her hand. She refuses, thus pointedly returning the snub.

Caroline Bingley invites Jane to dine. Mrs Bennett insists that she goes on horseback, hoping that it will rain and she will have to stay the night. Her wish comes true, but Jane catches cold, and has to stay for longer. Elizabeth visits her sister and also stays at Netherfield. Darcy's attraction to her deepens, against his better judgment. His pride repels him from the vulgarity of her family, and "She attracted him more than he liked."[521]

Mr Collins who is to inherit Mr Bennett's estate, comes to stay at Longbourn, professing that he intends to make one of his cousin's daughters "every possible amends". He is a pompous and ridiculous man who is at once nauseatingly deferential to his patroness, the Lady Catherine de Bourgh, but also puffed up with his clerical status. He is a "mixture of pride and obsequiousness, self-importance and humility."[522]

Elizabeth Bennett meets George Wickham, who has recently accepted a commission in the regiment now stationed in Meryton. She is attracted to him, and perceives an antipathy between him and Darcy. Wickham tells her that Darcy is the nephew of Lady Catherine. Wickham's father was the steward to old Mr Darcy, and the latter intended to gift him a living. However, on his death, Darcy dishonoured his father's commitment. Taking Wickham at his word, Elizabeth's prejudice against Darcy is deepened.

A ball is held at Netherfield. Darcy overhears Mrs Bennett's indiscreet comments about Bingley and Jane. Motivated in part by the apparent unsuitability of the match, and what he believes to be an indifference on the side of Jane, he counsels Bingley to leave Netherfield for town, and to forget her. After Christmas, Jane is invited by Miss Bennett's brother, Mr Gardiner and his wife, to accompany them back to London. Jane is delighted because she hopes to meet the Bingleys. However, she does not see Bingley, and when received by his sister is treated with coldness. She is now convinced that Bingley cares nothing for her.

Meanwhile, Mr Collins has proposed to Elizabeth, and is peremptorily refused, much to the displeasure of her mother. To the horror of Elizabeth, he is then accepted by her friend, Charlotte Lucas. After their marriage, Elizabeth goes to stay with them at the parsonage in Hunsford which abuts Rosings Park, the estate of Collins's patroness Lady Catherine. Whilst Elizabeth is at Hunsford, Mr Darcy comes to stay at Rosings with his cousin, Colonel Fitzwilliam. Fitzwilliam tells Elizabeth, unsuspecting any connection, that Darcy has recently saved a friend from a most imprudent marriage. Her prejudice against him is increased further.

One day Mr Darcy comes to the parsonage when Elizabeth is alone. He proposes to her. She would in any event have refused him. However, his manner of proposing is deeply offensive to her. He tells her that he loves her despite his sense of her inferior position and the shortcomings of her family; in short, against his better judgment. She angrily rejects him, and they have a heated exchange. She also cites his actions in destroying her sister's happiness, and his injury to Wickham.

The next day, deeply hurt by her recriminations, Darcy presents her with a letter to explain himself. Although he did not approve of a match between his friend and Jane, he genuinely did not believe that Jane had any particular regard for him. With regard to Wickham, Darcy explains that he is a rogue who had accepted £3,000, instead of the living, in order to train as a lawyer. He had then dissipated the money in drinking and gambling, and when it was gone demanded the living. When Darcy refused, he planned to elope with Darcy's fifteen year old sister, which was prevented in the nick of time. Although still resentful about Darcy's treatment of Jane, and the offensive manner in which he had proposed to her, Elizabeth realises that she has been deceived by Wickham, and that she had unjustly condemned Darcy. Her feelings towards Darcy begin to soften, although still "she could not approve him; nor could she for a moment repent her refusal, or feel the slightest inclination ever to see him again."[523]

In the summer, Elizabeth is invited to tour Derbyshire with Mr and Mrs Gardiner. She is a little apprehensive because it is the county of Darcy's estate, Pemberley. When they find that their route is taking them near to Pemberley, Mrs Gardiner is curious to see the house, little suspecting the history between its owner and her niece. Elizabeth, finding out from the inn in Lambton, where they are to stay, that the Darcys are away, is at last persuaded to do so. She is delighted with the house and the grounds, and hears reports from the housekeeper of Darcy's true nature which excite her "keenest attention".[524] She reflects, a little ruefully, how she might have been Pemberley's mistress. Darcy arrives earlier than expected whilst she and the Gardiners are still there. She is mightily embarrassed. However, Darcy is all civility and attention, both to her and to the Gardiners, and she is amazed and gratified by what she regards as the change in his manners. It is only now that she begins to entertain thoughts of "how far it would be for the happiness of both that she should employ the power, which her fancy told her she still possessed, of bringing on the renewal of his addresses."[525]

In the meantime, Lydia has been staying with Colonel Forster and his wife in Brighton where the regiment is now garrisoned. On the day that Elizabeth and the Gardiners are to dine at Pemberley, Elizabeth receives a letter from Jane which contains the shocking news that Lydia has eloped with Wickham. Mr and Mrs Gardiner entertain hopes that they are to marry. Elizabeth knows Wickham's true nature but is unable to divulge it, having been told by Darcy in confidence. Elizabeth and the Gardiners return to Hertfordshire immediately.

Later the news arrives at Longbourn that Wickham and Lydia have been traced by Mr Gardiner in London, and that he has struck a deal with Wickham which has persuaded him to marry Lydia. Given that Wickham was heavily in debt to all the tradesmen in Meryton, and owes numerous gambling debts too, the terms of the deal seem unaccountably easy. Mr Bennett fears that Gardiner has had to bribe Wickham out of his own pocket, and wonders how he will ever repay him.

Mr Bennett reluctantly receives Wickham and Lydia at Longbourn after their marriage. Lydia lets slip to Elizabeth what was supposed to be a secret, namely that Darcy was present at her wedding. Elizabeth, baffled by the news, writes to her aunt to find out what has happened. Her aunt explains that it was in fact Darcy who had traced Wickham, and it was he who bribed Wickham to do the honourable thing by paying off his debts, having held himself responsible for not having made Wickham's character more widely known. Mrs Gardiner suspects that Darcy might have had another motive, and that he did it for Elizabeth. Elizabeth's opinion of Darcy is now such that she bitterly regrets her behaviour towards him, and, in particular, her rejection. "How heartily did she grieve over every ungracious sensation she had ever encouraged, every saucy speech she had ever directed towards him."[526]

News now arrives that Bingley is to return to Netherfield Park. Elizabeth suspects, rightly, that he now has Darcy's blessing to renew his overtures to Jane. On the third morning after his arrival, he rides to Longbourn. To the amazement, and joy, of Elizabeth, Darcy is with him, although she has little chance to speak to him, and is mortified by her mother's behaviour. A few days later, Bingley and Jane are engaged. Then Lady Catherine pays a visit. She has heard a rumour that Elizabeth is engaged to Darcy, and wants to hear it contradicted. Elizabeth shocked by her rudeness, denies that she is engaged, but pointedly refuses to promise that she would not accept him.

When Bingley and Darcy return, Darcy contrives to walk alone with Elizabeth. She tells him that she knows what he has done, and he confesses his primary motive. "If you will thank me… let it be for yourself alone. That the wish of giving happiness to you might add force to the other inducements which led me on, I shall not attempt to deny."[527] He tells her that his feelings have not changed, and that one word from her will silence him for ever. The news from his aunt that Elizabeth had refused to promise she would not accept him had led him to hope. She tells him that her feelings have entirely changed, and they are swiftly engaged.

Again the driving mechanism of the plot in *Pride and Prejudice*, as in all Jane Austen's mature work, is the dependency of women. This is amplified bluntly, and ironically, in the very first sentence. "It is a truth universally acknowledged that a single man in possession of a fortune must be in want of a wife."[528] People are typically judged in this novel by their economic worth. The worthy and thoroughly decent Mr Gardiner, so unlike his sister, is still devalued by the fact that his money has been made in trade. "The Netherfield ladies would have had difficulty in believing that a man who lived by trade, and within view of his warehouses, could have been so well bred and agreeable."[529]

The Bennetts are looked down upon by Bingley's sisters

because they have an uncle who is an attorney, and another who lives in Cheapside, which "must very materially lessen their chance of marrying men of any consideration in the world."[530] Even Mr Bingley, with four or five thousand a year, is tainted by the fact that his money is new, inherited from his father, who made his money through trade, and never got around to buying an estate. Austen cleverly comments on the snobbery of Bingley's sisters, whilst at the same time pointing out that they are on the wrong end of this societal prejudice. Bingley's wealth is "a circumstance more deeply impressed on their memories than that their brother's fortune, and their own, had been acquired by trade."

But it is women, in particular, who are commodified. Wickham decides to abandon Elizabeth for Miss King, as Willoughby ditches Marianne for Miss Grey, and for the same reason: "The sudden acquisition of ten thousand pounds was the most remarkable charm of the young lady..."[531] When the execrable Collins finds out that Jane, his first choice, is practically engaged, he "had only to change from Jane to Elizabeth – and it was soon done – done while Mrs Bennett was stirring the fire."[532] His professed affection for Elizabeth is the last of the reasons he gives for proposing to her, almost an afterthought, and when she refuses him, he cruelly reminds her that her "portion is unhappily so small that it will in all likelihood undo the effects of your loveliness and amiable qualifications."[533]

Charlotte Lucas subscribes, and eventually surrenders to, the economic imperative. She urges Elizabeth "not to be a simpleton and allow her fancy for Wickham to make her appear unpleasant in the eyes of a man of ten times his consequence."[534] When Charlotte accepts Collins, Elizabeth finds it impossible to believe that her friend "would have sacrificed every better feeling to worldly advantage." Charlotte responds with the cold logic of the pragmatist. "I am not romantic you know. I never was. I ask only a comfortable home."[535]

But if Austen's earlier novel is a comedy of temperament, in which the humour and plot are driven by the ironical dichotomy of sense and sensibility, *Pride and Prejudice* is a comedy of manners, language and character, in which irony is used both internally in order to observe and comment upon the imperfections and improvements of the principal characters, but also as a structural framework for the novel as a whole, as in its predecessor. The dynamic of the novel is a progress from obfuscation and deception towards self-knowledge and enlightenment. In particular, whilst at the beginning of the novel the characters and opinions of Darcy and Elizabeth Bennett appear to be diametrically opposed; in the end, they join in a near perfect synthesis.

Elizabeth Bennett, one strongly suspects, is the heroine who is closest in temperament to her creator: intelligent and empathetic, self-aware and critical, affectionate – but also very funny, and with a talent for dissecting the world, and the characters who populate it, with humour, and the sharp scalpel of irony. *Pride and Prejudice*, more perhaps than any of the novels, explores character, and the flaws of the society from which which they are formed, and this exploration takes place through the eyes and ears of a modern woman, as liberated in spirit as any young woman could have been within the social restraints of the time. The manifesto of the narrator is articulated by this heroine in Chapter 24. "The more I see of the world, the more am I dissatisfied with it; and every day confirms my belief of the inconsistency of all human characters, and of the little dependence that can be placed on the appearance of either merit or sense…thoughtlessness, want of attention to other people's feelings, and want of resolution…"[536]

All of the principal characters in this novel are flawed, and these flaws are exposed, and frequently mocked, through the device of irony. The arrogance and self-regard of the rich, the "want of attention to other people's feelings", are personified in Lady Catherine who has no taste, nor manners, and, despite her rank, no breeding. After dinner, everyone is obliged to gather "round the fire to hear Lady Catherine determine what weather they were to have on the morrow, and she declares that "there are few people in England, I suppose, who have more true enjoyment of music"[537] than does she; despite the fact that she plays no instrument. Even her nephew, no stranger to arrogance, is ashamed of her ill-breeding. There is, I suppose, some moral difference between pride which has a foundation, and pride which has none.

Mrs Bennett is a woman of no merit or sense, and thinks only of herself, and her financial security, through the marriage of her daughters. Nor does she have any constancy. Her only concern when Lydia elopes with Wickham is that Mr Bennett will die in a fight, and they will be turned out by the Collinses. Such is her inconstancy that when she learns her husband is returning from London she wonders who is going to fight Wickham and make him marry her daughter. She has no sense to see the ruinous effect that the elopement will have, not just on Lydia, but on the marriageability of her other daughters. After news of the engagement reaches Longbourn, she refers to her "dear Wickham", and her only concern is arranging the procurement of the wedding clothes. She also, to the disgust of her daughter, dismisses the invaluable assistance of her brother by saying that if he had not had any children they would have had all his money anyway. Elizabeth, "sick of this folly, took refuge in her own room..."[538] This is a fickleness which is shared by the society which has formed her. After the double engagement of Jane and Elizabeth, the Bennetts are pronounced to be the luckiest family in the world only a few weeks after "they had been generally proved to be marked out for misfortune."[539]

Mr Bennett, although possessed of a great deal more sense, wit and intelligence than his wife, suffers from a "want of resolution". Like Mr Palmer, he has succumbed to the temptations of beauty and youth as a young man, and married a woman of no sense, "whose weak understanding and illiberal mind had very early in their marriage put an end to all real affection for her."[540] However, instead of trying to improve his wife, and curb her excesses, and those of his younger daughters, he laughs at the former, and indulges the latter. In short, he has given up: "For what do we live, but to make sport for our neighbours, and laugh at them in their turn."[541]

It is no surprise, perhaps, that as the creature of Jane Austen, Mr Bennett laughs at his wife, and ridicules her in front of his children, through the medium of irony. When she accuses him of having no compassion for her nerves, he responds in a manner which appears to contradict her but in fact justifies her complaint, "You mistake me, my dear. I have a high respect for your nerves. They are my old friends. I have heard you mention them with consideration these twenty years at least."[542] Similarly, when Mrs Bennett complains that Kitty's cough is getting on her nerves, he at once appears to upbraid his daughter whilst at the same time pointing out the arbitrariness of the complaint: "Kitty has no discretion in her coughs...she times them ill."[543] His skill as an ironist defeats his wife almost every time. When he suggests that she should send the girls by themselves to see Mr Bingley, in case he prefers her to them, her vanity is flattered rather than insulted. Often the only audience for his rather cruel wit is Elizabeth who has the compassion and wisdom to see through it. She had "never been blind to the impropriety of her father's behaviour as a husband."[544]

Laughter is the way in which Mr Bennett deals with the inconvenient truths of his life: his awful wife, his silly younger daughters, and his ridiculous and worthless cousin who is to inherit his estate. Collins too is subjected to the same treatment, and in reducing Collins to an object of ridicule he is, in Mr Bennett's eyes, an inconvenience which is rendered temporarily tolerable. Having suffered Collins's fawning praise of his patroness, he observes "...it is happy for you that you possess the talent of flattering with delicacy. May I ask whether these pleasing attentions proceed from the impulse of the moment, or are they the result of previous study."[545] The irony goes over the head of Collins, as it defeats Mrs Bennett.

The most sympathetic characters in the novel are Jane and Bingley; although even they are flawed in the sense that their inability to see any evil in others renders them particularly vulnerable. Jane falls prey to the amoral, snobbish and selfish Caroline Bingley. When the latter tells her that they hope her brother will marry Darcy's sister, Elizabeth is convinced that this is malicious, but Jane is too good natured to believe ill of her "friend", and thinks that she must have mistaken Bingley's affections. It is the "serenity of [her] countenance"[546] which causes Darcy's genuine belief that she has no real affection for his friend. Bingley himself is too easily manipulated in the hands of Darcy, albeit with the latter's good, but misguided, intentions. The sympathy with which Jane and Bingley are handled, however, renders them, taken in isolation, as two-dimensional.

It is the two principal protagonists, Darcy and Elizabeth, who are the most fully rounded characters, and whose personal development, and mutual coming together, is the centre-piece of the novel. Although in the bald terms of the title, they personify pride and prejudice respectively, these – like sense and sensibility – are not opposite, and certainly not mutually exclusive. Pride can be the source of prejudice, and prejudice can engender pride. Elizabeth is initially prejudiced against Darcy because she over-hears his remark to Bingley that she was merely tolerable, a remark which is the product of his pride. At the time she dismisses the remark with humour, but it is clear that she is hurt by it; later confiding in Charlotte that she "could easily forgive his pride, if he had not mortified mine." Her understandable prejudice is born.

Elizabeth is entitled to pre-judge Darcy's character on the basis of his insensitive remark. Prejudice, in the strictest sense, is not necessarily reprehensible. We are entitled to judge others, without knowing everything about them, so long as we keep our minds open to fresh evidence. It is the blind prejudice of the likes of Mrs Bennett which is reprehensible, a prejudice which cannot be mitigated by the facts, and is instantly removed upon Darcy's engagement to her daughter – "Such a charming man!...Pray apologise for my having disliked him so much before."[547] Likewise, the prejudice of Caroline Bingley against Wickham, although objectively justified, is formed in ignorance of the facts and on the basis of his "descent". Elizabeth does not fall into the same error, and deprecates it. "His guilt and descent appear by your account to be the same."[548]

Ironically it is Elizabeth's prejudice which, in the end, is the catalyst for the new evidence about Darcy's character which in turn dissolves that prejudice. She decides to disarm Darcy with wit. She says, "...if. I do not begin by being impertinent myself, I shall soon grow afraid of him."[549] She laughs at him, and mocks his self-importance. "Mr Darcy is not to be laughed at... That is an uncommon advantage, and uncommon I hope it will continue, for it would be a great loss to me to have many such acquaintance. I dearly love a laugh."[550] It is this liveliness of mind, and the intelligence in her eyes, which initially attracts him, and dissolves his pride. Caroline Bingley also tries to woo Darcy with wit, but her skill as an ironist cannot match that of Elizabeth Bennett, and her sarcasm leaves him cold. When she teases him on his apparent growing attraction for Elizabeth

- "You will have a charming mother-in-law, indeed, and of course she will always be at Pemberley with you" - he listens to her with "perfect indifference."

Darcy's pride is less easy to justify than Elizabeth's prejudice. He is entitled to be proud of his character, and, by the standards of the time, of his status, and what he does with it. (According to his housekeeper at Pemberley, he is kind to his staff, and the poor.) However, his pride has become ungoverned, which leads him to make insensitive observations which are insufficiently mindful of the feelings of others. The well meaning Sir William Lucas tries to engage him in conversation at a party, remarking that dancing is one of the first refinements of polished societies. Darcy coldly responds, "Certainly sir, and it has the advantages also of being in vogue amongst the less polished societies of the world. Every savage can dance."[551]

He is, however, increasingly attracted to Elizabeth Bennett, despite her connections which he regards, before his pride is tempered by her, as beneath him. It is her character, indeed, which is the closest to being unimpeachable. She has a lively, witty mind, is kind and generous, and has an admirable strength of character. She is the only person, probably including Darcy, who has had the courage to contradict Lady Catherine, and "suspected herself to be the first creature who had ever dared to trifle with so much dignified impertinence."[552]

It is Darcy who states at the outset of the novel that his good opinion once lost is lost forever but, in fact, this is a criticism more appropriately aimed at Elizabeth. Her prejudice towards Darcy is far more stubborn than his towards her. Indeed it is deepened by the false news of his behaviour towards Wickham, and the accurate news about his conduct towards her sister. She undoubtedly finds him attractive though, and is gratified to have inspired his affection in the wake of the proposal. However, his overt pride soon "overcame the pity which the consideration of his attachment had for a moment excited."[553]

Both Darcy and Elizabeth, unlike any of the other characters, have the capacity to change by recognising the faults within themselves. Elizabeth is prepared to change her opinion based upon the facts. Although her prejudice is as entrenched as ever on a first perusal of Darcy's letter, she studies its contents with reason, and concedes that she was wrong about Wickham, and the victim of his deceit, to the extent that her feelings begin to undergo a dramatic evolution. "She grew absolutely ashamed of herself. Of neither Darcy nor Wickham could she think without feeling that she had been blind, partial, prejudiced, absurd." And she has the self-awareness to recognise that the fault lay within herself; her vanity and her prejudice. "Pleased with the preference of one, and offended by the neglect of the other…"[554] She also concedes that there is much truth in what he had said about the impropriety of her family.

It might be remarked that this evolution, which does not reach its apogee until the end of the novel, and its mirror image in Darcy, are unrealistic. But Elizabeth's awakening love for Darcy is a gradual process. The first symptom of it is compassion, and there is a hint in Austen's language of the early flickerings of sexual tension engendered by it. "…her feelings…were at times widely different. When she remembered the style of his address, she was still full of indignation; but when she considered how unjustly she had condemned and upbraided him, her anger was turned against herself; and his disappointed feelings became the object of her compassion. His attachment excited gratitude, his general character respect."[555]

Her feelings are amended further by her first sight of

Pemberley. This is not, as Elizabeth later jokes, because of its economic value, it is because of what it has to say about the character of the owner. Here we have the first significant statement by Austen of her views about "improvements", which are developed further in *Mansfield Park*. "She had never seen a place for which nature had done more, or where natural beauty had been so little counteracted by awkward taste."[556] Austen here, through the eyes of Elizabeth, confers her approval on Darcy's honesty, propriety, taste, and rejection of artifice; as she later paid a similar compliment to George Knightley, and his management of the estate at Donwell Abbey.[557] It is in contrast to the pointless flamboyance of Rosings, a demonstration of wealth without taste. The interior "was neither gaudy nor uselessly fine; with less of splendour, and more real elegance, than the furniture of Rosings."[558] His pride, in her eyes, is being steadily mitigated. As the housekeeper tells her, "Some people call him proud; but I am sure I never saw anything of it. To my fancy, it is only because he does not rattle away like other young men."[559] The contrast with Wickham is stark. Wickham "has a pleasing address…a happy readiness of conversation"[560]. But it is all artifice, and Elizabeth, with an uncharacteristic lapse of insight, initially falls for it, supposing that his "very countenance may vouch for your being amiable."[561] Eventually, of course, she is disillusioned, and realises that "one has got all the goodness, and the other all the appearance of it."[562]

It is not just the physical manifestations of Darcy's taste which affect Elizabeth at Pemberley; it is also his changed behaviour towards her, and her relations, after his unexpected appearance. She had never seen him "so desirous to please, so free from self-consequence."[563] It is this change in him which finally leads her across the Rubicon: "…never had she so honestly felt that she could have loved him, as now, when all love must be in vain."[564]

Elizabeth realises in the end that Darcy is the perfect match for her. Whereas Jane and Bingley are a perfect match because they are so alike, the personal qualities of Darcy and Elizabeth ameliorate the flaws in the character of the other. "His understanding and temper, though unlike her own, would have answered all her wishes. It was an union that must have been to the advantage of both; by her ease and liveliness, his mind must have been softened, his manners improved, and from his judgment, information, and knowledge of the world, she must have received benefit of greater importance."[565] His veneer of pride is ameliorated by his love for her: "By you I was properly humbled."[566] Her prejudice is also appeased by his love for her, which in turn engenders her love for him. It is a synthesis of great beauty and symmetry. In the end, it is through his love that they are both redeemed.

XIX: MANSFIELD PARK

Jane Austen probably began to write *Mansfield Park* shortly after she had finished *Pride and Prejudice*, sometime around the spring of 1812. It is evident from Jane's letters to her sister in early 1813, around the time of the publication of *Pride and Prejudice*, that her new novel was in an advanced state. On 29th January, she wrote, "Now I will try to write of something else; - it shall be a complete change of subject – Ordination. I am glad to find your enquiries have ended so well. If you could discover whether Northamptonshire is a country of hedgerows, I should be glad again."[567] Cassandra was staying at Steventon with James and Mary, and it seems likely that Jane had asked her to do some research for the purpose of writing about Edmund Bertram's ordination, as well as the Northamptonshire landscape.

Mrs Austen was reading Sir John Carr's *Travels in Spain*, and Jane remarks that she had learned from the book "that there is no Government House at Gibraltar. I must alter it to the Commissioner's." This has to be a reference to the passage in the novel where Henry Crawford is talking to William Price about ladies' fashions, and refers to "the other women at the Commissioner's at Gibraltar." There is also a reference to the scene in Volume II, Chapter VII at the Parsonage, where, after making up the whist table, there are enough people for a round game, and Henry teaches Fanny how to play speculation. "As soon as a whist party was formed," she wrote to Cassandra, "and a round table threatened, I made my mother an excuse and came away, leaving just as many for their round table as there were at Mrs Grant's."[568]

In the spring of 1813, Edward's tenant, Mr Middleton, vacated the Great House in Chawton, and on 21st April, Edward and his family came to stay there for the whole summer whilst Godmersham was being refurbished. At around the same time, disturbing news had reached Chawton about the health of Eliza de Feuillide. It was a chronic disease. Jane wrote to Martha Lloyd in February that there had been no recent account from Sloane Street but concluded that "everything is going on in one regular progress, without any striking change."[569] It is likely that Eliza was suffering from the same disease that had killed her mother; breast cancer. The very day after Edward arrived at Chawton, he and Jane left for London, but by that stage Eliza's condition had reached a very advanced stage, and she died three days later. She was buried in the same grave as her mother and son. Jane came back to Chawton on 1st May but then returned with Henry to London a couple of weeks later. It was during this visit that she fancied she had seen her portrait of Mrs Bingley at the exhibition in Spring Gardens. Henry brought her back to Steventon on 28th May, to spend a couple of days with James and Mary, and they returned to Chawton by the beginning of June.[570]

This spring and summer of 1813, during which the first manuscript of *Mansfield Park* was finished, was spent with much social activity between the cottage and the Great House, as chronicled in Fanny's diary. Charles and his wife were also at Chawton for a time, with their new baby daughter, before going to Southend for a holiday. "Uncle & At. C.A. Miss Lloyd and Ats. Cass and Jane dined here. We had games &c in the eveng."[571] The secret of Jane's authorship was beginning to leak. Jane was apparently reading *Pride and Prejudice* aloud, to which it is so suited with its many dramatic passages of dialogue. Fanny records "At. J.A. as Miss Darcy," and, on 5th June she spent the morning with her niece reading it to her. The next day they had a very *interesting* conversation – with the word underlined. This may have been to do with the plot of *Mansfield Park* because the next day, Fanny and her family were going to the Portsmouth Dockyard, prior to a visit to the Isle of Wight.[572] James's son, James Edward, and Jane's first biographer, now fifteen, wrote a little verse to celebrate. "No words can express, my dear Aunt, my surprise; Or make you think how I opened my eyes; Like a pig Butcher Pile has just struck with his knife; When I heard for the first time in my life; That I had the honour to have a relation; Whose works were dispersed through the whole of the nation."[573]

In a letter to Frank on 6th July, Jane informed him that she was working on another book, and had used the names of his ships, but would remove them if he objected.[574] She seems to be resigned to the fact that her new novel would not be as successful as *Pride and Prejudice*. "You will be glad to hear that every copy of S & S is sold & that it has brought me £140 – besides the copyright, if that should ever be of any value. I have now therefore written myself into £250 – which only makes me long for more. I have something in hand – which I hope on the credit of P & P will sell well, though not half so entertaining. And by the bye – shall you object to my mentioning the Elephant in it, & two or three other of your old ships? I have done it, but it shall not stay, to make you angry. They are only just mentioned."[575]

On 18th July, Jane was confined to the house with "a bad face ache"[576], the nature of which is unclear, but it is something she did not fully recover from until the autumn. It was the first sign of the outer-penumbra of a shadow of ill-health. Then, in the middle of September, Jane returned with Edward's family to Godmersham. They broke their journey for three nights, staying in town with Henry at his house in Henrietta Street. They enjoyed a dinner of soup, fish, bouillée, partridges and an apple tart, prepared by Henry's emigrée housekeeper, Madame Bigion, before setting off for the Lyceum. They took a private box, Mr Spencer's, which was directly on the stage. They enjoyed "three musical things": "'Five Hours at Brighton' in three acts – of which one was over before we arrived, none the worse – and 'the Beehive', rather less flat and trumpery." The performance finished with "'Don Juan', whom we left in hell at half-past eleven – I have seen nobody on the stage who has been a more interesting character than that compound of cruelty and lust." They returned to soup, and wine with water, and to bed. Fanny and Jane had a bedroom with an adjoining dressing room, and were sharing Eliza's bed! Jane reported that she was feeling better, and had had no pain in her face since she had left Chawton. The following night they returned to Covent Garden to see 'Clandestine Marriage' and 'Midas', but "there was no actor worth naming. I believe the theatres are thought at a very low ebb at present."[577]

By 23rd September, they were in Godmersham. Jane was left in the library, with a good fire, writing to Cassandra, "mistress of all I survey". Jane told Cassandra that her complaint had got worse. She had caught a cold on her way down, and was experiencing pain in the evenings, "rather severer than it had been lately", but it had now worn off.[578] She was allowed to sit on her own in the library, with a good fire, to write, and she continued to perfect the manuscript of her new novel. Edward's twelve year old, Marianne, recalled her aunt working at this period. "…she would sit quietly working beside the fire in the library, saying nothing for a good while, and then would suddenly burst out laughing, jump up and run across the room to a table where pens and paper were lying, write something down, and then come back to the fire and go on quietly working as before."[579]

Jane also wrote again to Frank. He had apparently consented to her request to use the names of his ships, but had expressed concern that this might reveal her identity. Although she had attempted to keep her authorship a secret, by this stage she was past caring. "The truth is that the secret has spread so far as to be scarcely the shadow of a secret now - & that I believe whenever the 3rd appears [in other words *Mansfield Park*] I shall not even attempt to tell lies about it. I shall rather try to make all the money than all the mystery I can of it...Henry heard P & P warmly praised in Scotland by Lady Robert Kerr and another lady, and what does he do in the warmth of his brotherly vanity & love, but immediately tell them who wrote it. A thing once set going in that way – one knows how it spreads, and he, dear creature, has set it going so much more than once...let me here again express to you & Mary my sense of the superior kindness which you have shown on the occasion, in doing what I wished...There is to be a second edition of S and S and Egerton advises it."[580]

There was the usual round of socialising with the great and the good, and the not so good, from the local Kentish notables. In October there was quite the houseful, with a number of gentlemen guests. The Member of Parliament for Canterbury, Stephen Lushington, a future Secretary to the Treasury, and Governor of Madras, came to stay. Jane was impressed with him. "I like him very much. I am sure he is clever, and a man of taste. He got a volume of Milton last night, and spoke of it with warmth. He is quite an MP, very smiling, with an exceeding good address and readiness of language. I am rather in love with him. I dare say he is ambitious and insincere."[581] It is most unlikely that Jane's reference to being in love with him was anything other than a mischievous wink to her sister. She was now approaching forty, and contentedly resigned to spinsterhood. "I must leave off being young," she joked to Cassandra. "I find many *douceurs* in being a sort of chaperon, for I am put on the sofa near the fire, and can drink as much wine as I like."[582]

She was certainly dismissive enough of the other gentlemen callers. A Mr Wigram, the son of Sir Robert Wigram, the Tory politician and merchant ship builder, was "ill-looking, and not agreeable. He is certainly no addition. A sort of cool, gentlemanlike manner, but very silent. They say his name is Henry, a proof how unequally the gifts of fortune are bestowed. I have seen many a John and Thomas much more agreeable…We have got rid of Mr R. Mascall, however. I did not like him either. He talks too much, and is conceited, besides having a vulgarly shaped mouth. He slept here on Tuesday, so that yesterday Fanny and I sat down to breakfast with six gentlemen to admire us…I cannot imagine how a man can have the impudence to come into a family party for three days, where he is quite a stranger, unless he knows himself to be agreeable on undoubted authority…The comfort of the billiard table here is very great; it draws all the gentlemen to it whenever they are within, especially after dinner, so that my brother, Fanny and I have the library to ourselves in delightful quiet." She was glad when everybody had gone. Charles and his family arrived, and they were, to her delight, only a family party again. She wasn't even attracted by the idea of the Ashford ball. "I was very glad to be spared the trouble of dressing and going, and being weary before it was half over…"[583]

By early November, Cassandra was staying with Henry, and Jane was planning her return to Chawton. The original proposal was that she would go with Edward to Wrotham (on the Pilgrims' Way) on Saturday the 13th, spend Sunday there, and then go to London on the Monday. They would spend a couple of days in town before returning to Chawton on the Wednesday. However, it appears that Henry had not been well, which is the reason for Cassandra's visit. Although he was now on the mend, Jane was thinking of staying with him for a couple of weeks before going home. In the meantime, Jane had been to Canterbury with Edward, and had accompanied him in his inspection of the gaol as a magistrate. "I was gratified, and went through all the feelings which people must go through, I think, in visiting such a building."[584] On a lighter note she bought herself a ticket for a concert which she was to attend with a party from Goodnestone.

In her letter of 3rd November, Jane joked to Cassandra about her growing fame. "Oh! I have more of such sweet flattery from Miss Sharp. She is an excellent friend. I am read and admired in Ireland too. There is a Mrs Fletcher, the wife of a judge, an old lady, and very good and very clever, who is all curiosity to know about me – what I am like, and so forth. I am not known to her by name, however…I do not despair of having my picture in the Exhibition at last – all white and red, with my head on one side; or perhaps I may marry young Mr D'Arblay. I suppose in the meantime I shall owe dear Henry a great deal of money for printing, &c."[585] (Mr D'Arblay was the son of Fanny Burney).

It is probable that it was during a fortnight's visit to London, in the latter half of November 1813, that Henry presented the completed manuscript of *Mansfield Park* to Thomas Egerton. He offered to purchase the copyright but the offer was low, perhaps £150. It is likely that Egerton sensed the novel would be less popular than its predecessors. Jane refused. Her experience of the success of *Pride and Prejudice* had given her more confidence in her work. He then agreed to publish it on commission. To be fair, Egerton had a point, and to this day *Mansfield Park* is probably the least popular of Jane's novels amongst the general public. Its plot, characterisations, and message are more subtle, and less superficially sparkling and entertaining. This was as true at the time of its publication as it is today.

On 1st March 1814, Henry accompanied Jane back to London, presumably to finalise the arrangements for publication. On the way, Henry began to read her manuscript. "We did not begin reading until Bentley Green. Henry's approbation is hitherto equal even to my wishes. He says it is different from the other two, but does not appear to think it at all inferior. He has only married Mrs R [in other words he had got up to the passage where Maria marries Rushworth]. I am afraid he has gone through the most entertaining part. He took to Lady B and Mrs N most kindly, and gives great praise to the drawing of the characters. He understands them all, likes Fanny, and, I think, foresees how it will all be…He admires H Crawford: I mean properly, as a clever, pleasant man."[586] Jane sounds a little perplexed by her brother's reaction to Crawford, but she was looking forward to seeing Edmund Kean as Shylock in Drury Lane on the Saturday night following. By then Henry was on the third volume, and he was liking it better and better.[587]

On 21st March, Jane wrote to Frank to tell him that the book might be published by the end of April.[588] Cassandra joined Jane in London in late March, and she and Jane probably returned to Chawton together in early April. She was certainly back by the middle of that month, and Fanny records in her diary Aunts Jane and Cass dining at the Great House, and going for shopping trips into Alton, but on 27th April, Uncle Henry arrived unexpectedly at the Cottage, quite possibly to bring news from Egerton.[589] *Mansfield Park* was finally advertised on 9th May 1814 by *The Star* as "By the author of Sense and Sensibility, and Pride and Prejudice", and was priced at 18 shillings for the three volumes. The first print run extended to 1,250 copies.[590]

Although there were no published reviews for *Mansfield*

Park, Jane made notes about the reactions she had received: informal comments made almost in passing by her friends and family, reactions deliberately solicited by Jane from more distant acquaintances, and some more formal, written personal reviews from the literati.[591] The book was praised by the more eminent readership, including the publisher Mr Egerton, for its high moral principles. Lady Robert Kerr wrote: "You may be assured I read every line with the greatest interest and am more delighted with it than my humble pen can express. The excellent delineation of character, sound sense, elegant language and the pure morality with which it abounds, makes it a most desirable as well as useful work, and reflects the highest honour. Universally admired in Edinburgh by all the wise ones. Indeed I have not heard a single fault given to it."[592]

Lady Anne Romilly wrote to the Irish novelist, Maria Edgeworth, to ask her if she had read it. "It has been pretty generally admired here [in London], and I think all novels must be that are true to life which this is, with a good strong vein of principle running through the whole. It has not however that elevation of virtue, something beyond nature, that gives the greatest charm to a novel, but still it is real natural every day life, and will amuse an idle hour in spite of its faults."[593]

Some of the less esteemed readership also appear to have missed the message, and found it less inspiring than its lighter and more lively predecessor. Jane's notes reveal that Alethea Bigg thought that it had not the spirit of *Pride and Prejudice*, except for the Price family at Portsmouth! Her brother Frank, whilst considering it to be a worthy publication, did not "on the *whole*" think it equal to *Pride and Prejudice*. Charles thought that it "wanted incident". Edward, though, was "a warm admirer", and he was not alone, but Cassandra thought it "quite as clever, though not so brilliant as P & P." She appears to have entirely missed the point. According to their niece, Louisa

Knight, Cassandra tried to persuade Jane to alter the story and let Henry marry Fanny Price. She remembered her aunts "arguing the matter but Miss Austen stood firmly and would not allow a change."[594]

With the notable exception of Benjamin Lefroy, Fanny was generally regarded as a bit of a prig. Mrs Austen thought she was a bit insipid, and Anna could not bear her. Somebody called Fanny Cage did not much like it at all, thought the language was poor, and that there was nothing interesting in the characters, although it "improved as it went on." Mrs Augusta Bramstone "having finished the 1st vol. – flattered herself that she had got through the worst." George (Edward's son) was interested by nobody but Mary Crawford!

The fact that this third published novel is undoubtedly regarded less favourably than its predecessors is wholly unjustified. It certainly sold well enough. It was also produced cheaply by Egerton on thinner paper, and with more lines per page.[595] On 18th November 1814, Jane was able to tell her niece, Fanny, that the first edition was all sold. She had earned more than £310, which was a pretty penny for someone whose annual allowance was no more than £20 a year. She was thoroughly pleased with herself; although the money was not the only motivator. "Your uncle Henry", she wrote, "is rather wanting me to come to town to settle about a second edition; but as I could not very conveniently leave home now, I have written him my will and pleasure and unless he still urges it, shall not go. I am very greedy and want to make the most of it; but as you are much above caring about money, I shall not plague you with any particulars. The pleasures of vanity are more within your comprehension, and you will enter into mine at receiving the praise which every now and then comes to me through some channel or other."[596]

Three days later, she was encouraging her other niece, Anna, now married to Benjamin Lefroy, to "make everybody at Hendon admire 'Mansfield Park'."[597] She did go to stay with Henry at his new house in Hans Place towards the end of that month, and they were to meet Thomas Egerton to discuss the possibility of a second print run, but she was not optimistic. "People are more ready to borrow and praise than to buy, which I cannot wonder at; but though I like praise as well as anybody, I like what Edward calls "Pewter" too."[598] The fact remained that there had been no published reviews of the novel, and Egerton decided against taking the risk of a second edition. It was not until February of 1816 that a second edition was finally issued by John Murray, the publisher of *Emma*. However, Egerton's instincts were right, and the second edition lost money.[599]

Maria Ward, a woman of some means, marries well into the lower peerage, and becomes the wife of Sir Thomas Bertram of Mansfield Park in Northamptonshire. They have two daughters, Maria and Julia, and two sons, Tom and Edmund. Lady Bertram, a good natured but indolent woman, has two sisters. The elder married a clergyman called Norris, a friend of Sir Thomas, and granted a generous living by him on the Mansfield estate. Mr and Mrs Norris live at the Parsonage. The younger sister married unwisely, an uneducated lieutenant of marines called Price. He has become disabled for active service, and a bit of a drunk. Mr and Mrs Price, with their numerous children, live in Portsmouth.

Cut off by her imprudent marriage, Mrs Price has become estranged from her sisters but, after a number of years, contact is re-established, and an arrangement is made to relieve the burden on the Portsmouth household. Fanny, the oldest daughter of Mr and Mrs Price, and now nine years old, is to go to live with her relations at Mansfield Park. Quiet and sensitive, at first she is terribly homesick, unhappy, and neglected, but is soon put at her ease by her cousin Edmund, seven years her senior, and destined for the Church. He soon becomes her best friend, and is almost as dear to her as her beloved brother, William, who is a midshipman in the Royal Navy. Mrs Norris is widowed, and becomes more of a fixture at Mansfield Park. She is a malign influence, and resents Fanny's presence. Her favourite is Maria, who is thirteen. The living goes to Mr Grant, who moves into the Parsonage with his wife.

Sir Thomas has to leave for an extended period in order to tend to his estates in Antigua. During his absence, the semblance of order at Mansfield Park disintegrates. Maria becomes engaged to Mr Rushworth of Sotherton. He is very wealthy, but lacks all sense and judgment, and is unable to retain the respect of his fiancée, or anyone with whom he is acquainted. At around the same time, the half siblings of Mrs Grant come to stay at the Parsonage. They are Henry and Mary Crawford. Although they are on the surface very attractive, and charming company, they are, both of them, morally degenerate, having been brought up in the house of Admiral Crawford, a man who brought his mistress into the house as soon as his wife was cold in her grave. Mary reveals her brother's character early in the novel, although in doing so appears to be joking, when she declares him to be "...the most horrible flirt that can be imagined. If your Miss Bertrams do not like to have their hearts broke, let them avoid Henry...the Admiral's lessons have quite spoiled him."[600] Edmund, a man of high principles, becomes increasingly attracted to Mary, and is prepared to overlook her occasional improprieties. Fanny, a young woman of impeccable principles, disapproves.

A party is organised to Rushworth's estate at Sotherton. It is during this party that Henry Crawford starts to flirt with the beautiful Maria, despite the fact that she is now engaged to Rushworth. Only Fanny has the perspicacity to see this, and her dim view of Henry's character is irrevocably formed. Meanwhile, Edmund's attraction to Mary deepens, despite her speaking disrespectfully of the Church. She too is attracted to him, and when she discovers that he is to become a clergyman himself, she apologises.

With the arrival of his friend, John Yates, from an aborted amateur theatrical house party, Tom decides that Mansfield Park should stage some dramatics of its own. Edmund and Fanny object on the ground that this would be inappropriate in the absence of Sir Thomas, and whilst he is still potentially in danger on the high seas. The ultimate choice of the play, *Lovers' Vows*, adds to the impropriety, especially when Henry and Maria, whose flirtation has become more open, decide that they want to play opposite one another. Maria has fallen for Henry's charms, and secretly hopes that he will declare himself so that she can abandon the engagement to Rushworth.

Fanny is pressed to take on a minor part to make up the numbers, but is mortified and refuses point blank. Quite apart from the particular objections, the very idea of role playing offends her sense of sincerity. Edmund is asked to take on the part of the clergyman, Anhalt, which means he will be playing opposite Mary Crawford. At first he refuses, but, in another error of judgment, eventually relents, telling himself that it will prevent the greater evil of a stranger being brought in to play the part. Fanny has feelings of jealousy which she cannot comprehend. She is already unconsciously in love with her cousin. On the night of the first rehearsal, Sir Thomas unexpectedly arrives home. The play is at an end. They realise that what they have done is wrong. "To the greater number it was a moment of absolute horror."[601] Only Yates, who is too amoral, and Rushworth, who is too stupid, expect the play to continue.

With the return of Sir Thomas, life becomes more prosaic, and a semblance of order is restored. Henry returns to his estate in Norfolk. Maria, resentful that he makes no attempt to contact her, re-affirms her commitment to Rushworth, and they are married. They winter in Brighton, and Julia goes with them. In the absence of her two cousins, Fanny's consequence in the household correspondingly increases. She is invited to the Parsonage and becomes more intimate with Mrs Grant and Mary Crawford. However, she is still under no illusions about Mary's character. Her interest in the friendship is primarily because she is fascinated by the growing attraction between Mary and Edmund. She is confused by her own feelings for him which she still does not fully understand.

Henry Crawford returns to the Parsonage. He has a project to make Fanny Price fall in love with him. He is an accomplished actor but, although his attentions succeed in making her dislike him less, her settled disapproval of him, and her love for Edmund, is an inoculation against his attempts to woo her. Meanwhile, Fanny's brother William is on leave, and comes to stay at Mansfield Park. He is an exemplary young man, no doubt modelled by Jane on her brothers Frank and Charles, and he endears himself to Sir Thomas. A ball is planned in honour of him and Fanny.

Although Henry's project to woo Fanny started as an exercise to flatter his own vanity, he finds himself falling in love with her. He is attracted to her beauty, truth, goodness and simplicity, and has sufficient self-knowledge to know that she is everything he is not. He uses his influence with Admiral Crawford to secure William's promotion to Lieutenant, and tells Fanny that he has arranged it only for her. He asks her to marry him. She is delighted with the news about William but "...such were his [Crawford's] habits, that he could do nothing without a mixture of evil."[602] She is mortified by the proposal and rejects him.

Henry approaches Sir Thomas to intercede on his behalf, and

the latter, still ignorant of Crawford's real character, accuses Fanny of being wilful, selfish and ungrateful in refusing him. She cannot tell Sir Thomas the truth without exposing the improprieties of her cousins, especially Maria. Fanny, although timid and shy by nature, and mortified by Sir Thomas's opinion, stands firm and constant in her refusal. Sir Thomas, essentially a kind man, plans to send Fanny to stay with her family for a while in Portsmouth. She is delighted. She will spend time with William, see her brothers and sisters again, and be separated from the cares of, what she believes to be, the imminent engagement of Edmund and Mary. But Sir Thomas has an ulterior motive, to make her miss the comforts of a good income, and therefore more inclined to accept Crawford.

Fanny is shocked by the impropriety and disorder of her parents' house. She is even relieved to see Henry when he shows up to renew his entreaties. She is pleased to find him much improved but only insofar as it will make it more likely that he will desist from a suit so obviously distressing to her. Unlike the improvement which Elizabeth Bennett perceives in Darcy, which is a revelation of the truth, the improvement in Crawford is a concealment of it. The news eventually comes from London that Crawford has eloped with Maria. The true character of Henry Crawford is revealed, and Fanny's constancy vindicated.

Edmund comes to take Fanny back to Mansfield Park. He tells her of his last conversation with Mary. She regarded her brother's conduct as mere folly, that her objection to his conduct was only that he had allowed himself to be exposed, that he should have secured Fanny, and then carried on an occasional and surreptitious flirtation with Maria. The spell that Edmund has been under has been broken. After a while, he realises that it is Fanny he loves, and they are married. Order is restored at Mansfield Park.

In *Pride and Prejudice*, Elizabeth Bennett had articulated a moral manifesto. "The more I see of the world, the more am I dissatisfied with it; and every day confirms my belief of the inconsistency of all human characters, and of the little dependence that can be placed on the appearance of either merit or sense...thoughtlessness, want of attention to other people's feelings, and want of resolution..."[603] In *Mansfield Park*, Jane develops this manifesto through the world as observed and judged by Fanny Price, who is, without doubt, the Austenian character who comes closest to perfection. Fanny is kind, compassionate, deeply empathetic, reserved, modest, generous, profoundly moral, and, above all, constant in her principles. However, whereas in *Pride and Prejudice* this manifesto was explored through character alone, in *Mansfield Park* it is revealed in an ideal societal order. The *private* morality of Elizabeth Bennett is expanded into a *public* morality, as perceived and approved by Fanny Price. This more ambitious and developed moral consciousness may well be a result of the fact that *Mansfield Park* is the first of Jane Austen's novels to be wholly conceived, as opposed to extensively revised, in her maturity.

This social order is, at least at first sight, profoundly conservative, if not reactionary. The structure of this *public* morality is defined by statist and social institutions: primarily the family and the church. The structure of this *private* morality is defined by attitudes of mind: reserve, self awareness, integrity, compassion, and an appreciation of one's place in the eternal, natural order. It was written against a backdrop of moral degeneracy in the higher echelons of the British state. George III had entered his final bout of mental instability, and his son was appointed Prince Regent in June 1811. He proceeded to celebrate his elevation, and by implication his father's decline, with a party which cost the huge sum of £120,000, in the middle of a cost of living crisis precipitated by the war. Princess Charlotte was making a fool of herself by flirting with unsuitable young men. The Duke of Clarence, finally dismissed his mistress, the actress Mrs Jordan, who was the mother of ten of his children whilst making speeches in support of slavery in the House of Lords. His brother, the Regent, promptly appointed him Admiral of the Fleet at the end of the year. Such was the quality of the family at the apex of the British state.[604]

The family and the home are central to the Austenian idea of order. In the novel, as in its predecessor *Pride and Prejudice*, it is the defective domestic environment which is responsible for the flaws of character which permeate the novels. It is the improper conduct and indulgence of Mrs Bennett, and the indolence and passivity of her husband, which breed the defects of character in nearly all of their offspring. Only Elizabeth, and to some extent Jane, escape its legacy. In *Mansfield Park*, it is the aloofness of Sir Thomas and the indolence of Lady Bertram which have corrupted three of their children; with Edmund the honourable exception. Tom is dissolute and undisciplined, irresponsible and self-indulgent. Maria and Julia lack self-knowledge, generosity and humility, "the want of that higher species of self-command, that just consideration of others, that knowledge of [their] own heart, that principle of right which had not formed any essential part of [their] education..."[605]

Sir Thomas is essentially a good and kind man, and this becomes more apparent towards the end of the work, but he is not outwardly affectionate, "and the reserve of his manner repressed all the flow of their spirits before him."[606] More crucial still is that "...his cares had been directed to the understanding and manners, not the disposition."[607] His wife is useless. "To the education of her daughters, Lady Bertram paid not the smallest attention. She had not time for such cares. She was a woman who spent her days in sitting nicely dressed on a sofa, doing some long piece of needlework, of little use and no beauty, thinking more of her pug than her children..."[608] The greater, and more malign, influence on their characters, and especially upon Maria, comes from Mrs Norris.

The root cause of the loose morals of Mary and Henry is also their childhood home. They have been raised by Admiral Crawford, a man who was having an affair whilst married, and after the death of his wife, brought his mistress into the family home. He "hated marriage, and thought it never pardonable in a young man of independent fortune."[609]

When Fanny returns to her childhood home in Portsmouth, she is shocked at the ill-discipline, noise, confusion, and above all, the lack of order from which impropriety is the result. Her father is a drunkard who uses foul language and lacks basic manners, and the children and servants are out of control. At the centre of this chaos is her mother, who resembles Lady Bertram far more than she does her other sister, Mrs Norris. Whereas Lady Bertram is indolent without responsibility, Mrs Price is indolent with a household to run, and the result is a breakdown of order. She is "always behindhand and lamenting it, without altering her ways...a partial, ill-judging parent, a dawdle, a slattern, whose house was the scene of mismanagement and discomfort from beginning to end..." Fanny longs for the order of Mansfield Park: "The elegance, propriety, regularity, harmony – and perhaps, above all, the peace and tranquillity of Mansfield...everybody had their due importance; everybody's feelings were consulted."[610]

Both Edmund and Fanny are noble exceptions to the general tendency that character is formed in an ordered home. Both derive their character, in spite of the defects in their parentage, from other public institutions, most notably the established Church and the natural order, from the strength of their principles, and from the constancy of their private morality, which is very much along the lines expressed by Elizabeth Bennett. Indeed, it is in the very act of *defying* the parental authority of Sir Thomas, and refusing to accept Henry Crawford, that Fanny is at her most heroic. She also questions Sir Thomas about the slave trade, of which she quite clearly disapproves, and, in so doing, is challenging the very foundations of the home in which she has been raised. It is unlikely to be a mere coincidence that Sir Thomas's estate shares its name with the famous jurist, Lord Mansfield, whose famous judgment in 1772 had struck a blow against the very institution of slavery, and gave a crucial impetus to the abolitionist movement: "The state of slavery is...so odious, that nothing can be suffered to support it but positive law."[611]

The church, and in particular the established Anglican Church, plays a crucial role in the plot. Edmund is to be ordained, and that very fact is the dynamic at the centre of his relationship with Mary Crawford. For Jane Austen, Mary's disrespect for the Church, which of course played a crucial role in the life of the author, is a symptom and a consequence of her moral failure, and her rejection of the established order. When she hears at Sotherton that Mr Rushworth has discontinued regular services in the chapel, she says, "Every generation has its improvements." Fanny's view is quite the opposite: "It is a pity...that the custom should have been discontinued. It was a valuable part of former times...A whole family assembling regularly for the purpose of prayer, is fine!"[612]

Fanny's values are those of High Tory Anglicanism. Mary's tend to non-conformism, not through religious conviction, but through a more general moral weakness. She thinks it is safer to leave people to worship in their own way without obligation: "...if the good people who used to kneel and gape in that gallery could have foreseen that the time would come when men and women might lie another ten minutes in bed, when they woke with a headache...they would have jumped for joy and envy." Edmund's objection is informed by the same High Anglican values as Fanny. "Do you think the minds which are suffered, which are indulged in wanderings in a chapel, would be more collected in a closet?"[613]

The profession of a country parson is by its very nature a reserved and conservative one. Mary deprecates it by contrasting it with the activity of the army and navy: "...heroism, danger, bustle, fashion..."[614] William Price, a young naval officer, is the embodiment of heroism, but the quality of Mary's admiration of the services is revealed more by her last two epithets: bustle and fashion. She is more attracted to the trappings and appearance of heroism, not the still, quiet and unassuming service of the conscientious clergyman which could also, in his own way, be heroic within the context of Austen's rural England. Mary declaims that she "must look down upon anything contented with obscurity when it might rise to distinction."[615] But her kind of distinction is distinction for its own sake, for personal glory and preferment, a motive which is a threat to the Austenian ideal of order, just as much as Bonapartism was a threat to Regency England.

Reserve, sincerity and tranquillity are aspects of this idealised vision of the Church which manifest themselves too in Austenian private morality. Edmund observes to his likeminded cousin "...with you Fanny, there may be peace. You will not want to be talked to. Let us have the luxury of silence."[616] These virtues are not, of course, to be confused with the indolence of Lady Bertram, for whom "sitting and calling to Pug, and trying to keep him from the flower beds"[617] is the height of activity. Lady Bertram is inert, not just physically, but also morally. She is "one of those persons who think nothing can be dangerous or difficult, or fatiguing to anybody but themselves."[618] When Edmund expresses his concern about

Sir Thomas's absence being an anxious time for his mother, she is "sunk back in one corner of the sofa, the picture of health, wealth, ease and tranquillity...just falling into a gentle doze..."[619]

And so *moral* indolence is not to be confused with the virtues of reserve, sincerity and tranquillity, any more than activity is to be confused with heroism. Activity for its own sake, and for the projection of oneself, is deprecated in *Mansfield Park*. The most prominent exponent of being active for selfish advancement is Mrs Norris, one of the least attractive characters in the whole of the canon. She is busy where there is nothing to be busy about if only to be noticed. It is she who suggests to Sir Thomas that he should take in Fanny at the beginning of the novel, but this is not from any philanthropic motive. It is to appear important, and to have somebody to dominate and direct in order to *feel* important. She proceeds to interfere in Fanny's childhood and early adulthood with a malign activity; insisting, for instance, that she is dressed by housemaids, that she has an inferior horse, and that a fire is never made up in her room. In order to interfere with Fanny's pleasure in preparing for the ball, Mrs Norris is "entirely taken up at first in fresh arranging and injuring the noble fire which the butler had prepared."[620] The distinction between her activity and the activity of heroism is most apparent when her services are really needed. When her favourite, Maria Bertram, is in disgrace, she is good for nothing, even when Tom is seriously ill towards the end of the novel. "When really touched with affliction, her active powers had been all benumbed; and neither Lady Bertram nor Tom had received from her the smallest support or attempt at support."[621] Her pointless activity has degenerated into a worthless indolence.

After the unexpected arrival of Sir Thomas, Mrs Norris was "trying to be in a bustle without having anything to bustle about, and labouring to be important where nothing was wanted but tranquillity and silence."[622] Activity and busyness, as opposed to tranquillity and silence, are identified too as one of the principal faults of the Crawfords. Mary complains that resting fatigues her. At first she prefers Tom to Edmund because of his "liveliness and gallantry" before she discovers that this is all a bit of a façade. Her mind, indeed, is declared to be "too lively" by Edmund. But this restless temperament leads her into error. She is cynical about marriage, and it is she who encourages her brother to flirt with Maria. It is her upbringing, of course, in the house of Admiral Crawford, the adulterer, which has bred this cynicism. Of her upbringing she says, "Certainly my home at my uncle's brought me acquainted with a circle of admirals. Of *Rears* and *Vices,* I saw enough. Now do not be suspecting me of a pun, I entreat." This predictably causes Edmund to feel "grave".[623]

Henry's project to woo Fanny Price is fed by an unhealthy desire to conquer for selfish gratification. "I do not like the bread of idleness," he tells his sister. "No, my plan is to make Fanny Price in love with me."[624] His motive for activity is self-aggrandisement and, in his favour, he has sufficient insight to see the artifice, and to contrast it with true heroic activity. "The glory of heroism, of usefulness, of exertion, of endurance, made his own habits of selfish indulgence appear in shameful contrast; and he wished he had been a William Price, distinguishing himself and working his way to fortune and consequence with so much self respect and happy ardour, instead of what he was!"[625]

One symptom or consequence of a propensity to activity for self promotion is an inclination towards public performance, and, at the centre of the moral corruption which threatens the order of Mansfield Park, is the amateur theatricals which take place. They lead directly to the elopement of Maria and Crawford, Mary's tolerance of her brother's behaviour, the elopement of Julia and Yates, and even the compromise of

Edmund's principles. They are particularly improper because of the absence of Sir Thomas, and the potential intimacy of Maria, now betrothed to Rushworth, and Henry Crawford. However, the objections raised by Edmund and Fanny are more general than this. Edmund objects even to the admission of a stranger to the proceedings because of "the excessive intimacy which must spring from his being admitted among us in this manner...the more than intimacy – the familiarity."[626] Fanny is mortified by the very idea of acting. Edmund is ultimately prepared to compromise his particular objection to appease Mary; Fanny is prepared to compromise nothing.

Henry Crawford is an accomplished and enthusiastic performer. When he entertains the ladies by reading speeches from Shakespeare, he even captures the attention of Fanny. His enthusiasm for the theatricals is second to none, and he mourns their rude interruption. "There was such an interest, such an animation, such a spirit diffused! Everybody felt it. We were all alive. There was employment, hope, solicitude, bustle, for every hour of the day...I never was happier." Fanny's observation to herself is a simple one: "Oh what a corrupted mind!"[627]

It may be regarded as somewhat surprising that Jane Austen, through the eyes of her heroine, deprecates amateur theatricals, since these formed a significant part of her education. Again, however, it must be recalled that *Mansfield Park* is the first work to be wholly conceived in Jane's maturity. It was conceived and shaped years after Jane had left behind the more dramatic, epistolary form of writing, and years after the bloody consequences of revolution had become all too apparent on the continent, and around the globe. The language Henry uses in his exhortation to activity for its own sake is antithetical to Tory England; it is suited more to the mood of Republican or Bonapartiste France. Indeed, Henry's love of performance goes beyond the stage. He sees the profession into which Edmund is about to be ordained as a performance. "I could not preach but to the educated; to those who were capable of estimating my composition," he says. "Fanny, who could not listen, involuntarily shook her head."[628]

Even Edmund, in his infatuation with Mary Crawford, is infected by the insidious notion that it is the performance which matters, rather than the underlying integrity and truth. "Even in my profession," he opines, "how little the art of reading has been studied! How little a clear manner, and good delivery, have been attended to! I speak rather of the past, however, than the present. There is now a spirit of *improvement* abroad [emphasis added]."[629]

Edmund's observation brings together three of the movements which are deprecated in *Mansfield Park*: artifice, as expressed in performance; artifice, as it infects the clergy, and artifice as it assaults nature – in other words, *improvements*. When Rushworth declares his intent to improve Sotherton by hiring Humphry Repton, the author's disapproval is the thunderous. Whereas the great classical landscape contractor, Capability Brown, had created gardens which conformed to nature, eschewing formal settings, Repton had set the tone for the nineteenth century, re-introducing formal terraces, balustrades, and themed gardens, such as a cricket pitch and bowling green at Stoneleigh Abbey, of which Jane would have been well aware. Mrs Norris predictably approves of Rushworth's scheme: "Such a place as Sotherton Court deserves everything that taste and money can do."[630] Mary Crawford holds similar sentiments: "I should be most grateful to any Mr Repton who would undertake it, and give me as much beauty as he could for my money." Fanny, equally predictably, disapproves; "Cut down an avenue! What a pity! Does it not make you think of Cowper? 'Ye fallen avenues, once more I mourn your fate unmerited.'"[631] Edmund's sentiments are similar. When Henry shares his ideas for improving

Edmund's intended living at Thornton Lacey, Edmund dismisses them in favour of nature: "I must be satisfied with rather less ornament and beauty."[632]

The Austenian order contemplates the individual being at one in peace and tranquillity with the natural world, in contrast to artifice. Whereas Mary sees nature "with little observation; her attention was all for men and women, her talents for the light and lively"[633]; in contrast, Fanny "in observing the appearance of the country, the bearings of the roads, the difference of the soil, the state of the harvest, the cottages, the cattle, the children, she found entertainment that could only have been heightened by having Edmund to speak of what she felt."[634] Edmund draws a direct parallel between so called "improvements" to the natural order, and the ruination of character. He reflects upon Mary's upbringing: "This is what the world does. For where Fanny shall we find a woman whom nature had so richly endowed? Spoilt, spoilt!"[635]

Nowhere is this contemplation of man and nature more explicit than when Fanny, observing the brilliance of an unclouded night sky, declares her oneness with the universe. "Here's harmony!...Here's repose! Here's what may leave all painting and all music behind, and what poetry only can attempt to describe. Here's what may tranquillize every care, and lift the heart to rapture! When I look out on such a night as this, I feel as if there could be neither wickedness nor sorrow in this world; and there certainly would be less of both if the sublimity of nature were more attended to, and people were carried more out of themselves by contemplating such a scene."[636] She might have added that there can be no improvement to the night sky.

At the end of the novel, order is restored. Fanny is returned to Mansfield Park, useful, beloved and secure from Henry Crawford. Julia's match with Yates is deemed to be respectable. Tom regains his health, and, chastened by his illness, finally "...useful to his father, steady and quiet, and not living for himself."[637] Rushworth procures a divorce. The Grants leave the Parsonage for London with Mary; restored to her natural habitat. Maria and Mrs Norris receive their just reward in self-banishment to another country, and in perfect symmetry "their tempers became their mutual punishment."[638] Edmund is free of Mary's spell, and he and Fanny marry. "I entreat everybody to believe that exactly at the time when it was quite natural that it should be so, and not a week earlier, Edmund did cease to care about Mary Crawford, and became as anxious to marry Fanny, as Fanny herself could desire."[639] They move into the Parsonage which soon grows as dear to Fanny's heart, "...and as thoroughly perfect in her eyes as everything else, within the view and patronage of Mansfield Park, had long been."[640]

At the end then, a perfect order is restored both in the heavens and on earth at the hands of the omniscient and omnipotent author. "Let other pens dwell on guilt and misery," Jane concludes. "I quit such odious subjects as soon as I can, impatient to restore everybody, not greatly in fault themselves, to tolerable comfort, and to have done with all the rest...Time will do almost everything..." She might have added, as time will one day restore the planet to health when the presence of humanity is receding into geological history.

The artistic advantage that the novel enjoys over drama is its ability, through the authorial voice, to see into the souls of the men and women who populate it. The structural advantage it enjoys is its ability through the omnipotence of the author, to prescribe and impose an overarching and timeless order. In this sense, *Mansfield Park*, is the perfect English novel. It offers a vision of a singular and timeless moral order. It allows that order to be disassembled for the purpose of inspection, both in space and in time. It examines the constituent parts: the motives, the flaws, and the virtues of those who seek to disrupt it, and those who seek to conserve it. Finally it perfects it, reassembles the constituent parts, and restores it. In a sense, this novel is a microcosm of that creation with which Fanny Price feels at one.

XX: BACKCLOTH: INTERMISSION

Napoleon had finally over-stretched himself in 1812 by invading Russia. A combination of the fierce Russian winter, and the crippling problems of supply over vast distances, destroyed *La Grande Armée* as an effective fighting force, and the long and devastating retreat from Moscow began. The Russian army followed in its wake, and, at the beginning of 1813, entered East Prussia, occupying the city of Königsberg (modern day Kaliningrad). The Prussians, seeing which way the wind was blowing, declared neutrality but, in effect, came over to the allies. By 8th February, the Tsar had taken Warsaw, and Berlin by the beginning of March, at which point the Austrians too deserted Napoleon, and declared a truce. Napoleon launched a counter-offensive with a reorganised army, and made considerable progress in Germany with victories at the Battles of Lützen and Bautzen. This, however, prompted Great Britain to form a new alliance with the Russian Emperor and the Prussian Kaiser at Reichenbach. By October, the French had been forced west, out of Silesia to the Elbe. Then, after his defeat at the Battle of Leipzig, the largest battle which had ever been seen in Europe, involving half a million troops, Napoleon was forced to retreat towards the Rhine.

In the meantime, Wellington's Peninsula campaign was

reaching its climax. In May he marched from Portugal into Spain, thrusting north-eastwards from Freynada to Salamanca to Valladolid. The French, denuded of troops by the emergency in the north, retreated before his advance. In June his victory at Vitoria effectively expelled the main French army from Spain. By November the British were encamped south of the Pyrenees, ready to invade France itself. Russia, Prussia and Austria, by the Treaty of Chaumont, agreed to keep 150,000 men each in the field, and Great Britain agreed to divide a subsidy of £5 million between them and herself to provide a further 150,000 troops. Britain was at an unprecedented apogee in its power, thanks to its naval and economic strength, its military prowess under Wellington, and the diplomacy of great men such as Lord Castlereagh, the Foreign Secretary. "What an extraordinary display of power," he said. "This I trust will put an end to any doubts as to the claim we have to an opinion on Continental matters."[641]

In the March of 1814, when Henry Austen was evaluating the merits of *Mansfield Park*, Wellington was advancing into south-west France, taking Bordeaux, and in April Toulouse. In England the news was greeted with great joy. Thomas Sidney Cooper, the landscape artist, who was to live into the twentieth century, recalled in his autobiography being at school in Gainsborough at this time. "Our little town was kept in perpetual ferment by the news of the battles, and the street would be lined with people to see old Matthew Goy, the postman, ride in with his hat covered with ribbons, and blowing his horn mightily, as he bore the news of some fresh victory – Ciudad Rodrigo, or Badajoz, or Salamanca, or Vitoria, or St Sebastian, or Toulouse – Miller and I were pencilling soldiers and horses, or imaginarily, Wellington and Boney – for we had never heard the word 'Napoleon' at that time of day."[642]

The restoration of the Bourbon dynasty was proclaimed by

the Allies, and by the end of the month, Paris capitulated. On 5th April, Napoleon abdicated, was exiled to the island of Elba in the Mediterranean, and peace restored by the Treaty of Paris, roughly along the lines of the 1792 borders. On 9th April, the news was released by the Foreign Office in London that despatches had arrived "announcing the abdication of the crowns of France and Italy by Napoleon Bonaparte". The people went wild. Bells rang out all over the country which was lit up with illuminations from Lands End to John O'Groats. John Stonard wrote of his reaction to the bibliophile Richard Heber on 15th April. "What overpowering events! Surely there will never be any more news as long as we live. The papers will be as dull as a ledger and politics insipid as the white of an egg."[643] Prayers of thanksgiving were said that Easter, and celebrations went on for weeks. In Oldham, "the different manufacturers gave dinners and ale to their respective work people who paraded the streets with music and flags with different devices. A pair of looms were drawn in a cart where a person was weaving callico and a person representing Bonaparte was winding. Every degradation was used to insult the memory of the fallen monarch whose tyrannical career was at an end. The whole was conducted with the greatest harmony and good will, ale &c flowed in the greatest profusion."[644]

On 7th May Frank Austen signed off from HMS *Elephant*,[645] a dubious bonus from the peace, since he would now be on half pay until returned to active service. He and his family became tenants of Edward at the Great House, and lived there until the spring of 1816.[646] Thousands of soldiers began to return to the barrack towns of England. Benjamin Harris had served as a rifleman in the Royal Marines for six years. He later recalled the vicinity of Chelsea barracks where his battalion was marched for the purpose of disbandment. Thousands of soldiers were lining the streets, "and lounging about before the different public houses, with every description of wound and casualty incident to modern warfare. There hobbled the maimed light-infantry man, the heavy dragoon, the hussar, the artillery man, the fusilier, and specimens from every regiment in the service. The Irishman shouting and brandishing his crutch; the English soldier, reeling with drink; the Scot, with grave and melancholy visage, sitting on the steps of the public house among the crowd, listening to the skirl of his comrades' pipes, and thinking of the blue hills of his native land. Such were Pimlico and Chelsea in 1814."[647]

In June, the King of Prussia, the Russian Emperor, Prince Metternich, the Austrian Chancellor, and the heads of various minor German states, arrived in London for the peace celebrations. The whole route from Dover to the capital was to be illuminated. Cooper recalled that every house in Canterbury was lit up and flags hung across the streets. Tsar Alexander was bald, but had a round handsome face. The Prussian General Blücher "had bits of black like sticking plaster on his face – little tufts of hair I suppose, or perhaps small wounds."[648] Behind them came wounded soldiers, some on wooden legs or crutches, some with only one arm. "They were treated and cheered by the populace, who smoked and drank with them; and the city was kept in a state of conviviality and uproar until midnight." In London on the day of the grand procession, windows were let out for huge sums, bakers ran out of bread, and the cows in Hyde Park were frightened by the guns and cheers, and produced no milk. The Tsar and his sister, the Grand Duchess Catherine, took over Pulteney's hotel in Piccadilly. The Prince Regent was as profligate as ever, expending vast sums on parties, balls and fetes.[649]

The main event was an extravagant ball at Burlington House put on by White's club on 20th June. Betsey Wynne Fremantle, the diarist and wife of Thomas Fremantle, a close associate of

Nelson, recalled the splendour of the event. "The rooms were brilliant, and looked like a fairy palace...2,000 people set down without any inconvenience or confusion. I stayed till seven o'clock in the morning. And met almost everybody I know in London."[650] White's ball was rivalled by a masquerade attended by Byron dressed as a monk, "while Cam Hobhouse put on Byron's Albanian robes and Caroline Lamb appeared in mask and domino, flashing her green pantaloons."[651]

Cassandra had gone with her brother to the capital in the middle of all this mayhem on 13th June. Some of the London bankers had been invited to the ball, including Henry Austen. Jane was delighted when she heard. "Henry at White's! Oh, what a Henry!"[652] Edward and Fanny had arrived in London on the very day of the ball. Fanny wrote in her diary that they reached Henrietta Street in time to see the procession going to proclaim peace. They drove out in the evening. "Uncle Henry went to Whites Fete at Burlington House."[653]

Nor were the celebrations confined to the capital. In Oxford, the sovereigns attended a celebratory dinner in the Radcliffe Camera. There were balls and street parties all over the country. A ball was planned in Shrewsbury, at which Lord Hill was to play the emperor. In Bury St Edmunds, a feast was held for four thousand of the poor. "They came from all parts for 20 miles around...The whole of the meat was prepared a day or two before & of course was designed to be cold: the plum puddings hot. The tables were all set through the Butter Market & round the theatre, down to the Wool Pack." In Leeds there was a great procession carrying the proclamation of peace. In Gainsborough, the procession held figures representing Wellington, Blücher, Platov (the Russian general), the Tsar, and Napoleon, bearing a label, "Going to Elba". There were bands of music in the streets, a thanksgiving sermon and anthems at church, and feasting parties at the inns, during the day, with a general illumination, bonfire, crackers, and squibs at night.

There were celebrations in Alton too. Fanny Knight recorded in her diary going in the evening to see the illuminations, and "the poor at supper."[654] More exciting still was the prospect of the royal party progressing through Hampshire for the naval review in Portsmouth on 24th June. Jane wrote to Cassandra "…do not be trampled to death in running after the Emperor. The report in Alton yesterday was that they would certainly travel this road either to or from Portsmouth. I long to know what this bow of the Prince's will produce."[655]

All these celebrations were capped with a Grand Jubilee on 1st August to mark the centenary of the Hanoverian succession, and the anniversary of the Battle of the Nile. The Royal Parks were taken over. There was a revolving Temple of Concord, a Chinese pagoda, swings, roundabouts, wild-beast shows, a mock naval engagement on the Serpentine, a balloon launch from Green Park, and a firework display in St James's Park.[656]

Not everyone was impressed, including William Cobbett, the contemporary historian of the period, who appeared to deprecate the practice of people enjoying themselves "from the solemn and gawdy buffoonery of the freemasons down to the little ragged children at the Lancashire schools…Upwards of two thousand oxen were roasted whole and upwards of two thousand sheep. One boundless scene of extravagance and waste, and idleness and dissipation pervaded the whole kingdom, and the people appeared to be all raving drunk, all raving mad."[657]

The celebrations, of course, proved to be slightly premature. Castereagh's careful diplomacy, over the course of the following year at the Congress of Vienna, to establish a balance of power in central Europe, was shattered by the return of Napoleon on 1st March 1815, when he landed on the Riviera coast with a cohort of Imperial Guard, intent on reclaiming his throne. Castlereagh and Wellington determined to restore the peace as settled in Vienna, with a constitutional monarchy in France, and Great Britain again financed the cause with a subsidy of five million pounds. Napoleon was finally defeated by Wellington, supported by a Prussian force under General Blucher, at the Battle of Waterloo in June 1815.

XXI: EMMA

It was in early 1814 that Jane had begun, and through the course of this tumultuous period in English history that she completed, her next novel; namely, *Emma*. It was during that same period that her niece, Anna, now engaged to the son of her great friend Mrs Lefroy, sent her the manuscript of a novel which she was writing. Jane was happy to give her some advice, and four letters from Jane to her niece have survived from the summer of 1814[658]. Jane found it extremely entertaining and read it aloud to Mrs Austen, and her sister. They were "all very much pleased."

The naturalism of Jane Austen's style was well ahead of its time, and this prompts her to offer some gentle corrections to her much younger niece. "Devereux Forester's being ruined by his vanity is extremely good, but I wish you would not let him plunge into a 'vortex of dissipation.' I do not object to the thing, but I cannot bear the expression; it is such thorough novel slang, and so old that I dare say Adam met with it in the first novel he opened... I do not like a lover speaking in the 3rd person;...I think it not natural. If you think differently, however, you need not mind me...I have scratched out Sir Thos. from walking with the others to the stables, etc. the very day after breaking his arm; for though I find your papa [James] did walk out immediately after his arm was set, I think it can be so little usual as to appear unnatural in a book. Lynn will not do. Lynn is towards forty miles from Dawlish and would not be talked of there. I have put Starcross instead. If you prefer Easton, that must always be safe. I have also scratched out the introduction between Lord Portman and his brother and Mr Griffin. A country surgeon (don't tell Mr C Lyford) would not be introduced to men of their rank...They must be two days going from Dawlish to Bath. They are nearly one hundred miles apart...and we think you had better not leave England. Let the Portmans go to Ireland; but as you know nothing of the manners there, you had better not go with them. You will be in danger of giving false representations. Stick to Bath and the Foresters. There you will be quite at home." In other words, write what you know, and be original – excellent advice for any novelist.

Her advice on the development of the plot and character is revealing, given, as it was, in the wake of *Mansfield Park,* and during the maturation and perfection of *Emma.* "You are now collecting your people delightfully, getting them exactly into such a spot as is the delight of my life. Three or four families in a country village is the very thing to work on, and I hope you will do a great deal more, and make full use of them while they are so very favourably arranged...Henry Mellish will be, I am afraid, too much in the common novel style, - a handsome, amiable, unexceptionable young man (such as do not much abound in real life) desperately in love and all in vain." Perhaps she had in mind, as a contrast, her own, nascent Mr Churchill. "I wish you could make Mrs Forester talk more; but she must be difficult to manage and make entertaining, because there is so much good sense and propriety about her that nothing can be made very broad. Her economy and ambition must not be very staring." Here, one suspects, Jane was thinking of her own superior creations: Mrs Norris and Mrs Elton. "Miss Egerton does not entirely satisfy us. She is too formal and solemn, we think, in her advice to her brother not to fall in love; and it is hardly like a sensible woman – it is putting it into his head. We should like a few more hints from her better." In other words, the sort of subtle hints, and manipulations, of which her Emma would become the mistress.

There was even a little plagiarism it seems. "I do think you had better omit Lady Helena's postscript. To those that are acquainted with "Pride and Prejudice" it will seem an imitation...The last chapter does not please us quite so well; we do not thoroughly like the play, perhaps from having had too much of plays in that way lately (*vide* "Mansfield Park")." The precise extent and nature of this plagiarism (which from a niece and with notice prior to publication surely must be taken as a compliment) is unclear. There is no evidence that Anna ever submitted the draft to a publisher, and it was destroyed by her, apparently in a fit of frustration, much later in her life.

In the middle of that summer of 1814, Jane went to stay with her cousins in Surrey. The Cookes lived in Great Bookham, just a few miles from Leatherhead. Leatherhead was used by Jane as the model for Highbury in her new novel. She was familiar with it as a result of previous visits over the years. She would also have been very familiar with Box Hill, the vantage point just a few miles south, which features so prominently in the plot. It is likely that this visit was prompted by a desire to sharpen her recollections of the town, and to do some further research. It is clear, not least from the criticisms she gave to Anna, that she was very particular about realism, and factual accuracy with respect to geographical location.

By the end of March 1815, the manuscript of *Emma* had been finished. Egerton liked it but did not make a good enough offer, and Jane decided, no doubt with the assistance of her brother, to approach a new publisher, John Murray. Egerton was a specialist publisher of military books, whereas Murray was more mainstream, and prestigious. He had published Lord Byron, and also Walter Scott, including *Waverley* the previous year. Murray's editor, William Gifford, reported back that, "It will certainly sell well. Of *Emma* I have nothing but good to say. I was sure of the writer before you mentioned her." Gifford also suggested that Murray should try to obtain the copyright of *Pride and Prejudice*. "I have lately read it again – tis very good [but] wretchedly printed in some places, & so pointed as to be unintelligible."[659]

In the autumn of 1815, Henry fell ill, and Jane stayed with him at his London residence in Hans Place. This made special sense because she would be able to combine the stay with making arrangements for the publication of her new novel. In October, Murray wrote to Henry to offer the sum of £450 for the copyright of *Emma*, *Mansfield Park* and *Sense and Sensibility*. Jane, growing in confidence as a writer, rejected this offer, and contemplated self-publishing once again. Henry pointed out to Murray that his sister had made more from one edition of *Mansfield Park*. Shortly afterwards, however, Henry's condition deteriorated to the extent that Jane summoned her brothers, Edward and James, along with Cassandra, to London. For a while his life appeared to be in danger but after a week he had recovered sufficiently to allow his brothers to return home. Cassandra stayed to assist her sister.

Because of her brother's poor health, Jane negotiated directly with Murray who appears to have agreed to publish two-thousand copies of *Emma* on commission, together with a second edition of *Mansfield Park*; in other words, Jane would bear the risk of the publication of *Emma*. She was now increasingly taking charge of her own affairs, and was closely monitoring the production of her work. She was frustrated with delays, and wrote to Murray on 23rd November, "Is it likely that the printers will be influenced to greater dispatch and punctuality by knowing that the work is to be dedicated to the Prince Regent? If you can make that circumstance operate, I shall be very glad."[660]

At the end of the month she informed her sister that, "The printers have been waiting for paper – the blame is thrown upon the stationer; but he [Murray] gives his word that I shall have no further cause for dissatisfaction…A sheet came in this moment; 1st and 3rd volumes are now at 144; 2nd at 48. I am sure you will like particulars. We are not to have the trouble of returning the sheets to Mr Murray's any longer, the printer's boys bring and carry…I am advanced in Volume III to my arraroot, upon which peculiar style of spelling there is a modest query in the margin."[661]

With hindsight, Jane should have accepted Murray's offer. *Mansfield Park* had not been a success, and when the second edition appeared in February 1816 it had to be sold to wholesalers at a reduced rate. The losses were set off against the profits of *Emma*, and, as a result, she only made £38 profit for the work during her lifetime. It was not as popular as her earlier novels. Of the 2,000 copies which were printed, only 1,400 were sold in the first four years, and the rest were disposed of.[662]

Henry was treated by a Dr Matthew Baillie whose patients included the Prince Regent. It has already been noted that Princess Charlotte was an admirer of Jane's work. It turned out that her reprobate of a father was also a fan. Dr Baillie told them that the Prince was a great admirer of her novels, "read them often, and kept a set in every one of his residences."[663] When Dr Baillie informed the Prince that Jane Austen was in London, he commissioned his librarian, and domestic chaplain at his London residence at Carlton House, James Stanier Clarke, to seek her out around the time that *Emma* was being printed. Clarke invited her to visit him in order to view the Royal residence, rebuilt at huge expense by the architect Henry Holland, including its magnificent forty-foot library. During the course of the visit Clarke told her that the Regent had made it known that she could dedicate any future work to His Royal Personage "without the necessity of any solicitation on my part."

Austen, no fan of the Regent, to put it politely, was underwhelmed. She didn't want to do it, and told Cassandra that nobody should know of the proposed dedication "for fear of being obliged to do it."[664] She enquired of Clarke "whether it is incumbent on me to show my sense of the Honour, by inscribing the work now in the press to HRH – I should be equally concerned to appear either presumptious or ungrateful." Clarke having confirmed that it was indeed expected, a set of *Emma,* bound in red morocco gilt, was sent to Carlton House a few days prior to its publication with a dedication inserted at the beginning of the edition. "To His Royal Highness The Prince Regent. This work is, by His Royal Highness's permission, most respectfully dedicated, by His Royal Highness's dutiful and obedient humble servant." A couple of months later, Clarke passed on "the thanks of His Royal Highness the Prince Regent" and informed her that "many of the nobility" who had been staying at the Brighton Pavilion, the Prince's outrageously extravagant pleasure house on the coast, had paid Jane "the just tribute of their praise."[665]

Clarke had become a little besotted by Jane, and initiated an exchange of correspondence between them which lasted a number of months. He invited her to write a historical romance founded on the Royal House of Saxe Coburg. She politely, and with a touch of subtle irony, declined the honour. Such a romance "might be much more to the purpose of profit or popularity than such pictures of domestic life in country villages as I deal in. No – I must keep to my own style & go on in my own way; and though I may never succeed again in that, I am convinced that I should totally fail in any other."[666]

Being a little too pleased with himself as the domestic chaplain to the Regent, Clarke also suggested a book about "the habits of life and character and enthusiasm of a clergyman – who should pass his time between the metropolis and the country...fond of and entirely engaged in literature – no man's enemy but his own."[667] Jane was similarly unimpressed by his patronising tone, and indulged in a little ironic self-deprecation. "The comic part of the character I might be equal to," she said with a tongue firmly in her cheek, "but not the good, the enthusiastic, the literary...Such a man's conversation must at times be on subjects of science and philosophy, of which I know nothing – or at least be occasionally abundant in quotations and allusions which a woman, who like me, knows only her own mother-tongue and has read very little in that, would be totally without the power of giving – A classical education, or at any rate, a very extensive acquaintance with English literature, ancient and modern, appears to me quite indispensable for the person who would do any justice to your clergyman – And I think I may boast myself to be, with all possible vanity, the most unlearned and uninformed female who ever dared to be an authoress."[668]

By the end of November, Henry was on the mend. "Henry gets out in his garden every day, but at present his inclination for doing more seems over..."[669] They paid visits to her brother Charles's children in Keppel Street, now being looked after by their maternal aunt, Harriet Palmer, following the death of their mother in childbirth. They were visited in turn by Edward, and by Fanny, who had a flirtation with a Mr Haden, a medical man from Edinburgh who often came to dine. She wrote in her diary that "a delightful clever musical 'Haden' comes every evening & is agreeable." Jane seems to have approved. "Tomorrow Mr Haden is to dine with us," she wrote to her sister. "There is happiness! We really grow so fond of Mr Haden that I do not know what to expect...Fanny played, and he sat and listened and suggested improvements...It is Mr Haden's firm belief that a person not musical is fit for every sort of wickedness. I ventured to assert a little on the other side, but wished the cause in abler hands."[670] Later she gushed, "Mr H is reading 'Mansfield Park' for the first time, and prefers it to P and P."[671]

Cassandra appears to have been under the impression that Mr Haden was socially inferior, and not a suitable suitor for her niece. Jane had some fun teasing her in a letter of 2nd December. "You call him an apothecary. He is no apothecary, he has never been an apothecary; there is not an apothecary in this neighbourhood – the only inconvenience of the situation perhaps – but so it is; we have not a medical man within reach. He is a Haden, nothing but a Haden, a sort of wonderful nondescript creature on two legs, something between a man and an angel, but without the least spice of an apothecary. He is, perhaps, the only person not an apothecary hereabouts."[672]

In the meantime, Jane's fourth published novel had been printed. It was advertised in the *Morning Post* on 2nd December as a forthcoming publication. On the 11th, Jane wrote to Murray, and was clearly still very much in control of her own business, despite Henry's recovery. "I beg you to understand that I leave the terms on which the trade should be supplied with the work entirely to your judgment, entreating you to be guided in every such arrangement by your own experience of what is most likely to clear off the edition rapidly…The title page must be "Emma, dedicated by permission to HRH the Prince Regent." And it is my particular wish that one set should be completed and sent to HRH two or three days before the work is generally public…I shall subjoin a list of those persons to whom I must trouble you to forward also a set each, when the work is out; all unbound, with "From the Authoress" in the first page."[673]

She returned to Chawton on the 16th,[674] and then, on 23rd December 1815, a week after Jane's fortieth birthday, an advert appeared on the front page of the *Morning Chronicle*, declaring that amongst the books published that day was *Emma*, a novel by the author of *Pride and Prejudice.*" Two thousand copies were issued, and it was printed in three volumes at the price of one guinea.[675] Jane was apprehensive about the reception. In December 1815, she wrote to Clarke of her anxiety "that this 4th work should not disgrace what was good in the others...I am very strongly haunted by the idea that to those readers who have preferred P & P it will appear inferior in wit, & to those who have preferred MP very inferior in good sense."[676] She was not far off the mark.

As she had done for *Mansfield Park,* Jane made notes recording the opinions of *Emma* expressed by those of her immediate acquaintance, and family.[677] Her brother Frank "liked it extremely, observing that though there might be more wit in P & P - & an higher morality in MP - yet altogether, on account of its peculiar air of nature throughout, he preferred it to either." Charles was delighted with it, "more so I think than even with my favourite Pride & Prejudice, & I have read it three times in the passage." He was proud of Jane. On 12th August he wrote to a Mrs Liston in Edinburgh from Broadstairs, where he was on holiday with his children, and said, "Have you seen my sister's last novel *Emma.*"[678]

Cassandra liked it "better than P & P – but not so well as MP," whereas her mother "thought it more entertaining than MP – but not so interesting as P & P." A Mrs Guiton thought it "too natural to be interesting" which may be a testament to Jane's realistic style. The general opinion, however, is that it did not quite meet the standards set by her two previous novels. This may have been due, in part, to the fact that the leading lady is more morally ambiguous than Austen's other heroines; Fanny, for example, "could not bear Emma herself."

It is the Scottish novelist, Susan Ferrier, who may have written the most perspicacious assessment, although it is unclear if it ever came to Jane's attention. "I have been reading *Emma* which is excellent; there is no story whatever, and the heroine is not better than other people; but the characters are all so true to life, and the style is so piquant, that it does not require the adventitious aids of mystery and adventure."[679] It is true that the plot of *Emma* lacks the richness of the other novels. Its appeal lies more on character and dialogue, and a startling naturalism which was an important milestone in the development of the novel as an art form. The subtlety of this appears to have passed by the notice of a number of reviewers. The *British Lady's Magazine* was bored by Miss Bates, and the *Augustan Review* agreed, complaining of too little action, and too much of Miss Bates's gossip.[680]

However the naturalism of *Emma* was ostensibly appreciated by a more illustrious source. John Murray apparently asked Sir Walter Scott to write an article on Jane's work in his periodical, the *Quarterly Review*. The article praises the art involved in "copying from nature as she really exists in the common walks of life, and presenting to the reader, instead of the splendid scenes of an imaginary world, a correct and striking representation of that which is daily taking place around him...quiet yet comic dialogue, in which the characters of the speakers evolve themselves with dramatic effect."[681] Some doubt has been raised, however, as to the authorship of this article. Murray never informed Jane that the article had been written by Sir Walter Scott, and the writer unaccountably appears to have been unaware of *Mansfield Park*. A textual analysis suggests it may in fact have been written by John Whately, later the Archbishop of Dublin, who subsequently wrote a review of Austen in 1821.[682]

Emma Woodhouse, "handsome, clever and rich"[683], lives with her widowed, and hypochondriacal, father at Hartfield in the village of Highbury, some sixteen miles from London. It is a large and populous village and the Woodhouses are the "first in consequence"[684]. Emma, who has been over-indulged by her weak but loving father, is kind and well-meaning, but she also has a quality of mischief about her which, when coupled with her predilection for interfering in the lives of others, leads to trouble.

Emma, now twenty-one, is the younger of two daughters. Her sister, Isabella, has married John Knightley, an attorney in London. His brother, George Knightley, is the local squire, a man of 37 or 38, who holds the grand estate of Donwell Abbey in the adjoining parish. Emma has known him all her life, and has looked up to him as an older brother. He is very fond of her but "one of the few people who could see faults in Emma Woodhouse, and the only one who ever told her of them."[685] Neither of them appear to realise, let alone to articulate, that their feelings for each other are far more than the fraternal.

At the beginning of the novel, there are four other principal characters. Miss Taylor, Emma's beloved governess, whom Emma looks upon as an older sister, has married Mr Weston who lives at Randalls, just half a mile away. Emma congratulates herself on having been responsible for the happy match, and it is that success which goes to her head. Two of the subjects of her future attempts at match-making are Mr Elton, the village parson, and Harriet Smith, a foolish but good-natured girl of 17, and of unknown parentage, "the natural daughter of somebody"[686], who has been boarding at Miss Goddard's school for young ladies.

Miss Goddard introduces Harriet to Emma. Emma seizes upon Harriet as a substitute for her lost companion, Miss Taylor. Assuming Harriet to be of genteel birth, an assumption based more on hope than substance, Emma sets herself the project of "improving" Harriet, as if she were an outsourced finishing school. This includes trying her hand at match-making once more. She incites Harriet to think of Mr Elton by being a little creative with the truth. She repeats "some warm personal praise which she had drawn from Mr Elton, and now did full justice to..."[687]

In the meantime, Harriet has received a proposal of marriage from Robert Martin, a local farmer, who is at the lower end of gentility, and in whose household Harriet has boarded for a couple of months. Harriet is very fond of Mr Martin. She is excited by the proposal and is inclined to accept. However, Emma, a terrible snob, is horrified, and tries her best to alienate Harriet from her suitor: "...if she were not taken care of, she might be required to sink herself forever."[688] Emma means well but, in truth, is also selfishly motivated by imagining the sort of people she might be required to mix with. She persuades Harriet to turn Martin down. George Knightley, who throughout the novel is Emma's moral conscience, is angry when he hears of Emma's manipulations. Indeed, it was he who advised Mr Martin to make the proposal. He believes that Emma is over-estimating Harriet's social status in thinking her a good match for Elton.

Emma's sister, Isabella, and her family come to stay for Christmas. Her husband, John Knightley, a cynical lawyer, much in the same mould as Mr Palmer in *Sense and Sensibility*, suspects that Elton's attentions are really directed at Emma herself. This proves to be true. When Harriet is unable to go to Randalls for a Christmas party because of a bad cold, Elton, much to Emma's surprise, is indifferent. Later, when Emma and he share a carriage, Elton, who has had too much wine, declares himself to her. She refuses him, and says that she thought his attentions were directed at Harriet. Elton tells her that he regards Harriet as being below him. George Knightley has been proved, not for the first time, by far the better judge.

There are three other characters who enter the narrative from outside Highbury. Frank Churchill is the son of Mr Weston by his previous marriage some twenty years earlier. Frank was adopted by his uncle, in much the same way that Edward Austen was adopted by Mr Knight. Frank is due to visit his father and new step-mother, Miss Taylor at Randalls. There has always been a certain tension about the prospect of Frank meeting Emma, and Mr Weston clearly has unspoken hopes of their marrying. Emma is conscious of this weight of expectation: "...if she were to marry, he was the very person to suit her in age, character, and condition...she had a great curiosity to see him, a decided intention of finding him pleasant, of being liked by him to a certain degree, and a sort of pleasure in the idea of their being coupled in their friends' imaginations."[689]

The second intruder is Jane Fairfax. She is the niece of the kindly but verbally incontinent Miss Bates, whose mother is the local widow who has fallen on hard times. After the death of her father, Jane was brought up by Miss Bates and her mother in Highbury but was then taken in by a friend of her father to be educated for a governess. She has been absent from Highbury for two years. Emma is jealous of Jane, partly because of her acquaintance with Frank Churchill, but also because, as Mr Knightley once told her, "...she saw in her the really accomplished young woman which she wanted to be thought herself."[690] The third intruder is Miss Augusta Hawkins. Elton, following his rejection by Emma, goes to Bath to escape his embarrassment. It is there that he meets Miss Hawkins and they marry.

Frank arrives for a fortnight. Emma likes him. He is certainly determined to please her, and he appeals to her vanity. Later she reflects that her "...vanity was flattered, and I allowed his attentions."[691] His attentions, however, are false, and are, in effect, a blind to conceal his secret engagement to Jane Faifax, who would never be acceptable to his capricious aunt, Mrs Churchill. An early sign of Frank's flaws is when he takes the thirty-two mile round trip to have a hair cut in London.

Emma is prepared to excuse him but Knightley, perspicacious as always, takes it as proof that Frank is 'just the trifling, silly fellow I took him for."[692] In truth, Knightley's dislike of Frank is also fuelled by a sub-conscious jealousy of his friendship with Emma.

Frank and Emma plan a ball at the Crown Inn but he is called home by his aunt before it can take place. Before he leaves he is about to tell Emma something of importance, and she thinks it is a declaration, about which she is uncertain, and therefore puts him off. In fact, he was about to tell her of his secret engagement to Jane. Having convinced herself that she is not in love with him, Emma then sets about trying to pair Frank with Harriet, an even more unsuitable match than with Mr Elton.

Mr and Mrs Elton return from Bath following their marriage. The palpable awkwardness is summed up by the first meeting between the Eltons and Emma, who brings Harriet with her to cure Harriet of her infatuation with Elton, brought about by Emma's ill-judged match-making. "Mr Elton was in being in the same room at once with the woman he had just married, the woman he had wanted to marry, and the woman whom he had been expected to marry, she must allow him to have the right to look as little wise, and to be as much affectedly, and as little really easy as could be."[693] Harriet, who has the constancy of a mayfly, begins to put Elton out of her mind. She starts to talk of someone whom she admires but who is too far above her. Emma thinks she is referring to Frank; in fact she is thinking of George Knightley.

The Churchills are staying in town, and Frank is expected to spend much of his time at Randalls. Two social events are organised for successive days: strawberry picking at Donwell Abbey, followed by a cold supper, and a picnic at Box Hill. At Donwell, Jane Fairfax is in a state of distress, and walks back to Highbury on her own in the heat of the day. Unbeknown to Emma, she is distressed by the absence of her secret fiancé. Later, Frank attends, in a similar state of distress at Jane's absence. Emma, clueless as to the reality, still intends to make a match of Frank and Harriet.

Mrs Elton manages to secure Jane a post as a governess. She reluctantly accepts, having despaired of ever being united with Frank. Hard on the heels of this event, however, is the death of Frank's aunt, the chief obstacle to their marriage. Frank reveals his engagement to the Westons. They, believing Emma to be attached to Frank, summon Emma to convey the news, only to be relieved to discover that she is indifferent to him, and, in fact, delighted by it.

However, Emma dreads having to convey the news to Harriet, who she believes to be in love with Frank. She is perplexed when Harriet receives the news with equanimity, and Emma then realises, to her great distress, that the person of superior qualities to whom Harriet has been referring is none other than George Knightley. It is at this point that Emma consciously realises that she is in love with Knightley herself. "It darted through her with the speed of an arrow that Mr Knightley must marry no one but herself."[694] Emma now appreciates that her attempts, albeit well-meaning, to manipulate the lives of others have been badly mistaken. "She was sorrowfully indignant; ashamed of every sensation but the one revealed to her – her affection for Mr Knightley – Every other part of her mind was disgusting."[695] She even begins to regret her initial success in separating Harriet from Mr Martin, and realises that they were a perfect match after all.

Knightley also believed Emma to have been in love with Frank Churchill. On hearing of the engagement between Frank and Jane Fairfax, he goes to Emma with the purpose of consoling her, but also imbued with a new hope for his own chances. He is on the point of declaring himself to her but Emma, thinking that he is about to declare his affections for Harriet, stops him in mid-flow. This almost derails the whole project but Knightley, in the end, proposes, and Emma accepts.

The perfection of Emma's happiness is still impeded by two factors. First, she cannot bring herself to leave her father, and resolves to stay unmarried whilst he lives. Secondly, she feels guilt over Harriet whom she has led up the garden path three times, and apparently destroyed her chance of happiness. Both these issues are resolved. Knightley declares that he will move in with Emma and her father at Hartfield, "so long as her father's happiness – in other words his life – required."[696] Meanwhile, Harriet has gone to stay, at Emma's suggestion, with Isabella in London. Here she fortuitously encounters Robert Martin. He renews his proposal, and she accepts. He has in truth always been the object of her affections, and it has only been the ill-judged interventions of Emma which have planted unattainable and unsuitable fancies in her mind.

Jane Austen withholds her approbation from Emma Woodhouse more obviously than she withholds it from her other heroines. This is proclaimed from the very beginning. "Emma doing just what she liked; highly esteeming Miss Taylor's judgment, but directed chiefly by her own...the power of having her own way, and a disposition to think a little too well of herself."[697] Elinor Dashwood, Elizabeth Bennett, Fanny Price, Anne Elliott, and even Catherine Morland, are the recipients of their creator's, almost unqualified, approval. Emma is not. She is the most morally ambiguous of all Austen's heroines, and her actions cause instability rather than order, and confusion rather than concensus.

Emma, in contrast to Mrs Elton, is never malicious, nor is she consciously unkind. However, she is vain, selfish and (if it is not too anachronistic to say so) a snob. She looks down upon Mr Martin as a yeoman, and her principal motive for discouraging Harriet's attachment is so that she can retain her, whom she has collected as a replacement for Miss Taylor, within her social circle. Mr Knightley, often Emma's moral conscience, can see what she cannot, or will not. "You will puff her up with such idea of her own beauty, of what she has a claim to, that in a little while, nobody within her reach will be good enough for her."[698]

The fact that Austen does not approve of Emma is in fact essential, not just to the plot, but also to the style of this novel, because the disalignment of author and character facilitates the perfection of the ironic authorial voice. This is the device which had been honed in the earlier novels, but which reaches its apogee in *Emma*, as a result of this divergence between author and heroine. It is the very essence of Jane Austen's art. When Emma persuades Harriet to turn down Mr Martin by explaining that she would never be able to visit her, for example, Austen brilliantly punctures Emma's vanity with a quill dripping with irony. "Harriet had not surmised her own danger, but the idea of it struck her forcibly."[699] Emma's manipulative tendencies are ruthlessly critiqued by Austen through this device of irony. The effect is amplified further in this novel because Emma, in seeking to manipulate the fates of those around her is, in a sense, acting the role of the novelist herself. The effect is not dissimilar to that of the painting of the artist painting a picture of the artist at work.

At first glance, the author appears to be with Emma, approving of her behaviour, but in fact mocking it. When Emma manipulates Mr Elton into taking Harriet's portrait to be framed in London: "'He was too good – she could not endure the thought! She would not give him such a troublesome office for the world' – brought on the desired repetition of entreaties and assurances, and a very few minutes settled the business." In order to facilitate the intended alliance between Harriet and Elton, she manipulates Harriet into a decisive rejection of Robert Martin: "Emma continued to protest against any assistance being wanted, it was in fact given in the formation of every sentence...it was particularly necessary to brace her up with a few decisive expressions..."[700]

The moral ambivalence of Emma's behaviour is brutally exposed and examined. Emma convinces herself on one level that her project of trying to alienate Harriet from Mr Martin is the right course, but on another she knows it to be wrong. "She would have given a great deal, or endured a great deal, to have had the Martins in a higher rank of life. They were so deserving that a little higher should have been enough: but as it was, how could she have done otherwise?"[701] Ultimately she knows that she is being intellectually dishonest. It is only through the device of the ironical authorial voice that this can be so effectively dissected and examined. "She leaned back in the corner, to indulge her murmurs, or to reason them away; probably a little of both – such being the commonest process of a not ill-disposed mind."[702]

Emma's hypocrisy in finally convincing herself to attend the Coles' *soirée*, notwithstanding their perceived social unacceptability, is ruthlessly exposed: She is at once scornful of their social standing but offended when she thinks she has been omitted from the guest list: "She felt she should like to have had the power of refusal."[703] When she finally receives an invitation, she convinces herself to go by a process of self-deception: "...all that she might have lost on the side of dignified seclusion, must be amply repaid in the splendour of popularity. She must have delighted the Coles – worthy people who deserved to be made happy! – And left a name behind her that would not soon die away."[704]

It is also in *Emma* that one sees most vividly the naturalism which had become typical of Jane Austen's style, and which marked an important development in the English novel; a development which would lead to the realism of Charles Dickens, the Brontës, and Thomas Hardy later in the century. This is also reflected in the dialogue. There is a degree of naturalism for which there was little precedent. This is evident in the banter between Emma and Knightley, notably more naturalistic than that between, for example, Elizabeth Bennett and Mr Darcy. And so there is the following exchange between Emma and Knightley about Emma's attempts to improve Harriet.

"'Come,' said he, 'you are anxious for a compliment, so I will tell you that you have improved her. You have cured her of her school girl giggle; she really does you credit."

'Thank you. I should be mortified indeed if I did not believe I had been of some use; but it is not everybody who will bestow praise where they may. You do not often overpower me with it.'"[705]

This realism is evident too in the dialogue between Frank and Emma; for example, when they are feeding off each other's gossip about Jane Fairfax and Mr Dixon.[706] This naturalistic style, though is still in development, and it does lead in certain passages to vapidity. In particular, we are treated a little too often to the vapid chatter of Mr Woodhouse about the evils of marriage[707], and his concerns for other people's health[708]. This tries the temper of John Knightley to breaking point, and has a similar effect on the reader. Even Emma's attempts to stop her father are in vain. It is these passages of proto-naturalism which perhaps prevent *Emma*, contrary to the assertions of many critics, from being Austen's greatest novel.

But it is the middling characters such as Miss Bates and Harriet who speak in the most naturalistic style; see, for example, Miss Bates's stream of consciousness at the Crown Inn ball[709], or Harriet's description of her chance meeting with the Martins in Fords[710]. They speak as real people speak in everyday life; not in fluent constructed and finished sentences, but rapidly flitting from topic to topic, with digressions, repetition, meaningless oratorical interpolations, and assumptions about the prior knowledge of the interlocutor.

Emma, to a greater extent than any of the other other novels, describes the stable and pyramidical society in which Jane was writing.[711] The work is both broader in its expansive cast of characters, but also deeper in its portrayal of the many layers of the English class system in the early nineteenth century. At the top of the pyramid is Mr Knightley, the local squire, resident at the great estate of Donwell Abbey. Mr Woodhouse and Mr Weston just below, at Hartfield and Randalls respectively, form the second tier of gentility. Beneath them comes the clergy, in the form of Mr Elton, and Mrs Bates – the widow of a vicar, although since fallen on harder times. She and her daughter are reduced to living on one floor in a house which "belonged to people in business."[712] Jane Fairfax, Miss Bates's niece, has been brought up in genteel society by the Campbells, but is destined to be a governess. It is their origin which in turn distinguishes them from the Coles who, although wealthy, and second only in material terms to Mr Woodhouse in Highbury, are looked down upon by Emma because they are of "low origin, in trade, and only moderately genteel."[713] Harriet Smith is assumed by Emma to be of genteel birth, simply because Emma wills it to be so. She would not wish to mix with anybody of a lower pedigree.

Then there are those who are just below the minimum threshold for social acceptability, in the sense of being included, or potentially included, within the same social circle. These include the likes of Mr Perry who, whilst being Mr Woodhouse's highly valued and esteemed physician, would never be invited to dinner, and Robert Martin the farmer who, whilst keeping an upper maid, two parlours and a summerhouse, is regarded by Emma as no more than a yeoman. There are also the tradesmen. Fords, the village store, is featured in a couple of scenes. Frank decides to buy a pair of gloves, "…sleek, well tied parcels of Men's beavers and York Tan were bringing down and displaying on the counter."

The next layer are the servants, perhaps portrayed in this novel, together with their thoughts and feelings, more extensively than any other in the Austen canon. There is Knightley's housekeeper, Mrs Hodges, and his man, William Larkins, who comes over with the large basket of apples for Mrs Bates and her daughter. Miss Bates reports, in her inimitable style, that she spoke to William, "and said everything, as you may suppose. William Larkins is such an old acquaintance! I am always glad to see him. But, however, I found afterwards from Patty [Mrs Bates's occasional maid] that William said it was all the apples of that sort his master had; he had brought them all – and now his master had not one left to bake or boil. William did not seem to mind it himself, he was pleased to think his master had sold so many; for William, you know, thinks more of his master's profit than anything; but Mrs Hodges, he said, was quite displeased at their being all sent away. She could not bear that her master should not be able to have another apple-tart this spring. He told Patty this, but bid her not mind it, and be sure not to say anything to us about it, for Mrs Hodges would be cross sometimes, as long as so many sacks were sold, it did not signify who ate the remainder."[714]

Then there are the indigent poor. John Abdy was clerk to old Mr Bates, but is now an old man fallen on hard times, bed-ridden and very poorly "with the rheumatic gout in his joints", who is reliant on relief from the parish.[715] And then there are the poor and the sick who live in the cottage a little way out of Highbury, whom Emma visits to bring relief. "She understood their ways, could allow for their ignorance and their temptations, had no romantic expectations of extraordinary virtue from those, for whom education had done so little... and after remaining there as long as she could give comfort or advice, she quitted the cottage with such an impression of the scene as made her to say to Harriet, as they walked away, 'These are the sights, Harriet, to do one good. How trifling they make everything else appear.'"[716]

At the very bottom of this pyramid are those in the penumbra of society – beggars, thieves, and vagrants; personified by a party of gipsies "on a broader patch of greensward by the side...a child on the watch" who begs; "...an invitation to attack could not be resisted, and Harriet was soon assailed by half a dozen children, headed by a stout woman and a great boy, all clamorous, and impertinent in look...she was followed, or rather surrounded, by the whole gang, demanding more."[717]

It is from the door of Fords that Emma observes the whole panorama of village life, in a passage of sparkling realism: "...Mr Perry walking hastily by, Mr William Cox letting himself in at the office door, Mr Cole's carriage horses returning from exercise, or a stray letter on an obstinate mule, were the liveliest objects she could presume to expect, and when her eyes fell only on the butcher with his tray, a tidy old woman travelling homewards from shop with her full basket, two curs quarrelling over a dirty bone, and a string of dawdling children round the baker's little bow-window eyeing the gingerbread, she knew she had no reason to complain..."[718]

At the beginning of the novel, this social structure is stable and unthreatened, as is Emma's life. She has "a comfortable home and happy disposition, seemed to unite some of the best blessings of existence, and had lived nearly twenty-one years in the world with very little to distress or vex her."[719] At the pinnacle of this society is George Knightley who personifies its conservatism. As in *Mansfield Park*, Jane Austen draws a comparision between the conservation of the natural order and the preservation of social order. Emma admires, in particular, Mr Knightley's husbandry. "She felt all the honest pride and complacency which her alliance with the present and future proprietor could fairly warrant, as she viewed the respectable size and style of the building...its ample gardens stretching down to meadows washed by a stream...and its abundance of timber in rows and avenues, which neither fashion nor extravagance had rooted up...it was just what it ought to be, and it looked what it was – and Emma felt an increasing respect for it, as the residence of a family of such true gentility, untainted in blood and understanding."[720]

It is the middling classes, however, who are at the heart of this community. Miss Bates, although ridiculous, is kind and compassionate, and insightful, and perhaps something of an *idiot savant.* She is a gossip, and it is gossip which binds the community together: "a great talker upon little matters, which exactly suited Mr Woodhouse, full of trivial communications and harmless gossip."[721] Moreover, it is she who values the community above all else. "If ever there were people who, without having great wealth themselves, had everything they could wish for, I am sure it is us. We may well say that, "our lot is cast in a goodly heritage."[722]

However, the stability of this structure is threatened by intruders, most obviously Frank Churchill, unreliable, duplicitous and restless, and whose "indifference to a confusion of rank, bordered too much on inelegance of mind."[723] It is Emma's childish impulse to conspire with Frank in mischief that leads her into uncharacteristic unkindness. She is tempted into malicious gossip about Jane Fairfax, and is hurtful in her remarks to Miss Bates at the Boxhill picnic which attracts the ire of George Knightley. It is only when Emma learns of Frank's surreptitious engagement to Miss Fairfax that she appreciates his subversive influence. "So unlike what a man should be! None of that upright integrity, that strict adherence to truth and principle, that disdain of trick and littleness, which a man should display in every transaction of his life."[724] She might have added, "unlike Mr Knightley".

Mrs Elton is almost as subversive. She calls Mr Knightley "Knightley", is self-important, vain and ill-bred, and "had a little beauty and a little accomplishment, but so little judgment that she thought herself coming with superior knowledge of the world, to enliven and improve a country neighbourhood..."[725] Again, the contrast with George Knightley, and his distrust of 'improvements', is obvious. She is critical of his household, and "would not have such a creature as his Harry stand at our sideboard for any consideration."[726] She is intent on reforming the society into which she is a mere novitiate. She considers it to be "a good deal behind hand in knowledge of the world, but she would soon show them how everything ought to be arranged."[727]

It is not just the intruders who exert a subversive influence on the stability of the social structure. Emma, with her ill-considered meddling, is also in danger of disrupting it by encouraging Harriet to look beyond her natural station. It is only at the end of the novel that Emma realises her error. "What a connection had she been preparing for Mr Knightley – or for the Churchills – or even for Mr Elton! – the stain of illegitimacy, unbleached by nobility or wealth, would have been a stain indeed." It is coincident with her engagement to Mr Knightley that the natural order is restored, and she encourages Harriet to revert to Robert Martin: "...in the home he offered, there would be the hope of more, of security, stability and improvement."[728] Whereas in *Mansfield Park* there is a disintegration and inspection of the moral order, followed by its restoration; so in *Emma* there is an inspection and a restoration of the social order.

In the end Emma is revealed to be, at least in the eyes of Mr Knightley if not objectively so, "...faultless in spite of all her faults."[729] Like a complex piece of art, she is flawed in some of the brushstrokes, but when the observer stands back and regards the whole, she is perfect. Perhaps the same can be said for this novel itself, and for the conservative and pyramidical society it portrays. It is fitting perhaps that its publication coincided with the supposed restoration of the old order in Europe after the revolutionary wars; however fleeting and illusory that restoration turned out to be.

XXII: PERSUASION

It was in the early August of 1815, some four and a half months before the publication of *Emma,* that Jane began her final completed work, *Persuasion.* The novel was written against the backdrop of an increasingly dark period in the fortunes of the Austen family. Not only had they recently experienced the sad death of Charles's wife in childbirth, and the ill-health of his daughter Harriet (she had 'water on the brain'[730]) but Jane's financial security was once again thrown into doubt.

Although Jane had invested her profits so far (about six-hundred pounds) in five per cent Navy stock, and so would avoid penury, the apparent failure of *Emma* and the second edition of *Mansfield Park* must have caused her to doubt that she could make a good living from her writing. Moreover, two worrying events threatened the financial security of the family more generally. First, Edward was facing a challenge in the courts with regard to the legality of the inheritance of his Hampshire properties from the Knight family because he was not their blood relative. These properties included, of course, the Chawton Great House and the Cottage. The legal action was only settled in 1818 when Edward paid off the claimants by raising £15,000 from cutting down much of the timber in Chawton Park. Therefore, for the rest of her life, Jane's home was under threat.

Secondly, Henry, who had already made some bad business

decisions, was a victim of the economic crisis which came with the coming of peace; the fall in demand from the government for foodstuffs, cloth, and other goods, the resulting deflation, and the significant drop in the value of monies being handled for the army by his bank. The bank was badly over-extended. He went bankrupt in March 1816, and left London. He was to take orders to be a curate at Chawton, and divided his time between Steventon, Chawton and Godmersham, but not before making a hopeless visit to Restoration France to see if he could recover some of the de Feuillide property.

Edward, on top of his other woes, lost £20,000 with the collapse of the bank. Charles and James lost hundreds, and it had cost Jane the twenty-five pounds in her account; not a fortune, but a sizeable amount by her standards. Neither Henry, nor Frank, who was now on half pay, could maintain their annual contributions of fifty pounds to their mother's household, which they had made since their father's death. According to Fanny's diary, "The principal event of this year has been the failure of Uncle H Austen's bank & consequent distress to most of the family." Jane wrote to her publisher asking him to communicate directly with her in future at Chawton, "in consequence of the late sad event in Henrietta Street."[731]

In early 1816, as well as continuing to work on *Persuasion*, Jane re-purchased the manuscript of *Susan* from Crosby & Co anonymously. According to her nephew, she harboured a lingering resentment at Crosby for leaving this work on the shelf, and a degree of pleasure in the irony of its re-acquisition. "One of her brothers [presumably Henry who showed a remarkable lack of contrition following his bankruptcy] undertook the negotiation. He found the purchaser very willing to receive back his money, and to resign all claim to the copyright. When the bargain was concluded and the money paid, but not till then, the negotiator had the satisfaction of informing him that the work which had been so lightly esteemed was by the author of *Pride and Prejudice*."[732]

Jane continued to work on *Persuasion*, and tinkered with the draft of *Susan,* changing the name of the heroine to Catherine, which was to be published, after her death, as *Northanger Abbey*. As early as March of 1816 she wrote to Fanny about these two projects. "'Miss Catherine' is put upon the shelf for the present, and I do not know that she will ever come out; but I have a something ready for publication, which may, perhaps, appear about a twelvemonth hence. It is short, about the length of 'Catherine'...You will not like it, so you need not be impatient. You may perhaps like the heroine, as she is almost too good for me."[733]

But Jane's health was beginning to fail. Back in 1813, she had been suffering from pain in her face. On 18th July of that year, Fanny Knight recorded in her diary: "At. J. confined to the house with a bad face ache in the eveng. I staid with her, the others walked." On the 24th, "At. Jane came to see me and caught fresh cold in her face." On 1st August she reported that Jane's face had been "very indifferent all this week." The next day she "suffered sadly".[734] The cause is unknown but it may have been sinusitis, or trigeminal neuralgia which can result in severe shooting pains. In the days before paracetemol and antibiotics, these were not minor complaints. Nor it seems were these transient conditions. Fanny's sister later recalled that her aunt would sometimes walk along the path to the Great House with her "head a little to one side, and sometimes a very small cushion pressed against her cheek, as if she were suffering from face-ache, as she not unfrequently did in later life."[735]

From early 1816, Jane, who was generally of a stoical disposition, even by the standards of the time, began to mention her ill-health in her letters. She referred to it as 'rheumatism'. On 20th February, she wrote to Fanny, "I am almost entirely cured of my rheumatism, - just a little pain in my knee now and then to make me remember what it was, and keep on flannel. Aunt Cassandra nursed me so beautifully."[736] In March, though, it appears that there were issues with her mobility. She was "tolerably well again, quite equal to walking about and enjoying the air, and by sitting down and resting a good while between my walks I get exercise enough. I have a scheme, however, for accomplishing more, as the weather grows spring-like. I mean to take to riding the donkey; it will be more independent and less troublesome than the use of the carriage, and I shall be able to go about with Aunt Cassandra in her walks…"[737]

In a letter to her niece, Caroline, she wrote, "I have taken one ride on the donkey, and I like it very much, and you must try to get me quiet mild days that I may be able to go out pretty constantly – a great deal of wind does not suit me, as I still have a tendency to rheumatism." Caroline recorded in her *Memoir* the visible signs of her aunt's failing health. "In my later visits to Chawton Cottage, I remember Aunt Jane used often to lie down after dinner – My grandmother herself was frequently on the sofa – sometimes in the afternoon, sometimes in the evening, at no fixed period of the day, - She had not bad health for her age, and she worked often for hours in the garden, and naturally wanted rest afterwards – There was only one sofa in the room – and Aunt Jane laid upon 3 chairs which she arranged for herself…"[738]

On 23rd May, Jane and Casssandra went to Cheltenham in Gloucestershire for a week or two[739], at that time in its heyday as a spa town, with assembly rooms, theatre, concerts and libraries. In all probability this was for reasons of health. Visitors, which included Princess Victoria, the Duke of

Wellington, and Lord Byron, would take the waters at either the original spa, or one of the rival spas at Montpellier and Pittville. Several of the spas had tree-lined walks, rides and gardens in which bands of musicians would perform. There were public breakfasts, entertainments, and firework displays. There were balls and concerts at the assembly rooms, and plays at the Theatre Royal. It was, in fact, a Regency alternative to Bath, a town of which Jane and her sister had probably had quite enough.[740]

On their return, they stayed with their old friends the Fowles at Kintbury. Caroline later recalled a conversation with Mary Fowle who told her that "Aunt Jane went over the old places, and recalled old recollections associated with them, in a very particular manner – looked at them, as my cousin thought, as if she never expected to see them again – The Kintbury family, during that visit, received an impression that her health was failing..."[741] This observation may, of course, have the tincture of hindsight, but it is poignant nonetheless.

Jane completed the manuscript of *Persuasion* in the summer of 1816 but it was not published until the end of 1817, along with *Northanger Abbey*, some six months after her death. It is not clear why the manuscript was not submitted to a publisher sooner. The truth may lie in an observation made by Henry Austen in his Biographical Notice. "For though in composition she was equally rapid and correct, yet an invincible distrust of her own judgment induce her to withhold her works from the public, till time and many perusals had satisfied her that the charm of recent composition was dissolved."[742] Henry was, after all, best placed to know this as her agent.

She certainly did revise the conclusion of the novel. On 8th July 1816, she started work on the first draft of Chapter 10 of Volume Two, and wrote "Finis July 16 1816" at the end of the manuscript. The first draft of Chapter 10 is included in her nephew's 1871 *Memoir*. In this, Anne Elliott and Captain Wentworth become engaged at Admiral Croft's lodgings. But this draft of Chapter 10 was cancelled, and substituted with the final Chapters 10 and 11, which were completed in August. As her nephew recorded, "her performance did not satisfy her. She thought it tame and flat, and was desirous of producing something better. This weighed upon her mind, the more so probably on account of the weak state of her health; so that one night she retired to rest in very low spirits. But such depression was little in accordance with her nature, and was soon shaken off. The next morning she awoke to more cheerful views and brighter inspirations: the sense of power revived; and imagination resumed its course. She cancelled the condemned chapter, and wrote two others, entirely different, in its stead. The result is that we possess the visit of the Musgrove party to Bath; the crowded and animated scenes at the White Hart Hotel; and the charming conversation between Capt. Harville and Anne Elliot, overheard by Capt. Wentworth, by which the two faithful lovers were at last to understand each other's feelings."[743] Jane's creative powers, then, were still, despite her illness, in their full glory, and as a result of these amendments (her very last literary output) we have one of the most moving scenes of the whole canon.

Sir Walter Elliot, Baronet, of Kellynch Hall in Somerset, has been widowed for 13 years. He is a conceited and rather silly man; "vanity was the beginning and end of his character".[744] He has three daughters. Elizabeth is the oldest at twenty-nine, shares her father's vanity, and remains unmarried. Mary, the youngest, is married to the amiable Charles Musgrove of Uppercross, and has a young family. It is the middle daughter, Anne, who is the heroine of this novel. She is (almost) as virtuous as Fanny Price, with a warm heart, a sweetness of character, and an elegance of mind. However, unlike the saintly Miss Price, she is approaching the age of danger, being 27, and has been emotionally scarred, and to some extent embittered, by experience. Her father and older sister, with whom she lives, have little affection for her, and her only ally is Lady Russell, her godmother, and friend of the family, who is resident in Kellynch Lodge.

The rightful companion of Sir Walter's vanity is his extravagance and, since the removal of the restraint imposed by his wife, has lived beyond his means. Much to his displeasure, he has to find some way to "retrench". Eventually he is persuaded to let Kellynch Hall, and move to Bath, a social environment in which he hopes his rank will preserve his dignity. The first applicant for the letting is a naval man, Admiral Croft. He is acceptable to Sir Walter who regards him as high enough in rank to be just about worthy to reside at Kellynch Hall but low enough not to threaten his dignity and overwhelming self-importance.

It is the naval connection which is the key to the plot. The Admiral's wife, Mrs Croft, turns out to be the sister of a distinguished naval officer, Captain Wentworth, who is also connected to the Musgroves; their hapless, deceased brother, "poor Richard", having served for six months on his frigate. When she hears the name of Wentworth, profound emotions are conjured in Anne Elliot because it was none other than the same Frederick Wentworth who was the cause of Anne's heartbreak some eight years previously, and from which she has never recovered.

Wentworth was a hero of the Battle of St Domingo in 1806, the battle in which Frank Austen had seen action after his disappointment at Trafalgar. He had been made a commander, and had come to live for six months in Somerset at his family's home in Monkford. He was "a remarkably fine young man, with a great deal of intelligence, spirit and brilliancy; and Anne an extremely pretty girl, with gentleness, modesty, taste and feeling."[745] In short, they were a perfect match, and fell in love. Wentworth proposed to Anne, and she accepted; they were engaged. But then they encountered, perhaps predictably, opposition from Sir Walter who regarded the marriage as beneath his status. His dignity prevented him from altogether withholding his consent, and the engagement might have survived, save for the *persuasion* of Lady Russell. Anne was only 19 and looked up to Lady Russell as a mother. It was Lady Russell who persuaded her, at that tender and impressionable age, that Wentworth had nothing to recommend him, had no connections, and no prospects in an uncertain profession, subject to the vicissitudes and dangers of war. She was also persuaded, perhaps decisively but disingenuously, that it was also for the good of Wentworth himself. Anne withdrew from the engagement. He left the country, heartbroken, and embittered, and Anne had spent the intervening years weighed down by the chronic ache of regret and disappointment which had "clouded every enjoyment of youth; and an early loss of bloom and spirits had been their lasting effect."[746]

By the time of Wentworth's return, Lady Russell's judgment has been proved to be displaced, at best. He has distinguished himself further, been promoted Post-captain, and made a handsome fortune in prize money. Anne is still in love with him, and has never loved another, and nor does she have any reason to believe him married. Although she does not acknowledge it even to her self, she harbours, perhaps, in her inner soul, the faintest of hopes, but her more prosaic emotion on hearing of his proximity is merely a relief that their engagement is known only to the immediate family, and that therefore there will be no awkwardness in her acquaintance with the Crofts.

After her father and Elizabeth move to Bath, Anne stays behind and divides her time between Lady Russell at Kellynch Lodge, and her sister Mary at Uppercross. Mary, although less vindictive than Elizabeth, has inherited "a considerable share of the Elliot self-importance"[747], wallows in hypochondrial self-indulgence, and claims that she cannot do without Anne to tend to her every need. Anne is to go to Bath later with Lady Russell.

Meanwhile, Captain Wentworth is expected to visit the Crofts at Kellynch Hall, and Anne half hopes and half fears that she will see little or nothing of him. However, his first appearance is unexpected. Whilst visiting Mr and Mrs Musgrove at the Great House at Uppercross, he also drops into the Cottage, where Anne is staying with Charles and Mary. Their first meeting in eight years is brief and strained. "Her eye half met Captain Wentworth's; a bow, a curtsey passed,"[748] and that is all. After he is gone, Mary, unconscious of the pain she is causing, but too insensitive to guard against it, tells Anne that Wentworth remarked that she was so altered he would not have known her again. "Anne fully submitted in silent, deep mortification."[749] From that time on, they are repeatedly in the same social circle but "there was no conversation together, no intercourse but what the commonest civility required."[750] Wentworth is still very bitter. Perhaps he has convinced himself, as a means of self-preservation, that he has no desire of seeing her again, and her power over him has gone. If that is so, he is deceiving himself. He remains every bit as much in love with her as she is with him.

There are two early hints to Anne that Wentworth is not entirely indifferent to her, and which begin the process of nurturing her faintest hopes. One morning she is alone at Uppercross Cottage with the Musgrove children. Wentworth drops in, hoping to see Charles. He is embarrassed to find himself alone with her, and turns to the window. She, in order to mask her own embarassment, busies herself with the boys. One of them is bothering her and getting on her back. Wentworth comes over and helps her by picking the boy up and lifting her off. Although nothing is said between them, it is the faintest bat-squeak of enduring regard.

Then there is the walk to Winthrop a day or two later. Anne has already had to bear the pain of hearing her sister and brother-in-law talking about which of his sisters, Louisa or Henrietta will do for Wentworth. They are both attractive in their own way – Henrietta is the prettier, and Louisa has the livelier disposition. Anne overhears Wentworth praising Louisa for being decisive. "It is the worst of evil of too yielding and indecisive a character that no influence over it can be depended. You are never sure of a good impression being durable. Everybody may sway it; let those who would be happy be firm."[751] Although he has no idea that he is within earshot of Anne, there can be no mistaking who or what has inspired such an observation.

Almost immediately after this, Louisa tells Wentworth that they had hoped Charles Musgrave would marry Anne instead of Mary, but that Anne had refused him. Wentworth then shows a keen interest in this news, and when it had happened (in other words, whether it was after his rejection by Anne). Anne "saw how her own character was considered by Captain Wentworth; and there had been just that degree of feeling and curiosity about her in his manner, which must give her extreme agitation." Hard on the heels of this, is his evident concern, expressed to Mrs Croft, that Anne may be fatigued, and should have a seat in the carriage for the return trip. He then assists her into it.

Although these events begin to nurture Anne's hopes, they are still very latent. She sees it only as a remainder of former sentiment. "He could not forgive her but he could not be unfeeling...it was an impulse of pure, though unacknowledged friendship; it was a proof of his own warm and amiable heart."[752] It is during the excursion to Lyme

Regis when events gather pace. Wentworth's friend, Captain Harville, has settled with his wife and children in Lyme, and Wentworth's descriptions of the environs to the Musgroves inspire plans for a short, overnight excursion, albeit out of season in November. Anne, Mary, Charles, his two sisters, and Captain Wentworth, are to make up the party. An important cog in the plot is another friend, Captain Benwick, who was engaged to Harville's sister, but she died of a fever whilst he was at sea some six months before. He is staying with the Harvilles.

By chance, staying at the same inn as the Musgrove party, is Sir Walter's heir and Anne's cousin, William Elliot. He has been estranged from the family because he had snubbed Elizabeth some years before when it was supposed that they would become betrothed. Instead he married for money, and by now has been widowed for some months. Without knowing his identity, Anne passes Mr Elliot on the seafront. As they pass, Anne's face catches his eye, and he gives her an admiring look. Wentworth sees it, and it appears to cause him a pang of jealousy. "He gave her a momentary glance, a glance of brightness, which seemed to say, 'That man is struck with you, and even I, at this moment, see something like Anne Elliot again.'"[753] Of course, Wentworth's indifference has, all along, been only a façade for self-preservation.

The following morning, before leaving for home, the party goes for a walk on the Cobb, the sea wall which surrounds the small harbour. Louisa, a little infatuated with Wentworth, insists on jumping down from the wall so that he can catch her in his arms. However, she jumps too soon. He misses her, and she falls to the ground, apparently lifeless. Whilst everybody else is paralysed with shock, hysteria or guilt, even Wentworth, Anne alone keeps her wits about her. It is she who prompts Musgrove to go to Wentworth's assistance, and it is she who instructs Benwick, who knows the area, to go for a surgeon. "Anne, attending with all the strength and zeal, and thought, which instinct supplied, to Henrietta, still tried, at intervals, to suggest comfort to the others, tried to quiet Mary, to animate Charles, to assuage the feelings of Captain Wentworth. Both seemed to look to her for directions."[754] In short, her strength of character stands out like a beacon to all around her, and especially to Wentworth, in a moment of crisis. He turns to her for assistance, "speaking with a glow, and yet a gentleness which seemed almost restoring the past."[755] He has now been reminded at Lyme, both of her physical attraction, and her superior mind.

Louisa is taken to Harville's house, seen by the surgeon, and declared to be out of immediate danger. She is to be nursed by Mary, but effectively by Mrs Harville. Anne, Henrietta and Charles are escorted back to Uppercross by Wentworth, who again pointedly asks Anne for her advice on how to proceed. Her acquaintance with him, though, is cut short, and he returns immediately to Lyme. Anne then makes the move to Bath where her father and Elizabeth have taken a house in Camden Place, a perfectly respectable neighbourhood but a step down from Kellynch. They are attended by Elizabeth's friend, the widow Mrs Clay, who appears to have designs upon Sir Walter. Meanwhile, Mr Elliot has made pains to renew his acquaintance with Sir Walter, and has been paying his respects in Bath. Anne, although still finding him charming, wonders what his motives could be. His real object, unbeknown to Anne, is to prevent Sir Walter marrying Mrs Clay, and threatening his inheritance.

There is then a further development in Anne's nascent hopes. She receives a letter from Mary at Lyme announcing that Louisa has become engaged to Benwick. Anne had supposed there to be a growing attachment between Louisa and Wentworth, and so this news engenders "feelings which she was ashamed to investigate. They were too much like senseless joy."[756] Admiral and Mrs Croft arrive in Bath for the Admiral's gout. Wentworth's arrival is imminent, although Anne has little reason to believe it is on her account rather than his sister's. Sheltering from the rain in a shop, Wentworth comes in and sees Anne. He offers his services in getting her home but it causes her much pain to admit that she is waiting for Mr Elliot, a man he can only see as a rival. She walks home with Elliot, but can think only of Wentworth.

That same evening there is a concert at the Assembly Rooms. Anne and Wentworth are both early arrivals and they converse. Their conversation is poignant because he reflects upon the fact that Benwick has become engaged so soon after the death of his fiancée, Harville's sister. "A man does not recover from such a devotion of the heart to such a woman! He ought not – he does not." The message is clear enough, and after he moves away Anne is "struck, gratified, confused and beginning to breathe very quick, and feel an hundred things in a moment."[757] At the end of the evening, Anne's suspicions about Wentworth's jealousy appear to be confirmed. Anne is paid attention by Elliot, and Wentworth leaves, telling her that there is nothing worth his staying for.

Anne meets Wentworth again at the Musgroves's hotel, the White Hart. He shows a keen interest in any conversation to do with Elliot, and she goes out of her way to express her indifference to the latter. Wentworth again makes a deliberate move to converse with her, and refers pointedly to the length of time for which they have been separated.

The almost unbearably moving climax of the story comes a day or so later, also at the White Hart. Anne and Wentworth, unable to speak directly, as so many lovers before them, speak by proxy. Anne is in conversation with Captain Harville, whilst Wentworth sits at a desk barely within earshot to write a letter, ostensibly to another, but in reality to her. Anne and

Harville are discussing Louisa's engagement to Benwick, and the subject turns to the permanence of love. Anne is conscious that Wentworth is straining to hear their conversation, and she is desperate for him to hear her because it is to him that she is really speaking. She expresses her opinion that women are as constant as men. To forget, she says, "would not be the nature of any woman who truly loved."[758] At that point she notices that Wentworth drops his pen, and she takes the chance to drive her message home, hoping desperately that he will hear her. "All the privilege I claim for my own sex…is that of loving longest, when existence or when hope is gone."[759]

Wentworth surreptitiously places a letter in front of Anne before leaving. In it he renews his declaration of all those years before. " I offer myself to you again with a heart even more of your own than when you almost broke it eight years and a half ago…I have loved none but you…"[760] Anne is in a state of profound happiness and agitation. She is terrified of anything which might separate them again. She has nothing to fear. They meet again very soon on the street, and within a few minutes are as happy as ever they were.

Anne Elliot has more in common with her creator than all of the other heroines. She has an elegance of mind, as have Elizabeth Bennett, Eleanor Dashwood, and Emma Woodhouse; she has an unambiguously morally virtuous disposition, as have Fanny Price and Eleanor; she has been uprooted from her childhood home, as have the Dashwoods and Fanny, and, what is more, to "all the white glare" of Bath, a place she regards as little more than a prison. She thinks of "all the precious rooms and furniture, groves and prospects, beginning to own other eyes and limbs"[761] at Kellynch, and she bemoans the "littleness of a town."[762] She has a sweetness of character, coupled with a lively wit. She is practical, and realistic. It is she who urges retrenchment upon her profligate father. However, unlike the other heroines, she is older, more experienced, and emotionally scarred.

It is Anne's age, and her experience, which give this novel an atmosphere which has been described as elegiacal. There is certainly something of the autumn about it: "that season of peculiar and inexhaustible influence on the mind of taste and tenderness"[763]. The story begins in the autumn. As she leaves Kellynch, she grieves to forego "all the influence so sweet and so sad of the autumnal months in the country."[764] It is difficult to avoid the conclusion that this quality in the novel may well have been influenced, consciously or unconsciously, by Jane's failing health, and her growing appreciation of her mortality. As Anne listens to Wentworth praise Louisa's constancy, "…the sweet scenes of autumn were for a while put by – unless some tender sonnet, fraught with the apt analogy of the declining year, with declining happiness, and the images of youth and hope, and spring, all gone together, blessed her memory."[765]

However, there is potentially a more poignant reason yet for the autobiographical timbre of *Persuasion*, and that is the profoundly moving way in which it treats the theme of lost or unrequited love. Although the relationship between the sexes, and the subject of courtship, are at the heart of all of the other novels, love as a subjective emotion is largely avoided. In *Persuasion*, Jane examines it intimately, and with an insight and sensitivity which strongly suggests that she must have been writing from experience. Consider this very simple statement, early in the novel, when the love between Anne and Wentworth is first described: "They fell rapidly and deeply in love."[766] To the readers of today this sentence is not at all remarkable. It is *clichéd*. But within the context of the early nineteenth century novel it is ground-breaking. There is no more emphatic description of love in Jane Austen's work: "…there could have been no two hearts so open, no tastes so similar, no feelings so in unison, no countenances so beloved."[767]

Jane is able, in describing Anne's subjective experience of an imminent close encounter with somebody whom she loves, to convey a very deep understanding of that condition from what must have been first hand experience. On first hearing the news about Mrs Croft being Wentworth's daughter, Anne "left the room to seek the comfort of cool air for her flushed cheeks; and as she walked along a favourite grove, said with gentle sigh, 'a few months more, and he perhaps may be walking here.'"[768] She observes Mrs Croft "to watch for a likeness, and if it failed her in the features, to catch it in the voice, or the turn of sentiment and expression."[769] She expertly portrays the tortured debate which goes on in Anne's mind as to whether there is any conceivable prospect of them being united. "Had he wished ever to see her again, he need not have waited till this time...Eight years...all must be comprised in it; and oblivion of the past...Alas! with all her reasonings, she found, that to retentive feelings eight years may be little more than nothing."[770]

And then there is the bitter and sweet pain of the first meeting, after their long separation. At first it is the apparent cold indifference which hurts her the most. "His cold politeness, his ceremonious grace, were worse than anything."[771] She studies his slightest expression for thoughts and feelings which are invisible to everybody else, and is acutely sensitive to whether he is looking at her, and what he is speaking to others about, straining to hear any reference to what may pertain to her. She is moved even to be "actually on the same sofa"[772], albeit separated by the considerable obstacle of Mrs Musgrove. Sometimes her eyes simply fill with tears.

The all-consuming pleasure, pain, self-abasement and irrationality of unrequited love are described so vividly, that they are surely composed by a writer seared by the lived experience. She sees him through the window walking along the Milsom Street in Bath, and "instantly felt that she was the greatest simpleton in the world, the most unaccountable and absurd! For a few minutes she saw nothing before her. It was all confusion. She was lost." As he enters the room, it is "agitation, pain, pleasure, a something between delight and misery."[773] And when she has to leave with Elliot, "she had never found it so difficult to listen to him...she could think only of Captain Wentworth...sick of knowing nothing... if she could only have a few minutes conversation with him again."[774] When she arrives at the White Hart and finds him already there, she is "deep in the happiness of such misery, or the misery of such happiness, instantly."[775] And then there is the wistful introspection at what might have been. "These would have been all my friends,[776]" she says, on meeting his naval colleagues at Lyme. Almost groundless, and sometimes irrational, causes of hope are seized upon. On finding out that Benwick has become engaged to Louisa, she is ashamed to feel "joy, senseless joy". When she finds out from Admiral Croft that Wentworth has no attachment to Louisa, she looks down to hide her smile.

Jane's descriptions of Anne's reaction to the first signs that Wentworth is not indifferent to her are striking. She is sensitive to the faintest signs. His considerate behaviour towards her during the walk to Winthrop is "a remainder of former sentiment; ...an impulse of pure, though unacknowledged friendship; ...a proof of his own warm and amiable heart, which she could not contemplate without emotions so compounded of pleasure and pain, that she knew not which prevailed."[777] And then there is the profoundly moving climactic scene in which Wentworth re-affirms his love for her. It is all the more effective because of its theatrical nature. One can sense the dramatic proscenium space, with Wentworth sitting just barely within earshot of Anne's crucial conversation with Harville. Even after Anne has read Wentworth's letter, her restless heart is determined to leave nothing to chance, and she impresses on her friends that they must tell both Harville and Wentworth that she hopes to see them at the party that evening. It is the most moving of all Jane's *denouements*, and the end of her most poetical, beautiful and perfect work.

Can it really be the case that this novel was written by somebody who had never known lost or unrequited love. Surely it is far more likely that Jane's most vivid and profound portrait of love is borne from personal experience. This explanation is added further weight by the central role played by the town of Lyme Regis in the plot. This is a place which meant a great deal to Jane, and there is some evidence that she fell in love with a young man during a visit to the area in the early years of the century.[778] She certainly rhapsodises poetically about the town and its environs. "These places," she writes, "must be visited, and visited again, to make the worth of Lyme understood."[779]

This novel, although undoubtedly elegiacal in many respects, also looks to the future. It is telling that the flawed judgment of Lady Russell in persuading Anne to end her engagement to Wentworth owed much to her "prejudices on the side of ancestry; she had a value of rank and consequence, which blinded her a little to the faults of those who possessed them"[780], and, one might add, to the virtues of those who didn't. It is precisely for this reason, eight years later, that she tries to exercise her powers to persuade Anne to look favourably on William Elliot. She regards him as "steady, observant, moderate, candid, never run away with by spirits or by selfishness..."[781] – an evaluation which is wrong in every respect. At the end there is nothing less for her to do "than to admit that she had been pretty completely wrong, and to take up a new set of opinions and hopes."[782]

It is a "new set of opinions and hopes" to which Jane looks forward in the wake of the long, revolutionary period of war from which she and Great Britain had emerged. It is Sir Walter Elliot who represents the old England, crippled by debt, decline and inflexibility, and it is the navy which represents the renewed England. It is Sir Walter who is steeped in a reverence for rank, and appearance, but it is the naval heroes who represent the vitality of action and merit. Admiral Croft and his wife are the epitome of this new order. Although expressing himself politely, the Admiral can hardly disguise his contempt for Sir Walter's vanity: "…such a number of looking glasses! Oh Lord! There was no getting away from oneself."[783] "His goodness of heart and simplicity of character were irresistible."[784] His wife, who lived on board ship with her husband, as did Fanny with Charles Austen, is no less a picture of this new virility. In marked contrast to the hypochondria of Mary Musgrove, she declares that "I have always been blessed with excellent health, and no climate disagrees with me…as long as we could be together, nothing ever ailed me."[785]

Anne is very much with the new. She disapproves of her father's desire to ingratiate himself with the Viscountess Dalrymple and her insipid daughter, inferior in every way other than their rank, and she deprecates William Elliot's value of rank and connection. "My idea of good company," she tells him, "is the company of clever, well-informed people, who have a great deal of conversation."[786] When Admiral Croft is named as the likely applicant for the tenancy, her buffoon of a father makes a joke at his expense: "I take it for granted that his face is about as orange as the cuffs and capes of my livery."[787] He dislikes the navy because it raises "persons of obscure birth into undue distinction."[788] In contrast, Anne regards Wentworth and his like as the heroes that they are, and the wave of the future; not a subversive wave, but a wave of the prudence, courage, pragmatism, mercantilism, and good common-sense which would see Great Britain through the century of nationalism and revolution to come. And yet, even at the end of the novel, there is a note of pessimism for Anne: "the dread of a future war was all that could dim her sunshine."[789] Jane was conflicted: for her country the future looked bright, for her person the shadows were approaching.

XXIII: SEA CHANGE

In the late summer of 1816, Cassandra returned to Cheltenham with her sister-in-law, Mary Lloyd, who was also in poor health. On 8th September, Jane wrote to her sister. Plans were being made for Charles and his children to stay later in the month. Frank and his family had visited, and they had had a pleasant day in Alton with the Digweeds. "We had a beautiful walk home by moonlight." She appears at this stage to be in reasonable health but she had been suffering with her back, and was receiving medical attention. "Thank you," she says, "my back has given me scarcely any pain for many days. I have an idea that agitation does it as much harm as fatigue, and that I was ill at the time of your going from the very circumstance of your going. I am nursing myself up now into as beautiful a state as I can, because I hear that Dr White means to call on me before he leaves the country." [790] This is the last surviving letter from Jane to Cassandra. They were not separated again until her death.

There is a hint, in this final letter, that her energy was ebbing away, including her enthusiasm for writing. Her nephew, Edward, had been staying at the Cottage and, although she enjoyed his company, "I was not sorry when Friday came. It had been a busy week, and I wanted a few days quiet and exemption from the thought and contrivancy which any sort of company gives. I often wonder how you can find for what you do, in addition to the care of the house; and how good Mrs West [the novelist Jane West] could have written such books and collected so many hard words, with all her family cares, is still more a matter of astonishment. Composition seems to me impossible with a head full of joints of mutton and doses of rhubarb."[791]

By the end of the year, her condition had worsened. On 16th December she wrote to her nephew, a budding writer in his own right, joking about the suggestion that she might have stolen part of his manuscript. "What should I do with your strong, manly, spirited sketches, full of variety & glow? – How could I possibly join them onto the little bit (two inches wide) of ivory on which I work with so fine a brush, as produces little effect after much labour?" Her mind was still sparkling but her body was now failing it. She went on to say that Ben Lefroy had invited her to dine but she was forced to decline – "the walk is beyond my strength (though I am otherwise very well) & this is not a season for donkey carriages."[792]

However, in early 1817, there was a respite. She wrote to Alethea Bigg and Mary Lloyd: "I have certainly gained strength through the winter and am not far from being well; and I think I understand my own case now so much better than I did, as to be able by care to keep off any serious return of illness. I am more and more convinced that bile is at the bottom of all I have suffered, which makes it easy to know how to treat myself… I feel myself getting stronger than I was half a year ago, and can so perfectly well walk to Alton or back again without the slightest fatigue that I hope to be able to do both when summer comes."[793] Indeed, she was able to find sufficient energy for one last literary effort. On 27th January she began to write *Sanditon*, her final, and uncompleted, work.

Mr Tom Parker, a pleasant young man of 35, is a speculator "with more imagination than judgment"[794], who has become obsessed with the Regency craze for sea-bathing, and the health-giving properties of the coast, and has invested in the development of a new resort on the Sussex coast in the vicinity of the parish of Sanditon. Needing to recruit a medical man to render the resort more attractive to potential residents and tourists, he journeys with his wife, Mary, to nearby Willingden. He has seen notices in the London newspapers to do with the dissolution of a medical practice in that village.

Typical of his rash but boundless enthusiasm is his insistence, much to the distaste of their driver, to take an unmade road in order to speed their progress. The carriage is duly overturned, and Parker sprains his ankle. They are attended by the local squire, Mr Heywood, and his family who live nearby. Parker's need, now a personal one, for a medical man reveals that he has in fact come to the wrong Willingden. His lack of judgment is not remedied by his delightful wife because "whether he were risking his fortune or spraining his ankle, she remained equally useless."[795]

The Parkers are taken in by the Heywoods until Tom is fit to walk again. They are royally treated, particularly by the eldest daughter, Charlotte, and they become firm friends. Parker invites the Heywoods to come to Sanditon, lauding the health giving properties of the sea. The Heywoods are too attached to their home to be tempted to move. However, it is arranged that Charlotte, 22 years old, will accompany them to Sanditon for an extended visit.

The matriarch of Sanditon is Lady Denham, now an elderly lady of 70. She started life in a humble way as Miss Brereton but married the wealthy Mr Hollis who left her all of his considerable property upon his death. She had inherited her title from her second husband, Sir Harry Denham, of Denham Park in the neighbourhood of Sanditon. It is Lady Denham who is Parker's collaborator in the development of the resort, although she acts as a restraint on his wilder, more profligate, plans, much to his frustration.

There are three sets of potential claimants to Lady Denham's fortune. First, the Hollis family, resentful that she had inherited all of the property; secondly the Denhams, and, thirdly, her own family, the Breretons. The Breretons had played the better game and had ingratiated themselves with Lady Denham to the extent that she had invited Clara Brereton, a charming young woman with no fortune, to join her as a companion at Sanditon House.

The beneficiary of the Baronetcy of Sir Harry is his nephew, Edward. Sir Edward visits Sanditon with his sister, Esther. Charlotte is initially attracted to Edward who is handsome and superficially charming. However, upon further acquaintance, it is apparent that he is a buffoon, not far superior to Mr Rushworth in *Mansfield Park*, whose weak mind has been corrupted by sensational literature. Tom Parker's younger brother and two sisters also arrive. Diana Parker has come, in particular, to facilitate the arrival of a family from the West Indies, and a party of French schoolgirls. Her frenetic energy and organisational fervour belie her complaints of ill-health.

At that point the manuscript, written between January and March of 1817, ends, after about 24,000 words. It is tantalising because there are the makings of a great novel. A number of intriguing characters are introduced and promised who are going to interact in a closed society about money, manners and sex. It finishes, however, after Chapter 12, before the plot gets going.

The work is intriguing because it hints at an evolution in Jane's style. Some of the dialogue is almost impressionistic in the sense that the literal meaning of the words takes second place to the overall impression which they create. An example of this comes right at the beginning of the text in a passage which describes the attitude of the driver to being ordered to proceed along an unmade road.

"He had grumbled and shaken his shoulders so much indeed, and pitied and cut his horses so sharply, that he might have been open to the suspicion of overturning them on purpose (especially as the carriage was not his master's own) if the road had not been indisputably become considerably worse than before, as soon as the premises of the said house were left behind – expressing with a most intelligent portentous countenance that beyond it no wheels but cart wheels could safely proceed."[796]

Brian Southam argues that the apparent awkwardness of this passage is a contrived effect "to enforce our sense of the driver's recalcitrance, the difficulty of the road, and the foundering of the coach."[797] Another example of a passage which could be described as impressionistic is that in which Sir Edward Denham regales Charlotte with his literary theories.[798] The words make little sense, taken at their face value, but their impression is of a young man who is intoxicated with the sensibilities of an incipient movement of which he has little understanding – namely Romanticism.

One objection to this analysis is that these passages are not a deliberate contrivance but a result of the fact that the work is an unfinished draft. This argument is not convincing because, as Southam points out, the original manuscript had been heavily corrected and revised. Another objection is that the passages are not a contrivance, but merely evidence of the unravelling of Austen's powers of literal expression due to her failing health. But if this is a deliberate development, then it is comparable to the evolution in fine art from the Classical to the Romantic of the kind perhaps most clearly exemplified by JMW Turner, whose life and work spanned the transition. One can compare Turner's work from the late eighteenth century with works such as *Rain, Steam and Speed* (1844), for example, to appreciate the full scope of this change. It is possible that in *Sanditon* we can see the first stirrings of a comparable evolution.

Jane Austen was acutely conscious of the societal and cultural changes taking place in Britain, and across Europe, in the post-war period. *Sanditon* is about the tension between the old and the new, between stasis and change. The novel begins, not with a description of a village, or a family, or a community, but with rapid movement. The work is throbbing with the promise, or the threat, of energy and ambition for change, from Parker's enthusiasm for building and developing, to Diana's bustling and oppressive energy to get things done, to the elemental forces of the sea and the weather.

There is little doubt, however, where Jane's sympathies lie. In short they had not changed since she had completed *Mansfield Park*. Her attitude, whilst recognising the inevitability of change, is suspicious of it, and deeply nostalgic for home and for the past. Sir Edward's proto-Romanticism is mocked as the ramblings of a rather silly man. After his pretentious lecture to Charlotte about literature, she responds laconically, "If I understand you right…our taste in novels is not at all the same."[799]

The development of the resort which Parker envisages will be to the detriment of the old village of Sanditon which he deprecates and ridicules as a "contracted nook, without air or view"[800] because it is away from the sea. As he approaches the coast, having driven through the old village, he cries contemptuously, "Civilisation, civilisation indeed." But Parker is a man of poor judgment, symbolised by his reckless behaviour at the beginning of the work. His development will sacrifice tradition for profit, as will the industrial revolution. The ancient social fabric embodied in carefully preserved family estates is about to be torn apart. The coastal resort is a place for the transient, for the passing traffic, not for a stable and static community.

In contrast, the Heywoods love their home, and take no pleasure in change or movement. They are suspicious of the claim that the sea is a panacea for sickness. "We have been so healthy a family that I can be no judge of what the habit of self-doctoring will do."[801] Even Mary Parker looks back wistfully upon their old home, symbolically through the rear window of the carriage "with something like the fondess of regret…'One loves to look at an old friend, at a place where one has been happy'".[802]

Sanditon looks towards the future, then, albeit with apprehension and suspicion, but it also looks back. There are echoes of Jane's earlier works in this novel. Charlotte Heywood, like Catherine Morland, is a reader of novels which "supply her imagination", and, in an echo of Catherine's fantasies at Northanger Abbey, she fancies that Clara, with no fortune, is subject to the persecution of Lady Denham "which ought to be the lot of the interesting Clara."[803] She too is looking for the complete heroine of the Gothic novel but is obliged to accept that her hopes are misconceived. On one side there was nothing but protecting kindness, and on the other grateful and affectionate respect. The Denham siblings are a throw back to the burlesques and grotesques of even earlier works in the *Juvenilia*. Perhaps this is another expression of her nostalgia. The American critic Arthur Walton Litz has speculated that this may have been a defence mechanism against illness and depression.[804]

The work does have a particular poignancy, of course, because we know what we know of Jane's condition when she was writing it. In short, she was dying. She did not want to accept that she was dying, and probably did not know. She didn't even want to accept that she was seriously ill, and typically took a stoical view of her condition. The subject of health plays an important role in the plot. Parker's sisters and younger brother are all hypochondriacs. Diana complains of 'spasmodic bile"[805]. Susan suffers from her nerves, and is treating her headache with six leeches a day for ten days. Arthur is languid with a dodgy liver, and is given "a turn for being ill" and "encouraged to give way to indisposition."[806]

We know from the manuscript that *Sanditon* was begun on 27th January 1817, and that, at the end of the twelfth chapter, Jane entered the date "18 March". This suggests that she did not just leave off writing with a view to picking it up later, she very consciously put an end to it. She realised, by this stage, that she was not going to finish. It is notable that a couple of the pages of the manuscript are unusually written in pencil, easier to manipulate than an ink pen in a reclining position.

Just five days later, on 23rd March, she confided to Fanny that she had certainly not been well for many weeks, and "about a week ago I was very poorly. I have had a good deal of fever at times and indifferent nights; but I am considerably better now, and am recovering my looks a little, which have been had enough – black and white and every wrong colour." [807]

On 26th March, she wrote to Caroline: "I have taken one ride on the donkey and like it very much – and you must try to get me quiet, mild days, that I may be able to go out pretty constantly. A great deal of wind does not suit me, as I still have a tendency to rheumatism. In short I am a poor honey at present. I will be better when you can come and see us."[808]

Jane's illness was described by the English physician, Sir Zachary Cope in 1964, as Addison's disease, a hormonal disorder of the adrenal glands that leads to extreme fatigue, sometimes caused by a tubercular infection, which in the early nineteenth century was eventually fatal. The tubercular infection would typically affect the lungs, bowels and spine and so could account for abdominal and back pain. However, a more recent textual analysis has suggested Hodgkin's lymphoma, a type of cancer which attacks the body's immune system.[809] Both conditions could cause the discolouration of the skin, referred to in Jane's letter to Fanny, but with Addison's disease the effect is long lasting. The fact that Jane had recovered her looks is support for the Hodgkin's theory. She added poignantly, "I must not depend upon being ever very blooming again. Sickness is a dangerous indulgence at my time of life."

On 28th March 1817, Jane's uncle, Leigh-Perrot, died. The terms of his will were not favourable. The sum of £1,000 was left to each of the Austen children who should survive his wife, meaning that there would be no immediate amelioration of their financial position. With the bankruptcy of Henry, and the continuing law suit against Edward's estate, this was deeply disappointing. Jane's health deteriorated further. On 6th April she wrote to her brother, Charles. "I am ashamed to say that the shock of my uncle's will brought on a relapse, and I was so ill on Friday and thought myself likely to be worse that I could not but press for Cassandra's returning with Frank after the funeral last night, which she of course did, and either her return, or my having seen Mr Curtis, or my disorder's choosing to go away, have made me better this morning. I live upstairs for the present and am coddled."[810]

Her niece, Caroline, recalled, fifty years later, that she visited her aunt shortly after Mr Leigh-Perrot's death but she was too ill to receive her in the house. The next day Caroline went up to visit Jane in her room. "She was in her dressing gown and was sitting quite like an invalid in an arm chair – but she got up and kindly greeted us – and then pointed to seats which had been arranged for us by the fire, she said, 'There's a chair for the married lady, and a little stool for you Caroline'…those trifling words are the last of her's that I can remember…I was struck by the alteration in herself. She was very pale – her voice was weak and low and there was about her a general appearance of debility and suffering; but I have been told that she never had much actual pain…She was not equal to the exertion of talking to us, and our visit to the sick room was a short one – Aunt Cassandra soon taking us away. I do not suppose we stayed a quarter of an hour; and I never saw Aunt Jane again. "[811] On 26th April, Mary Lloyd noted, "Jane rather better,"[812] but the very next day, Jane Austen made her will. She left everything to Cassandra.

Cassandra was to survive her sister by almost thirty years, dying of a stroke in Portsdown, having gone there to see Frank off to his command in the West Indies. By her will she divided Jane's remaining manuscripts between the family. Volumes of the *Juvenilia* went to Charles, Frank and James Edward. *Lady Susan* went to Fanny, by then Lady Knatchbull, *The Watsons* to Caroline, and *Sanditon* to Anna. Anna attempted to finish the story but gave up after writing 20,000 words of indifferent merit. The original manuscript was finally published in 1925 under the title *Fragment of a Novel*.[813]

XXIV: CURTAIN

Jane's condition was now such that she needed to be close to the best available medical care in Winchester. This was Giles King Lyford, the chief surgeon at the Winchester Hospital, founded in 1736, and one of the best in the country, attracting medical students from London.[814] She wrote to her friend, the old governess at Godmersham, Anne Sharp, two days before she left Chawton for the last time. She said that she had been too ill to respond to her letter but was recovering her strength. It appears, however, that by this stage she was pretty much resigned to her fate. She told Miss Sharp that she would soon go to Winchester for treatment by Mr Lyford, and that Mrs Heathcote had hired lodgings for her.[815] "If I live to be an old woman", she said, "I must expect to wish I had died now, blessed in the tenderness of such a family, and before I had survived either them or their affection."[816]

She agreed to be taken by her brothers James and Henry, accompanied, of course, by Cassandra, to the lodgings at No 8 College Street, a pleasant house standing between the school buildings and the old city wall, and almost in the shadow of the Cathedral and the medieval castle. According to Henry, none even then dared to hope that she would be cured but she was as stoical as ever. "She supported, during two months, all the varying pain, irksomeness, and tedium, attendant on decaying nature, with more than resignation, with a truly elastic cheerfulness. She retained her faculties, her memory, her fancy, her temper, and her affections, warm, clear, and unimpaired, to the last. Neither her love of god, nor of her fellow creatures flagged for a moment."[817] Apparently, Mr Lyford told Mary Lloyd that there could be "no hope of recovery", but that "the duration of the illness must be very uncertain – it might be lingering or it might, with equal probability come to a sudden close – and that he feared that the last period, whenever it arrived, would be one of severe suffering – but this was mercifully ordered otherwise."[818]

They arrived on 24th May. They had the first floor, two sitting rooms, and two bedrooms at the back. They had plenty of visitors: the widowed Mrs Heathcote, previously Elizabeth Bigg, and her sister Alethea, lived nearby in Cathedral Close, where Jane and Cassandra had stayed at the Christmas of 1814. It was they who had arranged the accommodation. Her brothers Henry, Charles, and James all visited, and Mrs Austen and Mary Lloyd helped Cassandra to nurse Jane from time to time. James, no stranger to bad health, had made out his will the previous day, leaving money to Henry, Frank, Cassandra and Charles. Ominously, there was no reference to Jane.[819]

Shortly after her arrival, she wrote to her nephew, James Edward, on 27th May, "no longer, alas! in her former strong, clear hand". She claimed with her usual fortitude to be getting better but "I will not boast of my handwriting; neither that my face have yet recovered their proper beauty, but in other respects I gain strength very fast. I am now out of bed from 9 in the morning to 10 at night: upon the sofa, it is true, but I eat my meals with aunt Cassandra in a rational way, and can employ myself, and walk from one room to another. Mr Lyford says he will cure me, and if he fails, I shall draw up a memorial and lay it before the Dean and Chapter, and have no doubt of redress from that pious, learned and disinterested body. Our lodgings are very comfortable. We have a neat little drawing room with a bow window overlooking Dr Gabell's garden…God bless you my dear E. if ever you are ill, may you be as tenderly nursed as I have been. May the same blessed alleviations of anxious, sympathising friends be yours: and may you possess, as I dare say you will, the greatest blessing of all in the consciousness of not being unworthy of their love. I could not feel this." [820]

This was her last letter, save for a fragment written shortly afterwards, and preserved in Henry Austen's biographical notice upon the publication of her last works. Her mood had grown darker. "I will only say further that my dearest sister, my tender, watchful, indefatigable nurse, has not been made ill by her exertions. As to what I owe her, and the anxious affection of all my beloved family on this occasion, I can only cry over it, and pray God to bless them more and more."[821]

On Friday 6th June, Mary wrote in her diary, "I rode to Winchester to Mrs Heathcotes."[822] It seems likely that she had been sent for. On the Sunday, Mary dined with the Austens and stayed with Jane whilst Cassandra went to church. The following day she recorded that Jane was worse, and that she had sat up with her. On the Tuesday she wrote, "Jane in great danger."[823] On 12th June, Charles was sent for from Keppel Street. A hastily written note in his pocket book reads, "A rainy morning. Received a letter from Henry acquainting me with Dr. Jane's illness [sic] took a place in the mail for Winchester."[824]

At around the same time, James Austen wrote to his son at Oxford to tell him that the situation was hopeless, and that the symptoms which had come on after the first four or five days in Winchester had not subsided. My Lyford had told them that her case was desperate. "It is some consolation to know that our poor invalid has hitherto felt no very severe pain – which is rather an extraordinary circumstance in her complaint. I saw her on Tuesday and found her much altered, but composed and cheerful. She is well aware of her situation…Lyford said he saw no sign of immediate dissolution, but added that with such a pulse it was impossible for any person to last long."[825]

There was then, however, a brief rally in Jane's condition. Mary recorded on Friday 13th June that she had begun to get better. By the following Tuesday, a better account of Aunt Jane had reached Fanny at Godmersham. It was recognised, though, that this was but a temporary respite. Two days later, Charles wrote at Winchester, "Jane a little better. Saw her twice in the evening for the last time in this world as I greatly fear, the Doctor having no hope of her final recovery."[826]

She remained stable for a few weeks but on Sunday 13th July Mary, who had gone back to Steventon, returned to Winchester "to nurse Jane."[827] Henry was expected on the Tuesday. It was on that day, at least according to the manuscript[828], that Jane found the remarkable strength to write, or at least dictate, her last literary output, a six stanza poem about the Winchester races which were to take place that day. It was in the evening of the same day that her condition worsened. Cassandra later recorded that her sister "slept more and much more comfortably, indeed…she was more asleep than awake. Her looks altered and she fell away, but I perceived no material diminution of strength and though I was then hopeless of a recovery I had no suspicion how rapidly my loss was approaching."[829] On the Thursday, Mary recorded in her diary that "Jane Austen was taken for death about ½ past 5 in the evening."[830] In other words, there had been a sudden and rapid deterioration in her condition.

Cassandra later recorded the final scene. "I returned about a quarter before six and found her recovering from faintness and oppression, she got so well as to be able to give me a minute account of her seizure and when the clock struck 6 she was talking quietly to me. I cannot say how soon afterwards she was seized again with the same faintness…She felt herself to be dying about half an hour before she became tranquil and apparently unconscious. During that half hour was her struggle, poor soul! She said she could not tell us what she suffered, though she complained of little fixed pain. When I asked her if there was anything she wanted, her answer was she wanted nothing but death and some of her words were 'God grant me patience, pray for me oh pray for me.' Her voice was affected but as long as she spoke she was intelligible… Mr Lyford had been sent for, had applied something to give her ease and she was in a state of quiet insensibility by seven o'clock at the latest. From that time till half past four, when she ceased to breathe, she scarcely moved a limb, so that we have every reason to think, with gratitude to the Almighty, that her sufferings were over. A slight motion of the head with every breath remained till almost the last."

Cassandra sat with a pillow on her lap, supporting Jane's head which was almost off the bed for six hours. Mary took her place at about one in the morning, and then Cassandra resumed her position at half past three for the final hour of her sister's life. "There was nothing convulsed or which gave the idea of pain in her look, on the contrary, but for the continual motion in her head, she gave me the idea of a beautiful staue, and even now in her coffin, there is such a sweet air over her countenance as is quite pleasant to contemplate." [831] Mary recorded more prosaically that "Jane breathed her last ½ after four in the Morn: only Cass and I were with her. Henry came."[832]

The most eulogistic account of the end comes from James Edward's Memoir, albeit written half a century later. It was his mother, of course, who was a first hand witness. "While she used the language of hope," he writes, "she was fully aware of her danger, though not appalled by it." She was prepared for death by James and Henry, now also an ordained clergyman in the wake of his bankruptcy. "Her sweetness of temper never failed. She was ever considerate and grateful to those who attended on her. At times, when she felt rather better, her playfulness of spirit returned, and she amused them even in their sadness. Once, when she thought herself near the end, she said what she imagined might be her last words to those around her, and particularly thanked her sister-in-law for being with her, saying: 'You have aways been a kind sister to me, Mary.' When the end at last came, she sank rapidly, and on being asked by her attendants whether there was anything that she wanted, her reply was, 'Nothing but death.' These were her last words, In quietness and peace she breathed her last on the morning of July 18, 1817."[833]

Jane Austen was buried in Winchester Cathedral on Thursday 24th July, near the centre of the north aisle, almost opposite to the tomb of William of Wykham, the fourteenth century Bishop of Winchester, referred to by Jane in her final poem as having given faint approval to the races. Present were her brothers Edward, Henry, and Frank. James was too ill to attend, and was represented by his son, James Edward. As was customary for the time, the ladies did not attend and remained at the house in College Street. Cassandra stood at the window, and was typically stoical. "I watched the little mournful procession the length of the street and when it turned from my sight and I had lost her for ever – even then I was not overpowered."[834] But later Cassandra wrote movingly of her loss. "She was the sun of my life, the gilder of every pleasure, the soother of every sorrow, I had not a thought concealed from her, and it is as if I had lost a part of myself."[835]

An obituary in the *Hampshire Courier* on 22nd July, and written by Henry, identified Jane Austen, publicly for the first time, as the authoress of *Emma, Mansfield Park, Pride and Prejudice,* and *Sense and Sensibility.* In her will, save for two bequests, Jane left her worldly goods to Cassandra. In monetary terms this amounted, essentially, to the £600 she had invested in "Navy Fives", in other words bonds which yielded five per cent a year. She also left £50 to Henry, who had done so much to publish her work, and £50 to Madame Bigeon, who had been Eliza de Feuillide's long-serving maid – a clear sign of the enduring regard which Jane had for her cousin. There was also the copyright on the published works, and two manuscripts: the manuscript which had been provisionally given the title 'The Elliots', and the manuscript of *Catherine,* written at the turn of the century, sold to Crosby in 1803, but still unpublished. The rights to this had been re-acquired in 1816.

Cassandra had been made the executrix of Jane's will, and she and Henry soon got to work in getting the manuscripts published. They were both published by John Murray on commission, in December 1817, as a four volume set, and now called *Persuasion* and *Northanger Abbey.* The reviews were mixed. The *British Critic,* which had clearly not moved with the times in terms of literary development, complained about the author's lack of imagination and invention, and that her works were all drawn from experience but it went on to say that they "display a degree of excellence that has not often been surpassed." It praised the realism of the characterisation and dialogue, and described *Northanger Abbey* as "one of the very best of Miss Austen's productions." It judged *Persuasion* as "a much less fortunate performance" but this was less a comment on the literary merits of the work, and more a judgment on its morality "which seems to be that young people should always marry according to their own inclinations and upon their own judgment."[836]

Blackwood's Edinburgh Magazine (perhaps surprisingly) was a little less priggish, and appears to have regarded the absence of "imagination" as a virtue. It did not offer an individual critique of the novels but praised her work more generally. "The singular merit of her writings," it opined, "is that we could conceive, without the slightest strain of imagination, any one of her fictions to be realised in any town or village in England...We have always regarded [her] works as possessing a higher claim to public estimation than perhaps they have yet attained." The article went on to suggest a reason for this, namely that they had been written in an age when the public taste was for 'the highest seasoned food...the prevailing love of historical, and at the same time romantic incident, - dark and high-wrought passions...yet the time, probably, will return, when we shall take a more permanent delight in those familiar cabinet pictures...When this period arrives, we have no hesitation in saying that the delightful writer of the works now before us will be one of the most popular of English novelists."[837] It was precisely such "dark and high-wrought passions" that Jane had parodied almost twenty years earlier, in the work now just published.

Murray's edition sold well in the first year, making £500 for Cassandra, but sales then declined, and the remaining 282 copies of the 1,750 run were remaindered. Egerton had also published a third edition of *Pride and Prejudice* shortly after Jane's death. It was fifteen years before another publisher reprinted her works in England.[838]

Shortly before her death, her brother Charles was stationed in Italy, and he wrote to tell Jane of an admirer. "Books became the subject of conversation, and I praised Waverley highly, when a young man present observed that nothing had come out for years to be compared with *Pride and Prejudice, Sense and Sensibility*, etc. As I am sure you must be anxious to know the name of a person of so much taste, I shall tell you it is Fox, a nephew of the late Charles James Fox."[839]

It is not known whether Jane had the pleasure of reading this before her death, but in the 1820s, her works were out of print. Countless visitors to Winchester Cathedral walked over the large, black, marble slab in the north aisle with no idea to whom it was dedicated. In 1832, Henry negotiated, no doubt with the agreement of Cassandra, with the publisher Richard Bentley for the sale of five of the copyrights. They were sold for a total of £210. Bentley acquired the rights to *Pride and Prejudice,* which were still at that point held by Egerton, and printed all six novels in single volumes. Nevertheless, Jane's reputation grew very slowly during the early and middle part of the nineteenth century which was dominated by Dickens, Thackeray, Trollope and the Brontës. She had not been forgotten. In 1843, the *Foreign and Colonial Quarterly* published an article which described her as "the greatest of all female novelists."[840] In the same year, Macauley wrote an article in the *Edinburgh Review* on Fanny Burney, and compared Jane Austen's skill in creating characters who appear both commonplace and unique with Shakespeare.[841] Her reputation had crossed the Atlantic by the middle of the century, and her works were reputedly enjoyed by the Chief Justice of the US Supreme Court.[842]

But fifty years after her death, her nephew was still able to write in his memoir, "A few years ago, a gentleman visiting Winchester Cathedral desired to be shown Miss Austen's grave. The verger, as he pointed it out, asked, 'Pray sir can you tell me whether there was anything particular about that lady; so many people want to know where she was buried.?'"[843] Then, after the publication of this memoir in 1869, both public and critical interest in the novels increased. According to James Edward's daughter, writing in 1920: "When this book appeared, a singular change took place. It not only brought into being a large number of articles, notices and reviews concerning its subject and her works, but it also brought to himself a variety of interesting letters from unknown correspondents, both English and American, describing the effect that its perusal had produced upon the writers' minds."[844]

New editions were published, and by the end of the century there were numerous affordable editions to fuel a mass market. In that very last literary output, the poem about the Winchester races, Jane wrote these lines in the voice of St Swithin, so unconsciously prophetic: "Henceforward I'll triumph in showing my powers...When once we are buried you think we are dead, But behold me immortal."[845] Two centuries after her death, millions of people from all over the globe travel to see that large, black marble slab in Winchester Cathedral, precisely because they know to whom it is dedicated. There can be no finer testament to her memory than that.

SELECT BIBLIOGRAPHY

Adams, Oscar Faye, *The Story of Jane Austen's Life* (Boston 1891)
Adams, Samuel and Sarah, *The Complete Servant,* (London 1825)
Adkins, Roy, *Trafalgar* (London 2004)
Adkins, Roy and Lesley, *Eavesdropping on Jane Austen's England* (London 2013)
Amy, Helen, *The Jane Austen Files* (Stroud 2015)
Anon, *The Improved Bath Guide* (Bath 1809)
Anon, *The Jane Austen Quickstep Travel Guide: Missing Manydown* (10th January 2022)
Aspinall, Arthur., ed. *Letters of the Princess Charlotte 1811-1817* (London 1949)
Austen, Caroline, *My Aunt Jane Austen: A Memoir (1867)* [References are to CAM, as reproduced by Kathryn Sutherland.]
Austen, Henry,
- *Biographical Notice of the Author (1818)* [References are to HABN, as reproduced by Kathryn Sutherland.]
- *A Memoir of Miss Austen (1833)* [References are to HAM, as reproduced by Kathryn Sutherland.]

Austen, Jane, [Everyman Edition]
- *Sense and Sensibility,* (London 1992)
- *Pride and Prejudice,* (London 1991)
- *Mansfield Park,* (London 1992)
- *Emma,* (London 1991)
- *Persuasion,* (London 1992)

- *Northanger Abbey,* (London 1992)
- *Sanditon and Other Stories,* (London 1996)

Austen-Leigh, JE, *A Memoir of Jane Austen (2nd edition 1871)* [References are to JEAL, as reproduced by Kathryn Sutherland.]

Austen-Leigh, Mary Augusta, *Personal Aspects of Jane Austen (1920)* [References are to MAAL, as reproduced by Helen Amy.]

Austen-Leigh, Richard Arthur, *Austen Papers, 1704-1856,* (Colchester 1942)

Austen-Leigh, William and Richard Arthur, *Jane Austen, Her Life and Letters, A Family Record* (London 1913) [References are to W & RAAL, as reproduced by Helen Amy.]

Bigg Wither, Reginald Fitzhugh, *Materials for a History of the Wither Family* (Winchester 1907)

Black, Maggie and Dierdre Le Faye, *The Jane Austen Cookbook* (London 1995)

Brabourne, Lord Edward, *Letters of Jane Austen, Edited with an Introduction and Critical Remarks,* (London 1884) [References are to Brabourne, and as reproduced by Helen Amy.]

Browne, Joseph, *Account of the Wonderful Cures Perform'd by the Cold Baths* (London 1707)

British Critic, The (1812)

Brydges, Sir Egerton, *The Autobiography, Times, Opinions and Contemporaries of Sir Egerton Brydges* (London 1834)

Byrne, Paula, *The Genius of Jane Austen* (2nd Ed, London 2017)

Charlton, Deborah, *Archaeology Greets Jane Austen* (2017)

Cobbett, William, *History of the Regency and Reign of King George the Fourth* (London 1830)

Coleman, Terry, *Nelson* (London 2001)

Cooper, Thomas, *The Life of Thomas Cooper, Written by Himself* (1872)

Copeland, Edward & Juliet McMaster, *The Cambridge Companion to Jane Austen*

(Cambridge 2nd Ed 2011)

Critical Review, The (1812)

Davenport, RJ, JP Boulton, J Black, *Infant Mortality by Social*

Status in Georgian London, (London 2013)
Egan, Pearce, *Walks Through Bath* 1819
Fanny Knight's dairies [References are to FKD, as reproduced in Amy].
Feltham, John, *A Guide to All the Watering and Seabathing Places* (London 1803)
Garside, Peter; James Raven, and Rainer Schöwerling (eds), *The English Novel 1770-1829: A Biographical Survery* (Oxford 2000)
Gilson, David John, *A Bibliography of Jane Austen* (Oxford 1982)
Gore, Ann & George Carter, *Humphry Repton's Memoirs* (Norwich 2005)
Grey, J.David, *The Jane Austen Handbook,* Athlone Press (1986)
Hall, Edward (ed), *Miss Weeton: Journal of a Governess* (Oxford 1939)
Harris, Benjamin, *Recollections of Rifleman Harris* (1848)
Hayley, William, *A Philosophical, Historical and Moral Essay on Old Maids* (London 1786)
Hill, Constance, *Jane Austen: Her Homes and Her Friends*, London (1902)
Cheltenham Borough Council, *Historic Cheltenham* (cheltenham.gov.uk)
Horn, Pamela, *Life and Labour in Rural England* (London 1987)
Honan, Park, *Jane Austen Her Life,* New York (1987)
Hubback, Catherine-Anne, Family history notes: Jane Austen's House, Chawton [References are to Hubback notes]
Hubback, JH and Edith C, *Jane Austen's Sailor Brothers* (London 1906)
Jane Austen Society of North America (jasna.org) [JASNA]
Lascelles, Mary, *Jane Austen and her Art* (Oxford 1954)
Le Faye, Dierdre,
- *A Chronology of Jane Austen and Her Family,* Cambridge University Press (2nd Ed. 2013) [References are to Chron.]
- *Fanny Knight's Diaries: Jane Austen Through Her Niece's Eyes*, (Journal of the Jane Austen Society of North America – Persuasions Occasional Papers No.2) [Ref: Diaries]

- *Jane Austen, A Family Record,* Cambridge University Press (2nd Ed. 2004) [References are to Le Faye]

Lefroy, Anna,
- Quarto volume of notes on the family's history, compiled c. 1855-1871 [References are to Lefroy notes]
- *Recollections of Aunt Jane (1864)* [References are to ALR, and as reproduced by Kathryn Sutherland.]

Litz, A. Walton, *Jane Austen: A Study of Her Artistic Development,* London and New York (1965)

Mandal, AA, *Making Austen Mad: Benjamin Crosby and the non-Publication of* Susan, published in *The Review of English Studies,* New Series, vol.57, no 231 (2006) pp507-25

MacCarthy, Fiona, *Byron: Life and Legend* (2002)

Mudrick, Marvin, *Jane Austen: Irony as Defense and Discovery* (Princeton and London 1952)

Nokes, David, *Jane Austen: A Life* (London 1997)

O'Byrne, William Richard, *A Naval Biographical Dictionary* (London 1849)

Porter, Roy, *England in the Eighteenth Century,* Penguin (2nd Ed. 1990)

Reitzel, Wiliam, *Proceedings of the Modern Language Association of America,* Vol 43 No 2 (June 1928)

Roberts, George, *The History and Antiquities of the Borough of Lyme Regis* (London 1834)

Rowbottam, William, *Most Dismal Times:William Rowbottam's Diary 1787-1789* ed. Alan Peat (1996)

Sabor, Peter (Ed), *The Cambridge Companion to Emma* (Cambridge 2015)

Schama, Simon, *Citizens* (London 2004)

Sherwood, Mary Martha, *The Life and Times of Mrs Sherwood (Ed. FJ Harvey Darton),* Cambridge (2011)

Southam, BC, ed. *Jane Austen: The Critical Heritage,* London and New York (1968)

Southey, Robert, *Life of Nelson* (London 1814, 1909 ed)

Sutherland, Kathryn (Ed), *A Memoir of Jane Austen and Other*

Family Recollections, Oxford (2002)

Tomalin, Claire, *Jane Austen: A Life*, London (2nd Ed. 2000)

Tucker, George Holbert, *A Goodly Heritage; A History of Jane Austen's Family*, Manchester (1983)

Uglow, Jenny, *In These Times: Living in Britain through Napoleon's Wars 1793-1815* (London 2014)

Upfal, Annette, *Jane Austen's lifelong health problems and final illness* (Medical Humanities 2005 31:3-11).

Vallance, Rosalind (ed), *Dicken's London* (London 1966)

Ward, William S, *Nineteenth Century Fiction*, Vol 26, No 4 (March 1972)

Watson, J.Steven, *The Reign of George III (1760-1815)* (Oxford 1960)

Webster, C.K., *The Foreign Policy of Castlereagh* (London 1924)

Wilson, Harriette, *The Game of Hearts: Harriette Wilson's Memoirs* (New York 1955)

Woolsey, Sarah Chauncey, *The Letters of Jane Austen* (London 1892)

Worsley, Lucy, *Jane Austen at Home*, (London 2017)

Wrigley, E.A, *English Population History from Family Reconstitution, 1580-1837* (Cambridge 1997)

Wynne, Elizabeth Fremantle, *The Wynne Diaries*, ed. Anne Fremantle (1935-40)

---

[1] Royal Collection Trust, Georgian Papers [GEO/ADD 15/8/157]

[2] Lefroy notes.

[3] Hubback notes.

[4] JEAL (Sutherland p11)

[5] JEAL (Sutherland p15)

[6] Lefroy notes

[7] Woolsey p230

[8] Lefroy notes

[9] *George Austen to Susanna Walter, the wife of his half-brother, William Walter.*

[10] W & RAAL (Amy p473)

[11] JEAL (Sutherland p15)

[12] JEAL (Sutherland p14)

[13] JEAL (Sutherland p23)

[14] Le Faye p21

[15] Hubback notes

[16] Le Faye p21

[17] JEAL (Sutherland p26)

[18] Adams p5.

[19] *Cassandra Austen (snr) to Susanna Walter (26th August 1770)*

[20] *Cassandra Austen (snr) to Susanna Walter (9th December 1770)*

[21] *Cassandra Austen (snr) to Susanna Walter (21st July 1771)*

[22] W & RAAL (Amy p474)

[23] W & RAAL (Amy p475)

[24] JEAL (Sutherland p16)

[25] JEAL (Sutherland p16)

[26] *Jack & Alice,* Sanditon & Ors p224

[27] Chron p116

[28] Sanditon & Ors p258

[29] JEAL (Sutherland p19)

[30] The Beachcroft deposit, Bodleian Library – Leigh family papers.

[31] Le Faye p59

[32] Sanditon & Ors p485-86

[33] ALR (Sutherland p160)

[34] JEAL (Sutherland p28)

[35] La Faye p36-38

[36] La Faye p39

[37] *ibid*

[38] W & RAAL (Amy p475), La Faye p64
[39] 1.1.4
[40] 1.6.31
[41] 1.7.34
[42] 3.8.391
[43] *ibid*
[44] 3.8.390
[45] 2.2.134
[46] 1.6.44
[47] *ibid*
[48] 42.226
[49] 2.14.233
[50] Sanditon & Ors p94-95
[51] MAAL (Amy p535)
[52] W & RAAL (Amy p483)
[53] Chron p126
[54] La Faye p50
[55] HABN (Sutherland p137)
[56] Chron p94
[57] Chron p101
[58] HABN (Sutherland p141)
[59] Chron pp126,133
[60] Tomalin p34
[61] ALR (Sutherland p160)
[62] 1.3.18-19
[63] Sherwood
[64] *ibid*
[65] *ibid*
[66] Chron p102-103
[67] 29.156
[68] Austen-Leigh, Richard
[69] Le Faye p57
[70] Le Faye p61

[71] Honan p50
[72] Honan p47
[73] Le Faye p59
[74] Brydges Vol 2 pp40-41
[75] *ibid*
[76] Grey p140
[77] 2.11.234
[78] Chron p119
[79] Sanditon & Ors p215-23
[80] Sanditon & Ors p264
[81] *Ibid* p242-252
[82] *ibid* p254
[83] *ibid* p243
[84] *ibid* p256
[85] *ibid* p256
[86] *ibid* p224-42
[87] *ibid* p224-225
[88] *ibid* p246-53
[89] Chron p119
[90] *ibid* p234-241
[91] *ibid* p225, 228
[92] *ibid* p225-26
[93] *ibid* p295-328
[94] La Faye p75; Chron p131
[95] Sanditon & Ors p359-370
[96] JEAL (Sutherland p71)
[97] MAAL (Amy p501)
[98] CAM (Sutherland p173)
[99] Le Faye p73
[100] Sanditon & Ors p274-88
[101] *ibid* p329-58
[102] *ibid* p405-17
[103] *ibid* p418-69

[104] In *Sense and Sensibility* and *Persuasion* there are no formal balls, although there is a fair amount of dancing at Barton Park and Uppercross respectively, which plays a similar role.

[105] *Mansfield Park* 2.11.284

[106] Sanditon & Ors p274-88

[107] Sanditon & Ors p289

[108] *ibid* p292

[109] *ibid* p393

[110] CAM (Sutherland p174)

[111] *Copeland* p73

[112] Chron p150

[113] Black and Le Faye p36

[114] Gore p118

[115] ALR (Sutherland p158-60)

[116] HABN (Sutherland 139)

[117] JEAL (Sutherland p70)

[118] JEAL (Sutherland p133)

[119] JEAL (Sutherland p134)

[120] 1.1.15

[121] Sanditon & Ors p135-207

[122] Chron p263

[123] Adkins p6

[124] Uglow p33

[125] Chron p154-156

[126] *ibid* p165

[127] *ibid* p285

[128] *ibid* p291

[129] Brabourne (Amy p299)

[130] Chron p173

[131] La Faye p90

[132] Chron p174

[133] Tomalin p109

[134] La Faye p92

[135] Brabourne (Amy p156)

[136] Brabourne (Amy p209)
[137] Tomalin p116
[138] Brabourne (Amy p211)
[139] Brabourne (Amy p205)
[140] *ibid* p225
[141] La Faye p94
[142] JEAL (Sutherland p48)
[143] CAM (Sutherland p186)
[144] MAAL (Amy p522)
[145] Wrigley p143
[146] Chron.p182
[147] *ibid* p183
[148] Worsley p148
[149] Brabourne (Amy p212)
[150] Vallance pp77-83
[151] Brabourne (Amy p213)
[152] Brabourne (Amy p215)
[153] Brabourne (Amy p216)
[154] *ibid* p218
[155] *ibid*
[156] Le Faye p98
[157] *ibid* p99
[158] *ibid*
[159] Brabourne (Amy p223)
[160] Le Faye p100
[161] ALR (Sutherland p158)
[162] Honan pp116-118
[163] *ibid*
[164] JEAL (Sutherland p105)
[165] Le Faye p104
[166] Le Faye p104
[167] Brabourne (Amy p239)
[168] Tomalin p130

[169] Honan p136
[170] Le Faye p118
[171] Chron p208
[172] *ibid* p206
[173] Honan p169
[174] *ibid*
[175] Egan p65
[176] *ibid* p48,54
[177] *ibid* p31
[178] *ibid* p34
[179] *ibid* p84
[180] *ibid* p68,86
[181] *ibid* p162
[182] *ibid* p183
[183] *ibid* p143
[184] *ibid* p182
[185] Honan p168
[186] *ibid* p127
[187] *ibid* p130
[188] *ibid* p60
[189] *ibid* p65-66
[190] 1.7.44
[191] Copeland p23
[192] I.3.25
[193] I.3.29
[194] I.4.33
[195] I.6.40
[196] I.13.98
[197] I.7.51
[198] Garside Vol 1, p629
[199] 1.1.1
[200] 1.2.18
[201] 1.8.53

[202] 2.2.141
[203] 2.5.159-160
[204] 2.5.161
[205] 2.5.162
[206] 2.8.182
[207] 2.6.164-170
[208] 1.5.37-38
[209] 1.3.27
[210] 1.14.112
[211] 1.14.111
[212] 1.14.111
[213] 2.4.153
[214] 1.14.114
[215] 1.7.49
[216] 1.7.48
[217] 1.14.106
[218] 1.10.75
[219] 1.11.85
[220] 1.11.87
[221] 2.8.187
[222] 1.12.95-96
[223] 2.1.130
[224] 2.5.155
[225] 2.5.155
[226] 2.7.176
[227] 2.15.247
[228] 2.15.250
[229] 2.13.227
[230] Worsley p158
[231] Adams p8
[232] Brabourne (Amy p221)
[233] Hill p202
[234] Brabourne (Amy pp222-225)

[235] Brabourne (Amy p226)
[236] *ibid* p225
[237] *ibid*
[238] Brabourne (Amy pp232-233)
[239] *ibid* pp233-236
[240] *Ibid* p236
[241] O'Byrne (entry for Francis William Austen)
[242] Brabourne (Amy pp237-240)
[243] *ibid* p242
[244] Chron p221
[245] Brabourne (Amy p243-245)
[246] Egan p137
[247] Brabourne (Amy p246)
[248] Chron p226
[249] Brabourne (Amy p245)
[250] *ibid* p247-248
[251] *ibid* p249
[252] Le Faye p115
[253] Le Faye p120-124
[254] Honan p150
[255] Le Faye p121
[256] Chron p231-232
[257] Honan p150
[258] *ibid* p152
[259] Chron p237
[260] *ibid* p243
[261] Brabourne (Amy p253)
[262] *ibid* p259
[263] *ibid* p255
[264] *ibid* p256
[265] *ibid* p258
[266] Honan p161-162
[267] O'Byrne (entry for Francis William Austen)

[268] Brabourne (Amy p255)
[269] Honan p156
[270] Tomalin p153-154
[271] *The Improved Bath Guide* p56
[272] Worsley p187
[273] Brabourne (Amy p271-272)
[274] Sutherland p185
[275] W & RAAL (Amy p476)
[276] Le Faye p128
[277] 1.5.27
[278] Brabourne (Amy p265)
[279] *ibid* p266)
[280] *ibid* p261)
[281] *ibid* p267)
[282] *ibid* p270)
[283] 1.5.26
[284] Brabourne (Amy p268)
[285] *ibid* p267)
[286] *ibid* p267)
[287] Le Faye p130
[288] Chron p255
[289] Brabourne (Amy p276)
[290] Le Faye p131
[291] Tomalin p170-173
[292] 2.2.135
[293] ALR (Sutherland p183)
[294] Brabourne (Amy p274)
[295] Egan p173
[296] Brabourne (Amy p275)
[297] *ibid* p276
[298] *ibid* p277
[299] W & RAAL (Amy p478)
[300] *ibid* p276

[301] *ibid* p278
[302] *ibid* p279
[303] *ibid* p278
[304] Honan p182
[305] Worsley p203
[306] Le Faye p135
[307] Worsley p204
[308] Brabourne (Amy p263)
[309] Feltham p283-284
[310] Brabourne (Amy p266)
[311] Le Faye p135
[312] Chron p262-263
[313] *ibid* p265
[314] *ibid* p267-270
[315] Le Faye p136
[316] *ibid* p137
[317] Chron p274-276
[318] *The Jane Austen Quickstep Travel Guide: Missing Manydown* (10th January 2022)
[319] Brabourne (Amy p238)
[320] Hayley p7
[321] Hall Vol 1 p178
[322] W & RAAL [Amy p471]
[323] Sutherland p191
[324] RF Bigg Wither p58-59
[325] Brabourne (Amy p319)
[326] Wilson p384
[327] JEAL (Sutherland p29)
[328] Honan p186
[329] Chron p262
[330] Le Faye p141
[331] Le Faye p139
[332] Roberts p183
[333] JEAL (Sutherland p60)

[334] Le Faye p142, Chron p301-303
[335] Le Faye p140-141
[336] Mandal p522
[337] Sanditon & Ors p131
[338] *ibid* p79
[339] *ibid* p79-80
[340] *ibid* p81
[341] 1.10.85
[342] Sanditon & Ors p85
[343] *ibid* p77
[344] *ibid* p111
[345] *ibid* p91
[346] *ibid* p97
[347] *ibid* p95
[348] Lascelles p99-100
[349] Le Faye p145
[350] Sanditon & Ors p485
[351] Honan p210
[352] Worsley p247
[353] W & R Austen-Leigh (Amy p481)
[354] Le Faye p146-147
[355] JEAL (Sutherland p61)
[356] W & RAAL (Amy p480)
[357] *ibid* p479
[358] FKD (Amy p557)
[359] *ibid* p557
[360] Tomalin p192
[361] Chron p315
[362] Brabourne (Amy p282).
[363] *ibid* p284-285
[364] FKD (Amy p557)
[365] Chron p319
[366] Brabourne (Amy p283)

[367] JH Hubback p144
[368] *ibid* p147-148
[369] Honan p220
[370] JH Hubback p150
[371] JH Hubback p154
[372] *ibid* p155
[373] *ibid* p156
[374] Southey p260
[375] Uglow p403-404
[376] Egan p144
[377] Worsley p255
[378] Brabourne (Amy p262)
[379] *ibid* p312
[380] Worsley p261-262
[381] Le Faye p155
[382] Chron p330
[383] Le Faye pp156-157
[384] Worsley p268
[385] Chron p327
[386] *ibid* p333
[387] Brabourne (Amy p 288)
[388] Tomalin p203
[389] JEAL (Sutherland p65)
[390] Brabourne (Amy p289-290)
[391] *ibid* p289
[392] Chron p332
[393] Worsley p284
[394] Brabourne (Amy p290)
[395] JEAL (Sutherland p66)
[396] *ibid* p66-67
[397] Brabourne (Amy p294)
[398] Chron p338
[399] *ibid* p339

[400] Tomalin p204
[401] Le Faye p162
[402] Chron p343-344
[403] Brabourne (Amy p557-558)
[404] Chron p344
[405] Le Faye p165
[406] Brabourne (Amy p300)
[407] *ibid* p302
[408] *ibid* p305
[409] *ibid* p312
[410] *ibid* p307
[411] Worsley p282
[412] Brabourne (Amy p313)
[413] *ibid* p318
[414] *ibid* p315
[415] *ibid* p316
[416] JH Hubbock Ch XIII
[417] Brabourne (Amy p316)
[418] *ibid* p317
[419] See Jane Becalmed (Chapter XII)
[420] Brabourne (Amy p318-319)
[421] Tomalin p207-208
[422] Brabourne (Amy p318). Jane unaccountably refers, in this letter, to Edward having completed his *thirtieth* year.
[423] Le Faye p169
[424] Brabourne (Amy p321)
[425] *ibid* p324
[426] *ibid* p326
[427] *ibid* p335
[428] Brabourne (Amy p330)
[429] *ibid* p336
[430] *ibid* p338
[431] W & RAAL (Amy p471-72)
[432] Fanny Knight Diary

[433] Chron.p371
[434] JEAL (Sutherland p67)
[435] Worsley p292-293
[436] JEAL (Sutherland p67)
[437] Tomalin p212
[438] JEAL (Sutherland p69)
[439] CAM (Sutherland p168)
[440] Tomalin p213
[441] JEAL (Sutherland p69)
[442] Le Faye p176
[443] Honan p270
[444] JEAL (Sutherland p70, 79)
[445] CAM (Sutherland p169)
[446] *ibid* p170-72
[447] Honan p254
[448] Worsley p306
[449] JEAL (Sutherland p81-82)
[450] Grey p50
[451] Copeland and McMaster p4-6
[452] HABN (Sutherland p140)
[453] Brabourne (Amy p352)
[454] *ibid* p354
[455] *ibid* p348-350
[456] *ibid* p353
[457] *ibid* p351
[458] Brabourne (Amy p360)
[459] Chron p408-410
[460] Le Faye p187
[461] Tomalin p220-221
[462] Sanditon p476-480
[463] Chron p414
[464] Aspinall 26
[465] Critical Review p149-157

[466] The British Critic p527
[467] W & RAAL (Amy p484)
[468] 1.6.31
[469] 1.12.62
[470] 1.7.35
[471] 2.1.140
[472] 1.2.12
[473] 2.9.223
[474] 2.9.226
[475] 3.1.267
[476] 3.5.296
[477] 1.9.41
[478] 1.16.88
[479] 1.9.42-43
[480] 1.9.45
[481] 3.8.331
[482] 1.10.51
[483] 3.14.378
[484] 3.9.338
[485] 1.3.17-18
[486] 1.4.19-20
[487] 1.4.21
[488] 1.8.39
[489] 1.15.77
[490] 1.16.83
[491] 1.1.7
[492] 2.7.185
[493] 1.19.104
[494] 3.9.333
[495] 3.7.315
[496] 1.1.6
[497] 1.22.131-134
[498] 3.1.264

[499] 3.12.363
[500] 3.14.376
[501] 1.16.85
[502] Chron p420
[503] ALR (Sutherland p159)
[504] Le Faye p191
[505] Honan p286
[506] Woolsey p154-155
[507] *ibid* p156
[508] *ibid* p157
[509] Chron p437
[510] Le Faye p196
[511] Honan p318
[512] Brabourne (Amy p372
[513] Tomalin p243
[514] HAM (Sutherland p150)
[515] *ibid* p149
[516] 1.3
[517] 3.9
[518] 4.12
[519] 3.9
[520] 6.20
[521] 12.55
[522] 15.65
[523] 37.200-201
[524] 43.231
[525] 44.248
[526] 52.307
[527] 58.345-346
[528] 1.1
[529] 25.132
[530] 8.33
[531] 26.142

[532] 15.66
[533] 19.104
[534] 18.86
[535] 22.120
[536] 24.128-129
[537] 29.158
[538] 49.288
[539] 55.331
[540] 42.222
[541] 57.343-344
[542] 1.3
[543] 2.4
[544] 42.223
[545] 14.63
[546] 35.186
[547] 59.358
[548] 18.90
[549] 6.20
[550] 11.53
[551] 6.22
[552] 29.157
[553] 34.183
[554] 36.196
[555] 37.200-201
[556] 43.228
[557] Emma 1.12.100
[558] 43.229
[559] 43.232
[560] 15.67
[561] 16.76
[562] 40.212
[563] 44.245
[564] 46.259

[565] 50.292-293
[566] 58.349
[567] Woolsey p155/Le Faye p198
[568] W & RAAL (Amy p482-83)
[569] Le Faye p200
[570] Chron p446
[571] *ibid* p444
[572] *ibid* p445-47
[573] Le Faye p201
[574] Chron p451
[575] W & RAAL (Amy p484)
[576] Chron p452
[577] Brabourne, W & RAAL (Amy p375-77, 485)
[578] Brabourne (Amy p382-83)
[579] Le Faye p206
[580] W & RAAL (Amy p486-87)
[581] Brabourne (Amy p391)
[582] *ibid* p401
[583] Brabourne (Amy p388-91)
[584] *ibid* p398
[585] Brabourne (Amy p400)
[586] Woolsey p204-205
[587] Brabourne (Amy p407)
[588] Chron p476
[589] *ibid* p477-78
[590] Honan p346
[591] Sanditon & Ors p476-480
[592] *ibid* p478-479
[593] Le Faye p212
[594] Honan p343
[595] Copeland & McMaster p12
[596] Woolsey p231
[597] Woolsey p233

[598] *ibid* p240
[599] Copeland & McMaster p13
[600] 1.4.43
[601] 2.1.176
[602] 2.13.302
[603] 24.128-129
[604] Tomalin p227
[605] 1.9.91
[606] 1.2.19
[607] 3.17.463
[608] 1.2.18-19
[609] 2.12.292
[610] 3.8.389-91
[611] *Somerset v Stewart* (1772) 98 ER 499
[612] 1.9.86
[613] 1.9.86-87
[614] 1.11.109
[615] 2.4.214
[616] 2.10.278
[617] 1.7.74
[618] 1.3.32
[619] 1.13.126
[620] 2.10.273
[621] 3.16.448
[622] 2.1.180
[623] 1.6.60
[624] 2.6.229
[625] 2.6.236
[626] 1.16.154
[627] 2.5.225
[628] 3.3.341
[629] 3.3.339
[630] 1.6.53

[631] 1.6.56
[632] 2.7.242
[633] 1.8.81
[634] 1.8.80
[635] 3.16.455
[636] 1.11.113
[637] 3.17.462
[638] 3.17.465
[639] 3.17.470
[640] 3.17.473
[641] Webster p228
[642] Cooper p17-18
[643] Uglow p599
[644] Rowbottam (April 1814)
[645] Chron p479
[646] *ibid* p484
[647] Harris p189
[648] Cooper p21
[649] Uglow p603
[650] Wynne (Vol 3 p372)
[651] MacCarthy p217
[652] Brabourne (Amy p413)
[653] Chron p483
[654] *ibid* p483
[655] Brabourne (Amy p412)
[656] Uglow p604-5, and quoting from the diaries of James Oakes, and from Thomas Cooper's biography
[657] Cobbett (5.277)
[658] Woolsey p218-227
[659] Sabor p8
[660] JEAL (Sutherland p100)
[661] Brabourne (in Amy p418-20)
[662] Copeland & McMaster p13-14
[663] Adkins, R & L p245-46

[664] Brabourne (in Amy p420)
[665] Worsley p369
[666] JEAL (Sutherland p96)
[667] *ibid* p93
[668] *ibid* p94-95
[669] Brabourne (in Amy p421)
[670] *ibid* p418-419
[671] *ibid* p420
[672] *ibid* p422
[673] JEAL (Sutherland p100)
[674] Chron p522-524
[675] *ibid* p525
[676] JEAL (Sutherland p94)
[677] Sanditon & Ors pp481-484
[678] Chron p545
[679] Gilson p71
[680] Ward p469-77
[681] Southam p58-69
[682] Reitzel p487-493
[683] 1.1.1
[684] 1.1.3
[685] 1.1.7
[686] 1.3.20
[687] 1.4.32
[688] 1.4.25
[689] 1.14.119
[690] 2.2.167
[691] 3.13.436
[692] 2.7.209
[693] 2.14.275
[694] 3.11.418
[695] 3.11.423
[696] 3.15.460

[697] 1.1.1
[698] 1.8.62
[699] 1.7.51
[700] 1.7.52
[701] 2.5.190
[702] 2.5.191
[703] 2.7.211
[704] 2.9.234
[705] 1.8.56
[706] 2.8.219-221
[707] See for example 1.10.94-96
[708] See for example 2.11.252-254
[709] 3.2. 330-332, 337-338
[710] 2.3.180-181
[711] See Chapter 1: *Backcloth: Overture*
[712] 2.1.155
[713] 2.7.210
[714] 2.9.242
[715] 3.8.392
[716] 1.10.86-87
[717] 3.3.342
[718] 2.9.236
[719] 1.1.1
[720] 3.6.367
[721] 1.3.18
[722] 2.3.176
[723] 2.6.201
[724] 3.10.407
[725] 2.15.285
[726] 3.16.469
[727] 2.16.294
[728] 3.19.493
[729] 3.13.443

[730] Woolsey p260
[731] Tomalin p258
[732] JEAL *Memoir* p112
[733] Woolsey p259, 261
[734] Chron pp452-454
[735] Oscar Faye Adams p176
[736] Woolsey p255
[737] *ibid* p255
[738] CAM (Sutherland p177)
[739] Chron p539
[740] *Historic Cheltenham*
[741] CAM (Sutherland p178)
[742] HABN (Sutherland p138)
[743] JEAL (Sutherland p125)
[744] 1.1.4
[745] 1.4.26
[746] 1.4.28
[747] 1.5.37
[748] 1.7.59
[749] 1.7.60-61
[750] 1.8.63
[751] 1.10.88
[752] 1.10.91
[753] 1.12.104
[754] 1.12.111
[755] 1.11.114
[756] 2.6.167-168
[757] 2.8.183
[758] 2.11.232
[759] 2.11.235
[760] 2.11.237
[761] 1.6.47-48
[762] 2.3.138

[763] 1.10.84
[764] 1.5.33
[765] 1.10.85
[766] 1.4.26
[767] 1.8.63-64
[768] 1.3.25
[769] 1.6.48
[770] 1.7.58-60
[771] 1.8.72
[772] 1.8.68
[773] 2.7.175
[774] 2.7.178-180
[775] 2.11.229
[776] 1.11.98
[777] 1.10.91
[778] See Ch XII 'Jane Becalmed'
[779] 1.11.96
[780] 1.2.11
[781] 2.4.146-47
[782] 2.12.249
[783] 1.11.128
[784] 1.11.127
[785] 1.6.48
[786] 1.4.150
[787] 1.3.22
[788] 1.3.19
[789] 2.12.252
[790] Brabourne (Amy p424)
[791] *ibid* p425
[792] JEAL (Sutherland p123)
[793] JEAL (Sutherland p126)/W & RAAL (Amy p489)
[794] 2.14
[795] 2.14

[796] 1.5
[797] Grey p370
[798] 8.48
[799] 8.48
[800] 4.22
[801] 5.31
[802] 4.23-24
[803] 6.35
[804] Grey p341
[805] 5.29
[806] 5.32
[807] Brabourne (Amy p439)
[808] W & RAAL (Amy p490)
[809] Upfal
[810] Le Faye p247
[811] CAM (Sutherland p178-79)
[812] Chron p567
[813] Le Faye p271, 283
[814] Worsely p391
[815] Chron p570
[816] Tomalin p268
[817] HABN (Sutherland p138)
[818] CAM (Sutherland p179)
[819] Chron p570
[820] JEAL (Sutherland p129-30)
[821] HABN (Sutherland p142)
[822] Chron p572
[823] *ibid* p574
[824] *ibid* p574
[825] JEAL Memoir p270-71
[826] Chron p574
[827] *ibid* p577
[828] Sanditon p496

[829] Tomalin p272
[830] Chron p578
[831] Le Faye p253-54
[832] Chron p578
[833] JEAL (Sutherland p130-31)
[834] Honan p407
[835] Tomalin p274
[836] JASNA
[837] JASNA
[838] Tomalin p277-78
[839] W & RAAL (Amy p490)
[840] Le Faye p269
[841] Tomalin p279
[842] JEAL (Sutherland p114)
[843] *ibid* p91
[844] MAAL (Amy p515-160
[845] Sanditon p497

ABOUT THE AUTHOR

Christopher Richard Kerr

Christopher Kerr read law at Brasenose College, Oxford. He is a practising barrister, and lives with his wife and two daughters in London.

He is the author of a novel - A Conspiracy of Serpents (Austin Macauley 2022)

Printed in Great Britain
by Amazon